GARSINGTON
REVISITED

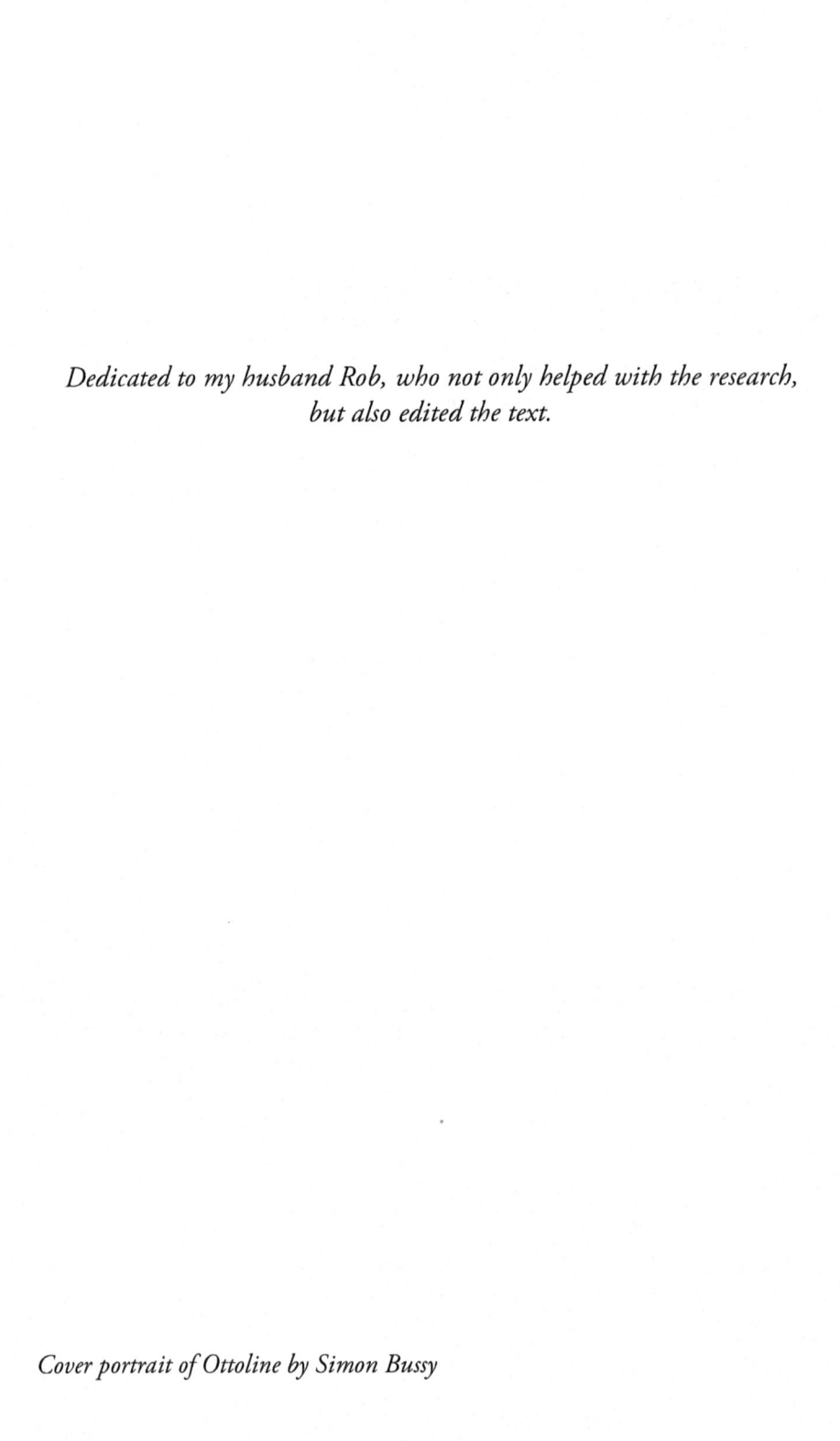

Dedicated to my husband Rob, who not only helped with the research, but also edited the text.

Cover portrait of Ottoline by Simon Bussy

GARSINGTON
REVISITED

The Legend of Lady Ottoline Morrell
Brought Up-to-Date

Sandra Jobson Darroch

JL

British Library Cataloguing in Publication Data

Garsington Revisited. The Legend of Lady Ottoline Morrell Brought Up-to-Date

A catalogue entry for this book is available from the British Library

ISBN: 9780 86196 737 7 (Paperback)
ISBN: 9780 86196 941 8 (Ebook)

This book was first published as *Ottoline: the Life of Lady Ottoline Morrell* by Coward McCann Geoghegan (New York) in 1975, and by Chatto & Windus (London) in 1976. Cassell (London) published the Paperback Edition in 1982.

This later edition, *Garsington Revisited*, is a revised and updated version of the original biography and contains additional vignettes and interludes, including accounts of interviews with a number of Ottoline's contemporaries. It is published by John Libbey Publishing Ltd, in association with Svengali Press & ETT Imprint in print and ebook formats. Apart from any fair-dealing for the purposes of private study, research, criticism or review (as permitted under the Copyright Act), no part may be reproduced by any process without written permission. Any inquiries should be addressed to trilby@svengalipress.com.au

---

Published by
John Libbey Publishing Ltd, 205 CrescentRoad, East Barnet, Herts EN4 8SB, United Kingdom
e-mail: john.libbey@orange.fr; web site: www.johnlibbey.com

Distributed Worldwide by **Indiana University Press**,
Herman B Wells Library – 350, 1320 E. 10th St., Bloomington, IN 47405, USA.
www.iupress.indiana.edu

© 2017 Copyright Sandra Jobson Darroch. All rights reserved.
Unauthorised duplication contravenes applicable laws.

Printed and bound in the United States of America

CONTENTS

	INTRODUCTION	i
Prelude	*A Blow-in From the Colonies*	1
Chapter 1	THE LEGEND OF OTTOLINE	5
Interlude	*Hook 'em Horns*	8
Chapter 2	THE DAUGHTER OF A THOUSAND EARLS	11
Interlude	*Stalked by the Dook*	19
Chapter 3	HUNT'N, SHOOT'N & FISH'N	21
Picture Spread	*The Early Men in Her Life*	28
Chapter 4	THE BUTTERFLY SPREADS HER WINGS	29
Interlude	*The Druce-Portland Case*	46
Chapter 5	TALL, DARK AND HANDSOME, BUT NO MR D'ARCY	49
Picture Spread	*On Honeymoon*	58
Chapter 6	MARY FOTHERINGHAM: OTTOLINE'S FIRST APPEARANCE IN PRINT	59
Interlude	*The Centre of the World*	70
Chapter 7	OTTOLINE LAUNCHES HERSELF ON THE SEA OF LONDON	73
Interlude	*The Hostess with the Mostest*	85
Chapter 8	THE GREAT LADY OF BEDFORD SQUARE	87
Picture Spread	*44 Bedford Square*	98
Chapter 9	THE ARCH-PRIEST OF BLOOMSBURY	99
Interlude	*The "Bloomsbury Group"*	107
Chapter 10	BERTIE STAYS THE NIGHT	109
Interlude	*A Lamb in Wolf's Clothing*	126
Chapter 11	FURTHER ENTANGLEMENTS	127
Interlude	*Mixing Beethoven with Mozart*	140

Chapter 12	NEWS OF THE SCANDAL SPREADS	143
Interlude	A "Thumbs-up" From Michael Holroyd	163
Chapter 13	THE GATHERING STORM	165
Interlude	My Introduction to Bloomsbury	185
Chapter 14	THE STORM CLOUDS BREAK	187
Interlude	Lunch with Duncan Grant	197
Chapter 15	THE WORKING-CLASS LAD FROM NOTTINGHAM	199
Interlude	"Why Don't You Look Into Lawrence?"	210
Chapter 16	ESCAPE TO THE COUNTRY	211
Picture Spread	At Garsington	226
Chapter 17	STICKING PINS INTO OTTOLINE	227
Interlude	My First Glimpse of Garsington	251
Chapter 18	BITING THE HAND THAT FED HIM	254
Interlude	I See a Ghost	272
Chapter 19	THE WORST YEAR OF HER LIFE	274
Interlude	A Brief Moment in the Limelight	297
Chapter 20	BERTIE GOES TO GAOL	300
Interlude	The Men in Her Life	317
Chapter 21	TIGER, TIGER	320
Interlude	A Visit to Hatfield House	340
Chapter 22	THE YOUNGER BRIGADE	342
Picture Spread	10 Gower Street	367
Chapter 23	THE DEAREST LITTLE DOLLS' HOUSE	368
Interlude	My Strange Visit to Pamela Diamand	404
	Appendix: "The Lady and the Pug"	407
	Acknowledgements	408
	Bibliography	411
	Key To End-notes	415
	End-notes	416
	Index	436

INTRODUCTION

FOUR DECADES have now passed since I wrote *Ottoline - The Life of Lady Ottoline Morrell* (published in New York in 1975 and in London in 1976). I explain below the unusual circumstances of how this came about. It was to be the first biography of one of the 20th century's most exotic literary figures, and only the second "Bloomsbury biography", following Michael Holroyd's 1967 life of Lytton Strachey. Since then much has been written about the literary and artistic milieu in which Ottoline cut such an outstanding figure, and in which she became a catalyst for some of the century's most important literature (in which she herself sometimes played a leading role). It was time, I felt, to revisit my biography, and tell about the people - almost all of them now dead - whom I was fortunate to meet and obtain their first-hand accounts of Ottoline and her circle. So, interposed throughout this revised-and-updated text, I have added a number of interludes and vignettes about people I interviewed, places I visited, and the progress of my research from 1972 to 1975. More interestingly perhaps - because of the time that has elapsed - I am now able to be more forthcoming about what I learnt "in confidence" from some of these encounters (such as what David Garnett told me about what he called "the skeletons in Ottoline's cupboard").

I was only in my twenties when, back in the 1970s, I began delving into Ottoline's life (as I describe below). So I thought that it would be useful now to look back on Ottoline and her world from the perspective of today and the values of the present era. I wrote my original biography at an exciting moment in biography. With his *Lytton Strachey*, Holroyd had broken through the barriers of prissy, old-fashioned biography, leaving hagiography in his wake, and ushering in a new world of candid truthfulness in the depiction of the lives of famous people. It was also at the beginning of the "Bloomsbury cult", which has lasted as a literary and biographical phenomenon to the present day.

Looking at photographs of Ottoline in her 30s and early 40s, I see her quite differently today. When I first wrote my book, she seemed to me quite old. Now she looks much younger. In her heyday she was a very beautiful and attractive woman. Yet her later detractors knew her only after her prime had passed, when she had become a caricature of her former self. So in awe and jealous were many of her contemporaries of her aristocratic background that they failed to understand that Ottoline was far from wealthy, and that her bountiful behaviour was an act of generosity, not that of a rich woman bestowing largesse.

I have kept most of the early part of this book substantially the same as the first book, adding embellishments here and there, correcting errors in dates, clarifying that which was unclear, and focusing anew on aspects of Ottoline's early life. As well, a number of subsequent works have helped fill out the picture I originally drew of Ottoline, particularly Miranda Seymour's 1992 biography, *Ottoline Morrell. Life on the Grand Scale* (and which I acknowledge more fully below). The publication by the Cambridge University Press of D.H. Lawrence's *Letters* allowed me to see many letters from Lawrence to people other than Ottoline, and these helped me present a fuller account of Lawrence's troubled relationship with her, and the break-up of their friendship over his portrayal of her in *Women in Love*.

Lady Ottoline's Album, a collection of photographs taken by Ottoline and published shortly after my book with an introduction by David Cecil, I found useful for his reminiscences of Ottoline (whom he found "at once very beautiful yet somehow grotesque"), and of Oxford's undergraduate days. Also valuable was Julian Vinogradoff's account in the *Album* of her mother's professional approach to photography, detailing the types of

INTRODUCTION

cameras she used, and her insistence on using the best photo-labs to develop and print her captured images.

Although Miranda Seymour's 1992 biography was far-more-comprehensive than mine (the word thorough comes to mind, in a most complimentary sense), we tended to emphasise different aspects of Ottoline's life. However, we based our research on much the same primary material. (I was especially pleased to see that she made use of my discovery of John Adam Cramb's early relationship with Ottoline.) Having had access to Ottoline's manuscript Diary (which had been denied to me - see my Julian Vinogradoff Interlude below), she revealed two important new pieces in the Ottoline jigsaw. The first was the names of two women who each bore Philip Morrell a son. I had mentioned this in my biography, for David Garnett had told me about Philip's liaisons and their resulting progeny. But I had not named the two women because both sons were then prominent in their fields — medicine and diplomacy— and I did not want to compromise their careers. The second new item was the revelation by Seymour of a late affair Ottoline had with a young stonemason, Lionel Gomme. I have updated my new volume accordingly, acknowledging the source. However, I find myself hesitant to share Seymour's emphasis on the importance of this affair. Although no doubt something did occur, I believe it may have been, to a some extent, a reflection of Ottoline's disturbed mental state at that time. It may not have been as "physical" (Ottoline's euphemism for sex) as she made out. Ottoline was in desperate need of a new relationship, and Gomme apparently provided it. Yet she spent six months away in Europe in the middle of the affair, and appears to have enjoyed herself thoroughly, apparently exhibiting few signs of missing him.

In her book, Seymour expressed sympathy for me in not having had full access to Ottoline's letters to Bertrand Russell until the day before they were released from embargo by McMaster University (where they were housed at that time), and that consequently I had only one day to peruse them. I must now confess that I misled Ms Seymour on this. Six months prior to the ending of the embargo, an anonymous benefactor at McMaster supplied me with illicit microfilm copies of Ottoline's letters, and thus I had ample time to decipher the convoluted arabesques of Ottoline's handwriting. However, to protect this benefactor, I had been obliged to say I had only seen the letters a day before the embargo was lifted.

After an absence of more than 40 years, my return to Ottoline — to "*Revisit Garsington*" — has reinforced my regard for her remarkable courage and character. She abandoned the comforts of an aristocratic life to join a lower world of Bohemian artists and writers (to the undisguised distain of her fellow aristocrats). Yes, she could appear to be a flibbertigibbet at times, and manipulative at others; but she possessed a fine, intuitive artistic sense, and she was, in her unique way, very intelligent. A man like Bertrand Russell, himself an aristocrat and thus immune to her aristocratic allure, would not have remained in love with her for so long if she hadn't possessed very special qualities. His 2,500 letters to her are a testimony to both the strength and sincerity of that relationship.

Compared to today's shallow celebrities, Ottoline — "the daughter of a thousand earls", as Lytton Strachey described her — brought a richness of tradition and a depth of sensibility to her chosen role as hostess, and this made her unique. She was at one and the same moment a "one-woman show" and the stage-manager of a cast of hundreds at Bedford Square and Garsington (and later also at Gower Street) in the first three decades of the 20th century.

PRELUDE
A Blow-in from the Colonies

Julian and Ottoline

TO THIS DAY, I do not know why Ottoline's daughter Julian Vinogradoff chose me – allowed me – to write the first biography of her mother. For many years she had been fending away other far-better-known prospective biographers. She believed that a full-scale biography of her controversial mother would be too intrusive. For her, this was very sensitive territory. At the very least she had been putting off any attempt to tell the story of her mother's tempestuous – and scandalous – life.

My nose had been put on to Ottoline's exotic scent in the early 1960s at the University of Sydney, where I was attending lectures in British History given by Marlay Stephen, a descendant of one branch of the Stephen family (which included Virginia and Vanessa, two of Bloomsbury's leading ladies). Marlay spoke about the Bloomsbury Group from a personal perspective. I remember the day Marlay, returning from a trip to England, told me: "I bumped into E.M. Forster in the fog on Clapham Common and he said'Marlay, old boy, could you lend me a bottle of ink?'" Marlay lectured us about the non-conformist, libertarian Clapham Sect, which was an important tap-root of "Bloomsbury". Yet it was only in 1971, when I read Bertrand Russell's three-volume autobiography, that I learned about Ottoline's involvement with Bloomsbury. It was Russell's unflinching prose that first introduced me to the larger-than-life figure of the notorious London salonniere, Lady Ottoline Morrell (who, despite having – in Russell's words – "a face like a horse", was to be his lover, and to haunt for many years one of the greatest minds of the 20th century).

When I left Australia for the UK in 1971 I already had one book under my belt. It was *Once Upon a Vase,* which retold the stories of Homer taken from the famous François Vase. In March 1972 in London I was casting around for a second book to write. I wondered if anyone had written a biography of Ottoline Morrell. Some preliminary research soon showed me that nothing very substantive had in fact been published on her, certainly no full-length biography. Ever since Michael Holroyd's magisterial biography of Lytton Strachey – in which Ottoline figured prominently – had been published five years earlier in 1967, interest in Bloomsbury had been growing. Surely such an obvious gap would have been filled by now? If not, was there any chance that an outsider from Down Under might have the opportunity to fill it?

My agent Peter Grose of Curtis Brown approached one of England's most-established publishers, Chatto & Windus, who (surprisingly) weren't put off by my lack of familiarity with British society. Norah Smallwood, Chatto's editorial director, arranged for me to travel up to Julian Vinogradoff's country house at

Banbury to be vetted by her. (Ms Smallwood, indicatively perhaps, also happened to be Julian Vinogradoff's literary agent.)

As I travelled on the train to Banbury for my first visit to Julian at her home, Broughton Grange, my mind was full of doubts. Would she look down her nose at me as a lower-class yokel from far-off Australia? It was vital I made a good impression, for Julian not only owned the copyright to all her mother's writings and large collection of photographs, but she was the *sine qua non* of the entire project. Even if I managed to get her initial approval, she could at any stage withdraw her permission for me to write the book, were I to displease her. Yet I was determined to try to remain independent and write a fair and balanced account of her mother's life. *So* I adopted a very low-key approach. I would arrive with no literary pretentions, be ultra-polite, and be careful not to drop the butter knife.

When my taxi drew up in the gravelled driveway, I saw before me a mellow brick-and-stone house surrounded by a large garden. In the distance were the soft, green, rounded hills of the Oxfordshire countryside. Julian greeted me at the door, and when we got inside introduced me to her husband, Igor Vinogradoff, who (I later found out) dabbled in antiques. Over lunch I scrutinised Julian. She looked about 60, rather portly, with a florid complexion and large pale-blue eyes. I observed that her hair was dyed to echo its original blonde. Though she spoke with an English upper-class accent, it wasn't over-the-top. I could, however, discern little or no resemblance to her mother, who had been tall and willowy, with a (famously) large nose and chin, and dark auburn hair. Julian apparently took more after her father, Philip Morrell. He had been the scion of a well-off Oxford brewing and legal family, and who was a lawyer and Liberal MP. (Broughton Grange had been in the Morrell family for a hundred years or more.)

Julian's husband Igor was a large, fair-headed man, the son of a Russian émigré, Sir Paul Vinogradoff, a former Professor of Jurisprudence at Oxford. In 1916 Igor, along with his siblings, became a naturalised British subject. He too spoke with an upper-class English accent. Over lunch, however, he sat silently, occasionally smiling benignly. I later learned that he had first proposed to Julian in 1927, but Ottoline had put the kibosh on the match because Igor at that time was young and virtually penniless. She may well, too, have been miffed or jealous, as young Igor had been one of her "young men" at Garsington. Less than a year later Julian married Victor (later Sir Victor) Goodman, later Clerk of the House of Lords. In 1930 she gave birth to a daughter, Anne. In 1942, after her mother's death, Julian divorced Victor and married Igor.

On that first visit, Igor's silence was in sharp contrast to Julian's animated chattiness, which leapt froglike from one subject to the next, dropping along the way names which, at the time, meant nothing to me. She informed me, with some satisfaction, that she had turned down many would-be biographers "because they came from Oxford" (or else Cambridge). Such people, she told me, would be biassed against her mother. I, on the other hand, was an "outsider" (which, I was glad to learn, was a point in my favour). She believed that I would be untarnished by the catty gossip that had surrounded Ottoline, and which continued (she assured me) to tarnish her mother's reputation to the present day.

Julian informed me that she had recently sold all her mother's letters and papers to the University of Texas. The uncatalogued collection was now lodged in the university's Humanities Research Center (HRC) in Austin. Although I didn't manage to ascertain from Julian any indication as to the size or content of the collection, I realised straight away that, assuming I got her permission to write the book, a trip to Texas would be my next step.

After the lunch was over, Julian escorted me to the front door (where a taxi was waiting for me), telling me that she would consult with her close friend Juliette Huxley about my proposed biography. Then, if the two of them agreed, she would contact my agent Peter Grose to inform him of their decision. After a nervous wait of several days, Peter rang to tell me we had her approval. He then set about negotiating a contract with Chatto & Windus for the (UK) publication of the book.

I was now the "official" – albeit unlikely – authorised biographer of Lady Ottoline Morrell…a position that was to open many important doors for me in the months (and years) that lay ahead.

CHAPTER 1
The Legend of Ottoline

Duncan Grant's portrait of the notorious Lady Ottoline Morrell

& there used to be a great lady in Bedford Square who managed to make life seem a little amusing & interesting & adventurous, so I used to think when I was young & wore a blue dress, & Ottoline was like a Spanish galleon, hung with golden coins, & lovely silken sails.[1]

THAT WAS Virginia Woolf's gilded vision of Lady Ottoline Morrell. Everyone who knew Ottoline thought she was remarkable. D.H. Lawrence pictured her as a grand lady, "a queen among women".[2] David Cecil called her an Elizabethan, rather like Queen Elizabeth herself.[3] Osbert Sitwell portrayed her as an oversized Infanta of Spain,[4] while Dorothy Brett said she had "a heart of gold and a yen for men".[5] It was Ottoline's extraordinary appearance that struck people first. She trailed, recalled Peter Quennell,[6] like one of the peacocks that followed her around Garsington, her high-arched nose, prognathous jaw, pale face and mahogany-red hair giving her an appearance both baroque and gothic. Stephen Spender was intrigued by her voice. He loved the way she emphasised syllables, transforming ordinary speech into "horn-like blasts", an effect echoed in her unique handwriting, the exquisite loops and arabesques of which elevated mere sentences into "a realm of pure ornament".[7] He conjured up a picture of her parading around Bloomsbury dressed like some aristocratic shepherdess, leading her Pekinese dogs on ribbons tied to the shepherd's crook she carried.

Leonard Woolf, Virginia's husband, also saw Ottoline taking the Bloomsbury air. He described her looking like some enormous bird, with her hair and clothes flopping and flapping around her, and whose brightly-and-badly-dyed plumage was in complete disarray, and no longer fitted her body.[8] He remembered her passing a trench in which some men were working. Seeing her, they roared with laughter, then whistled and catcalled; but Ottoline walked on, oblivious and impervious. "A very silly woman," was Woolf's summing up. For Woolf and many of his Bloomsbury colleagues, Ottoline was too fantastic, too scented, too exaggerated. Vanessa Bell said she talked "twaddle".[9] Clive Bell spread malicious stories about her; and even Lytton Strachey, who was truly fond of Ottoline, couldn't resist the customary Bloomsbury gibe, once describing her as *rongee* by malevolence, "every tea party in London to which she hasn't been invited is wormwood, wormwood".[10] David Garnett, then a junior member of Bloomsbury, first met Ottoline in 1913, and to him she appeared magnificent: glacier blue-green eyes, masses of dark Venetian red hair, a long straight nose, proud mouth and jutting-out chin; a "lovely, haggard face".[11] But Garnett also thought her overdone: "All her houses were a little too hothouse, too parrot-house. The rooms reeked of potpourri and oranges. I think in a way we exploited Ottoline. But it was fun to be invited and one didn't run down invitations. It was awfully nice for a scruffy young man to go to dinner at Ottoline's. But that's only adding to the legend."[12]

That is the legend that has come down to us today, much of it from the tongues and pens of Bloomsbury. They and their circle relished telling stories about her gatherings, first at Bedford Square, then at Garsington and later Gower Street. They portrayed her as a shallow society-hostess. They ridiculed her efforts to seek out and foster young poets and painters: "lion hunting" they sneered. Yet the legend is only part of the truth, and the gossip and sneers hardly touch the real Ottoline. She largely disappeared after 1918, retiring behind a facade that she and others erected around her declining years. But before then, at Bedford Square and (especially) Garsington, Ottoline lived an extraordinary life…much of which she kept to herself.

INTERLUDE
Hook'em Horns

The Humanities Research Center, Austin, Texas

WRITING A biography – and an "official" one at that – of Lady Ottoline Morrell was clearly going to be a major task. So my first step, after getting the "go-ahead" from Julian Vinogradoff, was to put together a research strategy, and work out how to fit it into my life. Chatto had given me a £1200 "advance", but that was not going to last long if – as I intended – this was to be a full-time project. Fortunately I had more than Virginia Woolf's "£500 and a room of my own". We had sold our house in Sydney before we came to London, where we intended to reside permanently. We bought an almost derelict three-storey terrace house in the more downtrodden part Notting Hill, and in mid-1971 moved into its renovated basement. That gave me my room of my own. With that asset, our local bank agreed to grant us an overdraft while I worked on the biography, and that would give us adequate money to live on (my husband Rob also had a job as a sub-editor on a Fleet Street magazine, which augmented our income, though he intended help me with the research).

There were three major areas of prospective research: reading what had been already been written about Ottoline; identifying and tracking down unpublished material (letters, etc); and trying to interview people who had known Ottoline, or had information about her. Much of the first four months or so was spent – primarily at the British Museum library – reading what other people had written about Ottoline, and using their bibliographies to identify other possible source material (the results of all of which went into my research card-index system). Yet we knew that the major research source was going to be Ottoline's letters, which Julian Vinogradoff had recently sold to the University of Texas. Nevertheless, by the time Rob and I flew to America in August 1972, I had a provisional picture in my mind of Ottoline and the circles – the milieu – she had moved in.

Prior to arriving in Austin, Texas, we had little or no idea what to expect. We gained some inkling, however, on the flight to San Antonio, when a voice from the cockpit said, in a slow Texan drawl: "Mary-Lou, when you're finished in the cabin, come up here and sit on ma knee." We caught the bus to Austin, where we had been booked into a 12-storey student hostel across the road – "the drag" – from the sprawling University of Texas campus. Next day we fronted up at the Humanities Research Center (HRC), which was one of the university's main research libraries, and housed what still is probably the world's major collection of English (and American, etc) literary documents and manuscripts. Some years before, oil had been struck on land owned by the university, and this had provided an annual income of (in those days) over $700 million. The HRC had been one of the beneficiaries of that flow of oil, which in turn allowed it to out-bid other libraries and research institutions for major caches of literary material (they had a Shakespeare First Folio, among many other literary treasures). I do not know what they paid for Ottoline's letters, but, as we say in Australia, it would have been a motza.

After signing in, we were allocated two desks in their modest reading-room, next to the main catalogue drawers (this was in the age before library computers). As Ottoline's papers had yet to be processed – they had only arrived a few months before we did – they had been temporarily stored in folders lodged in several filing cabinets. We started at the letter "A" and worked down the alphabet. We were not allowed to photocopy any of the letters, so had to take notes of anything we found of interest. I had brought along a portable typewriter, and so typed my notes (they gave me a special cubicle so I would not disturb other researchers), while Rob used his primitive shorthand to record his notes. (I looked after the major figures, while he covered the lesser ones.)

And what names were there! It was like opening a literary treasure-chest. There were more than 150 letters from Lytton Strachey alone; hundreds from Virginia Woolf; and scores from DH Lawrence and many of the other great names in English (indeed, world) literature. And to cap it all, there were more than 2,500 letters from Ottoline's lover, Bertrand Russell. Imagine it – 2,500 letters from one of the greatest intellects of the 20th century! If ever minds were boggled, ours were during that hectic month – working six days a week – at the HRC in Austin, Texas (while outside the temperature was in the 90s). The staff were very helpful and supportive, and we helped them by sorting some of the letters into chronological and other proper order.

We would arrive at 9am, break for an hour's lunch, then continue on until 6pm. We would then go back to our hostel and I would type up Rob's notes, before having dinner in one of the student eating-places that lined the Drag. On Saturday night, the Drag lived up to its name, as students in Porches and other expensive cars roared up and down the street, blowing their horns and shouting "Hook 'em Horns" (the catch-cry of the university's gridiron team, which strutted its stuff in the huge stadium down the road from our hostel). Directly across the Drag was the building where from its 27th floor in 1966 an ex-marine sharp-shooter, Charles Whiteman, had shot and killed 14 people, before he was gunned down.

Also in the campus opposite was the LBJ Presidential Library, built to resemble an Mayan temple, that housed his papers – 45 million of them (right down to his dry-cleaning tickets) – together with other Johnsonian memorabilia, including the gifts he had received as President, plus Lucy Baines' and Linda Bird's wedding dresses.

There was a lot of unrest on the campus when we were there – it was the height of the Vietnam War – and we attended several rallies and "peace" concerts on the Sundays we had off. The star of these was the campus darling, the one-toothed Kenneth Threadgill, a singer and guitar-player who had discovered Janis Joplin and launched the Austin brand of county-and-western music.

CHAPTER 2
The Daughter of a Thousand Earls

The young Ottoline

OTTOLINE WAS BORN in London on June 16, 1873, into a world of class and privilege. Victoria had been Queen for 36 years and was to reign another 28. Ottoline's parents were paradigms of the Victorian age. Her father was Lieutenant-General Arthur Bentinck, colonel of the Seventh Dragoon Guards, a big, bearded patriarch with a deep voice and booming laugh. Her mother was Augusta Mary Elizabeth, a dark-haired Anglo-Irish beauty, daughter of the Very Reverend and Honourable H.M. Browne, Dean of Lismore. Augusta, who was seriously religious, was the general's second wife. They had three older children: Henry, William, and Charles, and the general had an elder son, Arthur, by his first wife. A few weeks before her last confinement Augusta Bentinck, who was 39, sat down and wrote to her eldest son, Henry, who was ten:

> *My Henry – My Darling,*
> *If God takes me from you this is to bid you farewell. I pray to God to comfort you, if I go, as I pray him to spare me to you if it is His will…But if God takes me, His will is best. He and your own dear Father will in time comfort you. Papa will be as kind to you as I ever was, and God will take care of you if you ask Him, and never forget my darling to read your Bible and to say your prayers, wherever you are, for God loves those who love Him…Be persevering in your studies, and try when you are older to do good in the world, to make a name worthy of your ancestors and of yourself…Keep my little Willie in the right path…I think you will be happy at the schools we have chosen for you both, Cheam and Eton, and that you will go to Oxford.*[1]

Yet Mrs. Bentinck was spared, and her child, a daughter, was christened Ottoline Violet Anne Cavendish-Bentinck (though the family preferred to use plain Bentinck). Ottoline – the unusual name was a legacy of her Dutch ancestry – spent her first four-and-a-half years cocooned in the safe, ordered, narrow way of life then enjoyed by the English upper-class. They had a house in the country; a summer residence in London; servants in the attic; coachmen in the mews; and Nurse Powell in the nursery. An early family photograph shows Ottoline as a pudding-faced infant dressed up in a white lace dress with a sort of junior bustle and curling hair cut in a fringe. When the family came to London for the Season, her father would take her to Hyde Park, where he held her by a broad pink sash as she galloped out in front of him in her patent-leather shoes. When in the country, he took her for rides in a pony-trap down winding lanes, and on evenings when important visitors came, she would sit on his knee and hide her head on his shoulder.

The family was very comfortably off, the general's army pay being supplemented by an allowance from his distant cousin, the Fifth Duke of Portland. Moreover, due to a series of dynastic mishaps, the general was now the Duke's heir, and as Portland was old and ailing, it was assumed that at any moment Ottoline's father would become the Sixth Duke, inheriting the family seat, Welbeck Abbey, together with other property and extensive estates in Nottinghamshire, Derbyshire, Northumberland, Ayrshire, Caithness, and London itself.

In 1877, however, these secure expectations were dashed when General Bentinck unexpectedly suffered a heart attack, and died aged 59. For his widow Augusta, this was a double blow. Not only was she left to bring up a large family alone; but the prospect of becoming Duchess of Portland was gone, as the dukedom would now go to her stepson, Arthur, a 20-year-old officer in the Coldstream Guards. After the funeral, Mrs. Bentinck spent her period of mourning with her children in the country, only returning to London for the summer Season in 1878. She took a relatively modest house in Grosvenor Crescent, off Belgrave Square, paid for by a small allowance from the (still extant) Fifth Duke. From the windows of the house Arthur and his half-brothers and half-sister used to watch through lace curtains as splendidly-dressed guests arrived at the Duke of Richmond's much grander residence opposite. Mrs. Bentinck had not been granted an army pension, so the family's circumstances were consequently reduced, and there were fewer toys for Ottoline, and fewer servants below stairs.

This difficult period, however, lasted only a year. In December 1878 Arthur turned 21 and the Fifth Duke re-entailed his estates to provide for his succession by the young guardsman, at the same time giving him a generous allowance (which Arthur spent on a stable of hunting horses and the lease on a substantial London house, 13 Grosvenor Place, at the rear of Buckingham Palace, for the rest of the family). Almost exactly 12 months later the Fifth Duke himself died, and Arthur became the Sixth Duke.

The family, who were staying in the country, came down to London and were put up at Claridge's, where boxes of grapes and peaches, wrapped in pink paper, arrived from the Welbeck greenhouses for the Abbey's new owners. Six-year-old Ottoline and her brother Charlie were taken to Cremer's toyshop in Regent Street and told to choose anything they wished. Two weeks later the family travelled up to Welbeck to enter into their inheritance. Charlie meanwhile had fallen ill and had to be carried off the train at Worksop station, watched by a crowd of locals, who had come out on the cold wintry night to see the young Duke and his family arrive.

To a natural interest in the doings of the Portland dynasty was perhaps added an interest to see if there was any sign of oddness or eccentricity. For the late Fifth Duke had had a reputation in that direction. Neither Mrs. Bentinck nor Arthur had ever met him, but rumours of his activities at Welbeck had filtered through, and as they drove up the long drive to the squat, dark Abbey they too were no doubt wondering what they would find. Their worst fears were perhaps realised when through the carriage window they saw silhouettes of decapitated trees and mounds of rubble; while even to reach the Abbey entrance they had to go over a bridge of planks, as the drive had been dug up. Inside, the hall floorboards also were up and more planks had to be negotiated to reach the stairs that led to the only habitable part of the building; a suite of rooms in which the old Duke had lived out his solitary routine, communicating with his servants through double letter-boxes cut in the doors.

Next morning Ottoline and Willie began exploring the Abbey, a 13th-century building which successive owners had added to over the years. It was soon apparent where the Fifth Duke's nickname, the "Burrowing Duke", had come from. The place was riddled with tunnels. Evidently when the late duke inherited the Abbey he had been eager to add to it, and rather than spoil the facade he decided to put his extra rooms underground. With Welbeck situated in coal-mining country, there were plenty of miners available to work on the tunnelling.

As time went on, the Duke's tunnelling developed into a mania, and eventually over 600 navvies were employed at Welbeck on his excavations and tunnelling. These he used to supervised personally, his tall figure crowned with a top hat and his trousers tied with string at the ankles. One tunnel was of truly titanic proportions. It stretched a mile-and-a-half from the abbey towards Worksop station and was wide enough for two carriages to pass abreast. The old Duke had also been installing a new plumbing and heating system, which was the reason for the trenches outside and the disrupted state within. And in a misplaced effort to improve the appearance of the grounds, he had had every tree on the estate lopped.

It was hardly a homely place that Ottoline and her brother explored. One subterranean passage they discovered led to a trapdoor opening into the riding school built by the first Duke of Newcastle, a 17th-century ancestor of Ottoline's. But a riding school it was no longer. The Fifth Duke of Portland had transformed the stark interior into a fairy-tale ballroom. The ceiling was painted sunset-pink and hung with chandeliers, and the walls were lined with mirrors. Yet no ball had ever been held there, and stacked around the room, like so many wallflowers, were Bentinck family portraits, their frames removed.

Soon the young Sixth Duke began to feel oppressed by his new residence – he wanted to shut it up and return to his home and club in London. His stepmother, however, was a strong-willed woman who saw that their duty lay in restoring Welbeck to its former position as one of England's great ducal houses. As well, the welfare of the several thousand people who were tied to the Welbeck estate and its satellite villages concerned her. Not that the old Duke had neglected his tenants. He had given them donkeys to ride to work, and umbrellas to keep the rain off. He even had a roller-skating rink built for the servants, and encouraged them to make use of it. If he had a reason to go into Welbeck itself, and would throw handfuls of coins to the village children as he went past. To Mrs. Bentinck, such capricious philanthropy was not enough, and she began a programme of visiting the estate cottages. She screened off one end of the riding school to institute Sunday morning church services. With the aid of experts summoned from London, she personally sorted out the Welbeck treasures, giving Ottoline lessons in the history of the family as she did so. As they sifted through the heirlooms, she illustrated her instruction with pictures of Talbot courtiers in Elizabethan ruffs; pantalooned Cavendishes from the court of James I; and Bentincks with severe Dutch faces.

On the family's distaff side three women stood out. The first was the prodigious Bess of Hardwick, founder of the Cavendish line, and one of the few people to get the better of Elizabeth I. The second was Margaret, first Duchess of Newcastle, called "Mad Madge", and remembered as one of the first of the bluestockings. The third was Margaret Cavendish-Holles-Harley, who in 1734 married the second Duke of Portland, uniting the Cavendishes with the Bentincks. Ottoline was fascinated by all three women. They stood out as being cut from a different fabric than she was familiar with. Of the three, however, her favourite was Margaret, the first Duchess of Newcastle, who had lived at Bolsover Castle, in the nearby county of Derbyshire, mixing there with philosophers and scholars, and writing poetry and plays (and wearing outlandish clothes; a trait that came down to Ottoline). Ottoline had fond memories of visits to Bolsover Castle, which was part of the Cavendish inheritance, where she would sit with her mother in the castle garden and hear tales about Margaret, who had decorated the castle with magical murals and had lined the wooden panelling with gilt (as Ottoline herself was to do many years later at Garsington). History became Ottoline's playthings – Henry VIII's dagger; the pearl earring Charles 1 wore at his execution; and a casket that belonged to William of Orange (and in which she kept her childish letters).

Welbeck Abbey was to be the home of Ottoline, her mother and her three brothers for ten years - important years in any child's life. Yet, despite such interesting playthings, her life was strange and lonely. She had no playmates, apart from her elder brothers when they were still growing up. Her only other companions were servants. Like most girls of her class, she never even learned to dress herself. Her maid combed her hair; twisted it into sausage curls; lowered her lace petticoats and frocks over her head; tied her sashes; and buckled her shoes. Cooking and other feminine domestic skills were likewise a mystery (and were to remain so for the rest of her life).

Her education was entrusted entirely to governesses, principally a Miss Craig, whose primary duty, under instructions from Ottoline's mother, it was to drum the Scriptures into her young pupil. Ottoline also learned to read and write (and embroider); but of literature, science, and politics she was taught virtually nothing. It was only when an older cousin, Cattie, came to visit did she have any real companionship. On these rare occasions the two would go out together in Ottoline's miniature phaeton, drawn by a pair of Shetland ponies, and gallop through the Abbey grounds, and even as far afield as Sherwood Forest. Portland, as Ottoline's half-brother was now called, was outwardly kind to her; but he was inclined to be a trifle pompous, and anyway was busy enjoying the role of the young and highly-eligible Duke. As they grew older, her other brothers became increasingly uninterested in their younger sister; their world was Eton and military college. When they came home to Welbeck on holiday, she would trail around after them trying to join in their pursuits and conversation. She hero-worshipped her youngest brother Charlie, but he called her disparagingly "Higgory Stiggins". Yet Ottoline was nothing if not persistent, and kept on trying to communicate with them. When she was nine and her 19-year-old brother Henry was away with the Derbyshire Regiment, she wrote:

> *My Dear Henry,*
> *Are you very nearly drowned and how do you like it. Charly was up for the day on Saturday and was photographed in the morning and went to a cricket match in the afternoon. I bought him a prearbook and a pice of old Windsor soap and a bottle of eau de cologne.*

No more to say Your loving Ottoline
Please write at once[2]

As her childhood years came to an end (and puberty loomed), Ottoline turned in on herself. She curtained off one end of her room to make a private place where she could have her own treasures, and to which she could retire when her brothers proved too insensitive. This was the first of her boudoirs. She was becoming a young adult, with all that entailed.

INTERLUDE
Stalked by the Dook

The underground ballroom at Welbeck Abbey

ONE OF THE first doors I wanted opened was at Welbeck Abbey, the ancestral home of the Dukes of Portland, where Ottoline was to spend much of her childhood and early adulthood. Welbeck was one of England's great stately homes, set in 17,000 acres outside of Nottingham, including much of Sherwood Forest. Originally a religious building (hence "Abbey"), it was appropriated by Henry VIII during the Dissolution of the Monasteries, and came via the Cavendish line into the Bentinck family (who came over with William of Orange). In 1715 the Cavendish-Bentinck earldom was elevated into a dukedom. Ottoline's half-brother Arthur was the Sixth Duke.

The Fifth Duke, the "Burrowing Duke", had been Welbeck's most famous, or infamous, occupant (see above). I had attempted to get permission from the Seventh Duke, Ottoline's nephew, to see Welbeck, but he didn't reply to my letter. So I contacted the British Army, which had taken over much of Welbeck for a cadet training-college (although the Duke continued to occupy one wing of the building). A friendly Army major invited me and Rob to come and see the place. It was a particularly hot day when we arrived at the Abbey, to be greeted by the major, who invited us for a tour of the Abbey grounds. He warned us about the Duke. "He is quite inquisitive and has a habit of following my car if he sees me driving people around," the major said. "Just remember you are supposed to be parents of a potential cadet." As we set off past a lake and through some fields, we noticed a small, rather battered car following us. The major explained: "The Dook is a lovely old chap, but a trifle eccentric. Once he drove his old car into Worksop and left it in the middle of the street because he saw a shop he wanted to visit." Now the Dook was about 100 metres behind us, slowing down when we slowed down. Finally he drew level and wound his window down. I could see a long face with a largish nose. "Good morning Major," he said, "could you take a look at the pets' graveyard. My daughter is having some work done on it. Could you see if it has started?" The major said he would inspect it.

We then drove on up a small rise to the Portland family chapel to see the graves of Ottoline and Philip. We saw their simple, white gravestones, carved, not in traditional gothic script, but Gill Sans, an elegant sans-serif typeface developed by one of Ottoline's Garsington guests, the sculptor Eric Gill. As we drove back towards the Abbey, the major stopped his Range Rover beside a field where several estate workers were busy with shovels and mattocks, apparently tidying up the pets' graveyard. "I've never see a pets' graveyard," said Rob, "let alone a ducal one." So he got out to have a look. As he picked his way around the 18-inch-high gravestones, he was stopped dead in his tracks by the name on one of them. It read "Carbine"; Australia's greatest racehorse, which was bought by Ottoline's half-brother, the Sixth Duke, for 13,500 guineas, and put to stud at Welbeck.

My visit to Welbeck gave a new dimension to my picture of Ottoline. It is only when you see at first hand the size and scale of such a grand house, and the immensity of its gardens and estate – not to mention the acres and acres of Bentinck countryside surrounding it – that the power and lifestyle of those ducal families can be appreciated. That Ottoline grew up there would have had a powerful influence on her. Yet this was what she was to willingly turn her back on.

CHAPTER 3
Huntin', Shootn' & Fishn'

Ottoline as a young woman

OTTOLINE'S UPBRINGING had been designed to fit her for one purpose in life: marriage to an aristocrat of approximately equal rank. Everyone assumed she would become one of the tribe of ladies who now began to flock to Welbeck, accompanying the huntin', shootin', and fishin' "bloods" that made up virtually all of Portland's friends, and a large part of the English upper-class generally. Welbeck's return to the circuit of great country houses was sealed in November 1881 when the Prince of Wales, later Edward VII, paid it a Royal visit. Like the rest of society, he had heard of the amazing Burrowing Duke and his troglodyte wonderland at Welbeck, and he was anxious to come and see it for himself. Portland ensured he was not disappointed. Edward arrived at Worksop by the Royal train and travelled to the Abbey through the Burrowing Duke's tunnel, which was specially gas-lit for the occasion. HRH brought his usual entourage, and while the ladies preened themselves, the men went out shooting. In two days Edward and his party accounted for 1,081 pheasant, more than 400 hares and rabbits, plus three woodcock (a record of such things was kept at country houses). In the evenings, the guests played cards or listened to Mrs. Reynolds singing operatic selections.

During the visit, which was judged an unqualified success, Ottoline asked the Prince for a donation for a local hospital, and Edward obliged with a gold sovereign and a peck on the cheek. It was on occasions like this that the utter vapidity of the life of an upper-class lady was etched on Ottoline's mind. She observed them coming down to breakfast in morning dresses with tight waists and lace fronts. They sat, she recalled, "and gossiped all the morning, then changed into tweeds and drove out to lunch with the sports. In the afternoon they donned pink satin tea-gowns from Paris, before changing into brocades and velvets for the formal dinner".[1] She used to hide behind some embroidered curtains and peep at them as they swept into the drawing-room prior to dinner, composing themselves and giving their dresses a finishing pat before making their entrance.

After Arthur became the Sixth Duke, the (then) Prime Minister Disraeli – whose political career had been greatly advanced by the Bentincks – prevailed upon Queen Victoria to bestow titles appropriate to full brothers and sisters of a duke on Ottoline and her brothers (who henceforth would be Lady and Lords respectively). Disraeli also persuaded the Queen – as a personal favour to him, and against all precedent – to create Ottoline's mother, who had remained plain Mrs. Bentinck despite the succession of her stepson to the dukedom, Baroness Bolsover (a junior Bentinck title). Nor was this the end of Disraeli's largess. He used his influence to obtain for Portland, while still a young man, the Order of the Garter (the nation's highest order of chivalry) and the important post of Master of the Horse (as such he was in charge of coronation processions, a role he was soon called on to perform).

Occasionally Portland and his friends would forsake Welbeck and travel up to Langwell in Scotland where they would continue denuding the countryside of its wildlife, before moving on elsewhere. Several months of the year were spent in London observing the annual summer ritual of the Season. Soon Ottoline would have to go through the formality of Coming Out. Portland (following his appointment as Master of the Horse) would take his young sister riding on Rotten Row, their horses proudly wearing the red headbands of the Royal Stables, and Ottoline carrying a whip engraved with her initials, O.V.A.C-B. During the Season, Lady Bolsover took her daughter to the opera and theatre, and Ottoline remembered seeing Sir Henry Irving in *The Corsican Brothers* and Sarah Bernhardt in *Frou Frou*. On another night she and her mother saw Oscar Wilde, sunflower in his buttonhole, at the premiere of Gilbert and Sullivan's *Patience* at the Savoy Theatre in the Strand. There were other excursions to art galleries to view the latest works of Poynter, Watts, and Whistler. And once a week Ottoline set off in a carriage from 13 Grosvenor Place to go to dancing class, which she didn't enjoy because the other girls sniggered at her elaborate appearance.

But for an event in 1889, Ottoline would probably have outgrown her reserve and duly fulfilled her destiny of marrying one of her brothers' circle. However, in June of that year Portland himself married, and as Lady Bolsover watched the new duchess come down the aisle, she realised her days as mistress of Welbeck were over. Shortly after the wedding she left to live in a house provided by Portland at St. Anne's Hill, Chertsey, and with her into exile went Ottoline, aged 16. The next two years were quiet. Lady Bolsover's health was failing (she had diabetes among other complaints) and the task of looking after her fell principally to Ottoline. During this time – when a girl could look forward to a widening circle of acquaintances – Ottoline retreated even further into herself; devoting her days to nursing, running the house and servants, and poring over the 15th-century teachings of Thomas à Kempis, whose book *The Imitation of Christ* became her guide and scourge. Over and over she read his precepts on having a humble opinion of oneself; on obedience and submission; on the inner life; on doing without comfort; and on what delight there is in spurning the whole world and becoming the servant of God. Ottoline became something of a religious fanatic herself, and even the quiet, dutiful, self-denying life she was leading began to seem almost profligate. She put away her prettiest dresses and took to wearing the plainest cloth she could find.

She thought food a weakness of the flesh, so she ate as frugally as possible. Books were also pleasurable, so they had to be shunned as well. Yet even these sacrifices were not sufficient. She took up a young gypsy girl, giving her some of the luxuries she denied herself, and teaching her to read and write. Yet still she was torn by inner conflict. How could she reconcile her love of beautiful things – the countryside in spring and the gaiety and excitement of the theatre – with her hunger for a more purposeful, serious existence? The carefree life her brothers pursued began to appear not just hollow, but downright profligate.

Over the next three years Ottoline and her mother crossed the Channel several times to visit spas and clinics; but Ottoline derived little enjoyment from these excursions. She was shy and pious and her mother made little effort to encourage her to meet people of her own age. Indeed, it seems that Lady Bolsover almost made Ottoline her slave. Besides, at 17, Ottoline was not particularly attractive; she was almost six feet tall and her nose, which was always strong, had become over-prominent. Later her features were to blend together better, but at this time she could derive no confidence from her appearance.

In 1892 Ottoline turned 19 and, despite her obvious lack of interest in society, Portland and her mother decided she should "Come Out". Lady Bolsover rose to the occasion and took her reluctant and awkward daughter through the Season's important events: Ascot; garden parties; and the balls held at Stafford House, Grosvenor House, Devonshire House, and London's other aristocratic residences. Here, under the twinkling chandeliers, Ottoline watched handsome happy couples swirling to the latest Viennese waltz tunes; and felt totally out of place. She shrank against the wall, and when someone asked her to dance, the walk across the polished floor was agony. Her only pleasant memories of that summer of 1892 were of the scents of the flowers arranged around the rooms.

Her brothers despaired of her. She had the choice, were she to make the slightest effort, of any number of eligible young fellows who would be happy to marry the half-sister of the Duke of Portland. One of her brothers told her: "There isn't a girl in England who wouldn't want to step into your shoes."[2] But Ottoline was growing into a very stubborn young woman. She refused to consider any possibility of marriage. Instead she decided to devote her immediate future to her frail mother and Thomas à Kempis.

The following year Lady Bolsover decided to go abroad to Italy to try a new cure in Florence. En route, they stopped off in Paris where, in a final burst of maternal energy, Lady Bolsover bought Ottoline some pretty muslin dresses and a valuable necklace of pearls. (This necklace, which many people were later to call "The Portland Pearls," had actually belonged to Marie Antoinette.) Perhaps at last Lady Bolsover was realising that her daughter was becoming too serious and dowdy. Yet on finally reaching Florence, it was Ottoline who fell ill. Doctors diagnosed typhoid fever and for several days her life hung in the balance. Recovering, she went to convalesce with her aunt, Louise Bentinck, now married to her second husband, Henry Scott (Mrs Scott was to be the grandmother of the future Queen Elizabeth, the present Queen's mother).

The Scotts owned a villa outside Florence where, pampered and petted, Ottoline was introduced to a new way of life, in which happiness and the appreciation of beautiful things were not frowned on. After several happy weeks, however, the idyllic sojourn came to an end, as Ottoline had to take her ailing mother home to England. The trip back to London, first by train and then ferry and train, was agony for Ottoline. Still weak from her own illness, she had to haul her mother in a heavy wheelchair in and out of railway carriages, when station staff were not available. Back in London, Lady Bolsover lapsed into a coma and died shortly afterwards.

Ottoline was numbed by her mother's death. Her brother, Lord Henry, took her into his house in Sloane Square, but she found little comfort there. Her brothers avoided mentioning the death, preferring to act almost as if their mother had never existed. Later Lord Henry and his wife took Ottoline north where they joined Portland's stalking party at Langwell in Scotland. But instead of entering into the fun, Ottoline spent most of her time closeted in her room, reading religious books while being conscious of the growing disapproval of everyone around her. Her brothers could not understand why their sister had to go about with such a long face.

With the death of her mother, Ottoline was left in a serious financial situation. She had no income of her own and was totally dependent on her half-brother, the Sixth Duke, who was still hoping that she would finally come to her senses and marry one of the young blades who came to Welbeck. But Ottoline was not to be deterred from her desire to carry out good works, and in an effort to find something more worthwhile to do, she began holding Bible classes for the footmen and estate workers in her sitting-room at Welbeck. Some came out of curiosity, others from boredom or duty; but in any event the classes were a definite success. Later Ottoline was to look back on them with amusement: "It was difficult to concentrate at times with twenty young men in the room, all chosen as footmen because of their good looks."[3]

In 1893, however, it was for 20-year-old Ottoline a serious business, and she followed up their success with a wood-carving class, Portland being prevailed on to supply a teacher. Many years later Ottoline would sometimes come across one of her former students, working perhaps as an attendant at the National Gallery or in a department store. They would step forward and introduce themselves: "I was one of your young men, your Ladyship."[4]

Ottoline also took to visiting cottages on the estate, as her mother had done, distributing gifts and doing other good works. Yet she herself was almost friendless. The only person she could talk to was the librarian at Welbeck, Arthur Strong, who gave her books by Browning, Locke, and Meredith. To Ottoline, Strong was "a being from another planet".[5] But he was to later run foul of Portland, when one day he lit a cigarette in the dining-room, unaware that in doing so he had breached some rule of etiquette. Portland dismissed him instantly.

Ottoline's only other relief from her unhappy existence at Welbeck and in London came from occasional trips to Ham Common, outside of London, to visit her Florence relative, Mrs. Scott, at whose London house she had met some interesting people, among them young Bertie Russell. She got on particularly well with Mrs. Scott's daughters, Violet and Hyacinth, despite they being a little too High Church for Ottoline's Evangelical taste. One day Hyacinth invited her to accompany her on a visit to an Anglican convent in Cornwall, run by the Little Sisters of the Poor. There Ottoline met a nun named Mother Julian who was to be her mentor over the next few years (and after whom she was to name her daughter). She discussed her worries with Mother Julian, particularly the problem of how she could reconcile the spiritual side of her nature with her romantic instincts. For a nun, Mother Julian had a somewhat worldly view of human nature, and she assured Ottoline that to love beautiful things and enjoy life was not evil. Though not completely convinced, Ottoline began to understand her mother's last gesture in buying her the muslin dresses and pearls. Mother Julian may have been the first step towards Ottoline's liberation.

THE EARLY MEN IN HER LIFE

Ottoline's father, Lieutenant-General Arthur Bentinck

The Bentinck family c1893 (l to r) Duke of Portland, Lady Bolsover, Lord and Lady Enniskillen, Lord Henry Bentinck, Ottoline

The Archbishop of York, William Maclagan

H.H. Asquith

Welbeck Abbey

Augustine Birrell

Axel Munthe

Axel Munthe's villa on Capri

John Adam Cramb

CHAPTER 4
The Butterfly Spreads Her Wings

Ottoline at Hampton Court (by Charles Condor)

ALTHOUGH IT would be gilding the lily to describe Ottoline as a butterfly; she was now, butterfly-like, starting to break out from her chrysalis. If she had been like other girls of her age and era, her main interest in life would have been men and marriage. Yet she had no home to need to escape from; and her mother was no longer around to match-make. Ottoline did not approve of the male company her brothers kept, and now, aged 21, she was no longer interested in youthful pursuits. Her concerns were much more serious, and spiritual. Nevertheless, while she herself was not showing much interested in the male sex, the older element of it was starting to show a great deal of interest in her.

Probably the first man to fall under Ottoline's spell was the 88th Archbishop of York, William Dalrymple Maclagan. In 1895 Maclagan came to Welbeck to officiate at a Bentinck family occasion. While there he made friends with the long-nosed sister of his host. As one of the Empire's principal religious leaders, he was socially equal, if not senior to her brother. Also Maclagan represented a way of life that Ottoline now felt to be superior to that at Welbeck. It was perhaps natural that she should seek his company and support.

Yet there was more to their friendship than a common interest. All her life Ottoline had a knack for attracting men years her senior. There was something in her makeup that proved almost irresistible to men like Maclagan. Soon she and the 69-year-old prelate were to be seen taking long walks together in the grounds of Welbeck, deep in conversation. They made an incongruous twosome: Ottoline, 21 years old, just on six feet tall, towering over the diminutive, white-haired Archbishop. After he returned to his palace at Bishopthorpe in York, they corresponded regularly. Having lost her father at an early age, and having been forced to rely on her brothers for advice, Ottoline turned to the kindly old archbishop as a surrogate father. She addressed him as Father and he called her My Dear Child, My Dearest, signing himself "Your Loving Father in God". Soon Ottoline was making regular visits to Bishopthorpe, so many that Maclagan had a room set aside for her in his palace, much to his wife's disapproval. He took it upon himself to supervise Ottoline's further education, preparing reading lists for her. He also took an interest in her classes at Welbeck for the estate staff, and her other good works. They exchanged gifts and she voiced her concern about his rheumatism. He asked her about her recurrent headaches. He wrote: "I truly believe God committed you to my care."[1] Years later Ottoline was to admit in her memoirs that Maclagan had been rather flirtatious "in a mild, fatherly way".[2]

During the spring and summer of 1896 they met frequently. Maclagan often came to address her classes, which had now been extended to London during the Season. Held in her brother's house at 13 Grosvenor Place, these extramural meetings were mainly for girls, possibly below-stairs staff whom Ottoline befriended, or shop-girls, with whom she had a remarkable rapport throughout her life. The following year, on June 3, 1897, Maclagan wrote to her:

> *I have made a note of Thursday 13th, Friday 16th and Tuesday 30th July at 5 pm. for your little gatherings. (P.S. I was not quite pleased with your look today. Please be very careful & self-indulgent – if you can!)*[3]

But the Tuesday date proved difficult, as he explained rather apologetically the following month:

> DEAREST OTTOLINE, *Alas! the Queen has fixed Tuesday next for receiving the Bishops of the Lambeth Conference at Windsor, and my attendance there is necessary. What can be done about my address to your friends? Would there be any chance of my seeing you Sunday if I were to call?*[4]

In 1896 Maclagan lent his support to a project that was to alter Ottoline's life profoundly. In June she turned 23, an age at which her brothers thought they had a right to expect some indication of her future intentions. Yet she showed no interest in any of the activities of a normal young woman of her class and position. "One thing I was quite clear about, clear with a sort of horror," she said in her *Memoirs*, "I could not marry any of the young men who came to Welbeck. I remember visualising myself with dread as the mistress of one of their large houses, entertaining shooting parties, and living with a man to whom I could never talk."[5] Her brothers had become used to Ottoline's absence from the gatherings they enjoyed. Now, however, she intruded into their lives again. The idea came not from her but from Miss Craig, her former governess, who had stayed on at Welbeck and kept in touch with her erstwhile pupil. Concerned that Ottoline was looking tired and unhappy, she told her: "You are being starved. You must go abroad. You must get away."[6]

The possibility of travelling abroad had not occurred to Ottoline, probably because her previous trip to the Continent had ended in the tragedy of her mother's final illness. Now she screwed up her courage to ask Portland's permission to go (for he would have to finance the trip). At first he raised objections: "Why do you want to go? Are you not happy here?"[7] Then there were the logistics. Ottoline could not be allowed to go travelling around Europe unaccompanied. The brothers met in a family conclave to discuss the problem, and it was only after Miss Craig found a friend, Miss Rootes, a learned lady of impeccable respectability as companion-chaperone, that Portland finally gave his imprimatur to the adventure. The Archbishop smiled on the plan and recommended Cortina in the Dolomites as a congenial destination.

Ottoline's maid, Ellen, started packing. Before embarkation, a fourth member was added to the party: the Honourable Hilda Douglas-Pennant, a tall, prim, fussy young woman with a prunes-and-prisms expression. Ottoline had known Hilda only slightly; but one day she asked her if she would like to come to the Continent, and Hilda jumped at the idea. So, as the summer of 1896 faded, the party of four – laden with air cushions, clocks, smelling salts, and fans – travelled via Victoria Station to Dover, thence to Ostend and Brussels. Hilda was amazed by Ottoline's large red cape, which was in fact a travelling library; Ottoline having sewn pockets around the interior, into which she crammed the works of Ruskin and other writers recommended by the Archbishop. As they progressed, Miss Rootes, white of hair and long of tooth, would comment on passing items of interest. Cathedrals were examined from nave to crypt; art galleries toured; sites of historical interest diligently visited. Ottoline took notes on everything in her leather-bound travel notebook. From Brussels the party proceeded at a leisurely pace by way of Wurzburg, Munich, Innsbruck, and Ratisbon to Cortina. Ottoline was in a daze, revelling in her new-found freedom. She and Hilda became firm friends; and not even Hilda's undisguised distaste for the omniscient Miss Rootes soured Ottoline's enjoyment.

In October the weather in Cortina began to close in, so the party moved on south to Venice. While Ottoline was immersed in Ruskin's *Stones of Venice*, the friction between Hilda and Miss Rootes grew. Ottoline was in a dilemma. She appreciated the older woman's erudition – it was she who had opened her eyes to classical literature – but Hilda wanted Ottoline all to herself. Finally, Miss Rootes appreciated the situation and departed, leaving Ottoline, Hilda, and maid Ellen to continue on deeper into Italy. As the luscious countryside drifted past, Ottoline began to blossom. Padua, Bologna, Ravenna, Urbino, Siena, Perugia, Assisi; the romance, mystery, colour, and beauty of Renaissance Italy flooded into her dry puritan soul. Italy became for Ottoline a pulsing symbol of freedom. The richness of the land and the richness of its past overwhelmed her. "I drank then of the elixir of Italy," she said in her *Memoirs*. "I drank so deeply of it that it has never left me."[8] Ottoline and Hilda had arranged to join Ottoline's aunt Mrs. Scott in her villa in Florence and to stay with her and her daughters for the rest of the winter. Usually Ottoline relished their company; but this time, liberated as she was from Welbeck and her past, they seemed too serious for her new mood. Even so, she enjoyed these months spent walking through cobbled streets and squares; watching sunsets; and visiting churches and galleries with Hilda.

In March 1897 the two reluctantly made their way back to London, the prospect of which appalled Ottoline. Now that the rash, romantic element in her personality had been awakened, she felt she must "do something". In Italy she and Hilda had talked long and seriously about life and the future, without coming to a firm conclusion. Hilda had introduced her to poetry – to Keats in particular – and now Ottoline thirsted for further mental stimulation. Back at Grosvenor Place she took up some of her old threads, reconvening her classes for young girls and inviting Maclagan to come down from York to deliver his little sermons.

However, it was an advertisement in a newspaper that provided Ottoline with her next step towards independence. It gave details of preparatory courses for St. Andrews University in Scotland. The estimable Miss Rootes had raised the possibility of tertiary education, and now Ottoline resolved to follow her recommendation and go to St. Andrews for the coming academic year. This drastic step required another family conference, as it was thought no well-bred girl should, or would want to, go to university. The spectre of their eccentric sister turning into a bluestocking and becoming the source of unkind remarks among their circle haunted the brothers. Ottoline, however, found an unexpected ally in Portland's now mother-in-law, Mrs. Dallas-Yorke, who spoke up for the plan, and whose support proved decisive. So Ottoline travelled north, stopping off at Bishopthorpe to see the Archbishop, then continuing on to Scotland, accompanied by a retinue consisting of Hilda Douglas-Pennant; two dogs; the maid Ellen; and Miss Hurblatt, a lady tutor whom Mrs. Dallas-Yorke had provided for Ottoline and Hilda (who was also bent on higher education). They all moved into lodgings at No. 5 Murry Park, near the university.

This was to be Ottoline's first extended excursion outside her upper-class world, and she was understandably nervous about it. In the university register she entered her age not as 24, but as a coy 17. At St. Andrews she was, in every way, an outsider. Her first mistake was the subject she and Hilda chose, or rather Miss Hurblatt chose for them: logic. Ottoline's mind never had been logical, and never would be. This dry, unexciting course was decided on mainly because Miss Hurblatt had heard that its professor, D.G. Ritchie, was the best at the university. Ottoline, with her debutante's schooling, was utterly unprepared for anything like this; and even Miss Hurblatt's diligent coaching could do little in the teeth of the fact that both young women were utterly out of their depth. Worse, Hilda conceived another of her dislikes, this time for the hapless Miss Hurblatt, which did little to assist their studies. What the other students thought of the ménage at Murry Park, and the sight of Ottoline's tall gaunt figure, cape flapping against her legs, scurrying around the cold, windswept town, can be imagined. She tried to make contact with them; but Hilda frowned on too much fraternising. Also, Ottoline's well-meant efforts, abetted by the local bishop, to organise Bible classes for her fellow students fell rather flat. Still, she confessed in her *Memoirs* to having appreciated her time at St. Andrews. Her fellow undergraduates had a habit of shuffling their feet if someone of whom they disapproved entered the lecture-room, but Ottoline recorded: "I am thankful to say I was never shuffled at."[9] Finally the rigours of the Scottish climate, and the even harsher rigours of formal logic, plus a general feeling of ill-health (which had pestered her since the typhoid attack in Italy in 1892) convinced her that syllogisms and St. Andrews were not worth returning to after the summer vacation. She wrote a note to Professor Ritchie thanking him, and he replied that he was sorry she had found his course too dry. (Typically, Ottoline and the professor continued to correspond for some years.)

Despite her failure at St. Andrews, the experience was another step away from Welbeck; and the summer of 1898 was the first London Season Ottoline enjoyed. Although well-beyond the debutant age, she went to many of the Season events, and helped her sister-in-law, Lady Henry Bentinck, entertain at 13 Grosvenor Place. Also, the previous Christmas, Ottoline had met another older man who was to play a significant role in her life: Herbert Henry Asquith, one of the leaders of the Liberal Party, and a major figure in British politics. Married now to his second wife, the formidable Margot Tennant, Asquith had been Home Secretary in the last Liberal Government, and would follow Campbell-Bannerman as Prime Minister in 1908. He was a handsome man of 45, with a fine classical intellect and had something of a weakness for women, particularly young women (a weakness he was to indulge even while at No. 10 Downing Street). Ottoline, down from St. Andrews for the Christmas vacation, met Asquith at a dinner at Grosvenor Place. He was immediately attracted by her austere beauty; her obvious intelligence; her aristocratic background; and her unorthodox outlook on life. Also, she was 24, and unmarried.

In the following weeks, Ottoline saw more of Asquith. He visited her in her sitting-room on the top floor of 13 Grosvenor Place, and their talks ranged far and wide. An inveterate correspondent, he lectured her on the merits of letter-writing, a lesson she was to take very much to heart. They used to sit together, Ottoline recalled, on a deep sofa against white muslin cushions that had belonged to Lady Bolsover. They discussed religion, poetry, literature, and politics. He also lent her books by radical authors. Over the several months of 1898 their friendship deepened, and in August he wrote to her:

> *A year ago nothing cd. have seemed less likely than that, in the ebb & flow of the social tide, you & I would ever have been floated or washed into a creek of our own. But it has been so – has it not? I don't know how you feel & think about it, but for my own part I don't wish to lose touch & to be drifted away & apart again in the stream of chance.*[10]

However, Asquith had temporarily to take a back seat to another older man who in August 1898 swept into Ottoline's life like a comet from outer space. This celestial invader was called Axel Munthe. Outwardly Munthe was not attractive – very ugly was Ottoline's description of him – though he possessed an athletic, supple figure, remarkable hands, and charm you could cut with a knife. There hung about Munthe an air of mystery that most women – and he knew a lot of women – found well-nigh irresistible. A Swede, he had studied medicine in Paris, becoming – so he claimed in his best-selling autobiographical book, *The Story of San Michele* – the youngest MD in French history. Later he became a society doctor in Rome, specialising in nervous ailments, a condition which rich women seemed particularly prone to. Munthe had also built a superb villa, which he called San Michele, high above Capri.

That summer he was visiting London, and inevitably became the target of every society hostess. Lady Henry Bentinck managed to lure him to lunch at Grosvenor Place; and it was there that Ottoline first saw this fascinating satyr. Munthe's mystery, the romantic stories about him, and his slightly insolent manner attracted her; and they were soon discussing the beauty of the regions around Rome and Florence. Ottoline had an added reason for taking an interest in the tall, bearded doctor: her headaches. For if Munthe was an expert on anything, it was ladies' headaches. A touch of his long, sensitive fingers on the brow; a look from his cornflower-blue eyes; a few confident words; and the most recalcitrant migraine would vanish. Ottoline's cousin Violet Bentinck was also prone to headaches, and this gave Ottoline an excuse for writing to Munthe and asking if he would go down to Ham Common to examine Violet. Of course, Ottoline offered to accompany him. They met at Waterloo Station, and during the journey found they had much in common: both were descended from Dutch families; both loved Italy; and both had a high sense of duty, though Munthe's sense was less ingenuous than his companion's. Ottoline found she could talk easily and openly with him. She decided that he was not what she called in her *Memoirs* the "cardboard-pattern sort of person" she normally encountered in London society. After the Ham Common trip, he came to see her in her sitting-room (in Victorian times, a popular place of assignation) and at the last party of the Season he almost literally swept her off her feet, asking her to visit him at Capri. That night, for the first time, Ottoline was sorry to be leaving a party; and as she went out the door she flashed a triumphant smile at her sister-in-law.

Ottoline, however, could hardly let on to Portland why she wanted to go off to Europe again (it is not known whether she happened to mention Capri). Instead, she told her family that she and Hilda were going to visit a French health spa. In fact her brothers were quite happy to see the back of her. In France she received a letter from Munthe repeating his invitation; and offering her a villa of her own on Capri. Ignoring Hilda's strenuous objections, Ottoline resolved to go. Munthe, she reassured Hilda, was perfectly respectable and quite elderly (of which he was neither). Twenty years later Hilda recalled what happened that hot Italian summer in August in 1898:

> *Now – once upon a time in the Year One – long ago lost in the mists of forgetfulness, there lived a maiden Ottoline Violet Anne by name. And it came to pass that she persuaded another damsel called Hilda the Haughty to wander alone with her for many years over the face of the earth. And as they went on their way they sang for joy & lightheartedness & carried no burdens save books – many & heavy – until they came to the island of Shadows set in the midst of the Shining Sea where dwelt a great & powerful magician & weaver of spells – Then...*[11]

No wonder Hilda drew breath, for when she saw Munthe, far from being a safe old gentleman of at least 80, he was obviously in the prime of life; and over the next few days Ottoline became his willing captive. The villa he installed them in was exquisite, with a floor tiled in blue marble, and a fountain garlanded with flowers. Ottoline appeared to be in a trance, and as the days went by, Hilda and Ottoline's maid Ellen grew increasingly alarmed. Gradually, Hilda's disapproving glances began to tell. Ottoline told Munthe: "It is too good here. I must fly."[12] What happened over the next few days isn't clear, but Ottoline agreed to stay a little longer. "I knew that he loved me," she wrote in her *Memoirs*. "I had been filled with a spiritual and transcendental desire to pour love into this man, had poured out everything in my heart to him, but now for the first time in my life, I realised the usual feelings of love."[13] They went for a trip to Sorrento and Pompeii, and there Ottoline and Munthe managed to elude Hilda and wander off into the woods alone. Ottoline's memoirs are not explicit about what they did next. She says their hearts "mingled." She wrote: "The physical side of my love was barely awake, only enough to give the abandonment of the heart with complete and passionate warmth."[14] (The word "physical" was Ottoline's euphemism for sex.) Later they slipped back to Capri in a fishing boat with Ottoline lying covered over with Munthe's jacket.

Several days later, accompanied by the now-even more scandalised Hilda, Ottoline returned to England. She felt "numbed with emotion" (she recorded in her *Memoirs*); but on arrival in London a reaction set in. Doubts about whether she should or could love such an unusual and unpredictable man assailed her. Munthe was very proud and she feared he would not face her brothers' wrath by asking for her hand. She sensed too that he harboured reservations. Before she had left Naples he held her arm and said, "I feel there is something in you that you will never surrender to me."[15] Also she began to worry about their spiritual compatibility. Once, when Munthe had come upon her praying in an Italian church, he made some slighting remark about the intensity of her faith. Yet despite these doubts, Ottoline was deeply attracted; and so she decided to travel back to Italy to see him again.

Arriving in Rome, she went to his surgery, taking her place in the waiting-room. There she saw, left out on a table for all to handle, a white vellum-bound copy of Browning which had been her personal gift to him. And when she went in to see him he was cold and cutting. He told her she was neurotic. "I could never marry a religious fanatic," he told her, "I have quite enough nerve cases among my patients. To have one as my wife would be too much."[16] That was the end of Munthe; almost. Ottoline retreated to her aunt's villa near Florence to nurse her wounds. She spent days wandering the streets, slowly recovering her spirit. Sometimes a friend of her aunt's, Violet Paget (an intellectual who wrote under the name of Vernon Lee), took her for drives in a pony carriage. Later, Ottoline returned to England and Grosvenor Place, where she found her Bentinck sister-in-law not especially understanding. Portland was also unsympathetic. He was thankful Ottoline hadn't run off with Munthe; but he still feared she might retreat to Cornwall and become a nun, which would be almost as bad. When Ottoline later discovered that her brothers had actually written to each other discussing this possibility, she was furious. "Why didn't they ask me?" she complained in her *Memoirs*.[17] She would have told them it was the last thing she had in mind. In the coming years, however, they were to have occasion to wish she had disappeared into a nunnery.

Instead, in April 1899, Ottoline decided to give education a second chance, and another family conference was convened to approve her plan to go to Somerville College, Oxford, as a home student. This time she would not let Hilda come with her, probably because of her inhibiting influence at St. Andrews. Ottoline took rooms in Oxford and attended lectures on Roman history, also being tutored by a Miss Deverell on political economy. This was much more to her liking. Miss Deverell introduced her to socialism and other avant-garde ideas, once taking her to London to hear the anarchist Prince Kropotkin speak. Throughout the summer of 1899 Ottoline remained in Oxford, bicycling around the cobbled streets with a pile of books strapped on the back. Several times she was invited to tea by a member of local society, Mrs. Frederic Morrell, wife of the university's solicitor. It was at the Morrells' other Oxfordshire house, Black Hall, that Ottoline first met the man she was to marry two years later – the Morrells' elder son, Philip.

In December or January she made the decision to leave Oxford, giving as her reason her headaches. But that seems a thin excuse. Perhaps she had had enough of academic learning, or perhaps she had got tired of life in Oxford in winter. Yet her decision might also have had something to do with the renewal of her friendship with Asquith. As soon as she returned to Grosvenor Place (post-Munthe), she began to see a great deal of him. There is even a possibility that she may have been seeing him before then, perhaps at Oxford. Though in her *Memoirs* Ottoline doesn't go so far as to call it an affair; it is certain something was going on between them. There are strong reasons why she should want to disguise the nature of their friendship. For one thing, Asquith was married and she was not; an affair publicised could ruin either or both of them. Also, later, after

Ottoline married, there was the additional consideration of not wanting to offend her husband. Then there was the difficulty that Asquith, though permissible dinner-company, was a high-profile political opponent of the Bentincks, Portland being a prominent member of the ruling Salisbury Conservative administration. He would not have been amused at a relationship between Ottoline and one of his leading political opponents; and she was still dependent on her half-brother for all her material circumstances.

It is not easy to gauge when the relationship with Asquith became more serious. Ottoline says in her *Memoirs* they became "really intimat" in early 1900, but "intimate" does not necessarily mean a physical relationship.[18] On the other hand, around this date Asquith began making regular visits to Ottoline in her sitting-room at Grosvenor Place. Of course, these visits could have been perfectly innocuous. In Edwardian times it was not unusual for gentlemen to visit ladies in their sitting-rooms between the hours of four and five, when servants were told not to enter unless rung for. Ottoline liked Asquith very much indeed, though she was never totally at ease with him, finding him neither spontaneous nor intuitive. Yet she was pleased that such a man-of-the world should pay court to her. She wrote later: "As I look back on this intimacy, I regret many things, above all that my hypersensitive conscience made me nervous about it, so that I was prevented from drinking its full pleasure and riches."[19] One Sunday Asquith took her to St. Paul's Cathedral and there, as she wrote later, assured her of his affections. This confession disturbed her, and she began to fear she might be getting in out of her depth. Disappointingly, details of this important period in Ottoline's life are sketchy. Apart from a few tantalising references in her *Memoirs*, our main source of information is Asquith's correspondence with Ottoline, which she preserved (though there is some reason to believe several of the letters have been lost). Before August 1898 (when she met Munthe), Asquith's letters are fairly formal. Then there is a hiatus until February 1900 when he suddenly abandons his normal didactic tone and, instead of opening "My Dear Lady Ottoline", there now is no preliminary salutation, and he ends his letters "Your loving friend", with no signature.

Most of his letters over the next 12 months are couched in slightly coy terms, with oblique references to some mutual secret; several contain gentle pleas for her to resume a relationship which she has apparently broken off. Three or four are addressed to Switzerland and Germany, to where Ottoline had fled in April or May, ostensibly because of her health. Before leaving England she spent some time in a nursing home run by a Miss Nelson Smith in Maida Vale, and several of Asquith's letters express his surprise that she had not yet left it. At Easter he wrote saying he wanted to see her especially "to talk about a – lots of things!"[20] A postscript has been ripped off this letter. In another letter he said he was anxious to see her soon: "Can I come to your retreat? or must I wait till you emerge? and when will that be?"[21] Another letter is signed, "I am always and everywhere your loving friend."[22] On June 21, 1900, he wrote to her in Switzerland:

> *How does the atmosphere feel up there? I write as a dweller in the plains. Does it make you feel as if you have escaped & emancipated yourself from the dim & damp & sometimes poisonous air of the plains? And do you feel that you have got above & beyond the sort of influences which – for instance – dominate Maida Vale? If so, I shd. be very sorry. For, after all, the time which you & I have spent together has been, in what Browning calls the 'level flats.' And I shd. miss something a great deal – if I were to realise that all this was something you had left behind & below! Is it so.*[23]

Then there is a gap until Boxing Day 1900, when Asquith wrote thanking her for a gift, saying: "I was glad to know from your Christmas letters that your anger had abated & been replaced by more Christian & more natural conditions."[24] With this letter, the more intimate part of the correspondence between them ends.

Such letters and the clues in Ottoline's *Memoirs* lend some support to an affair between them. Asquith's biographer Roy Jenkins told me that he knew of no evidence to support such a speculation.[25] Yet there is no doubt that Ottoline and Asquith were very close; and there are other hints that they did have a "physical relationship" later. There is as well an interesting reference made by Lytton Strachey in a biographical sketch he wrote about Asquith. Though Strachey was a notorious exaggerator, he mostly stuck to the facts when writing serious biography. In this sketch Strachey relates how he and Henry Lamb were with Ottoline one evening when she brought out Asquith's letters, preserved in a box. She told them: "He used to come and see me in the evening – right up at the very top of the house."[26] They began looking through the letters, and Strachey, after recalling that most of them seemed rather dull, goes on: "One letter, which promised to be more interesting, was at the last moment (owing to Philip [Morrell]) withheld. I gathered that he had made love to her – perhaps kissed, or tried to kiss her – and that she had objected, and he had written to apologise."[27] Indeed it seems quite likely Asquith did make some overtures to Ottoline; but how far she responded is impossible now to judge. On one hand, she had nothing to gain from an affair; but she also had little of importance to lose. And if, as seems likely, she did have sex with the middle-aged Munthe; then neither customary maidenly inhibition, nor Asquith's age, exclude the likelihood of something more than casual friendship. But whether it was just a kiss, or something more, we will probably never know.

In late summer or early autumn of 1900 Ottoline, accompanied by the now ubiquitous Hilda, left to go to Germany to consult a Professor Beigel. About 60, tall and aristocratic "like an old Jewish Rabbi," Beigel, too, fell under Ottoline's spell, and after one consultation he bent down and kissed her. In her *Memoirs* Ottoline said: "I do not think anyone has ever been so devoted to me."[28] On one thing, however, Ottoline was now determined: she would not willingly return to London, where the ashes of the Asquith business were still smouldering. Nor did the thought of Welbeck and Grosvenor Place beckon. With Portland

and her brothers and their way of life, she was now done. She was stifled by their continuous disapproval. She wanted to escape, to be free, to catch joy on the wing. Therefore she resolved to stay on the Continent for as long as possible.

Actually her brothers were probably nowhere near as interested in her doings as she imagined. The Boer War was raging and her youngest brother, Lord Charles, had been wounded at Mafeking. Another brother, Lord William, was to die in 1903 from an infection caught during the fighting in South Africa. As well, Portland and his wife had financed a field hospital to help the Imperialist cause. None of them had much time to worry about Ottoline's wayward activities on the Continent.

When Ottoline was still London, around Christmas 1900, the Druce-Portland Case was still in its early stages, but it nevertheless was attracting intense public interest, and was at the forefront of her family's attention [see following Interlude]. Consequently, Ottoline's desire to seek the means and permission to stay Italy had been of little consequence, and no hindrance was put in her way. While still in London, Ottoline and Asquith met again, probably for the first time since the previous February. But now they met as old friends, any ardour having cooled. They agreed to keep in touch, and met several more times in January before Ottoline departed for Germany and Sicily with Hilda.

The twosome travelled around Sicily for several weeks, usually in the company of a Professor Butcher and his wife. During this trip, Ottoline says in her *Memoirs* that she felt like a pent-up spring, releasing itself in fits and starts. In her heart she had an over-riding desire to be free, free of entanglements. She felt she had flown too close to the flame, and now wanted to find her own way in the world. But what could she do? She might continue to go around sampling in the sensual delights of the eye and mind, but what else? She discussed it with Hilda. Their answer was that when they returned to London they would take a house and live together, though leading independent lives. Hilda's companionship, however, was not enough for Ottoline.

She was looking for something or someone else.

In Florence they teamed up with an intellectual friend-of-a-friend, Maud Crutwell, and the three went off on expeditions into the northern-Italian countryside. What a strange trio they made...Ottoline, almost 28, tall, aloof, with a high-boned face, aristocratic nose, masses of titian hair; dressed always in slightly unorthodox clothes, and wearing a large hat and muslin veil to shade her from the sun...Hilda, looking like a spinsterish schoolmistress out on a Sunday jaunt...and Maud, the eldest at 45, wearing a man's shirt, sailor hat and a blue serge suit, sitting up in front holding the reins of their pony-cart, smoking a cigar; her round, pink, innocent face beaming. They toured Ravenna, Lucca, Pisa, Carrara, then back to Florence, before making a reluctant return to England...and, for Ottoline, the not-very-exciting prospect of setting up home with Hilda in London.

INTERLUDE
The Druce-Portland Case

THE BURROWING DUKE left one other legacy behind which was to cause his successor, the Sixth Duke, and the Portland family a great deal of trouble – trouble that was to spill over into Ottoline's early life. This was the infamous Druce-Portland case, a major cause celebre of the Edwardian era in England.

It owed its origin to the excessive – indeed paranoid – reclusiveness of the Fifth Duke. The trouble was that virtually no one had seen him, in the flesh, for over a decade prior to his death in 1879. There had been fleeting glimpses of him, both at Welbeck and at Harcourt House, the Portland London house. But few if any had caught a close-up glimpse of his face and features. No one could swear to what he looked like, nor if it were really him. It was this anomaly that the Druce family took advantage of.

Thomas Charles Druce (left) and a bust of the Fifth Duke

Thomas Charles Druce's origins were obscure. It was claimed that he was born around 1794, before the registration of births. He once stated, according to evidence in court, that he was born in a village near Oxford. He could well have been related to other Druces who could be found across the social spectrum in 19th-century England, from the legal profession to agricultural workers. His first confirmed appearance was as a stall-holder at an antiques-cum-flea-market establishment called the Baker Street Bazaar in north London. Apparently he prospered, and became well-off. He died in 1864, and was buried – supposedly – in the Druce family vault in Highgate Cemetery.

And there he would have peacefully lain, were it not for the second wife of his son Walter, Anna Maria, who had been Walter's sister's governess – and was soon to be his widow. For reasons that are now obscure, she developed a belief that the late Thomas Charles Druce had been in fact the Fifth Duke of Portland. She supported this unlikely claim with an even-more-unlikely story that the Fifth Duke had led a secret life, and that, while he was supposedly at Welbeck or Harcourt House, he was in fact maintaining a double existence, running a haberdashery stall at the Baker Street Bazaar. Moreover, that during this double life he had fathered a son, Walter, and consequently his widow, Anna, claimed her late husband, Walter, was the rightful Sixth Duke of Portland, and so the putative Sixth Duke – Ottoline's half-brother – should be deprived of his wealth, title and estates in favour of Walter (despite the fact that Walter himself had always denied any connection, on either side of the blanket, to the Portland name and inheritance).

Her outrageous claim may have had some connection with the infamous Tichborne inheritance case, which had been an equally-major *cause célèbre* several decades earlier in the 1870-80s, when a butcher from Wagga in Australia called Castro claimed he was the long-lost heir to the Tichborne baronetcy. His claim was eventually disproved, but the fact that it had been pursued for a number of years may have given Anna Maria Druce the idea that she could go bigger and try something similar with the dukedom of Portland. Without going into the complex, not to say labyrinthine, twists and turns of the several court cases that she initiated (all vigorously defended by the Portland legal team), the case was eventually thrown out, and she was soon committed to a lunatic asylum.

By the time that happened, however, other claimants had appeared on the scene, alleging some link to the original Thomas Charles Druce (having been married twice, and having surviving heirs). One came all the way from New Zealand, and another from Boston in America. A syndicate was formed of shareholders to finance various claims in prospect of a share of the Portland estate. The legal actions went on well into the Edwardian era until

Druce's grave in Highgate Cemetery was exhumed one stormy night to see who really was inside.

The Druce coffin is opened

To the surprise of very few – and the disappointment of the various claimants and litigants – it turned out to be none other than T.C. Druce himself (duly confirmed by one of his grandsons). The courts, now heartily sick of the whole Druce-Portland affair, threw out all legal claims, confirming that Ottoline's half-brother was the rightful Sixth Duke. Several of the litigants were convicted of perjury and fraud. Anna Druce spent the rest of her life in a mental asylum.

This brou-ha-ha didn't concern Ottoline substantively, except that it focussed unwelcome public attention on her family and their eccentric lineage, casting them in a rather comical light (which hopefully helped inure her to the notoriety she herself was soon to become the focus of).

CHAPTER 5
Tall, Dark and Handsome, but no Mr D'Arcy

Ottoline on the brink of matrimony

INDEED, it is not altogether clear why Ottoline decided to return to London in the autumn of 1900, and entanglements she had left England to put behind her. Perhaps Hilda had to come back, or maybe Ottoline needed to see her family again. Perhaps she sensed that grand tours and sybaritic exiles could not go on forever. Hilda was in a similar quandary, and during their discussions in Italy the two often considered how they might satisfy what Ottoline called "the inner life". Marriage – the only answer Hilda could think of – had no appeal for Ottoline. She was not prepared to exchange her hard-won liberty for a new sort of bondage.

While they looked around for more permanent rooms, Ottoline went back to Grosvenor Place, and took over her old sitting-room overlooking Buckingham Palace. Asquith came to see her several times, but now things were kept on a much-more polite footing. Nevertheless, it was probably Asquith who introduced her to another man of mature years who was attracted to her – the up-and-coming Liberal politician and literary essayist Augustine Birrell. Birrell, who was later to become Irish Secretary in Asquith's first Cabinet, took an instant fancy to Ottoline, and was to visit her several times in her Grosvenor Place sitting-room. But she did not encourage him. She was becoming wary of father-figures.

In those autumn-winter months of 1900-01 it must have been obvious to many that Ottoline, the habitual wall-flower, was in need of London society's help. Soon invitations began to arrive at Grosvenor Place to dinners and other social occasions at which she would be introduced to the current crop of eligible bachelors. One such invitation came from someone Ottoline particularly liked: the former Welbeck librarian, Arthur Strong (whom Portland had sacked for some smoking solecism). Mrs. Strong happened to know a young man whom she thought was in a similar situation to Ottoline, he also being at something of a loose-end.

His name was Philip Morrell, and it was he whom Ottoline found herself sitting opposite at the Strongs' dinner-table one evening that autumn. They had in fact met earlier in Oxford (as mentioned above), but on that occasion Ottoline had not taken any particulars notice of him. He was presentable enough – tall, dark and passably handsome, with crinkly hair and a largish nose – but he had nothing to make him stand out from any number of other eligible youngish men she had been introduced to.

He, on the other hand, had been very impressed with her. He had first seen her in Oxford, cycling around the town. Later, at the Morrell's Black Hall, he had talked to her about his interests – principally art, books, and music. Ottoline had responded politely, but showed limited interest in his activities. He had been very aware of the higher, more rarefied stratum she came from. He knew she was, in Lytton Strachey's delightful expression, "the daughter of a thousand earls". On the other hand, the Morrells, though well-off, were decidedly middle-class. One branch of the family were brewers (Morrells was Oxfordshire's most-popular beer), while his side of the family had been solicitors to Oxford University for generations...a happy family conjunction of trade and upper-middle-class professional, a milieu that Ottoline's people normally avoided.

It was her voice that he remembered most. He found it extraordinary; sometimes purring like a cat, then dipping and soaring like a bird. Making polite conversation over the Strongs' dinner-table, she asked him: "What, Mr. Morrell, do you think of the political situation?" He told her that he inclined to the Liberal side, unlike his family, who too were stolidly Conservative. His father had been the Mayor of Oxford in the Conservative and Union interest. One of his brewer cousins was the sitting Tory member for Mid-Oxfordshire.

Yet at Eton, where he had spent some of the happiest years of his life, he discovered that Liberalism was not the evil he had been brought up to believe. It was there he started collecting blue-and-white china and questioning the presumption he would go into his father's legal practice. Why couldn't his brother Hugh go into the family firm, instead of him, leaving him to study something he really wanted to, like literature? His parents, however, were adamant. His brother wasn't clever enough for law: it was to be the Army for him. So Philip went up to Balliol, where he spent a miserable time acquiring a third-rate degree. At one stage he suffered what was thought to be a nervous breakdown. He also developed a morbid fear he would die young (in fact, he had once contracted typhoid, and had nearly died).

After coming down from Oxford, he spent the next eight years working in his father's practice in Oxford trying to make a career of the law.

His father, however, rebuffed his efforts to reform the firm's archaic procedures. Finally, after a disagreement, he moved down to London to set up a branch of the firm in Bedford Row, near Gray's Inn. But the venture was not particularly successful, and Philip, now 30, was left with ample time to cultivate the artistic people he had always pined to meet. With an American friend, Logan Pearsall Smith, and another friend, Percy Fielding, he was dabbling in antiques, starting a little company they called Miss Top Lady. In his leisure time he frequented the Bohemian parts of Chelsea with Logan Pearsall Smith to visit artists such as Charles Conder.

So there Ottoline and Philip sat in the Strongs' dining-room: both past the first flower of youth, both to some extent failures and misfits. Later in the month Ottoline invited Philip to tea in Grosvenor Place, and they discovered they could converse quite easily (always a good start to a relationship). Sometimes Asquith's visits would coincide, and the three would sit and talk of life and politics, taking tea from a tray on a low stool. No question of anything serious arose until several weeks later when Mrs. Morrell, no doubt with match-making in mind, invited Ottoline to Black Hall for a weekend. Ottoline was too experienced not to be oblivious of Mrs Morrell's ulterior motives. The half-sister of the Sixth Duke of Portland would raise the Morrell social standing several notches. In her *Memoirs* Ottoline recalled feeling for the first time that Philip wanted to marry her. She later remembered: "I sat up all night in my bedroom by my fire trying to push away the feeling of pressure that was closing upon me. I felt his personality almost physically elbowing in on me."[1]

So Ottoline was by no means swept, Munthe-like, off her feet. At first the letters she wrote to him were hesitant and self-deprecating. She outlined all her faults. She was deeply religious, she told him. She was strong-willed. She had a mind of her own.

She also told him of her lonely childhood at Welbeck, and a little of the Munthe affair, confessing she had been caught up in the "boiling cauldron" of the doctor's emotions.[2] In another letter she broached more practical matters. She felt she ought to explain that she had an allowance from Portland of £1,500 a year (in those days a truly handsome sum; 11 years later Leonard Woolf found he could live quite well in London on £300 a year, while his wife Virginia, in a celebrated essay, said that "£500 a year and a room of one's own" was all that a female writer needed). By Christmas 1901, Philip's timid courting had brought Ottoline to the point of decision. She was due to go to Welbeck for Christmas; while he was going with his father to Italy. They said goodbye at Euston station, where he handed her a bunch of lilies-of-the-valley. At Welbeck she still felt unsure about matrimony, but the thought of Philip gave her a comfortable glow. Soon after Christmas she returned to Grosvenor Place and sent a telegram to Italy with two words: "Come back". Philip returned poste-haste to London, and proposed to Ottoline in her sitting-room, where he was duly accepted.

Her conversion from confirmed spinster to blushing bride-to-be had taken only a few months. Yet it had been no love-at-first-sight affair: she had had plenty of time – many weeks – to think about it. Why had her staunch independence crumpled so easily? It may well be that the decision forced itself upon her. She knew that marriage was almost her only alternative to the sour, empty life single women of that era were almost universally condemned to.

She realised that education offered no escape, nor was travel a long-term solution; while the "hurly-burly of the *chaise-longue*" had too many drawbacks. Besides, Ottoline at 28 was as ready for marriage as most of her contemporaries had been at 21. She was a late developer, both physically and emotionally. By now the rest of her face had caught up with her nose, and she was in fact now a very beautiful woman (as her portrait photographs show). Her travels and experiences had given her a patina of worldliness, which, combined with her innate aristocratic confidence, had made her a challenging and alluring figure. Yet there might also have been a more immediate reason for her forsaking her spinsterhood. From a letter Ottoline wrote to Bertrand Russell in 1911, it seems that Asquith was overly upset about the marriage. "He was annoyed with me I don't know why because I did not tell him before I was engaged to P – & I have hardly seen him since."[3] There is more than a hint in her *Memoirs* that Asquith had been pressing his attentions on her again, and that one outcome of her engagement to Philip was that it blunted any further unwelcome familiarity from that direction.

At the news of her impending marriage Ottoline's family were, not to put too fine a point on it, relieved tending towards overjoyed. Admittedly Philip was of lower rank; but at least he was presentable. They did not suspect his liberal leanings, though one of Ottoline's sisters-in-law had a nightmare that Philip was (horror!) a Radical. At the wedding Ottoline's youngest brother, Lord Charles (the one she hero-worshipped as a child), took Philip aside and told him confidentially: "I'm glad I'm not in your shoes. I wouldn't undertake her for anything."[4] (Nor, noted Ottoline in her Diary, did he undertake to give them a wedding present.)

The ceremony took place on February 8, 1902, at fashionable St. Peter's church in Eaton Square. Two of Philip's nephews were pages; while Ottoline's niece Lady Victoria Cavendish-Bentinck, her cousin Lady Violet Manners, and Philip's niece Dorothy Warren were bridesmaids. Portland gave her away and the Bishop of Rochester officiated. After the vows were exchanged, the choir sang *O Perfect Love*. Sitting on the bride's side of the aisle were the Marquis and Marchioness of Granby; the Countess of Bective; the Earl of Feversham; Lord and Lady Howard de Walden; together with all Ottoline's brothers and their wives. On the groom's side were his parents, Mr. and Mrs. Frederic Morrell, his sisters and their husbands, together with other Morrell relatives and family friends. Lady Ottoline Morrell, as she now was, walked out of the church into the sunshine of a new life; one which would resemble her old existence as little as the fun-loving,

Edwardian era resembled the claustrophobic Victorian age, which had finally expired with its Queen over a year before.

After a honeymoon in Italy, where Ottoline swam at the Venice Lido wearing a large hat (and where she lost her engagement ring), they returned to leased accommodation in Grosvenor Road, alongside the Thames. During the week Philip would go off to his Bedford Row office while Ottoline indulged her developing *outré* style, creating a pink and grey drawing-room and furnishing her boudoir with silk cushions and stocking it with her favourite books. Most days she would meet Philip for luncheon at a fashionable café in New Oxford Street, where they watched enviously the writer Laurence Binyon and his friends talking and laughing at a nearby table. In the evenings they stayed at home reading Gibbon and Macaulay together. After the first few months' marriage, Ottoline's hopes of a new life began to tarnish. Something was definitely lacking. At first she thought it was her husband's job. Philip, too, was dissatisfied, yet he was not prepared to give up his career and become some kind of drone living off his wife's income. He had rejected the idea of transferring to the Bar, as it involved trouble and risk, and he did not have enough self-confidence to chance it. What he really wanted to do was become a writer – a journalist perhaps, or a biographer – and he believed his success with essays at university provided him with some reason for hopes in this direction. He began keeping a writer's notebook and composing little biographical pieces. But such exercises, pleasant though they may have been, were no answer to the immediate problem of how to escape the deadening influence of the solicitor's office in Bedford Row.

In July 1902 a solution appeared from a direction neither had considered. One weekend at Logan Pearsall Smith's cottage at Haslemere they met Beatrice and Sidney Webb, who spoke about the fortunes of the Liberal Party, which was still recovering from its disastrous drubbing in the 1900 Khaki landslide election. Sidney Webb mentioned a new organisation called the Liberal League which had been formed to help finance young and likely candidates contesting Conservative-held seats (of which there were a vast number to choose from). Immediately, Philip and Ottoline were interested. Fighting the Tories and the middle-class imperialism of Joseph Chamberlain had appeal to them both. Ottoline dispatched Philip to see Asquith, who referred him to an official of the Liberal League, who in turn advised him to see Herbert Gladstone, the Liberal chief whip. But to Philip's consternation, the seat Gladstone offered him was South Oxfordshire, in the very heart of Morrell Conservative territory. After some initial hesitation, however, Philip agreed that closeness to home ought not deter him, if his Liberal convictions were strong enough. The next step was to be adopted by the local Liberal Association; and this was achieved in September when he addressed a meeting in Oxford. After that all hell broke loose. The local Tory press denounced Philip for a complete lack of principle and ability; taking consolation only in the fact that as the constituency had never returned a Radical – and never would – he had no chance of getting in. Philip's family were only slightly less hostile. His father and mother were aghast; while his cousin Herbert Morrell, the sitting Mid-Oxfordshire MP, never spoke to him again. Ottoline's family, though now more tolerant of their scatter-brained relative, were equally shocked; particularly as Portland was a past-president of the National Union of Conservative Associations.

Ignoring all this, Philip and Ottoline launched themselves into trying to win over one of the country's bluest-of-blue Tory seats. Though the next election was not due for several years, they started touring the constituency in a dogcart, visiting fetes and addressing meetings. For a while it was exciting and adventurous. Many a winter's night in 1902-1903 was spent dashing between tiny hamlets trying to convert a handful of voters. Once their dogcart was attacked and overturned by angry Conservatives. Yet as the months wore on the shine wore off; and electioneering began to lose its excitement. Ottoline again found herself bored and dissatisfied. As yet they had few friends, and almost their only form of entertainment – apart from dull political events – was attending Sunday concerts at Queen's Hall, where they paid 7/6 or 10/6 to hear Beethoven, Bach, Weber, or Liszt. No, this was not the sort of new life Ottoline had been looking forward to. (Yet those Sunday concerts at Queen's Hall were to open a new door for Ottoline.)

ON HONEYMOON

Ottoline and Philip spent much of their honeymoon in Venice, where they swam at the Lido

Philip took a series of holiday snaps of Ottoline bathing and sight-seeing

Ottoline about to take the plunge at the Lido

Taking a dip at the Lido with Goldie Lowes Dickinson (left) and Baroness Meyer

Ottoline with various companions at the Lido

Stepping into a gondola

Ottoline feeding the pigeons in St Mark's Square

Ottoline, strolling at the Lido

CHAPTER 6
Mary Fotheringham – Ottoline's First Appearance in Print

Ottoline in her Boudoir

OTTOLINE WROTE in her *Memoirs*: "The years 1904 to 1906 I will pass on one side – save to say they were disagreeable and painful, and at this time they do not appear to me very significant. Perhaps I shall return to them if days and health are given to me."[1] But Ottoline did not return, and that which she found so hard to say remained unsaid, in print. What could she have been referring to? The words "disagreeable and painful" could refer to her pregnancy in 1905-1906 and the death of one of her twin children, together with the period of illness which followed. That these events were sad and painful there is no doubt; but she did write about them – and at length.

Since her marriage, Ottoline had occupied herself mainly helping Philip woo the voters of South Oxfordshire. There were still regular visits to Welbeck and Black Hall, though these were less pleasant since Philip's defection to the "Radicals". Hilda Douglas-Pennant and several other friends would come to tea, and there was shopping and management of the Grosvenor Road household. But most of the time Ottoline was once more bored. By October 1903 she had been married for almost two years, yet she was far from reconciled to domesticity. For a man it wasn't so bad – he had his clubs, his cronies, and other outside interests – but for a sensitive, intelligent woman with an upper-class upbringing, being cooped up in domesticity was irksome.

Such a situation, more recognised nowadays, is the subject of a now-forgotten novel called *Cuthbert Learmont*, which was published in 1910. Its author, J.A. Revermort, describes how a tall, copper-haired woman named Mary Fotheringham breaks the bonds of her conventional marriage by having an affair with a Scottish divinity student, Cuthbert Learmont. Some of the details of Mary Fotheringham's fictional life are uncannily similar to the reality of Ottoline's life in 1903. The fictional Mary had married a reliable but rather dull husband. Finding herself expected to lead the life of a doll in a doll's house, she hungers for a more romantic existence, craving a companion with whom she can share the experiences of the soul. Cuthbert, whom she meets at a party, provides her with just such a kindred spirit. They meet again in the foyer of a theatre and agree to see more of one another. Mary, an elegant, artistic woman with a strange seductive voice and a weakness for dramatic hats, takes to having long intimate talks with Cuthbert, usually in her boudoir; where they discuss books, poetry, music, and spiritual matters. They also go to art galleries and curio shops together. Mary, who often signs her name with her initials, "an M curiously formed", suffers from intense headaches and sometimes goes off to seek cures at health spas.[2]

The parallel between Mary and Ottoline is obvious – which is not surprising when one learns that J. A. Revermort is the pseudonym of a Scottish-born academic named John Adam Cramb, and amongst Ottoline's correspondence are 94 letters from Cramb, most of them written in 1904. Were it not for these letters, which Ottoline kept in a bundle tied with pink ribbon, we would know almost nothing of her liaison with Cramb. In her *Memoirs* his name appears only once, when Ottoline in passing says that the writer Katherine Mansfield had once been a pupil of "my old friend Cramb".[3] Additionally there is a letter written in 1913 in which Ottoline asks Asquith to give Cramb's widow a pension (he did). There is also a cryptic reference to Cramb, without mentioning him by name, in a letter from Ottoline to Lytton Strachey on November 2, 1913: "Today I went to West Kensington to see the widow of a very wonderful and eminent man – who died lately – I knew him very intimately."[4]

Who was Cramb? Apart from his age, he was not like Asquith or Munthe; still less like Philip. In his late 40s, with a magnificent walrus moustache, he spoke seven languages and littered his letters to Ottoline – written in a crabbed hand on small notepaper from 55 Edith Road, West Kensington – with classical allusions and heavy allegory; interspersed with snippets of Latin, Greek, and Italian. With Ottoline he adopted a Biblical tone, addressing her as "thou." He called himself "thine adoring Raymonde of Ruyremonde" and similar courtly names. Like his semi-autobiographical hero Cuthbert Learmont, Cramb trained as a clergyman, but gave up before being ordained. In 1887, at the age of 26, he married Lucy Selby Lowndes, who later became an invalid. In 1892 he became a lecturer in modern history at Queen's College, Harley Street, moving up to professor the following year. (He turned down a professorship at King's College, London, because it meant having to subscribe to the Thirty-nine Articles.) At Queen's college, the oldest foundation of higher learning for women in England, he taught what he called "the whole life": painting, music, philosophy, as well as history. He was an ardent Imperialist, and later became Lord Roberts' speechwriter. And he often visited his students in their homes.

His chief recreation was attending concerts at Queen's Hall, and it was there, in the foyer, that Ottoline and Cramb probably met around the middle of 1903. He offered her a cigarette (a good opening gambit), which she accepted. They got into conversation and agreed to meet again. Soon they began taking regular outings together to art galleries and bookshops, and by April 1904 they were firm friends, planning expeditions to Richmond Park. One Sunday morning in April Cramb set off from Edith Road for a rendezvous with Ottoline on the District Line platform at Richmond. Apparently she didn't turn up, and in his next letter he chided her, calling her "stern demi-goddess".[5] On May 20 he arranged another expedition, this time to Ottoline's old home at St. Anne's Hill, Chertsey. He also sent her a copy of the Roland memoirs, asking her to turn to a certain page where she would see a picture of "a charming face".[6] (One wonders in passing whether Ottoline's predilection for men of mature years ran to walrus moustaches.)

Did Cramb visit Ottoline at home? Certainly Mary Fotheringham's boudoir in *Cuthbert Learmont* could very easily be a description of Ottoline's sitting-room at 32 Grosvenor Road. In the book Learmont visited Mary in her boudoir and "on afternoons separated by narrower and narrower intervals, they passed exquisite hours, in music, in reading, in strange talk, or in silences as strange".[7] In May 1904 Cramb had an emotional outburst "by the river westward towards Kew" and buried his head in her hands.[8] Ottoline realised then that perhaps it had been unwise to encourage him. May 28 saw a crisis. Cramb wrote three letters to her and referred to a telegram of the day before. Three days later Ottoline went to Black Hall and his letters were tactfully less personal, referring to general matters like conscription, labour, and tariffs. But by early June nothing would deflect Cramb's ardour. One Saturday he wrote her a particularly florid note:

Thy letter this morning was a throb of delight...O thou

sweet sister...couldst but read my heart today how thou wouldst see there all that feeling, all that tenderness which thou didst desiderate and demand![9]

His tight, cramped handwriting went on, page after page:

...and I accuse myself for saying that thing yesterday – for hadst thou been well, I feel that thou wouldst have flung it back at me or simply laughed – yet in spite of my own pain how infinitely sweet thou wert – O thou heavenliest, thou heavenliest sister – what shall I say unto thee? Thou must see, thou must see heaven, how could'st thou speak that word!

June 1904 saw the climax of their friendship. Cramb called it "her month", probably because her 31st birthday fell in June. They went to several more galleries together and for trips to Richmond Park. Then there was a silence from Ottoline. Cramb was distraught:

Thou hast not written? Hast thou a temper? I wish thou wouldst be sensible...I know nothing from thy wild statements.[10]

Then he asked her to dine with him – "an enchanting possibility" – and by June 20 he was happily calling her "Alvorissima". He wrote again on June 22, twice on June 23, once on June 24, twice on the 25th, and again on the 27th. He suggested a rendezvous at the Grafton Galleries to see the Manet exhibition. He pictured himself as a gazelle led by Ottoline on a chain. She invited him to accompany her to Henley. But by November 1904 their friendship had cooled. In a letter postmarked November 18 Cramb hinted that Ottoline had resolved to break off. He said this made him "*triste vraiment*".[11] By December 15 he was no longer affectionate. Nevertheless, the correspondence continued on and off in formal terms until 1910. He often mentioned the cigarettes he bought for her at Noteras, 113 Piccadilly; Ladies' No 1 Gold tipped. He had them sent to her home, and in one letter he told her that so often had he done this that the assistant knew her address by heart.

Ottoline may not have been aware at the time that Cramb was writing *Cuthbert Learmont,* but after it was published in 1910 he either gave her a copy or she bought one. If she recognised herself in the novel, she doesn't appear to have minded; a curious fact, for throughout her life she was inordinately sensitive to any portrayal of herself or her family. Indeed, it is likely that Ottoline would not have approved of the ending of *Cuthbert Learmont,* in which Mary Fotheringham leaves her husband and children to go away with Cuthbert. If her friendship with Cramb had taught her anything, it was that there was as much danger of being restricted by an affair as by marriage. Cramb had become too importunate; which was probably the reason why she decided to retreat from him. It was one thing to have a liaison with a man other than her husband; it was quite another for that relationship to dominate her life. Ottoline was accustomed to the civilised ways of aristocratic affairs, in which "commitment" played a minor part. Moreover, she had enough regard for Philip, and a sufficiently ingrained sense of duty, to realise that Cramb might jeopardise the other important parts of her life. As well, she seems to have had a number of disagreements with Cramb; most probably over politics and religion. Perhaps she poured cold water on his ardour simply because in the end she discovered she didn't really have enough in common with him. Yet Ottoline felt a great deal of affection for hi;, as is shown by what she said and did when he died suddenly in 1913. In her letter to Strachey she said: "He was as brilliant – & wonderful as anyone I ever met – & now there is a white urn in [Lucy Cramb's] library & it holds his ashes."

How much did Philip know or suspect? It is difficult to say, but the fact that Ottoline later went to some lengths to conceal her degree of involvement with Cramb indicates she thought Philip was largely ignorant. And even if he did know, he was not the type to initiate an open row about this sort of thing. As she had occasion to complain later, he was infuriatingly broad-minded (or aristocratic?). Ottoline's friendship with Cramb had provided her an outlet and contact with a mind that, to some extent at least, soared; but her conscience must have been sorely troubled in 1904. A constant theme in her life is the tussle between her puritanical conscience and her wild, adventurous romanticism. Neither side could dominate the other for any length of time; and as soon as one side had its day, the other was waiting in the wings to take over. Another pattern is the escape reflex. It happened with Munthe and it happened with Asquith; in fact whenever Ottoline had an emotional crisis, a trip abroad or a visit to a nursing home was sure to follow. Though there is no question she did suffer from illnesses; they were often precipitated by dramatic events in her personal life.

So after she broke off from Cramb it is not surprising to find her and Philip leaving for a holiday in Spain, returning to Grosvenor Road on a cold January day in 1905. The time in Spain, where they sat in cafes and joined in peasant dancing, may have been something of a second honeymoon; and their return to London may have been in the nature of a fresh start. One rainy afternoon Philip said: "We must make some friends. We haven't any friends."[12] This wasn't quite true, for they knew many people; the society painter Sargent, a large number of Liberals, a few literary people, together with old friends like Hilda Douglas-Pennant and Logan Pearsall Smith. But Philip's remark may have indicated that he realised that Ottoline's craving for communication and social contact, soon to develop into an obsession, had to be directed into safer, shallower channels. Perhaps Ottoline realised it too.

New friends soon appeared. One day Percy Fielding showed them a painting by an artist named James Pryde, and this sparked an idea to have Ottoline's portrait painted. Pryde, despite his name, was an extremely shy man; and when he came down from Oxford to inspect Ottoline, his courage failed. Leaving her sitting in her loveliest lace dress, he fled, returning a little later with a substitute, the photographer Cavendish Morton, who took some pictures of Ottoline. Later Pryde did paint a picture of her, though she didn't think it very flattering. Through Pryde, however, Ottoline met another artist, Charles Conder, whom Philip had met already. Ottoline went to Conder's Chelsea studio, where the atmosphere of paint, models, and moral freedom immediately attracted her. Soon the Morrells and Conder and his wife were dining together and making expeditions to Hampton Court. (There has been a suggestion that Ottoline had an affair with Conder, but there is no evidence to support this speculation.)

Ottoline also attempted to make new friends in other directions. She wrote to the novelist George Meredith and to the anarchist Prince Kropotkin, the latter declining an invitation to dine. Around this time, through her work on behalf of Philip's political career, Ottoline also got to know Ethel Sands, a cultivated American Liberal supporter who painted and held a weekly salon at her home in Lowndes Place, Belgravia. Miss Sands also held court at her Newington House near Oxford, and was a friend of Henry James and his psychologist brother William. Henry James, who was also a friend of Mrs. Morrell (who, it has been claimed, was the inspiration for Mrs. Gereth in James' *The Spoils of Poynton*), became a close friend of Ottoline, and later was to be a frequent guest at her Bedford Square salon. Ethel Sands' salons, particularly those held at Newington in the summer (where Ottoline observed such luminaries as Henry James and Edith Wharton strolling in the garden), were an example she yearned to emulate. Another friend of this period was Crompton Llewellyn Davies, a solicitor whose humanitarian views, particularly on land reform for agricultural labourers, were taken up by Ottoline and Philip. It was either Davies or the Webbs who introduced Ottoline to Charles Sanger, a member of the Cambridge University group called the Conversazione Society, though better known as the Apostles, or simply the Society; membership of which was extremely select, and limited to only the brightest undergraduates. A recently-married couple, Sanger and his wife Dora held an open house (or rather flat) for their friends each Friday evening. Sanger was also friendly with several people who were later to be members of what became known as the Bloomsbury Group. On her first visit to the Sangers' flat, Ottoline climbed the several flights of stairs and entered their sparse, matting-floored sitting-room high above the Strand to find Charles and Dora and warming themselves around a gas stove. Later, a tall, gangling young man with a high-pitched voice called Lytton Strachey arrived, and perched his awkward figure in a basket-chair, leaning forward to warm his hands while he talked animatedly about the Shaw play he had just been to see. The freedom and informality of such gatherings impressed Ottoline, and she resolved that she would try to start something similar herself.

With Ottoline's social activities burgeoning, the house at Grosvenor Road was beginning to prove too small; and so towards the end of 1905 she and Philip began looking for something larger (and where she might start her salon). But there was an added reason for needing more room: in October 1905 Ottoline made a discovery that pleased her not one little bit – she was pregnant. What to other women was a warm invasion; a fulfilment of their destiny; was to Ottoline an assault upon her person, a burden, and the breaking into her existence by an unknown foreigner. She reacted hostilely, and this hostility could have caused Philip to feel alienated; for Ottoline implies that there was some strain in their marriage at this time. She recorded in her *Memoirs*: "I felt classed with those unfortunates who have to bear the burden of a child alone, without a husband to share the responsibility."[13] Philip did however have other matters to occupy him at this time; a general election was to be held in January, at which he too was elected in the post-Boer-War Liberal landside.

His election coincided with the move to what was to be their new home: an imposing, spacious Georgian house at 44 Bedford Square, whose lease they bought for £1,800. This was in an area – the heart of London's Bloomsbury district – that had long appealed to Ottoline. Before her engagement, she and Hilda had been negotiating to take rooms in a house in the same Square. Up until the turn of the century, Bloomsbury was a combination of Georgian elegance and Bohemian shabbiness. It was made up of a number of squares around the British Museum, and was separated from the more-fashionable parts of London by the commercial areas of Oxford Street, Regent Street, and Covent Garden. In the latter years of the 19th century, however, Bloomsbury had started to look up. The cafés and restaurants of Percy and Charlotte Streets – in what was called Fitzrovia – were attracting artists, writers, and some younger intellectuals (such as Lytton Strachey). Middle-class people were beginning to move in. Two years earlier in 1904, the younger Stephens – Virginia, Vanessa, Thoby, and Adrian – had taken up residence in nearby Gordon Square. Yet of all the Bloomsbury squares, Bedford Square was probably the most distinguished-looking; and No. 44 a not-inappropriate residence for an up-and-coming prospective politician. A pair of green double-doors led into a wide hallway from which a noble staircase curved up to two large first-floor drawing-rooms. There, floor-to-ceiling windows overlooked the tree-filled private garden in the square below. The rest of the house was arranged on three floors, plus basement and attic (for the servants).

Here, in early 1906 Ottoline waited impatiently for her pregnancy to run its course; alternately annoyed at the prospect of becoming a mother, and guilty that she should be harbouring such thoughts. Her social engagements had to be curtailed and she filled the tedium with plans to renovate her new house. She also wrote to people like Birrell and Hilaire Belloc asking them to recommend books she might read while she waited. (Belloc replied, dauntingly, that Michelet on the French Revolution was as great as Tacitus.) Finally the long wait ended, and on May 18 she gave birth to twins. One was a boy, to be called Hugh after Philip's brother; and the other a girl, to be named Julian, after Mother Julian (not, it might be noted, Bentinck names). Three days later, however, the boy died from a brain haemorrhage. Julian was christened at St. Paul's Cathedral on July 5.

The boy's death shattered both Philip and Ottoline, and

Ottoline in particular took a long time to recover. But with the birth her maternal instinct asserted itself; and she did her best to see that Julian, who was not a strong baby, got proper care. The child spent most of her time with her nurse at Peppard Cottage, Henley-on-Thames, a modest country house that Ottoline and Philip had bought as a foothold in the constituency to which he had been elected. Back in London, Ottoline tried to busy herself with redecorating 44 Bedford Square; but her old verve was lacking, and her health continued to be a problem. One of her main symptoms was a sort of nervous condition that made life for Philip difficult. The doctors they consulted could only diagnose "nervous upset", but finally it was discovered she was suffering from a gynaecological problem which required an urgent operation. In February 1907 she went into Miss Nelson Smith's nursing home in Maida Vale for surgery. The operation, though not a full hysterectomy, meant that she was unable to have any more children; but as she had no marked aptitude for the maternal life, this did not greatly concern her. On the contrary, it gave her both an added reason for leading the sort of life she wanted to lead; and greater freedom to do so. After she recovered her health, she threw herself into helping Philip politically; joining women's associations, helping the district nurse, and taking an interest in municipal libraries. But her heart was not in it. "I am not suited to good works," she said.[14] So she turned instead to something she believed she would be good at.

INTERLUDE
The Centre of the World

London 1907 – Rotten Row and Hyde Park Corner

LONDON IN 1907, with a population of over seven million, was the biggest, most powerful, and most sophisticated city in the world. In fact, if British civilisation could be said to have had a peak, then 1907 has a strong claim to being its date. The long golden Edwardian summer had still three years to run, and seven more years would elapse before the outbreak of the war that would end Britain's world leadership. Already there were signs of decline. Since before 1900 Britain's commercial domination had been waning, and now Germany and America were equal if not ahead in production. But the London of 1907 ignored such sordid statistics. It was the pleasure ground of the rich. Lining the spacious squares and streets of Mayfair, Belgravia, and parts of Kensington were the mansions of the privileged minority who believed the world existed for their benefit.

In an inner crescent of suburbs, from Hampstead round to Greenwich, resided the only slightly less privileged middle classes, who were beginning to discover that they too could share the sophistications and leisure activities that previously had been the preserve of their betters. And, below them, in an ever-widening sea of suburban sprawl, lived the six million or more other Londoners to whom £100 a year represented riches beyond their ken.

To the more fortunate one million, London presented a pleasant prospect. With no income tax worth speaking of, life went on in a leisurely fashion, largely horse-drawn, circulating around the comfortable clubs of Pall Mall and Piccadilly, the well-stocked emporiums of Knightsbridge and Oxford Street, and that most civilised of institutions, the House of Commons, in which, thanks to the previous year's election, a solid rump of Liberal gentlemen was presiding over what was believed to be the transition from a stuffy, restricted Victorian England to a bright, new, modern and progressive state in which, through education and opportunity, the poor would better themselves. A spirit of reform and optimism was in the air. As Leonard Woolf said: "It seemed as though human beings might really be on the brink of becoming civilised."[1]

London 1907 - Mark Twain visits the Houses of Parliament

Behind this elegant Edwardian façade, the ladies of the well-to-do classes presided effortlessly over the day-to-day mechanics of society. Assisted by their servants, they spent their days arranging their homes to cater for the various social functions that were the focus of Edwardian life. With few restaurants, and outside evening entertainment confined to the occasional play, opera, or ballet, most social events took place in private houses. Though less convention-ridden than in late Victorian times, society still had a strict hierarchy of engagements: morning calls, luncheons, afternoon calls, teas, dinners, suppers, balls, and that most quintessential of Edwardian activities, the "at home". Being a hostess gave many women a chance to use talents and abilities that would otherwise have had no outlet. They turned their houses into cultural or intellectual oases, or merely centres of gossip. And a few did so in such a style that they qualified for the exalted title of "salonniere".

CHAPTER 7
Ottoline Launches Herself on the Sea of London

Ottoline in salonniere mode

OTTOLINE SPENT much of 1907 getting 44 Bedford Square in order. She and Philip planned the renovations together; Philip looking after the rearrangement of doorways and chimney-pieces and designing bookcases for the library, while Ottoline conceived a rather daring grey-and-yellow colour scheme for the drawing-rooms. Around the house she placed urns of golden chrysanthemums and piled the sofas with her favourite silk cushions. The early entertainments held in these rooms were mainly for Philip's political colleagues; but soon

Ottoline expanded her guest lists, hoping, she said, to "leaven the heavy political dough."[1] She had a solid core of old friends – Hilda Douglas-Pennant, Ethel Sands, Logan Pearsall Smith, Crompton Llewellyn Davies, the Sangers, and several others; and to these were added people she met when dining at friends' homes. She particularly admired the sort of people Ethel Sands mixed with. Miss Sands and her friend Nan Hudson (also a painter) held their salon in their Belgravia town-house, which was frequented by such people as Henry James, Max Beerbohm, Sargent, and Walter Sickert; just the brand of guest Ottoline was hoping to draw into her net.

By early 1908 she had started what was to be her famous Thursday evening "at homes". She chose the "at home" because it was a particularly flexible method of entertaining; and which delivered a wide range of guests. To be invited (you couldn't just "roll up") virtually the only qualification was some talent or interest in the arts. Acceptance assured a pleasant evening and the chance to meet someone famous, interesting, or promising (not to mention the chance of being seen there yourself). In her quest for guests, Ottoline searched the highways and byways of the capital. Other hostesses' guest-lists were ruthlessly plundered. She loosed showers of missives to writers, painters, and poets; praising their work and inviting them to Bedford Square. Each morning she would sit down in her boudoir and write to people she was getting to know. (She had a telephone, but preferred the post.) Her letters were written in a unique script full of loops and curlicues and written in a distinctive sepia ink that became her personal trademark. And at the bottom was what must be one of the most beautiful signatures ever composed. It took a cold heart – or an exceptionally timid one – to turn down one of these flattering enticements.

Ottoline didn't entertain every Thursday – some weeks she went out to other people's parties – but her "at homes" soon became fairly regular. Arriving at No. 44 between 9 and 10 pm, the guests would be ushered up the winding stairs by the parlourmaid. Twenty or more people might be there already (some had probably also dined at Ottoline's), standing in the double drawing-rooms on the Oriental rugs in casual conversational knots; or sitting on sofas drinking coffee and discussing politics, art, or the latest Shaw play. Usually there were snacks and sometimes champagne, but Ottoline was not keen on strong alcohol – it brought on her headaches – and often she merely served cider or cordials. In these early days she made many mistakes. Often her enthusiasm would run away with her, and the most incongruous people would find themselves staring at one another across the oriental rugs and an unbridgeable abyss of class, behaviour, and interest. The writers and politicians usually got on well together. Asquith, Ramsay MacDonald, Augustine Birrell, Charles Masterman, and other (usually radical) MPs enjoyed mixing with writers like James, critics like Max Beerbohm, and poets like Yeats. Where difficulty arose was when members of the Smart Set, inhabitants from Ottoline's old world, came to see the "scallywags" she was mixing with. These people tended to sit stiffly in their chairs, afraid to unbend. But as Ottoline's social technique developed, she managed to sort out her guests better; keeping sticklers for formality like Beerbohm and James away from the scruffy artists, and diverting any Smart Set people to the innocuous morning or afternoon visits.

Over the next seven years – from 1908 to 1915 – a strange but rich assortment of people began to regard the drawing-and-dining-rooms of 44 Bedford Square as probably the most civilised few hundred square feet in the London. For these people, some already famous, many soon to become so, Ottoline came to be a combination of friend, critic, patron, muse, *confidante* and goddess. There was a unique, exotic air about her house; a heady atmosphere many people found intoxicating. And at the centre of it all was the lady herself; so extraordinary a figure as to be almost an apparition (or, as Lawrence later decided, "a presentment"). Dressed habitually in a fashion verging on the bizarre – sometimes in a Grecian style, at others like a Cossack or an Oriental princess – she had a compulsive interest and enthusiasm for everything and everyone. She desperately wanted her guests to get to know each other; to mix, to exchange ideas. Her mind was forever busy dreaming up new combinations of people to invite. "Conversation, talk, interchange of ideas – how good it was," she wrote later.[2] Greedy for friendship, she was carried away with her new life; it was all so exhilarating, new, and exciting. And other people caught her excitement. The painter William Rothenstein was one. In December 1908, less than two years after the birth of Julian, he wrote to her: "You have the most delightful salon in London."[3]

Yet the list of famous names that fill page after page of Ottoline's visitors' book is only of marginal interest; a dozen other hostesses could boast of guest lists equally impressive. Yet what makes Ottoline unique is the role she played in the lives and careers of a relatively small number of these people. For she was not content to remain on the sideline and watch the throng of talent that beat a path to the green double-doors of 44 Bedford Square; nor was she happy just to pick up vicarious crumbs of glory dropped by the talented ones as they passed through. No, she also wanted something *from* them. Passionately, desperately, she yearned to infiltrate their lives; to help them, encourage them, champion them, to share their creative experience; her long-sought-after "experiences of the soul". In return she was prepared to give a great deal. And the extent to which she succeeded raised her far above the level of a mere hostess. She became, as Americans used to say, the "Hostess with the Mostest".

This success did not come cheaply. Later the price she had to pay proved high indeed. But in 1907 Ottoline saw none of this; although she did not lack for warnings. An explicit one came from that most fastidious observer, Henry James; who was a regular visitor to Bedford Square, and took a fatherly interest in her activities. One evening, after observing a boisterous group of young people at one of her Thursdays, he put his hand on her arm and said: "Look at them. Look at them, dear lady, over the banisters. But don't go down amongst them."[4] Ottoline commented: "I disobeyed. I was already too far down the stairs to turn back." Further warnings came from her family and their Smart Set friends. They thought Ottoline's activities bordered on the "fast". But such warnings fell on deaf ears, especially as, around Christmas 1907, an exciting prospect loomed – a meeting with the romantic, mysterious figure of Augustus John.

John was precisely the sort of person who appalled Henry James, who said of him: "He paints human beings like animals and dogs like human beings."[5] But Ottoline did not agree. She had first met John three years earlier in Charles Conder's studio when he was painting her. Then John had been the epitome of the struggling artist; so poor he had to stay in bed so that his wife, Ida, could darn his only suit. Conder had shown some of John's nude sketches to Ottoline, who confessed to being shocked by the expanses of bare flesh. Lately John had prospered; and, at 29, was on the verge of popularity, if not fame. On this particular evening, Ethel Sands had invited him to her home for dinner; and the other guests included the painter Walter Sickert, Prince Antoine Bibesco – and Ottoline. John was late, and while they waited for him they discussed his scandalous reputation. Ottoline remembered his dramatic looks: his pale, bearded face; dark auburn hair; eyes "like sea anemones"; delicate hands – more expressive even than Axel Munthe's; and gold earrings.[6] Someone mentioned John's torrid private life; of how his mistress, Dorelia McNeill, had moved in with John and his wife to live *à trois*; how Dorelia and Ida had both had children by John; and how, a year ago, Ida had died in childbirth. Finally John arrived, dressed to everyone's surprise in orthodox evening clothes, though still sporting his gold earrings. Miss Sands seated him next to Ottoline and the two spent most of the evening discussing John's current hobby: gypsies. Though deprived of actual Romany blood (as his father was a middle-class Pembrokeshire lawyer); John had done the next best thing and adopted gypsy dress, gypsy habits, and the gypsy mode of life. He had taken his unconventional ways to the Slade art school in London; where his draughtsmanship was considered second to none. Later his startling, black-cloaked figure was a familiar sight around Bohemian London.

To Ottoline, already attracted to the intuitive, relaxed world of artists, John seemed infinitely romantic; and his slightly aggressive manner and hesitating way of speaking made him no less attractive. And he was equally impressed by her. Suddenly he said: "Will you sit to me? Will you come? Tomorrow?"[7] Ottoline readily agreed, and next day she and Philip walked over to his studio in Fitzroy Street, a short distance from Bedford Square. After climbing a narrow staircase, they found John, dressed neatly in a grey suit with a silk handkerchief around his neck, standing in front of a large unfinished painting.[8] His studio – a large room in which he also lived and slept – was clean and tidy; but there was no sign of Dorelia, who was apparently in Paris looking after John's brood of children. A little later two more people arrived: a blunt-faced man with reddish hair and a pleasantly spoken woman with Grecian features whom John introduced as Clive and Vanessa Bell. (Bell was a young art critic and Vanessa one of the Stephen sisters.) Ottoline invited John to return for tea at Bedford Square and there Philip promptly commissioned John to paint Ottoline's portrait. Having previously told Ottoline of his desire to paint her, John readily agreed; but this scheme had to be postponed as he was due to leave in a day or so to re-join Dorelia in Paris, while Ottoline and Philip were due to go to Peppard Cottage with Julian.

However, Ottoline was smitten; and while snowed-in at Peppard she read Balzac and dreamed of John. By March she was writing long letters to him in Paris and sending him presents, including Wordsworth's poems. In his *Autobiography* many years later John recorded: "I had difficulty with her letters which were written in a character of her own invention, so original and precious as to be almost indecipherable."[9] He wrote back telling her: "I do not intend to allow you to forget the portrait suggested by Mr. Morrell."[10] They exchanged views on Dostoevsky and the French primitive painters. By April their letters had become more personal; she was impatient for him to return, and in reply he said the thought of London horrified him; perhaps he could transfer his studio, and her with it, to Paris? By May Ottoline was even more impatient. She wanted to know exactly when he would return, but added that she feared he might be disappointed with her. He reassured her he would not be, and said he was returning almost immediately. Finally, towards the middle of May, he did start back, telling her he was disaffected with Paris. "The gypsies have a saying," he told her, 'the dog who walks finds the bone."[11] Normally Ottoline would not have appreciated being likened to a bone; but the imminence of John's return put all else out of her mind.

Within days of his getting bac, she was going to his studio for regular portrait-sessions. It was a situation tailor-made for seduction. Few women could have resisted John; and indeed, over the years, few women did. By May 30, after several sittings both in his studio and at Bedford Square, he wrote to her dropping the formal "Dear Lady Ottoline " and signing himself "Elfin":

> *At last I am alone – in bed and can write to you Ottoline – as I promised. When you were in my studio to-day I wished I could cry – I should have felt more intelligent perhaps – with the delicatest & noblest of women loving me so infinitely beyond my deserts...I have always been so excessively anxious to feel myself quite alive that I have plunged with needless precipitation into the most obviously fast flowing channels where there are rocks & bubbles & foam & whirlpools & the water seems perhaps more watery if less pure...Since my wife's death there have been few opportunities of excitement [or] intoxication that I have let pass and this plan has saved me from deadly morbidity at any rate if it has not improved my complexion altogether. But one doesn't meet Ottoline everyday – we can't go on thus, darling that you are – you will only get unhappy & I shall hate myself. Don't let us spoil a beautiful thing...and let us be gay little heroes!*[12]

Their affair was not a protracted one, and probably reached its peak around July 1908. But they were happy months for Ottoline, who revelled in the spontaneity and impulsiveness of John's attentions; and flattered by his desire to paint and draw her. Between May and July they met several times a week, usually in his studio, where he made scores of sketches of her; most of which were ripped from his block and discarded on the floor (many of them were retrieved, however, and John subsequently sold them).

What did John see in Ottoline? It might be thought that his interest could have had commercial overtones; that he realised she could help his career. Help him she certainly did; but he was unquestionably attracted to her, as his letters to her indicate. Also in 1908, when she fell in love with John, Ottoline had become a very alluring woman. A snapshot taken about this time gives some idea of her appeal: it shows a long nose and strong jaw, challenging eyes, a soft mouth, and high cheekbones that betray her aristocratic background. The pose she strikes – sitting upright on a sofa, cigarette (a daring departure in those days) in her left hand – is rather militant, an impression reinforced by her military-style tunic and Cossack hat. She is certainly a figure to challenge a man and artist such as John. Why did she deceive Philip? Indeed, why did she embark on the affair? There has been a suggestion that Philip had tended to shun Ottoline since her operation, but this is rather hard to believe; more likely he simply was busy with his legal and parliamentary activities, and was content that his wife was occupied. (That was the way things were done in aristocratic circles.) Ottoline's motives were more complex. She apparently had the idea that in having affairs with people like John she was not only having fun, but performing a duty. She was acting as a mother and ministering-angel to the "creative flame". She herself recognised this, and in her *Memoirs* there is a revealing dialogue with "an old friend of John" called "Mary" ("Mary" of course being Ottoline's own better-self). The dialogue runs:

> *"I expect he says he loves you?" she said, turning simply to me.*
>
> *"No, never [Mary/Ottoline replied]. He may feel attracted by my being strange to him, but I am far too different to him. He could only feel at ease with one of his gypsy clan. If I was one of them perhaps he would let himself go, but he is afraid of a woman such as I am."*

Even so, Ottoline believed she could help John, if only fleetingly, and she tells the "friend":

> *"I cannot touch his melancholy. What I can give him is not what he wants. He calls for something strong, reckless and rampant, which will carry him off his feet, and he knows too well that it is not mine to give."*[13]

The "friend" says that she had heard John call Ottoline "an angel". This was a role that rather appealed to her; so Ottoline continued to hover angel-like over John, showering gifts on him from her heaven in Bedford Square. They exchanged rings and she gave him cushions, chocolates, books on poetry and Plato, lilies, and a small watch similar to the one she had given Asquith (which, John complained, broke down almost continuously). John was unlike anyone Ottoline had known before. His courtly, old-fashioned manner and romantic aura captivated her; and even when she wasn't with him, he would haunt her thoughts. "He would appear in my imagination as if he passed through the room, suddenly making the conventional scene appear absurd," she wrote in her *Memoirs*.[14]

In July, John went back to France to re-join Dorelia and his children in Paris. Ottoline continued to write, but soon the first indication of discord appeared. John apparently wrote something frivolous, and she upbraided him for it. In another letter he told her she did not have to prove her generosity to him (a lament of many people whom Ottoline befriended). By October John was back in England and thinking of taking a house in Chelsea.

Ominously, Dorelia was with him. Despite Ottoline's efforts, he was beginning to slip away. She tried to help some of his impecunious friends, including the American sculptor Jacob Epstein, who was in trouble over some figures he had carved for a building in the Strand. Ottoline and Philip went to see him and commissioned a garden statue. Epstein was overjoyed: "A garden statue sounds delightful; sculpture outdoors amongst trees and shrubs; it is reminiscent of Italy and France."[15] Ottoline also tried to help Henry Lamb, a young artist who was something of a disciple of John's. She sent a cheque for Lamb to John, but the latter returned it, saying Lamb wasn't that needy (he came from a well-off family). As well, Ottoline bought four sketches from John and tried to interest her brother, Lord Henry, and several of her friends in John's works. However, by the end of November Ottoline was accusing John of ingratitude; he replied:

> *Of course I like the ring & wearing it, but you give me so many things it makes me shy of accepting more and whether you like it or not I find pleasure in it – I have a natural taste for barbaric splendour; and your giving the ring doesn't make it less precious!...It is more difficult to receive than to give.*[16]

Now John began to miss appointments; but Ottoline was still prepared to forgive. On November 23 he denied he had found her dull and stupid the day before. In December he wrote saying he was sorry she was feeling miserable and asked if he could bring two of his boys to visit her one day. He added that a concert might be nice, and hoped he would feel the right way about it when the time came. But by the 9th he could not come after all; and he also apologised for having forgotten the Bells' luncheon; he had been shopping with Dorelia. In another letter, probably also in December 1908, he told her that Dorelia was the only person he loved and added that "in loving her I am loyal to my wife" [the deceased Ida]. He insisted Ottoline must not feel worthless: she was wonderful and there would always be some cord between

Ottoline Launches Herself on the Sea of London

them, despite Dorelia – a cord...

> ...*so fine, so fragile that to strain it would break it, or to ask more from it than from the faint zephyrs of the air, or a more audible more definable message than the glimmer of a star in flight, for ever...And you will not continue to suffer too much. You will have the fortitude of great hearts & unconquerable souls – and the sweetness of the music of Heaven will teach you to smile at last with the sweetest smile of all, and the profound-est. Bless you Ottoline – Elfi.*[17]

In the contest between Dorelia and Ottoline for John's affections, Dorelia held most of the cards. Ottoline might have background, title, culture, allure and whatever; but it was Dorelia who had proximity, for she was actually living with John. She was also the mother of two of his children (as well as being in charge of the rest). Moreover, she was a determined and capable woman. From November 1908 to March 1909, Ottoline continued to bombard John with almost daily letters and weekly invitations. Manfully he tried to juggle the two women; but in the end was unequal to the task. The pull of Dorelia proved too strong; and slowly John disengaged himself from his high-flown dalliance. Ottoline tacitly admitted defeat in March when she wrote to Dorelia asking her and John to dine and meet the Bells. Dorelia, a forthright woman with a strong streak of pride, declined:

> *Thank you for your invitation, but I can't come as I think it rather ridiculous to be introduced to people as Mrs. John. I do not know the Bells...John asks me to say he will be pleased to come.*[18]

A few weeks later Ottoline and Dorelia met at last when Ottoline came to John's new studio in Chelsea, to resume her portrait sittings. She decided that Dorelia had dignity and repose, and a firm grip on the John household. The ice between them melted and they were soon on the best of terms.

At Bedford Square, however, things were not so amicable. Finally, the ever-patient Philip had become not only suspicious, but hostile. As early as December 18, John had said in a letter to Ottoline: "I was really not surprised that Morrell should have been out of humour. I felt I was cutting rather an offensive figure in your house. I should be very sorry to disturb so admirable a personage as your husband."[19] And in January he wrote: "I think it evident that your husband don't like me."[20] So Philip, for one, was relieved as it became clear that John's interests lay elsewhere. At the end of March Ottoline asked John's boys to Peppard for Easter, and there she and Philip took them out on to the Common with Julian, now a lively toddler, to fly kites. The visit was a success, though Ottoline found the boys' unconventional upbringing had made them rather ragamuffinish. When she asked one of them what he normally ate at home he replied gruffly: "Bones".[21]

In July John invited Ottoline to come to visit him and his ménage where they had encamped in a meadow outside Grantchester. It sounded wonderfully romantic – a day with John gypsy-style – and Ottoline eagerly accepted, setting off on the appointed day. John, sporting a black eye from an altercation in a pub the previous night, met her at the station at Cambridge in a gig he had hired. There Ottoline was disappointed to find a flat, featureless field with Dorelia and her sister struggling to do the washing and cooking in the most primitive conditions, and in no mood for light conversation. It began to rain. Dinner consisted of a crust of bread and fruit, and afterwards Ottoline decided to call it a day, getting back to London damp and bedraggled. Yet their friendship survived even that hapless afternoon, and two days later John wrote calling her *"chère amie"* and asking her to sit to him when he got back to London.[22] But as time went on they saw less of each other. Nevertheless, they continued meeting on and off, and would occasionally dine together. For the rest of Ottoline's life they went on corresponding, although John confessed that he never learned to decipher her letters.

INTERLUDE
The Hostess With the Mostest

A literary salon in 18th century Paris

OTTOLINE WAS a salonniere in the sense that her "at homes" or "Thursday evenings" in Bedford Square, and later at Garsington and Gower Street, were part of a tradition of famous salons that dated back to 17th and 18th century France, when aristocratic ladies convened regular gatherings at which invited guests met and discussed political and cultural topics, informally moderated by their hostess, or salonniere.

In many ways, however, Ottoline was more of a patroness than a salonniere, in the more accepted meaning of that term. She was the maypole around which the more interesting and talented people of the metropolis gathered to meet, be seen, and converse. Her "salon" was different to the other famous London salons of the Edwardian and Georgian periods, still less were they like those of the "Roaring Twenties', when hostesses like Emerald Cunard and Sybil Colefax dominated the London Season. These "society" hostesses (or salonnieres) dressed expensively and courted other aristocrats and important political figures in their lavish dining-and-ballrooms. Ottoline, on the other hand, opened her green double-doors at Bedford Square primarily to writers and artists, many of them practically penniless – although she did, on occasion, play hostess to politicians such as her old friend Asquith, and the young Winston Churchill.

Two rivals to Ottoline – Nancy Curard (left) and Sibyl Colfax

Ottoline's Thursday evening "at homes" were more the "literary salon" rather than the "society salon"; although her events also often included frivolities such as dancing and card-playing. They usually convened around 9pm (so they were an after-dinner occasion). The drinks were mainly tea and coffee (although there would be whisky for people like Asquith or Churchill, and wine for others if they wanted it, served by Ottoline's resident staff). And whereas the platinum-plated Cunards and Colefax parties could feature string-quartets and famous pianists and singers, what music there was at Ottoline's would be provided by Philip pumping out popular tunes on the pianola. Thursday evenings at Bedford Square were casual and informal – though you had to have an invitation or introduction to turn up. Other leading salonnieres of the period included Edwina Mountbatten, Margaret, "Mrs Ronnie" Greville', and Lady Diana Cooper, wife of the writer and diplomat Duff Cooper, who remarked in his Diary that in London they had attended "every lighted candle".

CHAPTER 8
The Great Lady of Bedford Square

Ottoline, by Duncan Grant

AROUND MARCH 1909 Virginia Stephen wrote: "We have just got to know a wonderful Lady Ottoline Morrell, who has the head of a Medusa; but she is very simple & innocent in spite of it, & worships the arts."[1] It may have been that Virginia met Ottoline earlier than this, for her sister Vanessa and her husband Clive Bell had been dinner guests at 44 Bedford

Square since their first meeting with Ottoline in John's studio just over a year before. Virginia and Vanessa had been living in Bloomsbury since 1904, moving there with their brothers Thoby and Adrian after the death of their father, Sir Leslie Stephen. In November 1906 Thoby died suddenly, and within a few months Vanessa had married the art critic Clive Bell. They stayed at 46 Gordon Square while Virginia and Adrian moved to nearby Fitzroy Square to set up their own establishment. After Virginia and Adrian settled in to their new lodgings, they revived the Thursday-evening "at homes" that Thoby had started at Gordon Square for his Cambridge friends; and it is from this time that some people date that most discussed phenomenon, Bloomsbury. (Ottoline's Thursday-evening "at homes" could be distinguished from the Stephen sisters' ones by the fact that the latter were more "intellectual", and thus they had a rather different clientele.)

Ottoline's relationship with Bloomsbury fluctuated, and was deeper with some of its members – particularly Lytton, Virginia (later), and, for a time, Clive Bell – than others. That she was attracted to Bloomsbury is easy to understand. Their talk was a fresh gust in her drawing-room, and she admired their cleverness and talent. But that they should be attracted to her might seem slightly odder; particularly in light of the dismissive remarks they were to make about her later on. A younger Bloomsbury member, Quentin Bell, appears to be speaking for the Group when he described Ottoline as "extremely simple and not very clever".[2] Yet he went on to say that Bloomsbury members found Ottoline likable: "She brought petticoats, frivolity and champagne to the buns, the buggery and high thinking of Fitzroy Square."[3] Indeed, Ottoline gave Bloomsbury a chance to indulge its less serious sid;, and she herself was most friendly with its more frivolous element: Lytton, Virginia (early), and Clive, together with its younger brigade, which included Duncan Grant and David Garnett. The more serious members of the group – Leonard Woolf and Saxon Sydney-Turner, for example – found her far too exotic for their more refined palates.

It was more or less coincidental that Ottoline and

Bloomsbury moved into each other's orbits. They had friends in common – such as Augustus John – and they lived in the same part of London. On the other hand, Ottoline had her own world which she was to create at 44 Bedford Square, while Bloomsbury was only a part of it. Of some significance, perhaps, is that each of them were refugees from the smart and respectable sections of London society. Thus, given Ottoline's never-ending quest to track down talent and intelligence, it is not surprising that, following Ottoline's first visit to Fitzroy Square, her thank-you note asked for the names and addresses of all of their "wonderful friends."[4] Over the next few years, Ottoline and Bloomsbury were to see a lot of each other. She and Philip – sometimes accompanied by John or Henry Lamb – would drop round to Fitzroy Square; while Vanessa, Clive, and Virginia often turned up at Bedford Square to revel in what Virginia called "that extraordinary whirlpool".[5]

Ottoline's strongest link with Bloomsbury was painting. Moore's philosophy (a favourite Bloomsbury discussion topic) was a mystery to her; but she could and did appreciate contemporary French and English art. Yet in this, as in many things, she was out of step with popular and fashionable opinion, which at this time still clung determinedly to the Victorian Royal Academy style. It was for young, struggling artists that Ottoline felt a special sympathy; and she saw that here she might do something worthwhile. Early in 1909 she met the critic and painter (and later Bloomsbury member) Roger Fry and joined with him in an ambitious project to encourage English artists. She lent her patronage to the contemporary art scene, buying and championing such artists as John, Epstein, and Duncan Grant.[6] In March 1909 Fry wrote to D.S. MacColl, keeper of the Tate Gallery, proposing lunch with himself and Ottoline, saying: "She has been very good to me and has a real feeling for art. You know she has patronised John a good deal."[7] In April the three of them plus C.J. Holmes, a friend of Fry's, decided to launch a fund dedicated to buying works of current English artists. The fund was a success; and in 1910 it was renamed the Contemporary Art Society. Its first committee members included Fry, Clive Bell, Ottoline, MacColl, and Holmes. During its first three years the society bought works by such artists as John, Epstein, Conder, Sickert, and Henry Lamb. For a short time Ottoline acted as its buyer.

The pace of Ottoline's life was quickening. Not only did she have her household to run, and parties, dinners, and "at homes" to preside over; but her political entertaining on Philip's behalf was becoming more important as, towards the end of 1909, it was clear that another general election was looming. And if, as expected, the Tories were to make up some of the ground they had given up in 1906, South Oxfordshire would be one of the first Liberal seats to fall. Not only did Ottoline support Philip on the platform at several big Liberal rallies; but she also did her bit entertaining charabancfuls of Liberal women driven down from Oxfordshire to Bedford Square for afternoon tea and inspection of the baby daughter of their MP. As well, there were ritual pilgrimages to such shrines of Liberal patronage as Mells, home of the Liberal doyenne Lady Horner, where Ottoline felt distinctly uncomfortable (because it reminded her of Welbeck). A more pleasant visit took place in September 1909 when Logan Pearsall Smith took Ottoline and Philip to Bagley Wood, near Oxford, to see Bertrand Russell, who was married to Logan's sister Alys.

A year older than Ottoline, Russell also came from an old aristocratic family (many of the streets in Bloomsbury were named after either his or Ottoline's families). He was the co-author of *Principia Mathematica*, one of mathematics' seminal works. A man of outstanding intellect, he was also something of a prig, and had for some time harboured a poor opinion of Ottoline, mainly because he believed her use of scent and powder indicated she was a flibbertigibbet. However, his friend Crompton Davies, with whom Ottoline and Philip had worked improving the lot of farm labourers, caused him to revise this opinion. Recently Russell had interested himself actively in politics, becoming a courageous supporter of women's suffrage; and only avoiding being adopted himself as a Liberal candidate through his prospective supporters' last-minute discovery that he was a practising atheist. Nevertheless, he resolved to aid the Liberals somehow and, disliking his local Liberal candidate, offered to help Philip in South Oxfordshire. In the course of the subsequent election campaign he had many opportunities to get to know Ottoline, discovering – as he says in his autobiography – that she was "extraordinarily kind and much in earnest about public life."[8] However, both his and the Morrells' efforts were in vain, and when the results came out, Philip had lost his seat. He was back in the solicitor's office in Bedford Row.

Meanwhile, Ottoline's friendship with Dorelia had led in October 1909 to the two women going off to Paris together, where they stayed with the rich Mrs. Chadbourne, and went to see an exhibition of Post-impressionist paintings. Later Ottoline accompanied Mrs. Chadbourne to Matisse's studio where the artist showed them – rather commercially, thought Ottoline – some of his work, an example of which however, Mrs. Chadbourne wisely purchased. Then Philip came over and he and Ottoline visited the American writer Gertrude Stein, an occasion which Miss Stein recorded in her *Autobiography of Alice B. Toklas*, describing finding Ottoline on her doorstep, looking like some "marvellous female version of Disraeli."[9]

Although Ottoline may not have realised it, her separation from John received a distinct nudge from Dorelia. Perceiving that John was quite content to let the affair drift desultorily along, Dorelia took matters into her own hands, and cast about for some way of diverting her aristocratic rival. And in September 1909 she hit upon a brilliant idea. One day she prevailed upon Ottoline to go with her to see a school she was considering for John's sons. On the way there they happened to stop off at John's old studio in Fitzroy Street. Dorelia left Ottoline waiting in the taxi while she went inside, explaining that she wanted to leave a message for a young artist, Henry Lamb, who now lived there.

As she waited in the cab, Ottoline's mind drifted to memories of previous visits to Fitzroy Street, when it was John's studio. Suddenly a voice interrupted her reverie. "Won't you come in for a moment? Dorelia sent me."[10] Ottoline looked up and there, standing on the pavement, was a figure that seemed to have escaped from a vision of Blake's; a pale slim young man dressed in an old-fashioned mustard-coloured coat, a green-and-yellow silk scarf round his neck, with his pale golden hair swept back off his forehead. It was Henry Lamb in person. Ottoline followed him into the hall, up the steps, and into the studio she knew so well. There Dorelia was waiting – an innocent look on her face no doubt – with another young woman, Helen Maitland, who was Lamb's current mistress. Before departing, Ottoline invited Lamb and the two women to return to Bedford Square for tea. (Apparently the visit to the school was shelved.) Lamb was, if possible, an even more romantic figure than John. Dorelia, who had also been Lamb's mistress in Paris, was right in believing that introducing Ottoline to him would produce the result she desired. And indeed, straight away, Ottoline found Lamb physically attractive; and he apparently was equally taken with her. But for the moment their mutual interest had to wait on the election campaign and Ottoline's forthcoming trip to Paris. In the meantime she and Lamb exchanged polite notes. Fortunately, Ottoline kept all of Lamb's letters; and it is from them that a chronicle of their relationship can be pieced together.

It was Ottoline's custom in her *Memoirs* to omit the more personal details of her romantic escapades. She had a genteel disdain of anything that even remotely approached the salacious ("sex" to her was always "the physical side" of a relationship). When, for example, Lamb later referred in a letter to having spent two days with her, she irritably crossed out the words; as if the very ink offended her. The first of Lamb's letters – undated, but probably late 1909 – was quite formal. He addressed her as "Dear Lady Ottoline" and told her that he was off to Cornwall, but hoped to see her on his return. The second (possibly February 1910) was more friendly, but not yet intimate. He thanked her for some tulips ("You are far too angelic") and referred to a hurt he had given her; perhaps over the nature of his relationship with Helen Maitland, for he said: "You say my friends can be yours, if

I will – yes, but are you ready to make enemies of my enemies? Do not be rash!"[11] The next letter (probably March 1910) is plainly one only a lover could write: "I am insatiable for more life with you & in you," he told her. It is evident they were having trouble meeting, for he says: "I am sure it is folly to add to the circumstantial difficulties of seeing you: do let me see more of you, I pray you most earnestly (less often if it must be so, but *longer*)."[12] It is not known if she was going to his studio, but it does not appear so: perhaps Helen Maitland was ensconced there. He went on to say:

> *All the recent happy memories are of our free times together & all the horrors spring from interruptions: don't for ever postpone our privacy because of future possibilities...I get congealed in your armchairs & the multitude of visitors distracts me. Must I wait for the age & fame of a Henry James before I am allowed the general concession of private attention?*

He asked her to the opera. From this and another letter (probably March or early April 1910) it seems clear that most of their meetings were in cafes, or during walks, or at Ottoline's Thursday more-general "at homes". Nevertheless, Ottoline's maid Brenty was kept busy ferrying notes between Bedford Square and Fitzroy Street. Lamb was looking forward to some seclusion when he joined Ottoline, who was alone at Peppard.

Also obvious is that Philip was getting suspicious. Since his defeat in the January election, he had been busy with a new Liberal organisation called the Gladstone League, of which he was secretary. (Ottoline also was involved – in the unlikely capacity of office dogsbody: opening letters, sorting papers, and looking after the stationery.) Philip well knew that his wife was incurably addicted to romantic figures like John and Lamb. He could not do anything to alter this; so in all probability he said nothing. On the other hand, Ottoline did not want to do anything overt to hurt either Philip or her marriage; even though Philip had not been so attendant to her of late. She tried to be as discreet as her nature and exigency would permit. Thursday evenings, secretarial duties at the League, and the rest of her varied life went on as before; with Lamb fitted in as circumstances allowed.

It was Lamb's boyishness and immaturity that particularly attracted Ottoline, though there was obviously a maternal element in their friendship, as she admitted:

> *I was much older than he, and I had the instinct that I had something in me which would supply what he needed, some ingredient in which he was lacking. It was perhaps a maternal instinct that pushed me towards this interesting centaur.* [13]

Lamb had been too long in the shadow of John – aping him, painting like him, taking up with his mistresses – and was insecure; and Ottoline was good at boosting the confidence of insecure people, especially if they were artists or poets. Yet Lamb was temperamental, and resented too obvious or too generous a dose of assistance or sympathy. It seems likely that Lamb and Ottoline spent two days together at Peppard in mid-April, and a longer period in May or June. Ottoline had been at Peppard quite a lot recently; partly because Julian, who was still frail, was staying there with her nurse, and partly because Ottoline's doctor had urged the peaceful country life on her as a cure for her headaches and ill-health generally. As cottages go, Peppard was not particularly striking; two storeys, brick-and-tile, with casement windows opening on to the garden. Ottoline likened it to a "bathing box" and complained that it was too small to entertain guests properly. But Peppard had its compensations. The countryside and the common were pretty; there were some pleasant walks; and London seemed a long way off. By now, Ottoline, intent on leading her own life, was besotted with Lamb. As the warm weather advanced, so did their friendship. They went for expeditions into the woods and picnicked under the beeches. Ottoline found Lamb a complex, moody man, and difficult to manage. For half a day he would be a charming and delightful companion; then he would change and pour out accusing words at her. Then, after his wild rantings, he would break down and sob, clinging to her. Sitting under the trees on Ottoline's silk cushions they talked about art and books. Then they would have discussions about the ups and downs of their relationship. After one such debate he wrote to her: "Divine Ottoline, Have we not the principal treasure? These endless discussions as to what may or may not be lacking seems mean & belittling sometimes: forgive me for raising them so often."[14] A regular topic was the amount of time Ottoline spent with Philip and her other friends, which he begrudged her.

In April 1910 an event occurred that was to give a new perspective to Ottoline's life in the ensuing years. This one took place in a setting very different from the sylvan surroundings of Peppard. Up in the Lancashire industrial belt, the Burnley Liberal Party executive was meeting to discuss a minor crisis in the affairs of the local party branch. For years Burnley had been (with its working-class vote) a fairly-secure Liberal seat, but in the recent election the Liberal candidate had been narrowly defeated, and was not standing again. So the Burnley Liberals were in the market for an up-and-coming Liberal to contest the next election. They wrote to Liberal headquarters in London explaining their problem; and received back the name of the former MP for South Oxfordshire. Deciding that he might be a suitable candidate, they sent a deputation to London to interview Philip and ask if he would be agreeable to stand. For Philip their arrival was timely. The Gladstone League was proving less a means of helping the Liberal Party than a way of helping the circulation of the *Daily News*, the newspaper which sponsored it. So the scent of political battle was welcome to him. He met the Burnley delegation in his study at Bedford Square and told them he would be willing to stand. When he showed them a photograph of Ottoline, their leader said, "Yes, she will suit the Burnley democrats all right."[15] So while Lamb made plans to holiday with John in France; Ottoline and Philip went up north to inspect and be inspected. In

Burnley they were put up at a house belonging to Lady O'Hagan, a local Liberal bigwig. The visit was a success and on April 12 Philip was endorsed as Burnley's next Liberal candidate.

Ottoline went back to Peppard in a state of nervous exhaustion. She had put up a good show in Burnley; visiting local textile mills, attending meetings, and generally playing the part of a conscientious candidate's wife. But the effort, on top of the poverty and misery she witnessed there, were too much for her sensitive soul; so she took to her bed for several days. From France he wrote saying Dorelia was ill and that the hotel John had recommended (for her and Philip to stay in) was literally lousy. Turning to more personal matters, he said that what he really wanted was a new leaf to his life, with Ottoline at his side. In reality, however, it was Helen Maitland who was at his side. He suggested, surely playfully, that Ottoline and Philip should come to France to form a *ménage à six*.

On May 16 he was back in London but couldn't see much of Ottoline because he had a five-week commission to paint a Brazilian woman's portrait. Ottoline came down from Peppard several times for rendezvous in a coffee shop in Mayfair; after which they went for strolls in Hyde Park, Lamb looking most dashing in a new, pink, square-topped hat. When he could spare himself from the Brazilian lady, he and Ottoline would catch the train to Putney or Richmond and walk and talk in the woods. At the end of May he was looking forward to going to Peppard again. But Philip was obviously getting anxious; for, after another city rendezvous, Lamb wrote to ask if there had been "a great storm waiting" for her at Bedford Square.[16]

In June Lamb went up to Cambridge to see his brother Walter, who was a don. He didn't enjoy the visit; nor did he enjoy the fact that Ottoline was putting restrictions on the time she could spare him; and he returned to London feeling out of sorts and suffering from stomach pains. He wrote to her:

> *Obviously, I can only look forward to rare & short spells of that enchanted existence we enjoyed a few days ago & in*

> *the intervals I only waste time crying for the moon. Therefore I must marry Ethel Sands & have no more worry about my future. Does this conclusion convince you?"* [17]

On June 18 he wrote asking her to accompany him to Brest with Boris Anrep, a Russian ceramic artist. Ottoline was tempted; but Philip apparently placed some restrictions on the plan, for Lamb wrote: "If he could be made to be serious about sending you with a chaperone surely one could be found."[18] Instead, Ottoline and Philip themselves went off to the Continent together, intending to go to La Bourboule, where Ottoline was to take the waters. Before they set off, Lamb wrote telling her he had been riding on the downs in Sussex. "I got so wild with joy I shouted your name out loud," he told her. [19]

August, September, and part of October, Ottoline and Philip spent on the Continent; travelling from La Bourboule to Aix-en-Provence, where they joined John and Dorelia, whom they found sitting outside a cafe, John looking very dissipated with a square-cut beard and bloodshot eyes. Later, on the way back to London, Ottoline and Philip stopped off in Paris where they encountered Roger Fry at a small gathering. Desmond MacCarthy was also there and later recalled Ottoline entering, in a hat "like a crimson tea cosy trimmed with hedgehogs".[20] Afterwards Fry wrote to his friend Goldie Lowes Dickinson at Cambridge: "Lady Ottoline was with us in Paris, she is quite splendid. She talks of coming to Cambridge to see you. Will you get them lodgings & may I come too?"[21]

At Cambridge Ottoline and Philip spent a not especially exciting weekend meeting, apart from Dickinson, people like Russell, Lytton Strachey, E.M. Forster, Fry, Russell's colleague A.N. Whitehead, and Jane Harrison, head of Newnham College. At Miss Harrison's Ottoline suggested to Strachey, half-jokingly, that he might like to come to stay at Peppard. He pondered, drifted away, then came back and said, "Do you really mean me to come to Peppard?" Ottoline replied: "Of course I do."[22]

44 BEDFORD SQUARE

Augustus John

Ottoline, Julian and Philip

David Garnett

Bertrand Russell

44 Bedford Square

D'Aranyi Sisters

Young Winston

Virginia Woolf

Henry Lamb

CHAPTER 9
The Arch-Priest of Bloomsbury

Ottoline and Lytton

LYTTON'S ACCEPTANCE of Ottoline's invitation began a friendship that ended only with Lytton's death in 1932. Yet his initial reasons for accepting were selfish; partly he wanted to escape from London and the trammels of his family, and partly he was filled with desire for Henry Lamb, whom he knew to be a friend of his hostess, and a likely fellow guest at Peppard. Indeed, Ottoline, who probably knew of Lytton's penchant for his own sex, may have used Lamb as bait to lure him to Peppard; a ploy she was to make some use of later at Garsington. At any rate, for Lytton the invitation was timely; he was in need of a little patronage.

For most of the previous year he had been plagued by illness. "Mahomet's coffin," as he whimsically called his frail physique, had been particularly tiresome, forcing him to take several rest cures at Scandinavian health farms. In a continuing effort to find salubrious surroundings, he had been compiling a list of friends with suitable rural retreats to which he could propose himself for as long as their owners would take him. Peppard fitted nicely into this roster.

Lytton had first seen Lamb at one of the Stephens' Gordon Square functions, and had been captivated. He wrote afterwards to Leonard Woolf:

> *He's run away from Manchester, become an artist, and grown side-whiskers. I didn't speak to him, but wanted to, because he really looked amazing, though of course very very bad.*[1]

But hardly had his appetite been whetted when the object of his admiration was snatched away by Euphemia, the art student with whom Lamb had eloped to Paris. Now Lamb was back, and with Ottoline, so a visit to Peppard was doubly attractive for Lytton.

Almost as soon as she issued the invitation, Ottoline began to regret it. For she still didn't have much confidence she could mix on equal terms with "intellectual" people like Lytton. And, on the face of it, she didn't have much in common with the archpriest of the Bloomsbury Group. He was an intellectual who had dominated his contemporaries at Cambridge. He was also a homosexual and renowned for making witty remarks and being cruel to people who weren't as clever as he was. Now, at 30, he was beginning to make a name for himself as a writer; particularly of biography and criticism, and he was currently working on a series of essays on French literature. As Ottoline returned to London, she wondered how she would possibly entertain such a figure.

At Bedford Square, Ottoline and Philip found Lamb waiting for them. The plan had been for him to accompany them to Peppard, where a studio had been prepared for him, and accommodation arranged at the local inn, The Dog (Philip having vetoed his staying at the Cottage itself). Lamb had brought with him a large quantity of luggage – paintboxes, canvasses, clothes, etc. – and Philip, observing the pile, ventured to suggest that a separate taxi might be engaged to carry it, while they followed in another vehicle. To this sensible idea Lamb replied: "Why? Do you object to travelling with my luggage overhead?"[2] It was not an auspicious start to the holiday.

But things improved, and the day after the trio's arrival Lamb was established at The Dog, and Ottoline was waiting for Lytton's arrival. She had written to him confirming the offer of the spare room at the Cottage, "…which I hope you will prefer to Mr. Lamb's Public House. He is here. I cannot answer to his temper…but the thought of seeing you makes him very happy today."[3]

A few days later Lytton arrived and proved to be a model guest. His appetite perked up and in the extensive woods around Peppard Common he indulged his love of walking. He proved easily amused and Ottoline relaxed after it became evident that Lamb was steadfastly heterosexual, while enjoying Lytton's doe-eyed attentions. At night she would listen to the two men's voices in the sitting-room beneath her bedroom: "I heard the duet of their voices underneath, laughing and joking, Lytton playing with him like a cat with a mouse, enjoying having his own sensations tickled by Lamb's beauty, while his contrariness adds spice to the contact."[4]

After a week or so, Philip had to leave to go up to Burnley to begin campaigning for the election due in January, and a little later Ottoline left to join him. Lytton and Lamb stayed behind, Lamb setting about Lytton's portrait. Lytton described the setup to his younger brother James:

> *Fortunately Philip is absent, electioneering in Burnley. Henry sleeps at a pub on the other side of the green, and paints in a coach-house rigged up by Ottoline with silks and stoves, a little further along the road. She seems quite gone – quite!...How does the woman do it! Every other menage must now seem sordid...Ah! She is a strange tragic figure (And such mysteries!)*[5]

Lamb wrote to Ottoline in Burnley, telling her he could get on with his work much better when she wasn't there as an distraction. But he missed her nonetheless: "I burn to embrace you & cover all your body with mine."[6]

Shortly before Christmas, Lytton left Peppard, returning briefly to London before going to France where he was to spend the next four months with his sister Dorothy and her husband, the painter Simon Bussy (who was to do the famous half-face portrait of Ottoline, and which I have chosen as my cover-illustration). Lytton wrote to thank her for her stay, which he said had been perfect bliss, "an interlude from the Arabian nights".[7] Was this either a reference to Ottoline's oriental décor of silks and rich rugs, or was it a more oblique allusion to the way Lamb had staved off Lytton's advances by his endless witty conversation, like Scheherazade's stories in the *Arabian Nights*?[8] He called Ottoline *"chère Marquise"* and also thanked her for the orange vellum-covered notebook she gave him to copy his poems into (a gift which she was to repeat with many other writers down the years).

Up in Burnley, Ottoline took to electioneering with gusto. At one meeting she made what the London Press described as a "virulent attack" on her Tory brothers and their "worthless way of life". It was probably these speeches which led to the (almost certainly apocryphal) story that went the rounds of Bloomsbury in which Ottoline was depicted stretching out her arms to a meeting of Burnley mill-workers and saying, "*I love* the people – I married into the people." She spoke at meetings and helped distribute a campaign leaflet that featured a curious tableau – Ottoline sitting stiffly at a piano; Philip uncharacteristically fatherly; with little Julian standing angelically in the foreground (see Bedford Square picture-spread above). Ottoline again visited several of the local cotton-mills, where the noise of the clacking looms was so loud the mill-girls could only communicate with her by kissing her on the cheek.

Each morning she was there, Ottoline was awakened at 6am by the sound of thousands of iron-soled clogs rat-tat-tatting up the cobbled streets on their way to the mills. The election was expected to be a close fight, and so Asquith, now Prime Minister, came up to make two speeches at meetings in support of Philip. One meeting on December 5 attracted the biggest political audience in the town's history – 11,000 in the hall, and several thousand more outside. Philip and the local Liberals together spent £953. 3s. 1d. on the campaign, an outlay which had its just reward when Philip was elected with a majority of 173 over his Tory opponent.

Soon after their return to Peppard, a whole posse of guests arrived. First was Roger Fry, who was becoming increasingly friendly with Ottoline. Fry's wife Helen had gone mad and, after being treated in an asylum, had returned to live at home, but was unable to speak more than a few words. Several times Ottoline had visited Fry's house to help him cope with his domestic problems. Lately Fry had been very busy arranging the first Post-impressionist exhibition to be held in London; and several other people involved in this project also came to Peppard. To make the situation even more complicated, later the Russian mosaic artist Boris Anrep arrived to see Lamb, accompanied by Helen Maitland.

Among these four guests – Fry, Lamb, Anrep, and Helen Maitland – there were to spring up some complex relationships: Helen was soon to leave Lamb, become Anrep's mistress and then his wife; before going off to live permanently with Fry. Next, Clive and Vanessa Bell, who were also close friends of Fry, turned up, as did the critic and Bloomsbury member Desmond MacCarthy.

Lamb was beginning to cause Ottoline many heartaches. While the Bells were at Peppard, he took it into his head to be odious to her, mainly, she thought, because he was jealous of the attention she was diverting from him in the presence of critics like Fry, MacCarthy, and Bell. Ottoline wrote of him: "His temper grew more and more unreasonable, and the more I suffered from it the more he delighted in tormenting me."[9] She likened him to a vampire, sucking her life away; away from Philip and Julian and the important things in her life. But she could not bear to let him go. He had a charm and a mystery about him that she found in no one else.

Early in 1911, after a display of temper, Lamb took himself off to Paris with Anrep. From there he wrote to say he had found Dorelia and one of the John children, Pyramus, both ill in a hotel. A week or so later he wrote again complaining he had not received any letters from Peppard. Ottoline was using her aloof tactic, something she maintained had a beneficial effect on Lamb's behaviour. But a day or so later she did write, telling him she herself felt very depressed.

He replied rather callously; and on the back of his envelope Ottoline jotted: "No imagination...momentary pleasure – like a child."[10] She wrote to him saying he must go his own path without her. On the other hand in her Diary she wrote: "My weakness hopes for him not to obey, for I long for his affection and companionship."[11]

Virginia Stephen also stayed at Peppard for a weekend in February and she later wrote to Ottoline to tell her how the Bells were "forever going on about copulation"; a topic that, she said, bored her. She and Ottoline discussed artists, and both agreed they were brutes. Writers and poets were much finer, Virginia assured Ottoline. Yet soon Lamb was back in England, and seeing Ottoline frequently. But he was still acting ungraciously, she complained, and after one tiff he wrote explaining that "something made me do & say the opposite [to what he really felt]".[12]

Lamb by now was working on a full-length portrait of Ottoline clad in a green dress. But she found standing for long periods of time, while he painted her, was not only tiring, but boring.

Towards the end of February he still felt unhappy and apologised to her for his sulky behaviour. Ottoline did her best to raise his spirits by plying him with gifts of tobacco, pipes, sweets, and biscuits, and installing electric light in his coach-house studio at Peppard. However, all this did was to make him feel even more a kept man, and when she went off for a few days to Black Hall, he asked his friend George Kennedy to come and stay at Peppard. He knew Ottoline disliked Kennedy, and so this gesture of rebellion appealed to him.

On February 22 Ottoline went off for a seaside break at Studland in Dorset. There she walked barefoot on the beach and shared jokes with her maid Brenty. Philip came down from the House of Commons to join her and, though at first she was disappointed with his company, after a while they re-established their rapport.

On the way back to Peppard they called in on Roger Fry, who did a sketch of her in what she described to Lamb as "indifferent colours". Lamb told her he couldn't imagine anyone painting her in indifferent colours. He was sorry his letters nowadays seemed so settled in comparison with a year ago, but added encouragingly: "When we are both 50 you won't scorn the expressions of the sedate contentment you so largely procured for me."[13]

Back at Peppard, Ethel Sands turned up for a brief stay, and on March 9 Anrep's wife Junia arrived, and promptly chided Lamb for criticising Ottoline, whose portrait he was working on in the coach-house studio.

As the weekend of March 18-19 approached, Ottoline was relieved to be able to escape from Lamb and Peppard and return to London, where an important engagement awaited her. It was an appointment that was to change her life.

INTERLUDE
The "Bloomsbury Group"

The "Blue Plaque" in Gordon Square marking where "Bloomsbury" began

WHAT LATER became known as "The Bloomsbury Group" was in fact two groups – "old Bloomsbury" (whose heyday was the decade leading up to WW1) and its younger set, who emerged on to the scene in the years between the wars. It began as an informal cluster of friends who lived in the streets and squares around the British Museum, mainly in Georgian terrace houses built by the aristocracy on land granted to them by the Hanoverian monarchs. Some of them had family connections to the earlier Whig-leaning Clapham Sect. Initially "Bloomsbury" revolved around the Stephen sisters Vanessa and Virginia, and their relatives and Cambridge friends who had known their brother Thoby at the University in the early years of the new century. (Thoby, however, died shortly after the Stephen family moved into Bloomsbury.)

A number of them had been members of an exclusive Cambridge society called Apostles, who at this period were much influenced by the philosopher G.E. Moore and his theories about honesty in personal relationships. Their main concerns were ideas, art, music, and literature, and the group's principal tenets were freedom of expression and the supremacy of the individual. Although several of the group – notably Virginia Woolf, Lytton

Strachey, E.M. Forster, Vanessa's husband Clive Bell, and J. M. Keynes – produced work of major significance, probably what distinguished Bloomsbury most was its attitude to life, and its conversation (and, subsequently, its memoirs)

Bloomsbury's early members included not only Virginia and Vanessa and Clive Bell, but Lytton Strachey, Duncan Grant, Adrian Stephen, Maynard Keynes, and Saxon Sydney-Turner. Gradually its membership widened to include Roger Fry, Harry Norton, David Garnett, the Shoves, Molly and Desmond MacCarthy, Mary Hutchinson, and various others. Virginia Woolf's biographer Quentin Bell gives a flavour of the revolutionary nature of Bloomsbury talk. He quotes Virginia's account of an event that happened around August 1908:

> *It was a spring evening. Vanessa and I were sitting in the drawing room...At any moment Clive might come in and he and I should begin to argue – amicably, impersonally at first; soon we should be hurling abuse at each other and pacing up and down the room. Vanessa sat silent and did something mysterious with her needle or her scissors. I talked egotistically, excitedly, about my own affairs no doubt. Suddenly the door opened and the long and sinister figure of Mr. Lytton Strachey stood on the threshold. He pointed his finger at a stain on Vanessa's white dress. "Semen?" he said.*
>
> *Can one really say it? I thought & we burst out laughing. With that one word all barriers of reticence and reserve went down. A flood of the sacred fluid seemed to overwhelm us. Sex permeated our conversation. The word bugger was never far from our lips."*

It has been argued that this incident was the true start of Bloomsbury. Lytton's utterance opened the floodgates, not merely for conversation, but also behaviour and morality. Though Ottoline has been described as "the patroness of Bloomsbury" and the "high priestess of Bloomsbury," she was never an acknowledged member of the Group. Some of the Bloomsburies, particularly Vanessa Bell and Roger Fry, became antagonistic towards her, and as time went on contributed to the spiteful gossip about her.

CHAPTER 10
Bertie Stays the Night

Ottoline and Bertie

ON SUNDAY March 19, 1911, a small dinner party was held at 44 Bedford Square. It was arranged because Bertrand Russell, who was teaching at Cambridge, wanted somewhere to stay the night on his way to Paris where he was to lecture. Although he wasn't a particularly close friend of the Morrells, he had got to know them while campaigning for the Liberals in South Oxfordshire (he had been unable to help with the Burnley campaign because of lecturing duties at Cambridge), and they had extended to him an open invitation to stay with them. Yet now that he had taken up this invitation, Ottoline felt misgivings. Even for a hostess of her experience, the prospect of having so eminent an intellect staying in her house was a little forbidding, especially as Philip at the last moment had been called away to attend to some urgent constituency business in Burnley.

Believing she might have problems conversing with a man whose razor-sharp mind had earned him the name "The Day of Judgement", Ottoline cast around for some other guests to make up a scratch dinner-party for the evening. Fortunately she found two people she thought would be ideal. One was Ralph Hawtrey, a contemporary of Russell at Cambridge (and a fellow Apostle). The other was Ethel Sands, who was a practised hand at easing dinner-table difficulties (and a good friend of Russell's brother-in-law, Logan Pearsall Smith).

Russell arrived around 4.30 pm, was shown his room, and the subsequent dinner went off pleasantly enough. He relaxed in the congenial company, and his already enhanced opinion of Ottoline was further advanced by her obvious taste and amiable manner. As he records in his autobiography, he felt happier than he had for a long time. Around midnight the party broke up, taxis were called, and Hawtrey and Miss Sands departed. Ottoline and Russell returned to the drawing-room for a few moments before retiring. But neither made a move to go to bed. Instead they sat by the fire and continued to talk – about Paris, politics, about Philip's recent success in Burnley, and so on. Gradually the conversation became more personal. Ottoline was well-known for her facility for drawing people out – particularly people with problem – and she sensed in Russell a problem of some proportion. The last time they had met, in July, she recalled, he had turned to her at dinner and said intensely: "There is always a tragedy in everyone's life, if you know them well enough to find it out."[1]

Now, finding Ottoline receptive, Russell suddenly began to talk about his own personal life. He sat on the edge of his chair, his hands clenched and his back ramrod stiff. His face was distorted with emotion (Ottoline recalled in her *Memoirs*). He was desperately unhappy, as unhappy as any man could be. For nine years he had been living with a woman he did not love. He was starved of love, starved of sexual fulfilment. His existence was bare. He was sick of his puritan way of life and longed for beauty and passion. For nine years he had dammed up his emotions, and that night in Ottoline's drawing-room the dam burst.

Ottoline's sympathetic reaction surprised Russell, but he was even more surprise to find she didn't repulse his timid advances. Suddenly he was overcome with love when he realised to his delight that she would allow him to make love to her. They spent the remainder of the night talking and embracing, because, as Russell says in his autobiography, "for external and accidental reasons" they did not have full relations that time.[2] For both it was a crucial encounter, a climactic moment in their lives. Later Ottoline explained that she had been stunned and overwhelmed, but for the moment she was carried away by Russell's outburst of emotion, and everything else – Philip, Julian, her other friends – were swept aside in his raging torrent. They agreed to become lovers as soon as possible and, around 4am, finally retired to their separate beds.

To appreciate fully what happened that night under the calm, logical surface of one of Britain's greatest minds it is necessary to go back to 1902. In his autobiography Russell describes how, while bicycling one day near Grantchester, he suddenly realised he no longer loved his wife, Alys. She was five years older than him, a Quaker, and, although somewhat puritan in outlook, devoted to him. Very soon she perceived the change in his attitude, and was grievously hurt by it. Russell relates how every now and then Alys would come to him in her dressing-gown and beg him to spend the night with her. "Sometimes I did so, but the result was utterly unsatisfactory," he says. "For nine years this state of affairs continued."[3]

Stark and brutal as is Russell's description in his autobiography of this incident, and what followed, it barely touches on the misery he – and the hapless Alys – went through. A more accurate idea can be got from one of Russell's notebooks which Ottoline somehow acquired and kept (Russell probably gave it to her to prove that his marriage to Alys has broken down irretrievably). Dating 1902-1905, the notebook is in two parts. At the front are 20 or so pages of closely-packed mathematical symbols: some of Gauss' theorems which Russell was simply going through and working out to his own satisfaction. At the back are another 20 or so pages containing his diary of this period in his life. Here, with cold mathematical precision, he sets down the day-to-day horror of the destruction of his marriage.

He started, he records, by adopting a cold attitude towards Alys, "in the deliberate hope of destroying her affection".[4] In June 1902 Alys asked him directly what was wrong. He told her his love for her was dead. All that night he worked on *Principia Mathematica* while in the bedroom next door he could hear Alys' heartrending sobs. He noted in his notebook:

> *Oh the pity of it! How she was crushed and broken! How nearly I returned and said it had all been lies. And how my soul hardened from moment to moment because I left her to sob. In the middle of the night she came to my door to say she was calmer now and would hope – poor, poor woman.*[5]

A little later he adds:

> *I do not believe, in my soul, that I was justified; and I don't know whether I am justified now. But I have certainly effected a great moral reformation in her, and that depends upon keeping her hopes alive but unfulfilled. This requires vacillation – occasional great friendliness, occasional censure.*[6]

In November 1902 he wrote: "When I got home Alys had a crying fit; I know it is my fault, and I must manage better, but it is hard; she is too lonely – good God, what a lonely world it is."[7] A few weeks later he recalled an incident earlier in the year when he had picked a bunch of primroses and offered them to her as a little token of love. Both were "touched, deeply touched". He continues:

> ...for a moment hope whispered honeyed words; but in our hearts we knew they were lies; we knew that never again would the sun shine...The pathos of her love lived in my imagination in that moment, and I longed, with an infinite tenderness, to revivify my dying love. Almost I succeeded, but it was too late. The spring of which those poor flowers fondly dreamed never came, and will never come; in human lives there is but one spring, and winter, when it comes, is not thawed by gentle winds from southern seas, but deepens slowly into Arctic night.[8]

And deepen it did. On December 13 he wrote: "Last night when I went to bed Alys asked the time, which was 12:40. After the light was out she asked if I remembered the date at Cambridge – I had forgotten it was our wedding date. Her misery was uncontrollable."[9] On March 18, 1903, he wrote: "Last night for the first time I made the last possible sacrifice. In return I am to have three weeks' liberty."[10] And on April 8: "The last sacrifice to Alys was not adequately carried out, and failed totally. She hated it and didn't want a repetition. I shirked my duty on that occasion. I ought to have been more self-forgetful."[11] Around May 1903 Russell reached the depths of unhappiness. He was struggling with *Principia*, meeting mental obstacles he could not surmount, while his personal existence was a torment. He wrote: "day by day I wonder how another 24 hours of such utter misery can be endured."[12] But slowly Alys came to live with her misery and the new conditions under which she and Russell occupied separate bedrooms, yet were to the outside world still ostensibly married. In April 1904 he says that Alys had improved greatly. In January 1905 he is no longer miserable all the time, an improvement he attributed to the "modus vivendi" he had adopted with Alys: "I never look at her."[13] In March 1905 he wrote: "I feel that continence will become increasingly difficult, and that I shall be tempted to get into more or less flirtatious relations with women

I don't respect."[14] Three weeks later he noted: "She has given up kissing me morning and evening, which is a great gain. I look forward to a gradually increasing separation."[15]

Russell wrote in his autobiography of the ensuing years: "During all this time she hoped to win me back, and never became interested in any other man. During all this time I had no other sex relations."[16] Of all this Ottoline knew nothing, so it is understandable what a shock she experienced when, in her own words, she lifted the lid from this boiling cauldron. For, in spite of his unattractive exterior and inexorable intellect, Russell was a passionate man. His subsequent career provides ample proof of how, despite the power of his mind, the power of his heart was greater. Now, in the space of a few hours that evening at Bedford Square, Russell had fallen deeply and irrevocably in love – probably more deeply than he ever was to again. After all those years of abstinence and misery, he was prepared to overcome any obstacle to achieve his end. And his end was the body and love of Ottoline. She too was a passionate person. She also was ruled by her heart not her head. Unlike Russell, however, she had much to lose: she was married to a man she had a high regard for, even though by then their sex life had become occasional, if not perfunctory. And she had a child whose welfare she would not ignore.

The next morning Russell went off, dizzy with desire, like some love-sick teenager. Though they didn't see each other for several days, they wrote to each other by almost every post – often three times a day. The first letters in a correspondence that was to prove prodigious by any standard were full of expressions of love and devotion – and passion. Over the next few years he wrote more than 2,500 letters to her, and she wrote over 1,500 replies. Russell's letters, almost all of which Ottoline kept, give an idea of the change that had now overwhelmed him. No longer the cold, calculating machine, he was revelling in the joys of first love (despite the fact that he was 38 and Ottoline 37).

His first love letter to her (that she kept) was postmarked March 21, 1911 "in the train Tuesday". He wrote:

> My Dearest,
>
> My heart is so full that I hardly know where to begin. The world is so changed in these last 48 hours that I am still bewildered. My thoughts won't come away from you – I don't hear what people say. All yesterday evening Bob Trevi babbled on; every now & then I woke up & wondered who he was talking about just then. Fortunately yes & quite so & ah indeed were enough for him.... I love you very dearly now & I know that every time I see you I shall love you more.... It is altogether extraordinary to me that you should love me – I feel myself so rugged & ruthless, & so removed from the whole aesthetic side of life – a sort of logic machine warranted to destroy any ideal that is not very robust.... In Paris I shall have to try to collect my wits – it won't do to be thinking of you while the philosophers are making objections to my views.... Goodbye, my Dearest. I grudge the hours till I am with you again. With all my love,
> B [17]

By Wednesday, March 22, Russell was in Paris giving his lectures and staying at the Hotel Corneille, where a letter was waiting for him from Ottoline. As usual, after the first ecstatic surrender to emotion, she was beginning to have reservations. She told him she felt the hand of fate holding her back and wondered if her love could really mean something to him. In his reply, he brushed aside her doubts: "Dearest I love you, & everything else is dross." He told her that her love could give him happiness and peace:

> *All my life, except for a short time after my marriage, I have been driven on by restless inward furies, flogging me to activity & never letting me rest, till I feel often so weary that it seems as if no more could be borne. You could change all that if you were willing. You could give me inward joy & expel the demons.*[18]

In her following letter Ottoline tried a different tack. Realising the earnestness of his protestations, she now insisted they must either keep their affair secret, or else break it off altogether. Russell, however, his logical mind reasserting itself for the moment, saw the perils of subterfuge:

> *My serious & intended view is that our love would be degraded if we allow it to be surrounded by the sordid atmosphere of intrigue – prying servants, tattling friends, & gradually increasing suspicion. All this is inevitable if we attempt secrecy; we cannot hope to succeed in it. If your love were not so precious to me, I should mind less; but I cannot bear to have it degraded.*[19]

As to her alternative, that was even more out of the question:

> *But to sacrifice you altogether, just when 1 have found you, is too much; I can't face that. If you will tell Philip & let me tell Alys, I can acquiesce in your staying with him; then the deceit & sordidness is avoided. And then you can still help him politically. That seems to me the right course, as well as the most likely to minimize scandal. But whatever you say I shan't give up the hope of everything. I have been told, & I believe, that your obstinacy is incredible; so is mine.*

Ottoline next had misgivings about her intellect. Wasn't she a trifle out of his class? He brushed that idea aside too: "No woman's intellect is really good enough to give me pleasure as intellect...It is plain to me that I love you – absolutely, devotedly, with all the passion of a fierce nature long starved & lonely." He would hear no more of her doubts: "A great love is a great responsibility; do not degrade us both by not living up to the best...My life is bound up with you; it is my last chance of real happiness, or of a life that brings out my best. "

Russell returned to London on Friday, March 24, and the next morning went to see Ottoline on his way to Haslemere, where he and Alys had taken a house for the university vacation. At Bedford Square he met a very worried Ottoline. In an attempt to dampen his ardour she managed to get him to agree that they would not meet for a few weeks, during which time they would both have the opportunity to reflect and see if they still felt the same way about each other. Russell reluctantly agreed, but in return he extracted from her a promise that they would spend some time alone together at the end of the separation period. Ottoline would be going down to Studland (where the Morrells had taken a cottage) soon, and she agreed, reluctantly, that as soon as she could arrange things he could come down and stay with her. In the meantime he would break the news of their affair to Alys, and Ottoline would tell Philip. After Russell had gone Ottoline felt she might have been too strict with him, so she wrote him a note explaining that she was not trying to kill their love, merely trying to do the right thing by everyone.

At Haslemere Russell found Alys entertaining two of her young relatives, Ray and Karin Costello (Russell was coaching Karin in philosophy); so he decided to wait until Monday when the two visitors left before telling Alys about Ottoline. As might be imagined, it wasn't an enjoyable weekend. He did his best to put on a happy face, but he was feeling miserable. On Saturday night he wrote to Ottoline saying he feared she would choose duty before love. He assured her, however, that there were occasions when duty meant choosing one's own happiness rather than other people's. He went on: "There have been things in my life which I should have wished to tell you, but that I am not at liberty to do so; they would have illustrated why I am so certain of what I think right."[20] (A reference, no doubt, to the end-of-marriage diary entries in his Gauss notebook.) He ended the letter on a low note: "I cannot understand the wish for a future life – it is the chief consolation that in the grave there is rest." On Monday Russell told Alys about Ottoline and either on that day or the previous one Ottoline told Philip about Russell.

In her *Memoirs* Ottoline relates what Philip's reaction was: "When Philip returned, I told him all that had happened, and I was terribly hurt by his saying to me, 'Do you want to go? You must if you want to.'"[21] However, in a footnote Philip later appended in the *Memoirs* manuscript he said Ottoline's dating of this response was incorrect. Her revelation had come, not after his return from Burnley, but "some weeks later at Studland." He wrote: "When I returned to London from Burnley, so far from telling me 'all that had happened,' she told me very little: merely that Bertie Russell had said how unhappy he was with his wife, and asked for sympathy and support, which she felt she ought to give him, and to this…I rather reluctantly consented." Indeed, Ottoline may have also misled Bertie into thinking she had revealed all to Philip. Nevertheless, taking Lamb and John into account, there can be little doubt that Philip was to some degree resigned to allowing Ottoline a measure of freedom in her relationships with other men. Yet Ottoline was clearly in a state of emotional disarray. She had no intention of leaving Philip and Julian, regardless of what Russell might want to believe. What Alys said when Russell broke the news to her is not recorded. All he told Ottoline was: "I have told Alys who took it very well."[22] Both Philip and Alys no doubt realised there was little point in taking it otherwise.

If Ottoline were upset at Philip's reaction, Russell was dumbfounded. She told him Philip had agreed to let the status quo continue. This meant in effect that Russell and Philip would be competing for Ottoline's love. Russell found that most curious. He told her: "The situation is one I have not known of before in any case I have ever heard of."[23] Perhaps, he added, he might come to understand in time. Meanwhile all he asked was that Philip should not share her room. This meant a great deal to him, as he explained:

> *I dread my nature – I can do much with it in many ways, but where passion comes in it is difficult. I will not put myself where hatred would come to me, & I will not let its poison come into our lives. If I can overcome that, or if you can cease to share a room with him, all will be well. If not,*

it will be better to part.[24]

But Ottoline was not going to forsake Philip. Screwing up her courage, she wrote to Russell agreeing that the best thing would be for them to part. She proposed that they should have a final meeting at the house of Russell's *Principia* co-author Alfred North Whitehead in Carlyle Square, Chelsea. Russell agreed. But the meeting did not go off as Ottoline had apparently intended. As soon as they saw each other their fears evaporated and they fell into each other's arms. All Ottoline's firm intentions, so carefully nurtured in private, disappeared. Their love blazed up again, if anything stronger than before.

That night Russell wrote to her: "Dearest, my whole soul is flooded with joy – your radiance shines before me, & I feel still your arms about me & your kiss on my lips." He saw now that she could not leave Philip and said: "I will accept whatever of your time you feel you can rightly give, & will not ask for more."[25] He told her he was glad they were not going to snatch at happiness by the ruin of others, and he asked her for a snapshot of herself. She sent him a picture he found "delightful" – though he might not have found it quite so charming had he known it was taken while she was on honeymoon with Philip in Venice. He had gone back to reading poetry, he told her, and was happy that beauty had come back into his life. Ottoline, however, was anything but happy. On all sides she was beset by problems, and felt very ill and tired. Not only did she have Philip and Julian to worry about, but Lamb too. Additionally, as we will soon see, she had at this time yet another emotional crisis on her hands; one she could not divulge to anyone, least of all Russell. Little wonder she had a severe bout of crisis headaches.

On Saturday April 1, Russell returned to Haslemere in a better frame of mind. He discussed with Alys what their future relationship would be. He apparently told her that the shell that was their marriage would have to be broken up further, leaving only the merest form. She would not, he informed her, be returning with him to Cambridge when the Easter vacation ended on April 24. That night he wrote to Ottoline:

> *She is behaving very well. I do not think she is suffering much. All the real pain was nine years ago, when I told her I no longer loved her...Alys has great kindness, whenever there is competition, and she has times of real nobility – just now nothing could be better – I shall tell people that her rheumatism doesn't allow her to live at Cambridge. She seems to prefer to give the reason that we can't get on together, but except to intimate friends I don't feel I can say that.*[26]

The following day Alys was being less noble. The implications of her husband's decision were beginning to sink in, and she spoke to him (Russell reported that later night in another letter to Ottoline) "in a most harrowing way". Her pain, he wrote, "is like the pain of a wounded animal...At times I have thought I ought never to have told her I no longer cared for her, yet I feel that a life of active & constant hypocrisy would have been impossible and wrong. But giving pain deliberately is very terrible."[27]

His truthfulness was relentless. In the same letter he confessed that he had recently kissed a woman whom he had "known a long time". This confession was apparently activated by a letter the woman had just written him, asking him to come to see her. Of course he would not go, he wrote. He told Ottoline that he was telling her about this because, if it ever came to mind when he was with her, he should feel guilty, which would be unbearable. He admitted that this was a very egotistical attitude, but he wanted to be sure Ottoline would love him "without illusion". Russell returned to London on Monday, April 3, to attend a function at the House of Commons; an occasion he was dreading for fear of bumping into Philip. However, Ottoline had already promised to meet Bertie on Wednesday, and this balanced the former dread. In a letter to her he expanded slightly on the "harrowing way" Alys had spoken during the weekend: "I am afraid that if a serious scandal is to be avoided it may be necessary for me to remain on terms with her."[28] Alys apparently had written to Mrs. Whitehead demanding sympathy and an interview. Russell said that he had offered Alys half his income, but she indignantly refused. "This looks like trouble," he added. Alys had agreed, however, to a formal three-month separation, but on the condition that Russell would make no final decision until after the three months were up. She had also resigned from the various charitable committees she was a member of. "Altogether there may be much difficulty", commented Russell.

He was also concerning himself about where he and Ottoline could meet. He had thought Mrs. Whitehead might lend her Chelsea house for a rendezvous, but he told her that there were problems in this, as Mrs. Whitehead didn't want her servants or her teenage son to know. ("He is very perceptive, & if he saw you he would guess at once," Russell explained.) Other possibilities also had their disadvantages:

> *I think it is better to avoid places like Kensington Gardens, where we should meet all our friends. The only plan I can think of is to meet at some underground station exit, & take a cab to some out of the way place like Putney Heath.*

At the House of Commons on Tuesday Russell and Philip did see each other, but only at a distance. Russell dared not look him in the eye, but he did observe that Philip seemed upset at seeing him. At 3pm the following day Russell and Ottoline met at Bedford Square. Again it was a happy reunion, smoothing out problems and recharging the friendship. Back at Haslemere that night, Alys sat up after dinner, forcing Russell to retire to his bed to write to Ottoline in privacy: "I feel she is meditating something," he said.[29] Before he went to sleep he kissed Ottoline's photograph. On Thursday Alys seemed to have come to a decision and left for London; to see Mrs. Whitehead, Russell assumed. But she wouldn't find much sympathy in that quarter: "Mrs. Whitehead dislikes her – but Whitehead hates her."[30] Alys' absence gave him the chance to write a really long letter to

Ottoline, who was about to leave with Julian for a holiday at Studland. He told her:

> *I went [for] a long walk alone to-day. I felt so full of happiness and life that I hardly knew how to contain myself, I [wanted] to shout and sing like the morning stars and the Sons of God. Even the East wind seemed delightful. You won't like me if I become boisterous and jovial.*[31]

Before going to Studland Ottoline went to see Mrs. Whitehead, who alarmed her with talk of public scandal and the possibility of Alys committing suicide. Ethel Sands had somehow heard of the affair and Ottoline was concerned others might soon know. Russell told her he understood her fears, but tried to play them down. He said Alys was becoming resigned to the situation, "and will behave well in return for very small amounts of my society."[32] He thanked Ottoline for a box she had sent him (to keep her letters in) and looked forward to joining her at Studland in about ten days' time. On April 8 he wrote:

> *Tomorrow when you get this it will be three weeks since we found each other…O my heart, don't let us be kept by other people from what is possible. I love you, I love you, love you. We have had to wait for complete union, and if not at Studland it might be a long time.*

Later the same day he wrote again to tell her he had had a satisfactory talk with Alys. They had agreed to preserve appearance; he would spend occasional weekends with her, during which they would have visitors and be seen together. She had also agreed to go on taking his money. Most importantly, he had made her understand that if there came to be much scandal it would become impossible to even keep up these appearances. "Pride and prudence will combine to keep her silent, and though her family will guess that something is up, I feel sure she won't breathe a word, and I don't believe they will think of you."[33]

This last point was important to Ottoline. Alys's brother Logan was, after all, an old friend, and she shuddered to think what would happen if he were to discover that she was the woman for whom Russell had left his sister. (Ottoline's concern was to prove well-founded.) Russell tried to allay her fears: "She is I think now loyally anxious to do her part."[34] He also tried to put to rest Ottoline's fears about their spiritual compatibility. He was an atheist and she was still deeply religious. He said:

> *Dearest, there is no vital difference between us as regards religion. It is true I shall sometimes publicly attack things which you believe, but it will be for the sake of other things that you will also believe.*

On Monday April 10 he received a note from Ottoline telling him that if he wished, he could come to Studland that day rather than Tuesday week. After some soul-searching, he opted for the latter date, explaining: "I would rather come when you are rested as I fear you may find me not conducive to rest. I should have felt more certain [of the later date] except for the feeling that there's many a slip…But that seems only a superstition." The next letter he received from her told him she had been ill, so he was glad he had made the right decision. "I do hope you will soon be better. Only why should you imagine I should think you a 'wretched poor creature'? I believe people with really good health are never nice. My health is invariably perfect."[35] On a more serious note he talked about some of his personal misgivings:

> *It is a dreadful thing to cause so much pain. I am oppressed by the thought of all the pain I have caused in the course of my life, and by the foreboding that I shall cause more. Dearest I do most earnestly hope I shall not cause pain to you, beyond what the situation must involve. But sometimes I think I am fated to cause misery…But for all your firmness I might had done incalculable damage to you and P. and Julian – all this is obvious to me now, but at the*

> *moment I felt utterly reckless – the suppressed ego rebelled and clamoured for its desires.*

Over the next few days they exchanged long letters about their early lives. Russell told her that he had been almost always sad: "My natural view is that all human happiness is a mere interlude, & that sorrow is the normal lot of man."[36] Ottoline told him of her unhappy childhood and of a man she had once loved deeply (no doubt Axel Munthe). She also told him of a serious complication that had arisen at Studland. Logan Pearsall Smith, Alys's brother, had arrived to stay. "It is a nuisance about Logan," Russell replied. "You must manage to get him away before I come." (She did.) For neither Ottoline nor Russell were going to let Logan spoil a meeting both were looking forward to. On April 12 Russell wrote: "O my Dearest, I do love you with all my strength, with all possible love – I love dearly your outward beauty, and more dearly the beauty of your mind – your shy thoughts that you hardly dare speak of are wonderful. Goodbye my Dearest."[37] Russell took to going for long walks around Haslemere, trying to exhaust himself so as to get some respite from the physical and mental frustration of not being at Studland. He was almost frenzied with longing for Ottoline. He wrote 13 times during this week and she wrote almost as often, telling him in one letter that she had changed her hairstyle. He responded: "I should like to see you with your hair in two plaits and looking very wild. Oh how happy we shall be when I come – I shall feel like a boy fresh from school for the holidays."[38] Russell's good spirits were infectious, as he explained: "I know it is hard on Alys to see it, but I have been so full of gaiety these last two days that even she has been carried away and has grown almost gay too."[38] Ottoline was also having a beneficial effect on his intellect, as he told her: "Reading over the great philosophers, as I have been doing, I seem much quicker than usual to see what they mean."[39]

On the Saturday before he was due to go to Studland, Russell visited a dentist who told him he might have cancer of the mouth. But he told Ottoline none of this. Nor did he tell her what happened at Haslemere when he finally said goodbye to Alys to go to stay with Ottoline at Studland. In his autobiography Russell said Alys flew into a rage and that later he gave a lesson in Locke's philosophy to her niece Karin, adding: "I then rode away on my bicycle and with that my first marriage came to an end. I did not see Alys again till 1950, when we met as friendly acquaintances."[40]

Actually he did meet Alys again before 1950, but he is correct in saying his marriage ended with the melodramatic leave-taking at Haslemere. On Tuesday April 18 at 1.49 in the afternoon Russell arrived by train at Swanage, the station for Studland. He hired a pony-cart and drove out to where Ottoline was waiting for him on the hill under a group of fir trees.

INTERLUDE
A Lamb in Wolf's Clothing

A self-portrait of Henry Lamb (1914)

LADY PANSY LAMB, the widow of the man who was probably Ottoline's greatest passion - the painter Henry Lamb - was living in a modest basement flat in Ladbroke Grove, near Portobello Road, when I visited her in 1973

Lady Pansy, who was 69 when I met her, had decorated the walls of her little flat with ivy wallpaper to remind her, she told me, of the garden she used to have when she was growing up in the country in Ireland. She was the sister of the 7th Earl Longford, an Irish Catholic peer known as Lord Longford, who made a name for himself as a passionate social and penal reformer in Britain in the 1970s, 80s, and 90s.

So Pansy Pakenham became "Lady Pansy" by dint of being the sister of an Earl. She was 11 years younger than Lamb when they married, and a novelist and translator of French poetry.

Lady Pansy was Lamb's second wife. His first, Nina Forrest (known as Euphemia), left him soon after their marriage when he began associating with Helen Maitland, the mistress of the painter August John (with whom Ottoline also had an affair).

Lady Pansy had not known Ottoline in her prime at Garsington, still less at Bedford Square where Lamb first came into Ottoline's life. Lady Pansy first met Ottoline in 1929, when she and Henry visited her at Gower Street, where Ottoline described Lamb's new wife as "very nice…like a succulent plum".

CHAPTER 11
Further Entanglements

Ottoline escapes to Studland

OTTOLINE HAD not been altogether honest with Russell. She had told him nothing of John, and only the barest minimum about Lamb, whom she painted as a weak creature in need of her support. Also she told him nothing of another attachment which had been developing for some time, this time with the art critic Roger Fry. She had often visited Fry to help with his mentally-unstable wife Helen. Ottoline did not relish these harrowing visits but continued to go because she knew Fry was suffering greatly. In the early months of 1911 their friendship grew more intimate as Fry's admiration and gratitude deepened into affection. Ottoline admired the intellect of her Contemporary Art Society colleague and welcomed his friendship. Although Fry, who was 44, could seem rather stiff and dry – like some medieval saint, Lytton Strachey thought – he had a marked sympathy and understanding of women. Moreover, he was at this time especially lonely and vulnerable, as his wife had just been put into a mental asylum again. In March 1911, a week or so after the Russell eruption, Fry visited Ottoline at Bedford Square. He was just about to go off to Constantinople for a holiday with Clive and Vanessa Bell together with a mathematician friend, Harry Norton. We have no record of what happened at this meeting, but something obviously did, for around March 31 Ottoline received this letter from Fry:

> My Dear,
> I'm still all amazed and wondering…can't begin to think – I can only know how beautiful it was of you, how splendid – only how terrible to learn it like that. What terrifies me is that you should suffer for it – regret it in any way – you mustn't indeed dear, it was altogether beautiful and right.[1]

That was a letter only a lover could write. He told her he might be able to see her again before he left London, as Vanessa had suddenly taken ill, which could mean a postponement of the trip. He went on: "…but Oh Ottoline – no I can't fathom it yet or say anything clear or right or see the way for us, only it shall not be hard or bitter shall it my dear, it must mean more hope and love for us somehow." But Fry couldn't alter his travel arrangements, so next day he and Norton departed for Bruges, where they were to wait for Clive and Vanessa to catch them up. From there he wrote to Ottoline:

> My Dear Ottoline,
> I wish we hadn't come and stuck here, except that I may get a letter tomorrow. I don't think I can wait till I've heard from you, not properly. I'm still dazed and have only a

sense of immense wealth which I don't touch or investigate.[2]

And he signed it "Yr. Roger." The next day he wrote again, this time calling her "My dearest Ottoline ":

I know you will decide right for us...that now we can be much more to each other than would have been possible before, that our friendship will be more perfect, more precious, more complete, and that is after all the greatest value for us – tho' it hurts to think how much more it might be if life were not so difficult, so entangled with ties.[3]

He said he found it difficult to understand why she should think him wonderful – but it made him feel good that she did, adding: "...and the best is that it isn't based on some fancy of yours because you are too dear and serene in mind for that so I needn't dread to lose it." But serene in mind at that moment Ottoline was not. She had gone down to Studland to await the arrival of Russell, with whom she was maintaining an emotion-charged correspondence. Henry Lamb was hovering nearby at Corfe and Philip was due as soon as Russell's promised three days were up. Logan Pearsall Smith was also in the vicinity, as yet unsuspecting. Now, to further complicate a tangled skein of relationships, here was Fry pouring out love letters from Europe. Little wonder Ottoline complained of headaches.

As Ottoline and Russell walked together through the gorse and heather to her rented seaside cottage, their feelings for each other, strained by separation and the pressures on them from many quarters, burst into flame again. On his side this wasn't unexpected. For weeks he had been looking forward to this day, and he was prepared to run any risk for just a few hours' bliss; and hours could be all he might get if his doctor confirmed the diagnosis of cancer. In his autobiography he describes the next three days spent with Ottoline in Studland as "among the few moments when life seemed all that it might be, but hardly ever is."[4] On Ottoline's side the abandonment of any resolve to discourage Bertie was less understandable. By now she must have realised how strong was Russell's love for her, and what any encouragement would do to it. She must also have known that she wasn't dealing with a lover like Lamb or John, for whom an affair meant little more than a brief flirtation. Russell was competing with Philip not for her love, but her life. She was courting the destruction of her marriage and family; the obloquy of her relations and friends; probable unhappiness; and an uncertain future. She had every reason to put a damper on Bertie's ardour. Especially, as she says in her *Memoirs*, she did not take to his rather clumsy ways: "He assumed at once that I was his possession, and started to investigate, to explore, to probe. I shrank back, for it was intolerable to me to have the hands of this psychological surgeon investigating the tangle of thoughts, feelings and emotions which I had never allowed anyone to see. I felt like a sea-anemone that shrinks and closes at the slightest touch."[5] Yet during these three days she succeeded in making Bertie ecstatically happy; and it seems from her letters to him that she too enjoyed their seaside idyll. If there is any explanation for Ottoline's dual attitude it is probably to be found in that fundamental split in her character between her romanticism and puritan conscience. When she paused to think, her conscience could find any number of reasons why she should not love Bertie. But during those days at Studland her heart gave her little pause to consider the consequences.

In her *Memoirs* she claims that at first she was shy with Russell; but by degrees her defences fell. Julian, now almost five, was still at the cottage, so things had to be fairly discreet. Mostly they went off for long walks or sat under the trees and talked. They exchanged details of their childhoods, and Ottoline again told Bertie about her unhappy adolescence at Welbeck; while he told her of his lonely childhood after the death of his parents, when he lived with his grandmother in Richmond Park, almost being suffocated by the religious fervour of his grandmother's household. He also told her more about the misery he had suffered in the past nine years of his marriage to Alys. He also tried to explain to her his mathematical and philosophical work. Ottoline was very flattered that a mind such as Russell's should come and beg to commune with her. She knew Russell was an important man, probably a great man, and she believed him when he told her she could help him achieve greater heights in his work. But, as always with Ottoline, there were problems. Apart from the ones already mentioned, there was the matter of Bertie's appearance. Ottoline said: "To my shame, however much I was thrilled with the beauty and transcendence of his thoughts, I could hardly bear the lack of physical attraction."[6] Not only was Bertie strikingly unhandsome, he also lacked charm and gentleness and sympathy, qualities Ottoline always regarded as desirable in her intimate friends. In some ways this matter of unattractiveness was mutual: in his autobiography Russell described Ottoline as having "a long thin face something like a horse"; although he added that she had very beautiful hair and a gentle, vibrant, voice.[7] Yet Ottoline recognised Bertie's good points too. She described him as "rather short and thin, rigid and ungraceful, and would be unremarkable in a crowd. Then the exceeding beauty of his head would arrest me, for it gave the impression of perfect modelling: the skull thin and delicate, and the shape, especially when looked at from behind, always gave me a thrill as a very beautiful object".[8]

Finally it was time for Bertie to depart after their seaside idyll. He left in a pony-cart and Ottoline stood on a hillside waving to him until he was out of sight. In the train he wrote:

> *My Dearest Life – It is absurd to be writing to you now but I can't do anything else. You fill my heart and mind so completely that I can't take my thoughts off you for a moment. Our three days were an absolute revelation to me of the possibilities of happiness and of love. Each moment our union seemed to grow more complete and perfect.*[9]

After he returned to his room at Trinity College, Cambridge, he continued to shower Ottoline with daily letters, interspersing his romantic outpourings with further details of his earlier life and dissertations on philosophical subjects. Ottoline wrote back diligently, alternately joining the exchange of endearments, then fetching up the doubts that assailed her. In the following weeks and months they visited each other whenever practicable; and in fact their affair was to continue in varying degrees of warmth for the next five years. Soon a pattern began to emerge, a sort of mathematical ratio. Ottoline's love for Russell was inversely proportional to the distance between them. A future factor in the relationship would be his increasing interest in other women; whom he was to turn to from time-to-time, while still holding on to his love for Ottoline. In her *Memoirs* she admitted she had been swept a certain distance by Russell; but she nevertheless claimed that her response had been as restrained as she could make it in the circumstances:

> What was I to do? With all his intense passionate conviction and eloquence he urged it upon me as my walk in life to leave all and go forth with him to a new life. "I will give you a life that is worthwhile," he kept saying. He refused to realise that I would not consent. It was a nightmare.[10]

Looking back, Ottoline believed that if she had neglected Russell – if she had refused to "take upon me the burden of this fine and valuable life" – he would have just as easily found someone else to be the excuse for leaving Alys. In this she was probably right: Bertie was ready to break out. But things appeared very different in March and April 1911. And when many years later Ottoline asked herself what she would have done if she had to choose again; she admitted she would not have acted differently.

What was Philip's view of all this? Again we have to guess this from the attitude he adopted. It seems he and Ottoline had come to an understanding that she would remain his wife and live a normal married life, except in one respect; she could do what she could to give Russell the comfort and happiness he was so sorely craving. It might not seem a satisfactory arrangement from various points of view; but it was, to use Russell's phrase, a practicable *modus vivendi,* and disturbed the lives of the various participants least. Even so, it was a precarious compromise – and one that could be disrupted at any moment by the wrong door being opened.

While Russell had been having his three days of bliss, Henry Lamb was staying nearby with Lytton, who was about to succumb to the mumps. Lamb also visited Ottoline while she was at Studland; but she managed to arrange things so that Lamb's and Russell's visits didn't clash. Lamb and Ottoline were still very involved with each other, though their respective temperaments continued to make their relationship a stormy one. Before she came down to Studland, Lamb, expecting to see a lot of her, wrote to ask if she could attend to:

1. Tea
2. Black currant jam
3. Dirty ties [11]

Yet despite her problems, Ottoline managed to attend to Henry's needs. She sent him clay-pipes and socks and some bacilli for making sour milk. He was grateful for the gifts and apologised for appearing cold earlier. He said she mustn't feel hurt if he didn't mention his love for her every time, or forgot to call her "Ottolinotchka":

> *Why my good creature you have only to reflect that in something like a year's time you have managed to envelope me in every possible sense with your benevolence, you have clothed me from head to foot several times over in your livery: fed, doctored, nursed, housed, studioed & beflowered me; (nay have you not penned, papered, inked, chalked, painted me even?); you have advertised, secretaried, wire-pulled, bargained, heckled, haggled, persuaded, bewitched for me – in short, you have put me on such a footing that I*

can look at all material & most moral difficulties straight in the face; I can chirp, grow fat, live where I will & paint what I like: – Yet can you reflect on all this & then be hurt by my chirping.[12]

A difficult decision now faced Ottoline. Assuming she continued to see Lamb – as she fully intended to – how much more should she tell Russell about him, and, more importantly, how much about Russell should she tell Lamb? She eventually opted for a policy of minimal disclosure. To Lamb she said she was helping Russell, who was a tortured soul in need of a strong white arm around his neck. To Russell she gave an almost identical story about Lamb. Fortunately the existence of neutral Philip, in the middle so to speak, helped her to juggle Lamb and Russell so that this precarious illusion could be maintained.

For the moment, however, Lamb was about to depart to France to stay with Boris Anrep. So when Ottoline arrived back at Bedford Square towards the end of April, Bertie was her main worry. Throughout April and May Russell averaged one letter a day and one meeting a week. At first he came to see her at Bedford Square, but this soon became embarrassing; and so they took to meeting in railway waiting-rooms, then adjourning to various hotels around Bloomsbury for their more-private moments. Ottoline also had other things to think about. Julian was ill again and it looked as if she would have to be taken to the Continent to consult a specialist. Also Bedford Square was proving expensive to run, and Ottoline was contemplating moving to a smaller house. In the meantime she decided to hold fewer of her Thursday "entertainments".

Early in May Lamb wrote begging Ottoline to come over to Paris to visit him. He told her he was overwhelmed by her sublime strength, beauty, courage, and love. He wanted to submit to her and obey her in everything. Her flame and brightness dazzled him: "Though you know that what I am feeling for you at this particular juncture could only be expressed in our endless abandoned embrace. I kiss your face & your body all over."[13]

Further Entanglements

Ottoline wanted to go, but Philip demurred, again insisting she must be chaperoned. In the end she managed to override Philip's objections. She told Lamb she would leave around May 10 so as to return, as Lamb phrased it, "to be brilliant to Winston [Churchill] on the 18th."[14]

In Paris Ottoline found a changed Henry Lamb. Gone was the morose and difficult man she had become accustomed to in recent months; now he was vivacious and charming. News of Russell's rivalry (she had told him by now) had acted as an electric shock on him; but she told him his new attitude was to no avail...at least that was *her* story of what took place in Boris Anrep's Paris apartment. Lamb, in a letter to her a few weeks later, mentioned another version, in which she lay on a couch in "that incredible little room where you, holy woman, lay & received me."[15] Their farewell at the Gare du Nord was fond. On her return to London, Ottoline went straight to meet Bertie in a hotel off Tottenham Court Road. They spent the afternoon there; and he told her later that her economical soul would be glad to hear that the hotel only charged 2s. 6d. for the room, when it found out they were not staying the night.

The next evening, Ottoline held a scintillating dinner for Churchill at Bedford Square. The other guests included Massingham (editor of the *Nation*); Desmond MacCarthy and his wife, Molly; Virginia Stephen; Jos Wedgewood and his wife; and, back from Constantinople, Roger Fry. Winston arrived dressed for a court ball he had to go on to later, and entertained them all with talk of high politics, which to Ottoline was rather like Bertie's talk of higher mathematics. But the other guests enjoyed meeting the dashing, glamorous Churchill. Virginia made a diary note: "Winston Churchill very rubicund all gold lace and medals on his way to Buckingham Palace."[16]

A few days later Ottoline sent Bertie a telegram and a large bouquet of roses for his 39th birthday. Russell had some difficulty in explaining away the flowers to his bedmaker at Cambridge. That night he came down to London to meet Ottoline and see a show. Between meetings they kept up their correspondence.

Russell made a detailed study of the postal service, particularly box-clearing and delivery times, so he would know the exact moment to post each letter. He was now beginning to worry about the practical problems of having walked out on his wife. He told Ottoline that he had discussed it with the Whiteheads "until he was sick of the whole sordid coil".[17] The Whiteheads thought he should offer Alys the chance of a divorce with bogus evidence. He told Ottoline that if she felt she ought to break with him while there was still time, she should. Either Ottoline didn't take this proposal seriously, or decided that she was not prepared to give up Bertie. Her own doubts were of a different kind. She feared Bertie would find her mentally so inferior that he would soon tire of her. He tried to reassure her that her taste was "very exact" and her mind better than she realised: "At first I was afraid there would be a softness, & a fear of hard sharp outlines in your intellect, but I was wrong. I don't find any difference of intellectual taste."[18] He informed her that Alys now knew of their Bedford Square meetings and Studland, but nothing more. He had been trying to find somewhere to spend the summer and had at last found rooms at Ipsden from where he could easily come over to visit her at nearby Peppard. They would study Spinoza together. It would be an idyllic summer.

Since Roger Fry returned to London at the end of April, Ottoline had seen him several times, the latest being at her gala dinner for Churchill. He had written several times from Turkey and it was from these letters, still friendly and intimate in tone, that Ottoline learned of the disaster that had befallen the party in Byzantium. A day's journey from Constantinople, Vanessa collapsed, becoming so ill that Virginia had to hurry out from London to help Fry nurse her back to health, Clive apparently being useless, and Norton in despair. It was mainly Fry's commonsense and organising ability that got the party safely home. Ottoline did not have much of a chance to speak to Fry, but neither then nor at their previous meetings did she detect any change in his demeanour. She was, however, secretly glad that he had made no attempt to follow up the intimacy of their meeting

Further Entanglements

in March.

On Saturday morning May 20 Ottoline went with Russell to Heals store in Tottenham Court Road to help him choose a table for his rooms at Cambridge; after lunch Fry came to see her at Bedford Square. Ottoline described in her *Memoirs* what happened. "He suddenly turned on me with a fierce and accusing expression, commanding me to explain why I had spread abroad that he was in love with me. I was so utterly dumbfounded, for this thought had never entered my head – and I had certainly not uttered such an absurd thing to anyone."[19] No wonder Ottoline was dumbfounded, for she had every reason to believe, despite her protestations to the contrary, that Fry *was* in love with her. She had his letters to prove it. What she didn't know was the reason why he had suddenly become so sensitive on the subject. While in Turkey he and Vanessa Bell had fallen in love, and had begun what was to be a long liaison. So Fry would have been very angry indeed were Vanessa to hear that he was also in love with Lady Ottoline Morrell. And obviously he believed that Vanessa had either found out. or was in danger of doing so. From whom? The obvious sources of such gossip in Bloomsbury were Virginia or Lytton, both arch-gossips who would have delighted in spreading such a juicy morsel. Both had been at Bedford Square recently and Ottoline would not have seen much wrong in letting slip that Fry had made overtures to her. It would have provided a convenient smokescreen for Russell. In any case the gossip was out and could have come via Lytton or Virginia from one source only: Ottoline herself. No matter how hard she tried to expostulate, Fry's anger would not be appeased. Finally, after two hours, the interview ended with Fry stamping off and Ottoline in tears – a rare state for her. In one stroke she had now gained in Fry and Vanessa two formidable enemies. They were a powerful influence in the Bloomsbury Group, and their subsequent enmity was to do much to sully Ottoline's name in that quarter.

Shattered by the terrible scene, Ottoline told Russell about it. He said he was sorry to hear of it, but he was unable to get very indignant. Fry, he said, was overwrought, and Vanessa had a lot of power over him. Anyway Bertie had other worries at the moment: Alys was threatening to expose him as a public menace. Also he felt that he ought to speak to Logan about Ottoline. (Apparently Alys had promised not to tell her brother.) By May 23 Logan knew all. He went straight to see Ottoline and they had a bitter confrontation. He told her he was greatly pained by her behaviour. He was, he said, the helpless brother who had for many years witnessed his sister's misery, and there was much on his heart to say; but he would not say anything more unless she wished it. Obviously she did not, for next Logan went to Philip and discussed the matter with him. In her *Memoirs* Ottoline says Logan forced Philip into "denouncing" her and extracted a promise that she would not spend another night alone with Russell. Ottoline, oddly, agreed to this condition and, from now on, she and Russell spent only afternoons or early evenings together. (Perhaps, however, this more remote arrangement suited her anyway.)

Meanwhile, from Cap Finistere in France, Lamb was writing passionate letters recalling their last night in Paris. He said that the night after she left he had lain down in her bed and plunged his face into the pillow, breathing himself to sleep in her scents. "It was like dying – & the following night an attempt to repeat it resulted in something like an unsuccessful suicide! The smell of your hair was fainter & the perspective of our separation much clearer."[20] Ottoline told him of her troubles with Bloomsbury, and he replied that he was sickened by their squalid gossip. He was also sorry to hear of Logan's outburst. Four days later Lamb was drawing himself nude in front of the mirror, bewailing his lack of chest muscles, but admiring his feminine skin.

Logan soon paid another visit to Bedford Square and spoke to Ottoline very coarsely about the sexual side of her friendship with Russell. Logan's homosexuality, and the fact that he believed Ottoline had lured Philip, who was his best friend at Oxford, away from him, made his disapproval all the more venomous. Pressure was now mounting on all sides. The

Further Entanglements

Whiteheads advised Russell to resign his tutoring post at Newnham immediately – apparently it was thought that the young ladies there might be contaminated by the presence of a secret adulterer. Next, Ethel Sands joined (her neighbour) Logan to harass Ottoline. Ethel invited her and Philip to come to Newington for a conference on the affair. Logan came too, and for two days these two New England puritans pried into Ottoline's morals and behaviour. Ottoline felt herself the victim of some Salem witch-hunt.

They made her out to be a scarlet woman and told her she was killing Alys. Then Logan threatened that Alys would start divorce proceedings, naming Ottoline as co-respondent; thus ruining both Russell's and Philip's careers. While this inquisition was going on, Philip was out on the lawn playing croquet with Desmond MacCarthy. Finally he came in and stood up for Ottoline as best he could. That evening in their bedroom Ottoline and Philip stood by the window overlooking the moonlit garden and discussed what they should do. Ottoline said she felt as if she were covered in mud. Was she really the cause of Alys' unhappiness? Surely not, for Bertie hadn't loved Alys for many years. Eventually they decided that Logan's friendship must be given up, and Ethel's behaviour overlooked. Ottoline persuaded Philip that Russell was still suffering deeply and needed her support. Her amazing husband agreed, and they left Newington next day closer than they had been for some time. Yet if she and Philip had come to an understanding, Ottoline's relationships with others had taken a definite turn for the worse. She had now added to her list of enemies Logan Pearsall Smith. He was to prove an implacable foe, whose spite was to dog her for the rest of her life. It had not been a good week for Ottoline.

INTERLUDE
Mixing Beethoven with Mozart

Roger Fry's portrait of Bertrand Russell

WHEN I FIRST opened the filing cabinet for the letter "R" in the reading room of the HRC, I felt how Howard Carter must have felt when he broke into Tutankhamen's tomb in the Valley of the Kings. There I found what turned out to be more than 2,500 letters from Bertrand Russell to Ottoline.

Nobody, apart from Ottoline and perhaps Julian, had seen them before. As I read through them I realised that one of my primary duties was to tell the world about what was one of the great love stories of the 20th century. (I later read Ottoline's corresponding letters to her lover Russell on microfilm, kindly supplied by McMaster University in Canada, which held Ottoline's letters to Bertie.)

I would read Bertrand Russell's letters in the morning, and Lytton Strachey's or one of the other Bloomsburies in the afternoon. It was a bit like listening to Beethoven before lunch, and (as far as Lytton was concerned) Mozart after lunch.

Henry Lamb's famous portrait of a limp Lytton Strachey

Often Russell wrote to Ottoline three or four times a day, selecting, with a scientific rigour, the best mailbox from which to post his letters to ensure they would be delivered swiftly to Ottoline, wherever and whenever – at what hour – she happened to be. Bertie wanted to devote his life to Ottoline, his fellow aristocrat, despite the fact that she already had a family – Russell wanted children – and was married to Philip. He wanted her to marry him. But Ottoline was not interested in spending the rest of her life as Mrs Russell.

Given the other men in Ottoline's life, Russell was an unlikely lover. A towering intellect, he had little time for social graces. His charms were by no means obvious. He was, by no stretch of the imagination, comely. He had the most frightful bad-breath, which she did her best to cure (he took a long time to take her hints). His social graces were minimal to non-existent.

Bertie would arrange his rendezvous with her out in the countryside, or else at obscure suburban railway stations, where they thought they would escape notice. Yet the two must have made a strange spectacle: the diminutive Bertie looking – as Lytton described him – "like a Secretary bird" (a reference to a bird that had a hooked beak, resembling Russell's nose); and Ottoline, over six feet tall, dressed in her customary flowing gowns, often wearing one of her enormous hats. At other times, the two lovers wandered through the streets of Bloomsbury on the way to a "love nest" that Bertie had set up in a part of London where the streets and squares were named after their two aristocratic families: Bedford Square, Russell Square, Cavendish Square, Great Portland Street, and so on.

What Russell did not realise, however – as I found when I moved on to read the letters to Ottoline from Henry Lamb – was that she was conducting an affair with Lamb at the same time as her liaison with Russell. When Ottoline went to stay at Peppard, she arranged for Bertie to go back to London on the up-train, while Lamb was coming on the down-train. That took a lot of juggling.

CHAPTER 12
News of the Scandal Spreads

Ottoline, the hive round which the bees buzzed

BACK IN April, before she left Studland to return to London, Ottoline travelled over to Corfe to the Castle Inn, where Lytton was in quarantine with mumps. She stood under his window and called up to him, and when he leaned out she saw he had acquired a beard. Of this beard he was inordinately proud ("It is a red-brown-gold beard of the most divine proportions," he revealed to a friend). He did not need much encouragement to be talked into retaining it as a permanent facial feature.[1] After they had exchanged pleasantries, Ottoline blew him an elaborate kiss and departed. As soon as his mumps subsided, he returned to London where, over the next few months, he and Ottoline saw a lot of each other.

In some ways they had much in common (Henry Lamb being not the least). Indeed, Lytton would have liked to be even more like Ottoline; free to flirt with young men, to dress up in silks and rustling petticoats, and be frivolously feminine. "What a pity one can't now and then change sexes," he told Clive Bell. "I should love to be a dowager Countess."[2] Failing that, the next best thing was to be in Ottoline's company. Lytton's biographer Michael Holroyd says Lytton and Ottoline were at their best when alone together. "Each seemed to fulfil a need in the other, he wrote, "one hungering after secret confidences, the other so eager to impart them." Holroyd went on: "By themselves they were unaffected and relaxed. Yet introduce a third person into the room, and their relationship was immediately made subject to an uneasy strain." But when together, they carried on like a couple of high-spirited teenage girls – all giggling and high heels and titillating gossip. "Occasionally they would step outside the drawing-room to play at tennis in Bedford Square Gardens, their slow, huge lobs over the net being accompanied by such convulsive shrieks of laughter that a crowd of passers-by and residents would quickly assemble to behold these hysterical performances."[3]

Undoubtedly there was an element of flirtation in their friendship, for, despite Lytton's homosexual leanings, Ottoline believed he might yet be saved for the female sex. After all, he had proposed to Virginia Stephen (and what a couple they would have made!). At one time there circulated around Bloomsbury a rumour that Ottoline and Lytton were romantically involved. Michael Holroyd cites one item of evidence in support of this unlikely relationship. Henry Lamb once caught the two of them locked in a passionate embrace, and as they sprang apart he observed blood trickling down from Lytton's lip. It is just conceivable that Lamb did observe something like this. However, the story is rendered suspect by its similarity to another story that circulated around the Bloomsbury Group about this time. In this version it was Henry Lamb whom Ottoline was surprised with, and as they sprang apart, Ottoline allegedly explained: "I was just giving Henry an aspirin". (Pure Bloomsbury "false news".) Besides, given Lytton's chronic shyness, any possible relationship between them was likely to have been more stagey than real; what Holroyd called "good pseudo-robust Elizabethan stuff, flighty and rollicking."[4]

Yet there is little question that Lytton got on exceptionally well with Ottoline. She was the dominant, forceful sort of woman he professed to like. Ottoline told him once: "I often wish I was a man, for then we should get on so wonderfully."[5] As it was, she worked assiduously to convert him to more heterosexual ways until, realising her task was hopeless, she abandoned it; and playfully joined him in discussions on the relative merits of the groom's brother and the young postman. She was one of the first women to whom Lytton revealed his private thoughts on sex. Ottoline in her *Memoirs* remembered:

> *He talked a great deal about his friendships with young men. It is hard to realise that this tall, solemn, lanky, cadaverous man, with his rather unpleasant appearance, looking indeed far older than he is, is a combination of frivolity, love of indecency, mixed up with a rigid intellectual integrity. He is, I think, frivolous about personal life and serious about history...The steeds that draw the chariot of his life seem to be curiously ill-matched: one so dignified and serious, and so high-stepping, and of the old English breed, so well versed in the manners and traditions of the last four centuries; the other so feminine, nervous, hysterical, shying at imaginary obstacles, delighting in being patted and flattered and fed with sugar.*[6]

(This being an example of the sharpness of Ottoline's observational skill, and her ability to convert it into perceptive prose.)

Russell didn't like Ottoline's friendship with Lytton, not one little bit, and although they were brother Apostles, his heterosexual hackles rose whenever Lytton came near. In June, when Lytton was spending a weekend closeted at Peppard with

Ottoline, Russell wrote irritably: "Can't you make Lytton Strachey go Wednesday morning? Your guests can't expect to stay longer than they are asked for."[7] But Ottoline needed someone like Lytton to balance the missives that she was being showered with from Upper Wyche, where Russell had taken temporary rooms, before moving on to Ipsden, in the South Oxfordshire. Finally, to Russell's relief, Lytton did depart, going up to Cambridge to inspect the current crop of undergraduates. From there he wrote back to tell Ottoline that, in his taxi from the station carrying the box of chocolates and pot of marmalade she had pressed on him, he had felt like a pirate. He reported back on his progress at Cambridge. Most of his days, he told her, were spent lying in a punt beside King's College "propped up by innumerable cushions" and holding a sort of pastoral court:

> *Various nice young men are around me, and I have won their good-will by giving them langues-de-chat to eat. I wish you could look at the scene for a minute or two – it's really rather pretty with willows, sunshine, parasols, blue skies, and white flannels. But even I (such is the progress of my education) feel it would be still nicer if there were also some lace petticoats...Do you know though, that as my education progresses, my Terror also grows? The female sex – ! Oh dear, how alarming!*[8]

That summer Ottoline made one last attempt to convert him, and in doing so went more than halfway to meet his tastes, suggesting as a possible spouse Ethel Sands, who was a lesbian (but had a nice house in the country). Lytton gracefully declined: "So kind of you to think of Miss Sands for me. If only one could marry houses, it would be very convenient. As it is, I think I'll wait a little."[9]

While Ottoline was at Peppard receiving Lytton and Bertie and juggling Lamb, back in London lurid stories of her affair with Russell were circulating. Ottoline blamed Fry and Vanessa for this gossip – and indeed they probably started it – but the real villain seems to have been Vanessa's sister Virginia. An incorrigible gossip, she delighted in propagating and embellishing tittle-tattle about how the eminent philosopher was infatuated with the famous Bloomsbury hostess. Indeed, Vanessa felt constrained to caution her not to say too much because of the harm it could do Russell at Cambridge. Vanessa also wrote to Fry warning him to be particularly discreet with Virginia, who had already told her brother Adrian, "which means Duncan [Grant]".[10]

But Fry had little reason to be discreet. Like Alys and Logan, he too came of puritan stock, and he strongly disapproved of the damage Russell had inflicted on his hapless sister Alys. In June he went to see the Whiteheads (who were acting as go-betweens for Alys and Russell) to discuss the matter. Mrs. Whitehead construed what he said as jealousy. She reported to Russell that Fry was still fond of Ottoline. Russell, passing this on to Ottoline, added his own opinion that the trouble was that Fry had been hurt, and was hitting blindly back. Meanwhile, the Whiteheads and Alys were putting further pressure on Russell to give up his tutoring post at Newnham. Finally, faced with the threat of a public scandal, Russell did resign. But he refused to give up his fellowship at his beloved Trinity College. This wasn't enough for Alys and Logan, and they again threatened a gory public divorce, with Ottoline's name brought in. This goaded Russell into action, and in June he gave Alys an ultimatum – either she cease bothering him, or he would throw himself under a bus. Alys had reason to believe this might not be an idle threat, so she toned down her vengeance, retiring into a role which, according to Russell, she actually preferred: that of the silent, long-suffering martyr. On June 6 Russell was able to tell Ottoline: "We need fear Alys no longer."[11]

In spite of the split with Fry, Ottoline still played an active part in the Contemporary Art Society, of which Fry was a leading light. In the middle of June she arranged a large party for several hundred guests at Bedford Square to publicise the society's work. Yet some of her Society duties were less onerous, and during committee meetings she found time to write to Henry Lamb in France. He pictured her sitting with her tortoiseshell pince-nez – after suffering for some time with pains at the back of her eyes she had recently discovered she needed reading glasses – giving him a few moments between items of business. Ottoline replied: "You will never be able to kiss my eyes now – a great tortoishell [sic] rampart to protect them."[12] He also asked when he could see her – July perhaps? Or maybe she could come over to Brittany to Anrep's little pink house by the sea (Anrep sent a sketch of it)? Ottoline replied that she had no room for him in July and playfully (or perhaps sarcastically) asked for details of what housekeeping duties would be required of her should she decide to come to Brittany. Lamb assured her she would not have to make any beds. What about August? he asked, could he come to see her then? No, she replied, he would have to wait until September. Apparently Ottoline had pleaded duties and responsibilities to Philip as an excuse for not seeing Lamb; for in June he wrote: "I'm sure P can't demand it". He scolded her for entering the houses of "publicans and sinners" (perhaps a reference to rich Liberal supporters) and for leading a worldly life.[13] On each page of his letter Ottoline scrawled "ROT" and "Superior HL".

Most of the summer of 1911 Ottoline spent at Peppard. She wrote later of this time:

> *It was one of the few English summers that are day after day hot and cloudless. Bertie was staying at lodgings at Ipsden and came over every day to see me. We grew more and more accustomed to one another and more intimate.*[14]

Looking back, both of them regarded this period as one of the happiest in their lives. Each day they went out into the woods around Peppard, walking down shady paths and sitting under the trees, the hot sun beating down on them. As they sat and talked, Ottoline began to realise that here at last she had come across an intellect so powerful and expansive that not even *her* thirst for mental stimulation could exhaust it. Russell gave her daily lessons in philosophy, reading Plato and Spinoza to her, and setting her little exercises in logic. Perhaps, he told her, when she was 60 he might think of trying to show her how to apply logic to some of the simpler commonplaces of existence, such as "business is business" and "boys will be boys".[15]

Ottoline believed her friendship with Russell was leading her back to a more natural and serious world of thought, from which she had drifted away trying to please Henry Lamb, who liked to feel intellectually superior to his female friends. Ottoline felt Russell's intellect sharpening her mind, pruning away the fuzziness and forcing her to grasp things firmly, and examine them in depth. She believed that with Bertie's help she could ascend into that world of ideas and ideals which she had always been seeking. He wrote in her *Memoirs*: "The beauty of his mind, the pure fire of his soul began to affect me and attract me...his unattractive body seemed to disappear, his spirit and mine united in one flame, the flame of his soul penetrated mine."[16]

During that summer Russell suggested to Ottoline that they should write a book together in which his atheism and her religious beliefs could be addressed and perhaps reconciled. He proposed that he would do the writing and she could make comments and suggest corrections. The book was to be titled (tentatively) "Prisons". Unlikely as it may seem, the book was actually written; but when Russell's even-more-ruthlessly-logical student Wittgenstein read a draft of it, he criticised it robustly, perhaps deducing that Russell's fine mind had become clouded by his relationship with Ottoline (a non-unlikely supposition). Later, Russell published a chapter from the book – now renamed "Religion" – and Wittgenstein, who was becoming an ever-more important influence in Russell's life and beliefs, once again objected to it. Russell eventually cleaved to Wittgenstein's assessment and "Prisons" never saw the light of day; in part or whole. Later, and equally improbably, Ottoline and Russell were to collaborate on a novel, to be called either *Forstice*, or *The Perplexities of John Forstice*. This was to be some sort of fictional joint-autobiography. However, like "Prisons", it was finally abandoned; Russell, later deciding that it was overly sentimental (this was after he had distanced himself from Ottoline). It was finally published, after his death, as part of the *Collected Papers of Bertrand Russell*.

For most of that summer, Philip stayed in London attending to his parliamentary duties. Once Ottoline went up to London to hear him speak in the House, and a second time on June 22 to join him in Westminster Abbey to watch the coronation of George V. Occasionally Philip would come down to Peppard, so Russell had to be careful to time his visits accordingly. Yet there were occasional slip-ups. One occurred on the weekend of June 7-8 when Bertie accidentally met Philip face-to-face at Peppard for the first time since the affair began. Philip was polite and asked him to stay to tea. Russell told Ottoline later: "I thought that Philip felt my presence almost unendurable, and thinking so, I admired his behaviour very much indeed. I felt a sense of shame in his presence – not reasonably but instinctively. I am glad the first meeting is over – it will be easier another time."[17] It must have all been rather strange for Julian – this man who was not her father turning up and staying with her mother, watching the two of them going off for long walks and having such intimate, intense discussions. But perhaps Julian was by now unsurprised by the comings and goings around her. Still, it goes some way to explaining Julian's later attitude to any account of the life of her mother (it brought back painful memories).

One day Ottoline gave Russell a heart-shaped locket containing a lock of her hair. She told him she was shy about appearing sentimental. He assured her he was just as sentimental. They discussed the subject of children. (She had not told him of her inability to conceive.) He told her that he was very keen to start a family. However, when she told him she was unable to have any more children, he told her not to give another thought to the matter, saying that it was probably more convenient if they did not have a child. Despite his protestations of uninterest in fatherhood, Ottoline came to understand that a desire to have offspring ran deep in him (Alys also could not have children), and that things might have been different had she understood this better at the time.

Another problem led to their first quarrel, and which kept rearing its head – religion. No matter how much Russell tried to minimise the differences between them in this, it was something that continued to hang back in the shadows; but threatening to jump out any moment and provoke bitter exchanges. More serious was Russell's omnipresent fear that, no matter how happy they were, he knew she was not his. Once he overheard someone refer to Ottoline and Philip as "such a devoted couple", always putting their arms around each other and calling each other "darling."[18] This caused Russell to be tormented by jealousy, but there was little Ottoline could do to ameliorate his anxiety. She tried suggesting that he might cultivate other women friends. He rejected this out of hand. "Believe me," he told her, "I *know* I am right in saying it is better I should avoid intimacy with other women. You will make a grave mistake if you go against this knowledge."[19] Ottoline had another reason for suggesting other women friends. She was finding that Russell's physical demands on her were more than she could cope with. To her, sex was a means to an end: to Bertie, it was an end in itself. He tried by analogy to convey how much he needed it. He told her: "Young men who want to live decently have a frightfully hard time, it must be difficult for women to know how hard. At that age one's instincts never give one any rest night or day. All one's thoughts and feelings are coloured by them."[20] The question of their physical relationship continued to cause discord, and would dog their future just as much, and probably even more, than the matter of religion. Nevertheless, Ottoline did apparently derive some enjoyment from her "physical" relations with Bertie. She was to tell him: "I feel shy of speaking ever about *our* physical union – but it *is most* divine & today it seemed so almost more than ever before."[21] Not words aimed at deflecting Bertie's amorous intentions.

One of the main excuses Ottoline gave Russell, for not

wanting to make love as frequently as he wanted, was her ill-health. Excuse it may have been some of the time; but it was also the truth. Throughout the entire period of her friendship with Russell, Ottoline's health was exceedingly poor (though which was the cause, and which the effect, is open to question). Her doctors diagnosed neuritis, a rather meaningless term describing a general nervous condition. That summer at Peppard it seemed that she was almost constantly in the grip of neuritis.

The Contemporary Art Society party in June had exhausted her, and under the surface she was close to emotional and physical breakdown. Throughout June and July the entries in her Diary reflect moods alternating between joy and despair. Bertie did his best to cheer her up with quasi-mathematical jokes; for example:

The attraction between myself and another person is directly proportional to the merit of the other person and inversely proportional to the square of the distance between them; O. is an object of infinite merit; the distance between me and O. is zero.[22]

More interestingly, he also told her that she was now often featuring in his dreams. In one dream she had a small, insignificant face and a snub nose: clearly a reversal-of-reality dream. In another she was a man and he was a woman, and the dream went on to "the point where the difference was of the most importance" (he added that, as a woman, he behaved very sensually and remembered thinking it was lucky for her that he was not a man, or he should have been "brutal").[23]

In July Ottoline's doctors ordered her to get more sleep and to this end put her on a course of injections. Bertie told her: "I hope you will get 14 hours' sleep on all possible occasions – these do not include occasions when you have visits from eminent philosophers, do they?"[24] But the injections didn't help, and in August her headaches became so acute she decided to go to a spa at Marienbad for a cure. She came down to Bedford Square for a few days, where Virginia visited her. She reported back to Vanessa that Ottoline had told her she still wanted to be friends with Roger Fry, but that it was hopeless because Fry didn't want to be friends with her. Vanessa wrote to Fry urging him to make a friendly move: "Couldn't you write to Ottoline?" she asked.[25] But Fry did nothing. At the end of August Ottoline left for Marienbad. Philip remained behind in London, and Russell prepared to quit Ipsden, first calling at Peppard to say goodbye to Julian. He reported to Ottoline that Julian had told her nurse: "Mummie's gone and Daddie's going. It's a queer world."[26] Russell was hoping to join Ottoline at Marienbad as soon as possible. He wrote to her almost every day asking when he could come. In one letter he revealed that his friends were beginning to make sly digs at him over his "secret" friendship with her. It was funny, he said, how many people mentioned her name. Not everyone, however, knew. His bedmaker at Cambridge told him that the current theory around Trinity was that he was having an affair with a local Cambridge lady (his promiscuity was attracting attention).

Finally, Ottoline told Bertie that he could come and join her. But when he turned up, he ran foul of the manager of the hotel, an officious Prussian who frowned on this strange Englishman paying visits to the titled lady with the different name. The manager also complained about the way they got cigarette-ash all over the sofa. Eventually he banned Bertie from visiting Ottoline's room, a decision against which she appealed to Rufus Isaacs, the British Solicitor-General, who was also taking the waters. Alas, he could do nothing. Finally, around September 18, Bertie left, to be replaced almost immediately by Philip, who had arrived from London. The Prussian went out of his way to inform Philip of his wife's misconduct, and was most put out when Philip smiled and told him how pleased he was to hear it.

Back in England, Russell found trouble waiting for him. Somehow Alys had learned that Ottoline had gone to Marienbad without her maid, and that Russell had been there with her. (He suspected she had been using detectives.) Alys' wrath – vented, apparently, by letter or by way of the Whiteheads – was not pleasant. While Ottoline was in Marienbad she also received the sad news that Mother Julian had died. Russell telegraphed his sympathy, but she was inconsolable. A few days later she travelled on to Vienna, where her depression was too deep for her to enjoy sightseeing. Russell also wrote telling her that on her return to London they must meet in the first-class waiting-room at Euston Station, not Kings Cross, as planned, to avoid the Cambridge travellers, some of whom might recognise them. Ottoline wrote from Meran in the Tyrol telling Russell she was concerned that she was keeping him from his work (which idea he pooh-poohed), and that she was too weak a person to support him in his needs. Russell replied that there was nothing physically wrong with her a winter in an African desert wouldn't cure. In Paris Ottoline and Lamb had a brief and pleasant reunion.

While still in Paris, she received a letter from Russell relating how his friend Whitehead had asked to borrow a cake of soap she had given him. He couldn't bear to part with it, and instead scrounged up a small piece to give him. Later Whitehead remarked that Russell seemed to have more hair than usual, and asked if he had been using hair restorer. "It nearly made me blush!"[27] (Russell told Ottoline, apparently oblivious to the fact that Whitehead was teasing him). Before she left the Continent, Ottoline did some shopping in Paris and told Bertie: "I bought myself two petticoats which *you* [her emphasis] shall see!"[28]

After a reunion at Euston Station, Bertie and Ottoline went to room 28 on the first floor of the Grafton Hotel in Tottenham Court Road, which Russell had booked (for two days!). But so unsatisfactory did this arrangement prove that he promised to begin looking immediately for a more permanent place of assignation. First he tried Chelsea, but the Whiteheads advised against this area, as Alys and Logan planned to move there soon. Instead they suggested Bloomsbury. (The fact that this was closer to Bedford Square might have been another dig by the Whiteheads at the now-so-not-secret imbroglio.) Near Grays Inn he thought he had found an ideal flat; until he discovered that opposite was the firm of solicitors that had inherited a parlourmaid from him and Alys. Finally he found a flat in Bury Place, around the corner from the British Museum, in a building named (of all things!) Russell Chambers. In fact, almost every street and square through which Ottoline and Russell would walk to their new "love-nest" had names like Russell, Bedford, Tavistock; or Bentinck, Cavendish, Bolsover, and Welbeck. He told Ottoline of his delight: "It will be very nice – we shall have a great sense of liberty & I can have books there & means of making tea, & even peppermints in some secret recess!"[29] (Ottoline was addicted to peppermints – though their presence in the love-nest may have had something to do with Bertie's bad breath.)

Over the next three weeks they had a lot of fun fitting out the little flat in the crowded, rather ordinary red-brick building. Ottoline bought a rug and filled the rooms full of carnations and lilies-of-the-valley, while he moved in his most precious material possessions: his grandfather's desk and a small table made from Doomsday-Book-oak that had belonged to his mother, and on which he had written much of *Principia Mathematica*. Looking back on these days in late 1911, Ottoline wrote:

> *How much emotion those little rooms in Bury Place held – intense and burning and very tragic! Bertie demanded so much, and I could give so inadequately. He would stand at his window looking for my coming, growing tenser and tenser, counting the minutes if I was late. As I hurried along the street I dreaded to look up and see his face, pressed against the panes, looking for me.*[30]

Yet after she left Russell behind in those little rooms "unsatisfied and tragically lonely", she would return home to Bedford Square and skip for joy. She recalled in her *Memoirs*: "Often I dance round my bed-room and fling my arms out and sing, 'Free, free'."

Bertie, on the other hand, was ecstatically happy. On November 13 he wrote: "What a deliciously absurd time we had in the flat – I don't know when I have felt more silly."[31] A few days later Ottoline had to accompany Philip to Burnley where they attended a ball and she addressed several meetings. She wrote to Russell asking him to send her his views on the Persian situation and women's suffrage. Russell replied saying that until a woman had a vote she could not hope to have any dignity. (Ottoline may have agreed with this, though she was never an ardent advocate of votes for women, and later opposed the suffragettes after they pelted Asquith with rotten eggs.) While in Burnley she wrote to Lamb, who was now back in England, inviting him to meet her when she returned to London. They met on the platform at Euston and spent a happy day together (probably in his studio), after which he wrote to her: "It has all been so very wonderful, so revealing, transfiguring; I can still only ponder in bewildered joy."

He concluded:

> *I kiss*
> *your feet in reverence*
> *your knees in trust*
> *your hands in troth*
> *your mouth in courage*
> *& your heart in fiery penetration.*[32]

But three days later he was sulky again and apologising for his behaviour. It was caused by jealousy, he said. Ottoline went back to Burnley feeling ill and dispirited.

Christmas 1911 was spent at Black Hall, where Ottoline suffered from a cold, headaches, and a liver chill; and the patent disapproval of Mrs. Morrell, who too had found out about Russell. Ottoline wrote telling Lytton her troubles. He did his best to cheer her up. On Boxing Day she was sitting at the Jacobean table in the dining-room when the maid brought her a letter from Lytton, who wrote:

> *If it wasn't for…circumstances, I believe this letter would jump up from the breakfast-table, and throw its arms around your neck. As it is, a few tender glances are all that*

> *it will allow itself, while your hostess is engaged with the tea."*[33]

This letter was a contrast to the sort of mail she was getting from Russell during the festive season. They had had a bitter disagreement over religion. "What I don't understand," he told her, "is the purely intellectual parts – how you can think that it is true."[34] But he soon regretted his outburst and begged her forgiveness. He assured her that he would improve if only he could get the fanaticism of reason out of his soul. Yet it refused to be silenced.

> *I must go on writing – it is impossible to do anything else. I can already see better how it is. You do not believe that reasoning is a method of arriving at truth; I do. That is the root of the matter. Reduced to that, it does not much matter. You are wrong in thinking it will crop up worse & worse as time goes on; hitherto I have never said the worst; & so it kept on growing. Things unsaid are poisonous in my mind. When once I have grasped fully how your beliefs are incompatible with truthfulness I shall hardly wish them changed.*[35]

Ottoline then accused Russell of unworthy bigotry. He agreed abjectly and strove mightily to reconcile their differences. "Do you know," he told her, "that there is scarcely a word that I disagree with in your confession of faith. The only practical difference is that things which we both think possible but not certain seem to me rather less probable than to you."[36]

Ottoline's sojourn in Marienbad had done nothing to cure her headaches, and so in February she decided to go to Lausanne to see a Dr. Combe, who was said to be an expert on neuralgia. But before leaving she had another crisis with Lamb; this time over his semi-serious courting of Ka Cox, a motherly young woman who was also a friend of Rupert Brooke. But just before Ottoline left for Switzerland she and Lamb spent two heavenly days together, after which he waved farewell at the station. Lamb told her to take plenty of rest and, when she was running her finger down her present list of adorers, to stop and reflect a little on her youngest and former *"esclave favori"*, who still hoped and loved.[37]

Despite, or because of, Dr. Combe's drastic treatment in Lausanne (her nose was probed with a red-hot needle), Ottoline's headaches did not vanish; moreover her surroundings annoyed her. She complained to Bertie that the person in the next room at her hotel smelled. Then she had a tooth extracted. Then she suffered liver trouble. To make matters worse, Dr. Combe put her on a strict diet of starch and chicken. All she could do to relieve the tedium was read Spinoza and do her embroidery (Lamb had specially designed her a "Deirdre of the Sorrows" picture to sew). Russell wrote telling her he was pining for her and kissed her locket every night before bed. On March 19 she received another letter from him reminding her it was exactly one year since their first momentous evening together at Bedford Square:

> *You and I, dearest, belong to each other in a very eternal way: we are of those who are not passive to the world, but resolved to stamp it with the seal of divinity whenever it is possible. The flames of our inmost fires meet and mingle. 1 know your springs of living water, and my spirit drinks at them.*[38]

While Ottoline was away, Lamb had been getting to know Philip better, and went riding with him several times, along with Ka Cox and Leonard Woolf (who was soon to marry Virginia Stephen). Lamb told Ottoline that Philip was charming and mellow, but "unbelievably naif". "He has a way of making his weaknesses appear virtuous – by excessive frankness! I do like him so very much."[39] He asked Ottoline why it was Philip didn't have any friends, adding: "I suppose people are either too suspicious or patronising, & if neither *you* absorb them! What a sad sacrifice!"[40]

Ottoline had not allowed Bertie to join her in Lausanne, but he had been counting the hours until she returned. Yet instead of hurrying back to London to see him, Ottoline stopped over in Paris for an extra day "not to rest, but merely for pleasure," as he later indignantly complained. This "oversight" joined with "a host of things I have overlooked before" to produce a coldness in Russell that he expressed in a letter in April, 1912:

> *There is one thing you could do for me if you have time, and that is to look through my letters since the latter part of your stay in Lausanne, and see if there is anything in them worth remembering, and if so bring some of them round with you. I should like to talk about the things in them.*

He sounded like a stiff schoolmaster. He said her judgment about sex was "morbid and maladif...It seems to me one can only say that to some sex is spiritually important, to others not. Unfortunately you and I belong to different camps in this respect. But today I can hardly imagine what sexual feelings are like, as they are utterly dead in me."[41] Ottoline ignored the sarcastic tone and at their next meeting smoothed down his ruffled feathers. A few days later he sent her two poems he had composed. A stanza of one went:

> *My love is a burning fire*
> *From the flaming heart of mankind,*
> *The heart of a vast desire,*
> *Restless and ruthless and blind.*[42]

Russell told her that talking to her helped him gain an insight into how to explain his philosophy to his popular audience. This was the sort of work he was really interested in now, he told her. He would be happy to leave the "technical" work to others. Around this time he also started writing his autobiography, which he proposed to publish under the pseudonym Simon Styles. They went to concerts together, and after one he told her that her beauty was like the effect of a Beethoven melody. But the matter of sex continued to cause problems. At the end of April he drafted a letter saying it might be better if they parted, but he didn't send it. Later Ottoline asked how he would feel if either of them took another lover. He replied that it wouldn't help *him* and that if *she* took up with someone else he should suffer untold torments. However, he believed that their love might survive if the person she chose was someone he admired and respected, like Henry James (!).

A few weeks later Russell was feeling very depressed. He was still mulling over the Paris business and threatening the direst consequences should she decide to drop him. In May he wrote:

I feel that if we parted...the moment would come when in a sudden impulse I should put myself under a motor for the pleasure of hearing my backbone break. And if I avoided that, I should not avoid sexual crime, from mere desperation.

In April Lamb and Lytton went off together for a holiday in Dorset. Earlier they had had a tiff (possibly over Lamb's refusal to set up house somewhere together); but they made up, and from an inn in Dorset Lamb pleaded with Ottoline to join them. She declined, but offered to show him some dances she had learned at the Easter fair on Hampstead Heath. He replied: "I will learn anything which involves you hugging my neck!"[43] But their relationship was beginning to show signs of succumbing to its inherent strains. In May there was a misunderstanding over a painting which either she or her brother Lord Henry had commissioned from Lamb. Apparently Ottoline accepted it as a gift, then decided she didn't like it and sent it back with a cheque for £30. Later Robbie Ross bought it for the Contemporary Art Society and Lamb returned the cheque to Ottoline. (He also gave her another picture that was to lead to even greater trouble.) Then he returned a ring Ottoline had given him, a gesture for which she took him to task. Lamb replied, addressing her as "Dear

Ottoline" – a form of address he had not employed for years: "The returning of the ring was not an act of hostility, as you seemed to take it: indeed I should not have risked it if I hadn't thought the moment propitiously free from misunderstanding."[44]

In June Ottoline went off again to Lausanne to consult Dr. Combe. This time Russell accompanied her in order to see if their friendship could improve, as indeed it did. Bertie spent his mornings reading or writing in the garden of his hotel, and in the afternoons he and Ottoline would go for walks and read poetry together. She found that he was now more gentle and imaginative, less positive and definite, and she felt that they were happy again. While she was undergoing yet another of Dr. Combe's Draconian treatments – drinking for 30 days a daily dose of radium in milk – she received another of Lytton's morale-boosting letters. It was dreadful, he told her, to think of her in Lausanne without a maid:

> *I should love to come out and be your maid – I'm sure I'd make a very good one. I believe my real role in life would be that. I should arrange your petticoats most exquisitely, and only look through the crack of the door now and then. When are you coming back? – I'm afraid not for ages. I wish I could send you wireless telegrams of affection and laughter, dearest Ottoline. But really I do send them – Don't you see them glimmering in your radium? Oh yes, and dancing up your flight of stairs, and running into your room at the oddest moments? They don't even stop to knock at the door.*[45]

On her return to London Ottoline had a frightful scene with Lamb. The incident that sparked it concerned the other painting he had given her. Ottoline had accused Lamb's dealer of delivering the painting at an inconvenient moment. Lamb then told her that in sending the cheque for the first painting she had been trying to remove the painful associations it had for her. He told her to return the second one if she didn't wish to accept it as a gift. She went to see him and afterwards he wrote a bitter note, saying he now pitied her and signing "ever your 'little' Henry Lamb."[46] (This apparently was a reference to Philip Morrell's earlier comment that Henry was Ottoline's "little lamb".) Lamb's next letter was formal and cutting. She had insisted he accept her cheque and he replied sarcastically that it was much too big. He said he was sorry she had such bad headaches, but he couldn't see her, as he was off to Donegal, perhaps for a year.

However, he did see her once more, and at this meeting Ottoline took him bodily by the shoulders and shook him. Later she felt sorry and wrote to apologise, but he replied curtly:

> *Dear Ottoline,*
> *Many thanks for your advice & renewed protestations.*
> *I also venture to say that I know you well, & in my turn make you a few recommendations – gratis, like yours.*
> *Just try & keep for your own benefit a little of all this overflowing soul, spirit & help; you will really be surprised to find how they will have their work cut out for them. And when you have made a little progress towards manufacturing some self-control, you will perhaps be better prepared for the eclairissement which you seem so anxious to get from me.*
> *As for the "outburst" – Don't worry – Lobelia [Euphemia] used to use plates & dinner-knives –: Meanwhile I shall go on my way cheerfully – and slightly weathered, yet enormously wiser as to the validity of feminine assistance in Life.*
> *Yrs, HENRY L*[47]

INTERLUDE
A *'Thumbs-up'* from Michael Holroyd

*Michael Holroyd, shortly after I met him in 1972
(he was knighted in 2007 for his services to literature)*

JUST AS in the early years of the last century Lytton Strachey's famous biography *Eminent Victorians* changed the face of literary biography, so did Michael Holroyd's 1967 biography of Lytton change the face of modern biographical writing. Even more significantly for me, it was his precedent that not only delivered me the opportunity to write my book about Ottoline, but (I believe) it was his not inconsiderable imprimatur that ensured it was published.

Firstly, it opened up the subject of Bloomsbury to the modern literary world and brought its characters and activities back into contemporary relevance. That, I believe, was a factor in Julian Vinogradoff agreeing to let me write the story of her mother's life. And just as Lytton had written disrespectfully about such Victorian-age icons as General Gordon and Florence Nightingale, so Michael's frank discussion of the hitherto taboo subject of homosexuality lifted a cloud of hypocrisy from the more prissy forms of biographical writing.

But he did more than that for me. He became my unofficial mentor, guiding me towards the right people to talk to, and discussing with me the world of Bloomsbury his research had exposed. And when I finished my final draft, Julian Vinogradoff objected strongly to my reference, when quoting Lytton Strachey, to Ottoline's skirts swishing the floor at the National Gallery. Michael, of his own accord, wrote a letter to my publishers, Chatto & Windus, standing up strongly for my book, dispelling any reservations Chatto and their formidable Nora Smallwood might have entertained about It. Holroyd, the world's most eminent biographer, had given it his approval, who was to question his judgement?

At our initial meeting at his home in Ladbroke Grove W10, Michael gave me some sage advice on how to handle the gentle, rather unworldly people I was likely to encounter during my own research. He warned me: "Lunch with them amounts to a dry biscuit and a lettuce leaf, if you are lucky." My visit to one of the first people Michael gave me an introduction to, Alix Strachey, the widow of Lytton's brother James, confirmed his culinary fears. She was a very bright woman in her eighties, and lunch with her was as frugal as Michael Holroyd had predicted. Nevertheless, I enjoyed meeting her and seeing her beautiful mural drawings, as well as hearing her reminiscences of Ottoline and the world of Bloomsbury.

During my research I kept in touch with Michael and visited him several times. When many months later I finally completed my manuscript, he volunteered to read it. Dispatching it, I didn't hear back from him for about a week, and began to worry. Then he rang me and said: "Thumbs up!". His favourable response was a symphony to my ears.

When we later collaborated on an article for the *Times Literary Supplement* about literary estates (specifically D.H. Lawrence's), he rang me after its publication to tell me, with a chuckle, that his father had asked him if he was going to marry me! He was, of course, to marry the novelist Margaret Drabble.

CHAPTER 13
The Gathering Storm

Ottoline (by Augustus John) was now back at Bedford Square

IN THE SUMMER of 1912 Ottoline took up residence at 44 Bedford Square and reopened her salon again. Though she had been out of circulation for over a year, all her old friends – Asquith, Birrell, Henry James, Ethel Sands, Hilda Douglas-Pennant – flocked back, and once more the grey-and-yellow drawing-rooms came alive with laughter, gossip, and argument.

Nor had her flair for spotting and attracting new talent deserted her; and mixing with the more familiar faces were a number of new ones: the novelist Arnold Bennett, the painters Wyndham Lewis and Frederick Etchells, and the mathematician (and budding Bloomsburyite) Harry Norton, whom Ottoline had recently befriended. Bloomsbury itself was represented by Duncan Grant, Adrian and Virginia Stephen (who had married Leonard Woolf that August), and of course Lytton, by now almost part of the furniture. (Roger Fry and Clive and Vanessa Bell were conspicuous by their absence.)

But for Ottoline undoubtedly the most exciting new faces at Bedford Square that summer of 1912 belonged to Vaslav Nijinsky, Leon Bakst, and Sergei Diaghilev; for this was the summer of the Russian Ballet, and Ottoline had discovered a new setting in which to sparkle. Nijinsky she had met in Paris in 1910, without being overly impressed, and when Diaghilev brought his Ballet Russe to London the following year she had been away at Peppard reading Spinoza in the woods with Bertie. At first she rather dismissed the Ballet Russe, probably because everybody else was making such a fuss about it. But in July 1912 she went to Covent Garden and became a convert overnight. She was entranced with the wild music of Stravinsky; the bizarre Oriental sets and costumes of Bakst; and, above all, the faunlike genius of Nijinsky. Night after night she returned to drink in the excitement of *Thamar*; the splendour of *Scheherazade*; and the elegance of *Giselle*. In the intervals she and her friends gathered at the refreshment bars to discuss the merits of one dance over another; Ottoline's tall figure draped with a gorgeous cloak, and her dramatic outfit topped by a large leghorn hat decked with ostrich feathers. Through her friendship with the Ballet's patron, Lady Ripon, she was able to invite Nijinsky and Diaghilev to Bedford Square. Soon she became one of the few people in London whom the highly-strung and very shy Nijinsky would trust. Most Londoners had found it difficult to communicate with Nijinsky because of his minimal English; but Ottoline spoke fluent French, and was thus able to converse happily with him. Sometimes he and Diaghilev would come to tea, and afterwards wander round the gardens in the square. One evening they happened upon Duncan Grant and Adrian Stephen playing tennis in the Square in the twilight, and at the sight of their lithe bodies flitting over the shadows; Nijinsky exclaimed: *"Quel decor!"*[1] Another time he was overheard discussing Ottoline: "Lady Morrell is so tall, so beautiful, like a giraffe."[2] Fearing Ottoline might be hurt, Diaghilev tried to correct him; but the dancer insisted: "No, no, giraffe is beautiful – long, gracious...she looks like it." Diaghilev, too, was impressed with Ottoline's appearance, and once toyed with the idea of designing a ballet in which she would appear as herself – on stage and in person.

That summer Ottoline met everybody and went everywhere. And, perhaps to compensate for the comparative dullness of her marital life, she also went out of her way to wear outfits that were especially colourful and striking. Her entrance at a garden party given by Asquith caused a mild sensation; though she later confessed to Lytton: "I was awfully shy and cut most of the people I most wanted to talk to from sheer fright, but some came up and [were caught] in my magic ring."[3] Perhaps Nijinsky was right in likening Ottoline to some tall, slightly improbable inhabitant of the savannah. Certainly whenever she went out for a stroll, passers-by would stop to stare. She discovered that it was not wise to travel by bus because of the stir her appearance created. She told Lytton: "What an odd life I have, continually acting on the different stages of London."[4]

Another face absent from Ottoline's public functions was Bertie's (and a much more interesting face it was too, now he had taken Ottoline's advice and shaved off his prim moustache). Though his meeting with Philip at Peppard had been cordial, he still found it embarrassing to be seen at 44 Bedford Square. So Ottoline, preoccupied with her social whirl, ensured their meetings were restricted to occasional afternoons in 34 Russell Chambers. He couldn't even go to see the Russian Ballet with her; and had to go instead with a male companion. Even so, an embarrassing incident occurred. Just as he was sitting down he caught sight of Alys, sitting only a few seats away. Jumping up, he dragged his protesting colleague out into the street. But Alys had seen them, and followed them out. They met face-to-face and she gave him a look which, Russell told Ottoline, "was intended to pierce my heart, and did so." He was so upset he had to lean against some railings. "Darling, I can't tell you how awful it was," he added.[5] When at first he saw Alys in the auditorium, he had been struck by her good looks. But out in the street, she seemed old and tragic (he told Ottoline). Later he decided that her intense stare at him was not all tragedy, but was also "partly to see how I looked without my moustache." Throughout 1912 Russell's letters to Ottoline reveal a slight but distinct change in tone. His disappointment when she stopped over in Paris instead of coming to see him had hurt him deeply, and left a scar. He worshipped her still, but now his devotion was not unreserved. His calculating mind had reasserted itself. He began to devote more time to his philosophical and mathematical work. At a philosophy conference in London in August he enjoyed being praised and feted, particularly by the Americans there. Yet he was still deeply in love with Ottoline, and there were times when desire overcame him:

> *My Darling My Darling* – People were with me all the evening and now it is too late for the post. I had gone to bed not meaning to write till tomorrow, but the longing for you is too great – I must write a word of love, my dearest Heart – a sudden flood of yearning has overwhelmed me – such a hunger for you as is hard to bear. Dear Dear Love, I do try to be contented away from you, and to think how soon I shall see you again, but it is not easy.[6]

At other times his mind was occupied with things entirely flippant – his appearance, for instance. He told Ottoline: "My HAT has come. Do you like the crown pressed down or sticking up? This question is *very important.*"[7] But on other occasions he would grow maudlin and write: "Sometimes I think you and

Aunt Agatha are the only people who really care for me."[8]

Ottoline and Philip had sold Peppard in 1911, and since then had been looking around for a larger country house. While they searched, Philip's parents offered them the use of Broughton Grange, the Morrell country house near Banbury, outside Oxford. Philip talked Ottoline into spending a month there in August. It was, however, an unmitigated disaster. Most of the time it rained; Ottoline felt even more ill; and Mrs. Morrell spoilt Julian. Ottoline wrote: "It is secure and quiet, but deadly...purely hunting country."[9] (Which was a considerable put-down by country-raised Ottoline.) Still, there were diversions. On August 19 she received a telegram: *SHALL ARRIVE TOMORROW WIRE TRAIN LATER. IN NEED OF YOUR CORRAGIO AS WELL AS MY OWN. LYTTON*[10] It came from Ulster, where Lytton and Lamb had fetched up after an exhausting and progressively less-comradely tour of the British Isles. Earlier, Lytton, already weak from privations suffered in provincial guest-houses, had written from south of the border, where he and Lamb had gone to recuperate: "Don't be surprised if I suddenly arrive at Broughton pale and trembling."[11]

On August 20, duly fragile, he did arrive, falling into Ottoline's arms, an emotional and physical wreck. Ottoline set aside some rooms for him and did her best to raise his spirits. They spent hours together gossiping; then Lytton would put on her high-heeled shoes and totter around the room, both of them getting more and more giggly. Of such behaviour, Mrs. Morrell did not approve. Nor did Russell, who came down to Broughton for a day. He told Ottoline he liked neither Lytton nor Mrs. Morrell. "Nevertheless," he told her, "I think loathing for him quite pardonable, whereas I don't see why he should loathe her. He is diseased and unnatural, & only a very high degree of civilisation enables a healthy person to stand him."[12] Needless to say, Russell's visit was not a success, and all Ottoline remembered of it was a melancholy walk in a local churchyard. That may have been all *she* remembered, but the walk stuck firmly in Russell's memory, and from it he was to later date the beginning of his escape from Ottoline's thrall.

In September she went to stay at Churn, Berkshire, in a house lent by her brother, Lord Henry. There she took up watercolour painting and had another visit from Lytton, who was engaged in a walking tour of the Downs. He warned her of an exciting new development in his appearance:

> *Very exceeding secret. I shall be...in earrings! Yes! HUSH! It was the maddest lark – perhaps too mad for me even?? – but I was in a mood for **anything**, so don't jibe and think me quite grotesque or a mere imitation of John or anything else – only a very young youth on a gay holiday – reckless & debonair & not caring a brass farthing for the rest of humanity. – Do you understand? Oh, I like them very much – so far –. But of course civilized society – imagine its comments! – I shall therefore arrange my locks so that Pipsey shall not observe them. – and you are **not** to tell him or anyone else.*[13]

He signed the letter "Your eighteen-year-old Lytton" (actually he was 32). When he arrived, sporting a bright-yellow coat and orange waistcoat, he tried to persuade Ottoline to soften towards Lamb, whom he likened to a cat:

> *How I should stroke him! – And then up would come a soft pad onto my thigh – oh so soft & caressing! – and then – the sudden stiffening, and the claws starting out and drawing blood right through my trousers!*"[14]

To Lytton, Ottoline moaned that she had lost her youth and vitality. He tried to cheer her up by telling her it was only temporary – he suffered the same thing from time to time. He told her:

> *Of course, you have a splendid and glorious and vivacious and perpetually youthful future before you,* ma plus chere

de toutes les marquises – you mustn't doubt that. Your humble servant will always be there to assist you to the best of his ability – and you will do the like by him, I hope. Our great-grandchildren shall see us gallivanting down Bond Street as nonagenarians, and gnash their teeth with envy.[15]

In October Ottoline's health forced her to return to Lausanne for another session of Dr. Combe's radium cocktails. Lytton was deeply concerned:

Tea and radium! A horrid mixture! One day there'll be an explosion on your balcony, if you're not careful. The boots will rush up – too late! too late! Miladi will have been dissipated into a thousand fragments, and the reputation of Dr. Combe at last ruined for ever."[16]

Russell also wrote. He had had another dream about her, and this time she had turned into a cat – a very nice cat (he hastened to explain), very affectionate, purring and rubbing soft fur against him. He hadn't minded the strange transformation until he began to regret that she had lost the power of speech.

Less happy was a letter from Lamb, who was still in Ireland, accusing her of having given Clive Bell the wrong picture to hang in an exhibition at the Grafton Galleries. Apparently Clive had gone to Bedford Square to get some of Lamb's paintings and had taken the wrong one. A week later Lamb wrote to apologise, Clive having told him the error wasn't Ottoline's. Nevertheless, rumours of the mix-up had already spread round Bloomsbury, and Molly MacCarthy wrote to Clive Bell: "What *is* the Ottoline scandal? I am so distressed if she is being gossiped about, as I do love her, & don't mind what she does; she is a rare muddler I fear in her intense affairs. Don't let people say unkind things about her."[17]

In November Ottoline returned to London with the first decent piece of advice she had received from the medical profession: she was to rest in the country for at least two years.

Now she and Philip began looking in earnest for a suitable country house. In the meantime Ottoline retired to Breach House, Cholsey, in Berkshire, where Philip's sister-in-law had some spare rooms. Lytton was devastated by news of her impending exile. How would he survive without her parties? Bedford Square was the one place where he could go and mingle with the *beau monde*. She reassured him she wasn't shutting up house just yet. Ottoline remained at Cholsey for most of the winter of 1912-1913, which meant she saw Russell, who had duties in Cambridge, only irregularly. Though he was more or less reconciled to the necessity of her staying in the country; he still missed their afternoons together, and he continued to write several times a week. In one letter he told her he had heard that Philip was one of only four men in the House of Commons willing to speak out against the foreign policies of Sir Edward Grey. In another he defined the current state of their relationship:

> *Dearest, do believe that my real deep love is not less. I know passion is less, but that can't be helped. You explained before once how you have to keep me on an island in your life; for a long time I kept you in the centre of mine, but in the long run that was incompatible with one's duties, and I had to put you on an island too.*[18]

At this time Russell's main duty was trying to keep his star pupil, Ludwig Wittgenstein, from going mad; a task that was causing him some concern. By now Wittgenstein had met Maynard Keynes and several other Apostles who wanted to recruit him for the Society. Russell argued against this, but was overruled. Later Lytton and others put it about that Russell had been trying to monopolize Wittgenstein; but from Russell's letters to Ottoline it seems that this accusation was groundless. Russell was trying to shield the delicate Wittgenstein from all excitement to preserve his fragile mental equilibrium.

In November 1912 Russell accepted an offer of £600 to go to the United States in the spring of 1914 to lecture at Harvard. He told Ottoline that, though he was looking forward to seeing what America was like, he begrudged not seeing her for three months. Actually she was relieved Bertie would be absent for a while, for although her letters to him speak of her shortcomings and weaknesses, her Diary gives a different picture: "I wish I knew why he is not sympathetic to me...His hands are the hands of a bear. They have no expression in them, only force...I find it exhausting to keep in step with his intellect all the time, and also satisfy his heart. But after all one's spirit can endure and press on – stagnation is what I fear.[19] A little later comes another outburst: "Bertie has been very much annoyed with me lately for desiring quiet times in the day for reading, he expects me to be entirely at his disposal morning, noon, night, and becomes very angry if I am not. He told me that I could never accomplish anything important in life by *my* reading while I could help him by being with him."[20] Meanwhile, Lytton was learning to ride: "I shall come galloping into Bedford Square," he warned Ottoline, "in a peaked cap & striped silk breeches."[21] Especially was he proud of his appearance in breeches: "Full many a leg is born to blush unseen," he told her.

One of the main reasons Ottoline and Philip decided to stay in the country for so long a time was their financial situation. Ottoline had always expected she would inherit a substantial sum from an insurance policy for £100,000 taken out on himself by her half-brother, the Duke, in 1884. This sum was to be released to Lady Bolsover's children by her second marriage when it expired in 1912. However, for reasons unknown, Lady Bolsover had decreed that Ottoline was not to be included in the bequest: only her brothers were to inherit the money. All Ottoline received was £6,000 from her share of the proceeds of the sale of her mother's old house at Grosvenor Place, which was sold that year. Although £6,000 was still quite a substantial sum, the revelation of her reduced expectations came as a serious shock, and was one of the reasons why she and Philip had decided to start looking for a country residence where life would be less expensive than Bedford Square.

Ten miles away from where Ottoline was staying in Cholsey, Lytton was ensconced in the Chestnuts, a farmhouse Ottoline had booked him into as a paying guest. He had now discarded his earrings and was starting work on what was to become his most famous work, *Eminent Victorians*. As he delved into Cardinal Manning and the Oxford Movement, Ottoline kept his spirits up with gifts and pep talks. In January he felt particularly low and came to see Ottoline for a heart-to-heart talk. He was depressed about his writing, he told her. His voice was too thin for politics; and he was no good in company. Ottoline reassured him that writing was his real *metier*, and he should concentrate on that. In March, partly for want of anything better to do, he returned to Hampstead where Lamb began work on a new portrait of him. (The celebrated Lamb portrait, now in the National Portrait Gallery in London, showing Lytton draped limply in an armchair – see above.) By now, Ottoline was by having some regrets about her estrangement from Lamb, and for Christmas 1912 she had embroidered him a silk picture to hang over his fireplace. He thanked her for this, and also for sending him a cheque, adding the hope that the country air would restore her to health.

Ottoline and Philip's search for a country house ended in March 1913 when they learned that Garsington Manor, a somewhat ramshackle Jacobean house just outside Oxford, was coming up for auction. The Morrell family had owned land around the village of Garsington for more than 200 years, and Philip's sister owned some of the Garsington Manor farmland. Philip went to Oxford to bid and returned with the news that he had bought the lease on the house, and 360 acres of farmland that went with it, for £8,450. He and Ottoline scraped together the purchase-price with a £2,000 top-up loan from Ottoline's brother Lord Henry, augmented by the proceeds of a sale of a painting Philip owned. (This painting caused a rift between Philip and his mother, who had decided that the painting belonged to her. Philip had to go to some lengths to establish his right to it.)

Philip fancied himself a gentleman farmer, and promptly

made plans to start work on the farm straight away; even though the house itself would not be vacant for another two years, when the existing lease expired. Moreover, it would need considerable renovations and repair-work, for which (they calculated) they had just sufficient funds. Lytton was pleased at the news, but wondered about the two-year wait:

> *And then – 2 years hence! – where shall we all be by then? – and what? – infinitely grey-haired, respectable, crutch-supported antiquities – or bankrupts – or exiles with ruined reputations – I shudder to think of it. Or do you think we shall be altogether rejuvenated & sprightly? Or just the same as ever?"*[22]

On Russell's part, he could not work up much enthusiasm about the purchase, as he knew it would involve even more difficulties seeing Ottoline. To make up a little for this she visited him several times in March. He cooked scrambled eggs on toast for her and told her the past year had taught him to accept the fact that she would not leave Philip, and that he must be satisfied with what time, age, and health permitted her to allow him.

Ottoline returned to London in April and resumed her Thursday levees. Henry Lamb wrote asking to be allowed to attend, but Ottoline, fearing trouble, gently put him off. She did, however, attempt another reconciliation. At the Sickerts' one night she found herself talking to Vanessa Bell, and later they shared a taxi home. Vanessa reported to Fry that Ottoline was making friendly overtures. Next day Ottoline telephoned Vanessa and invited her to Bedford Square, where they had a touching reunion, Ottoline telling her that the whole quarrel had been dreadful. "Then," Vanessa told Fry, "she kissed me passionately on the lips!"[23] When Vanessa got up to go Ottoline pressed a silk handkerchief on her. "I think she is really very nice," Vanessa remarked, "though muddle-headed. One mustn't expect her to be over clear about anything." But hardly had Ottoline dealt with Vanessa, than Lytton began to fret. He was jealous over the interest "Our Lady of Bedford Square" was taking in Gilbert Cannan, a young writer who had been to school with Henry Lamb in Manchester. Ottoline wrote to Cannan praising his latest novel, and he soon became a regular visitor to Bedford Square; sometimes staying the night in a spare room. Bloomsbury tongues wagged, but there is no evidence the gossip had any substance. Nevertheless, it was indicative that Ottoline was beginning to seek younger friends.

In April Ottoline went north to Burnley to preside over a local bazaar. She tended a stall and raised £70,17.5d for local Liberal coffers, reporting to Lytton: "I sat & sold at the Bazaar for 4 days until 10:30 pm & altogether they made nearly £5000... *can't we go* into commerce?"[24] In May she went off to Lausanne again, this time taking Julian, who was still frail. While there Ottoline transferred her allegiance to a Dr. Vittoz, a psychiatrist whose specialty was eliminating unnecessary thoughts from the mind. Her concentration did wander for a moment, however, to Lytton, to whom she sent some pressed flowers and a letter: "You really must be dead. So I send you a few flowers to scatter on your grave. Where are you buried I wonder?"[25]

Throughout the summer of 1913 relations with Russell fluctuated. He was busy writing a substantial book on the theory of knowledge; and most of his letters to her, though still regular, were shorter and less intense. But whenever a meeting was in the offing, his passion would reignite. On May 2 he wrote:

> *The last two days I had been rather sad and listless, but today has been **quite** different. It seems odd that the prospect of an hour with you can alter the whole aspect of the universe – but it is so. You must prepare yourself for a dreadful blow! Thinking I shouldn't see you for six weeks, I have had my hair cropped quite short – it will horrify you, but I thought it would please all my relations.*[26]

A little later the 41-year-old philosopher's thoughts wandered to lighter matters: "My Darling Love...The night is hot and delicious, with just a sound of summer breeze in the treetops – a night that seems made for love – ah me..."[27] But Ottoline was still in Lausanne, so he reluctantly returned to William James' theory of consciousness. A few days later, on May 28, he made a disconcerting discovery. After spending months on his new book he ventured to show Wittgenstein a crucial part. "He said it was all wrong," Russell told Ottoline. "I couldn't understand his objection – in fact he was very inarticulate – but I feel in my bones that he must be right, and that he has seen something that I have missed...Well, well, it is the younger generation knocking at the door – I must make room for him when I can, or I shall become an incubus. But at the moment I am rather cross."[28]

From Lausanne Ottoline wrote breaking the news to Russell that he couldn't come over to see her, as he had been hoping. This, on top of Wittgenstein's criticism, depressed him severely. Caught between the hammer of Wittgenstein's keener mind and the anvil of Ottoline's insensitivity, he had a miserable summer; and when Ottoline returned he was a bundle of nerves. Just before she arrived he told her: "I can hardly let myself think of holding you in my arms once more and hearing your voice and kissing your dear eyes...O my loved one my Ottoline my soul is yours. I love you love you love you."[29] But after she arrived things didn't go at all smoothly, and Russell got so low he again contemplated suicide. "I must get myself in hand," he wrote to her, "and I will. Till then I am not fit for you to associate with."[30] He took himself off to Cornwall to try to piece together the shattered pieces of his emotions.

For Ottoline, probably the most important event of the summer was her meeting with Joseph Conrad. When Henry James learned that she intended to go down to Conrad's house at Ashford in Kent, he was appalled. He paced up and down her drawing-room, telling her:

> *But, dear lady...he has lived his life at sea – dear lady...he has never met a civilised woman...No, dear lady, he has lived a rough life and is not used to talking to..."*[31]

...and he raised his arms to indicate the sort of woman he imagined Ottoline to be. She also told Desmond MacCarthy of her intended visit, and he advised her that, as Conrad saw few ladies of fashion, she should wear something unusual for the occasion. This was not difficult for Ottoline. But on arrival at Ashford she found Conrad to be a perfect gentleman, and she returned to London full of his praises, which she proceeded to sing to Russell, who was still feeling morose. On her recommendation he later went to see Conrad, and they became lifelong friends.

Back in London, Ottoline found the Russian Ballet had returned, and that Lytton had fallen in love with Nijinsky. He persuaded her to arrange an introduction, and bought for the occasion a new dark-purple suit and an orange stock, though he was terrified of uttering a single word in French (in which he was fluent). Delighted at finding "Nij" no eunuch, he sent him basketfuls of flowers at his performance of *Le Sacre du Printemps*. They even attempted a game of tennis one afternoon on the Bedford Square court, which must have been a sight to see. But before long his bedazzlement faded and he began calling him "that cretinous lackey". He spread mischievous stories about Ottoline's worship, describing her as "gaping and gurgling" over Nijinsky "like a hooked fish". (Later, in the early 1930s when Nijinsky's mental stability degenerated, Ottoline and Philip worked to found the Nijinsky Foundation to help support him and his family.)

Meanwhile, Russell had taken himself off to stay in Cornwall. But this had done little to sort out his feelings about Ottoline; and in August he went to Italy, sending back bitter letters. On August 10 he told her:

I can't help feeling that what makes you less useful than you might be is a kind of selfishness...I am very sorry you miss my letters so much. I have felt the need of not thinking too constantly about you...when I care for people I like to be with them; yet you would rather ruin my life and work than be very much with me.[32]

He became more and more desperate. He told her he had been flirting with a German woman, Liese von Hattingberg. While he was in this mood, Ottoline took the opportunity to break the news about his breath. He told her that he would get his teeth cleaned and see a doctor about his breath as soon as possible (his earlier fear of mouth cancer had long been dispelled).

In August, before going to spend a few weeks at Black Hall, Ottoline held a reception at Bedford Square for a group of African chiefs who were visiting London. One of them, Chief Odunta Labinjo, was particularly impressed with Ottoline, and later wrote from Nigeria sending her a parcel of native cloth and his photograph (taken at Harrods and copied by a native photographer in Lagos). He and Ottoline continued to correspond for several years. In September Ottoline and Philip had to go up to Burnley for a month, and there, to help relieve the boredom, Ottoline would spend Saturday afternoons watching the local soccer team. Her favourite player was a little red-haired youth named Moscrop, who was later one of the few conscientious objectors in Burnley. Another diversion was Gladstone League rambles on which Ottoline made friends with the girl mill-workers, one of whom wrote to her:

> *It is with great pleasure that I forward the [bed] cover I promised...Dear Lady Ottoline you must excuse me for being so long as I have had to do it in my spare time in the evenings and it has taken me rather a long time as work in the mill occupies all my time during the day; hoping it will give you much pleasure in receiving, as it does me in sending, I Remain "Yours an earnest Gladstone League Worker." (It was signed "Bessie Burrows".)*[33]

After Burnley, Ottoline left for Switzerland to join Julian who was recovering from a chest infection at a sanatorium there. After Ottoline arrived, she wrote to Norton asking him to join her, but he declined. Meanwhile Lytton had taken a country cottage near Marlborough from where he wrote asking how she was getting on: "An escapade with John? Or an amorous adventure with an ice-cream boy?"[34] He declined to spend Christmas 1913 with her because he had a prior engagement with Lamb. Instead he sent her a spoon dated 1759: "The year *Candide* came out".[35]

For Ottoline the year 1913 ended on an uneasy plateau. Lamb was gone and Russell, who was scheduled to visit America the next year, was beginning to stray. Where was she to go from here? London beckoned, but she felt she couldn't respond to it with all her heart. The country beckoned, but she feared it wouldn't be the answer to her problems. In February 1914 she wrote in her Diary: "For many months I have felt a dire loneliness that nothing will ever relieve. I seem to have tried everyone and found them all wanting...At one time I seem to have plunged into others' lives – Roger Fry, Lamb, Lytton, Bertie – but from some cause they all seem to have come to an end."[36]

That month the most severe crisis so far in her friendship with Russell occurred. It was over Bertie's continued flirtations with "the German woman", and some hard words were exchanged; after which Russell and Ottoline agreed to part. But on February 5 he wrote to her:

> *My dearest I can't bear that we should part with bitterness on both sides it is too dreadful after what we have been to each other...The longing for children has grown & grown in me, & the pain of not having a child by you has been terrible...When you spoke the other day, the bitterness of all the pain & hunger I have suffered became just too much & I couldn't bear it any more...I must break with you, or I shall be broken – & I must not be broken yet...You think I no longer love you & that is why I break. That is an ABSOLUTE MISTAKE. I have no wish of any sort or kind to have anything to do with any other woman, that was only an attempt to bear the pain.*[37]

For several weeks letters between them were almost formal, then she sent him a telegram and went to see him in his flat. Within days they were back on the best of terms; just in time for Russell's departure to the United States. On February 25 he wrote: "It is quite extraordinary how deep and strong the tie is between us – such storms one would have thought would destroy any tie – yet it always emerged as living as ever."[38] On March 19 he wrote from Harvard: "America produces a type of bore more virulent, I think, than the bore of any other country – they all give one exactly the same information, slowly, inexorably, undeterred by all one's efforts to stop them."[39] Also, the large number of spittoons he observed everywhere surprised him. He was unimpressed with his fellow academics: "They were all barbarians, but some, who had been to Oxford, accentuated their barbarism by a Common Room veneer. Ygh!"[40] The only consolations were a bright young student named T.S. Eliot; the money; and a young lady named Helen Dudley, who had written to him on his arrival in America inviting him to stay at her parents' home. Russell told Ottoline that he found himself falling in love with her, and that she had agreed to return to England to live with him. Russell broke the news in a letter to Ottoline:

> MY DARLING,
> This is the last letter before I sail – thank heaven. I am longing to be with you again my Dearest. When I started I assured you I should not have any adventure here but I have had one, a rather important one.[41]

He went on to tell her about Miss Dudley, including the information that they had spent at least one night together, and that she would be following him to England in a few months. He added: "I do not want you to think this will make the *smallest* difference in my feeling towards you, beyond removing the irritation of unsatisfied instinct." What Ottoline would think of this he would have to wait to discover on his return.

When Ottoline arrived back from another trip to Lausanne,

she began to enjoy London with newfound zest. That spring the capital seemed more lively and interesting than ever. Nijinsky was back; with his own troupe, having quarrelled with Diaghilev, who had opposed his recent marriage. Ottoline stood at the door of Nijinsky's suite at the Savoy, her arms full of flowers, waiting to greet him and his young bride. Ottoline's entertainments at Bedford Square that year surpassed even those of the previous two. She was also growing more interested in Vanessa Bell's husband Clive, a development Lytton wasn't very happy about. He wrote to him: "Your new intimacy with the Lady O. alarms me."[42]

Later Ottoline was to look back on her activities during that summer of 1914 with a certain awe. She had begun to live her own legend – the extraordinary Lady Ottoline Morrell, the *grande dame* who caused crowds to form around her in the streets; the Scarlet Woman whom the gossips liked to tear to shreds; the woman who knew everyone *intimately*. One entertainment followed another, with bewildering speed. She held luncheons and dinners and soirees,; spent weeks up in Burnley helping Philip; and still found time to go to the ballet and opera and meet everyone of interest in the capital. She wrote: "What fun it all was that summer. Everything seemed easy and light, as if the atmosphere had something electric and gay in it, imbuing anything that was done with a lovely gay easy quality absorbing from it the worry and care and fret."[43]

Ottoline had recently been appointed buyer for the Contemporary Art Society for six months; and with the money entrusted to her she bought a large farmyard scene by a young artist named Gilbert Spencer, whom Henry Lamb had introduced to her, along with Gilbert's brother Stanley. Ottoline and Philip went to the Spencers' home:

> *One lovely hot Saturday afternoon we went down to Cookham to see them, and found the old father and mother in their little house. A disused bedroom upstairs was used by the two artist brothers as a studio. They had more the*

appearance of two healthy red-faced farm labourers with their rough shocks of hair and teeth protruding in all directions...Stanley, the elder one, who was smaller in stature, was the more remarkable of the two, more of a genius, more intense, and slightly crazy.[44]

There were several other brothers, one who became professor of music at Cologne and another a lion-tamer. When Ottoline and Philip left they hailed a passing London taxi; a gesture that so astonished the whole Spencer family that, according to Ottoline, they "nearly fell backwards with their canvas shoes in the air".

In May Ottoline held her most ambitious entertainment yet. Some whispered it was her last bid to secure an under-secretaryship for Philip – and, if subsequent events hadn't ruined all chances of such an appointment, she might have been successful. That evening she surpassed even her previous self. Lytton told his brother James of some of the people he saw there: Asquith; Lady Howard de Walden; Henry James; the Walter Raleighs; and Sir Matthew Nathan. Lytton himself was scooped up by his hostess and planted on a sofa with the Prime Minister, who talked about the worsening situation in Ulster. "My head spun round and round at finding itself cheek by jowl with so many eminent persons," Lytton told Ottoline.[45] But such occasions were very exhausting, as Ottoline told E.M. Forster, who sympathised: "Yes those evenings must be nervous work, I wouldn't even entertain white mice, were two or three of them gathered together."[46]

Around June 10 Russell arrived back in London and Ottoline immediately set about reclaiming him. Before he went away she had told him their relationship would have to be entirely platonic. She now saw that this had been the root of all the trouble. So she re-established normal physical relations with him; 7an easier proposition now his bad breath, the result of pyorrhoea, had been finally cured by American dentists. Russell says in his autobiography: "Ottoline could still, when she chose, be a lover so delightful that to leave her seemed impossible."[47]

She had just over six weeks before Helen Dudley's arrival. She told Russell she quite understood what had happened; and he in turn told her that already he was growing less fond of Miss Dudley. He said it was partly the American's ardour and partly the quality of her writing that had enamoured him. Ottoline invited him to a party at Bedford Square and they went for long walks in their old haunt, Richmond Park. Ottoline found Bertie less possessive; and in July wrote in her diary: "I feel tremendously alive, and very happy."[48] Russell was delighted by Ottoline's new attitude and told her:

> MY DARLING LOVE,
> *I cannot tell you how full of happiness I feel or what complete joy it is now when we are together. It all seems so easy and natural – there is not a trace of the constraint which had grown up...I thought at first it was due to H.D. but I don't think so now. I think it is much more due to my teeth being all right.*[49]

Ottoline had won round 1 and was in a good position for round 2 when Helen Dudley arrived. But, as it turned out, she had no need to worry; events elsewhere were beginning to overtake questions of personal happiness.

Late in July Ottoline was at an afternoon party at Asquith's country home where the main topic of conversation was the assassination of Archduke Ferdinand. Afterwards she and Asquith went for a stroll by the river and she asked him what he thought might happen. He replied: "This will take their attention away from Ulster, which is a good thing."[50]

INTERLUDE
MY INTRODUCTION TO BLOOMSBURY

David Garnett – a generous host

DAVID GARNETT was one of my first interviews with someone (apart from Julian Vinogradoff) who had actually known Ottoline personally. By 1972 he was one of the two members of the inner circle of the Bloomsbury Group who were still alive (the other being Duncan Grant, whom I met later down at Charleston, in Sussex - see my Duncan Grant interview below). I was most fortunate to have had the opportunity to meet Garnett "in the flesh" (before he died in 1981).

I first visited him on the banks of the Thames at Chelsea where he was living on a houseboat belonging to his estranged wife, Angelica, the love-child of Vanessa Bell and Duncan Grant. David Garnett had been present at the birth of Angelica and had declared (so the story goes): "I think of marrying it. When she is 20, I shall be 46 – will it be scandalous?". Twenty years later, he did indeed marry her. Angelica later alleged in her autobiography *Deceived with Kindness* that she was unaware of Garnett's long homosexual relationship with Duncan Grant, nor was she aware that it was Duncan Grant, not Vanessa's husband Clive Bell, who was her father.

To reach the houseboat I had to negotiate a series of gangplanks along the river bank. Garnett, a robust-looking man in his early 80s, greeted me at the door of the houseboat wearing a well-cut tweed jacket and an affable manner. He ushered me inside. On the walls were paintings by (he told me) Vanessa Bell and Roger Fry. He settled me on a sofa in the comfortably-carpeted galley and asked if I would like a sherry. Expecting a sherry glass, I was surprised when he then poured two large ships' tumblers of alcohol. Still standing, he drained his glass, then opened the conversation by asking: "Would you like to hear what Ottoline's voice sounded like?" He placed his hand on the lapel of his tweed jacket, as if he were going to make a speech, and said: "You know the French painter, Derain? Well, Ottoline pronounced his name Derrrrrraaaaiiin...Derrrrrraaaaiiin," he warbled, his voice gliding over the painter's name, sounding like a cow mooing. This rendition of Ottoline's voice must have been a favourite party trick in Bloomsbury.

He invited me to come back again, which I did, on one occasion accompanied by our Australian artist friend, Paul Delprat, who enjoyed meeting Garnett and discussing post-impressionist art with him. Over the following months, Garnett (who soon went off to live in the French countryside) corresponded often with me. His last letter described how the rain was pattering through holes in the roof of his cottage into an array of pots and pans he had arranged on the floor.

He told me about Ottoline's affairs with Russell and the painters Henry Lamb and Augustus John (among others). He also told me: "I think before you start on your book, you should know about the skeletons in Ottoline's cupboard." What he revealed was crucial to understanding Ottoline's behaviour as it highlighted two crucial periods in her life, which I will explain below.

David Garnett was not only generous with his reminiscences (and his sherry), he also told me how to contact other people who might help me, such as Lady Pansy Lamb, widow of the painter Henry Lamb and a sister of Lord Longford ("Lord Porn"). I made a mental note to contact and visit them all.

CHAPTER 14
The Storm Clouds Break

Ottoline, by Lamb, in pensive mood

ON JULY 28, three days after the Asquiths' party, Austria declared war on Serbia. Two days later France's ally Russia mobilised, and on August 1 Germany declared war on Russia. If France, Russia's ally, went to war, Britain was treaty-bound to go to war too; and in London war fever swept the capital. Within the governing Liberal Party, however, there was substantial opposition to intervention in Europe; and one of the leaders of this opposition was Philip Morrell. On Saturday August 1 Philip and Ottoline went up to Black Hall, intending to spend the weekend there. But the news from Europe was so grim that on Sunday morning Philip decided to hurry back to try to help rally anti-war sentiment in parliament. Though it was the weekend, Bedford Square was crowded. Groups of young men were parading up and down the streets of Bloomsbury singing patriotic songs. On Monday August 4 Germany declared war on France.

Russell, who came from a leading Liberal family, travelled down from Cambridge to lunch with Ottoline, and discuss the madness descending all around them. Why people wanted war was a mystery to them both. Russell thought hatred of Germany (with which he had strong academic links) was the main reason. "And yet," he explained to her, "for once Germany is wholly disinterested and guided by honour."[1] Later Ottoline went to the House of Commons where Philip was preparing to make his protest heard. She waited while Sir Edward Grey, the Foreign Secretary, warned Germany that Britain would not stand idle if France or Belgium were invaded. Grey sat down to shouts of approval and a waving of order papers.

Hansard reported[2] that when Philip rose to speak there were hostile murmurs and cries of "Sit down" from all sides. England was being asked, he told the House, to go to war merely because Germany had insisted on its rights (angry Tory jeers of "Rights?"). They were being asked to go to war because a few German regiments might be marching across a corner of Belgian territory (more hostile jeers). The real reason, he believed, was not honour, but fear and jealousy of supposed German ambitions. If Britain went to war it would be just as much to preserve Russian despotism; and little love as he had for Germany, he had less for Russia ("Hear, hear"). Other radical Liberals voiced similar sentiments, while the Labour member for Merthyr Tydfil, Keir Hardie, said honour was always the excuse used to wage war; and a flimsy one it was too. Philip's Liberal colleague Arthur Ponsonby told the House that the previous night he had seen a band of half-drunken youths outside a great club in St. James's Street being egged on by members from the balcony. Such speeches, however, fell on largely deaf ears. Philip and Ottoline walked away from the House in despair.

That night, like bedraggled seagulls in a storm, a small group of anti-war MPs came to Bedford Square to wait for Grey's ultimatum to Germany to expire. At midnight it did, and the country was at war. Over the next day or so 44 Bedford Square became a rallying point for the pacifist cause. All who gathered there were bewildered at the way their world – that civilised world for which Leonard Woolf and others had held out such high hopes – was collapsing. It was as if some highly contagious disease were sweeping the world, and Ottoline and Philip and a handful of others were the only ones immune. A week or so earlier Russell, aghast at the way Europe was drifting towards war, had begun collecting signatures around Cambridge to a statement against English involvement. On August 1 he told Ottoline he had not found a single person of any party or class who was in favour of the war: "*All* think it folly and very unpopular."[3] But four days later things had suddenly changed. Bertie had a letter from Mrs. Whitehead in favour of war; and he discovered that most of the dons who had signed his petition had had abrupt changes of heart. "We are terribly alone," he told Ottoline.[4] She herself detested the drum-beating and rabble-rousing of the warmongers, and was horrified that Europe could throw aside the moral and human code that had taken centuries to build. War was an ugly, evil force that would destroy everything fine in civilisation; and she opposed it as a Liberal, as a woman, and as a Christian. Above all, she was repulsed at the glorification of brutality. "Why is it," she asked, "that yesterday we called death by another man's hand murder or manslaughter, now it is called glorious bravery and valour?"[5]

Philip's August 4 speech in the Commons had been brave. He knew it might end his political career and all that that meant to him, yet still he spoke. And ruin his career it did. From now on most of his parliamentary colleagues treated him as a pariah. Yet up in Burnley his stand was at first welcomed, and the day after his speech the local Liberal branch met and the secretary told Philip that his speech had been perfectly correct and patriotic.

Philip had offered to come up and explain his views, but the secretary told him not to bother, because they were sure that in the end his view would be justified. Indeed, several committee members confessed they now thought more of Philip than before. The meeting passed a vote of confidence in him. However, their letter telling him of this asked him to keep the vote secret. It was an augury of what was to come.

Of the many sordid aspects of the war, one which particularly affronted Ottoline and Philip was a rabid campaign, fomented by the press, to stir up anti-German feeling in the country; as a result of which the Royal family changed its surname, Saxe-Coburg, to Windsor. Kindergartens became "infant schools", and German nationals were hounded and harassed. In individual cases of persecution brought to their notice, Philip and Ottoline did what they could to help. They also joined a society which supplied money to wives of interned aliens. One German wrote to thank Ottoline:

> *I beg to thank you very much indeed for your great kindness in helping us as you did and for the great interest you took in my family and myself.*
>
> *I have been trying hard to get some work or other, but impossible – they even refused to let me address envelopes in the big banking concern I used to be in*
>
> *I am afraid I have lost my brother. He was officer on one of the ships in Chinese waters.*
>
> *Dear Madam will you please accept the kindest regards from my family and the heartiest thanks from*
> *yours very respectfully,*
> MAX GIELAND [6]

The war caused deep rifts between Ottoline and some of her friends. Hilda Douglas-Pennant was only one of the many who no longer called at Bedford Square. Ottoline's warm relations with Asquith cooled, and a friendship with his daughter Violet nipped in the bud. A few months earlier in May, Violet had written to Ottoline: "I long...to be with you beyond all people. Goodbye dearest."[7] But on August 29 she wrote: "I haven't been because I heard you didn't want to see anyone who was in favour of the war – including me."[8]

Philip and Ottoline were now even more at odds with their families. Portland's son went off to join the cavalry, while Portland and his wife themselves did all they could to aid the war effort. Philip's relations were equally patriotic, and hard words were exchanged whenever Ottoline and Philip visited Black Hall. Of Ottoline's men friends, Henry Lamb was most influenced by the call of King and Country. He abandoned painting to return to his medical studies and become an army doctor. A bad knee prevented Augustus John from joining up, but he eventually did his bit in Lord Beaverbrook's band of war artists. E.M. Forster volunteered as a Red Cross observer in Egypt. Even Lytton, who was later to make a dramatic pacifist stand in court, made an effort, knitting scarves for the soldiers; although he quipped that he was learning German "in case the other side wins". Yet, taken as a whole, most of Ottoline's circle shared her convictions. An example of this anti-war feeling was expressed by Ottoline's young friend Norton, who wrote to her: "I find this war horrible – horrible in fact, horrible in imagination; in retrospect & anticipation, past present & future, hateful & hateful."[9]

Bloomsbury was fervently anti-war, and over the next two or three years Ottoline and members of the Bloomsbury Group were closer than at any other time. The war also brought Ottoline and Russell nearer. For the moment, Bertie had no thought for anyone else; certainly not Helen Dudley, who turned up in London with her father in mid-August. Ottoline wrote: "She came, poor girl, panting with high hopes and ardour, expecting B to welcome her with passionate love, and unfortunately the war had intervened." Or rather the war and Ottoline had intervened. She handled this latest peccadillo of Bertie's with consummate skill. Miss Dudley and her father thought that Russell was intending to put them up prior to a speedy divorce from Alys and a marriage ceremony soon after. But the Russell who greeted them was not the Russell they had said goodbye to in America a few months earlier. He told Miss Dudley bluntly that his attitude had changed, and plans of marriage would have to be postponed. He enlisted Ottoline's help to explain to the Dudleys that the war had so devastated him that all previous plans were void. But he cautioned her: "I don't think she realises *quite* what you and I are to each other, and now there is no reason why she should. It would be very unfortunate if she thought you had anything to do with my change toward her."[10] Ottoline agreed to do what she could and went to see the Dudleys, reporting back to Russell that she liked Miss Dudley. She recalled later: "She was an odd girl of about 27, rather creeping and sinuous in her movements; she had a large head, a fringe cut across her forehead, a very long chin, rather underhung, and thick lips."[11]

Ottoline felt sorry for the way Miss Dudley, through no fault of her own, was being treated, and once she discovered the girl was no threat, she went out of her way to be sympathetic. After Mr Dudley returned to America, she invited Miss Dudley to stay at Bedford Square. No sooner had she moved in than the two women began swapping stories about Russell. Miss Dudley brought out some of Bertie's love-letters which, to Ottoline's dismay, were couched in terms familiar to her. He'd actually repeated the same phrases he had used in letters to her! At first this upset her, and she told Russell so. He replied: "My Darling Love – I am very sorry that H.D. goes on telling things that bother you – *do* try to stop her – there is no use in her telling them and you really know all about it now."[12] Next, Ottoline complained (rather petulantly) that his letters to Miss Dudley were more passionate. He replied by showing her a letter he wrote to her in March 1912 when he was feeling particularly amorous. Yet it still rankled. "Why should one mind," Ottoline asked herself, "but one does...I feel somehow it is *too* discriminating. The same form, the special offering, to be used to two people as unlike as Helen and myself."[13] But Ottoline's anger did not last long. She recognised it was partially her own fault: "*Apres tout*, I have never given him enough, and so I cannot complain."

Despite the less than enthusiastic welcome she had received in London, Helen Dudley did not give up Russell without a fight. One day he and Ottoline were in his Russell Chambers flat when she knocked at the door (though Russell assured Ottoline he had forbidden her to visit him there). Ottoline recalled: "We heard knock, knock, knock, and hands banging on the door. B refused to open, as he was sure it was she, and I imagined I heard her panting outside."[14] The following day Miss Dudley told Russell she had heard breathing sounds when she knocked and he had to admit he had been in. Gradually, however, Miss Dudley realised Russell was a lost cause and began turning her attentions elsewhere. Unfortunately she happened to choose men whom Ottoline regarded as her preserve: Gilbert Cannan, for one. Worse, she conducted her operations in Ottoline's own drawing-room, amidst clouds of cigarette smoke. Very soon Miss Dudley was packed off to stay with some relatives of Philip's in the country. There Russell would sometimes visit her. (Later she was diagnosed with multiple sclerosis and returned to America, where she died insane.)

Meanwhile the war news from France was so painful for Ottoline that she could hardly bear to read it. It hurt both ways: the fighting offended her pacifist beliefs, yet each Allied victory made her feel guilty that she could not bring herself to join in the patriotic fervour. Nevertheless, she was not deaf to appeals to relieve the suffering in Flanders. John Masefield wrote to her asking for a gift towards £3,500 to equip a field-hospital in France. Ottoline complied, and Masefield wrote back: "Thank you very much indeed for your most kind generous help. It is most good of you to have got me all this money."[15]

Other things upset her too, in particular the sight of young women throwing themselves into war work. Against them she felt a sharp resentment that they should be gaining their freedom by freeing men to be sent out to the front as cannon-fodder. Ottoline tried to assuage some of her conscience by taking in Belgian and French refugees. Among these was a young Belgian girl, Maria Nys, who soon became almost one of the family at

Bedford Square. A plump, pretty girl, Maria developed an adolescent crush on Ottoline, following her around like a young calf. Bloomsbury spread a rumour that Ottoline conducted a Lesbian relationship, not only with Maria, but with certain other young women. However, though she was often seen with her arms around these women, and sometimes kissing them, there is no evidence that Ottoline ever had any Lesbian inclinations.

In November 1914 Ottoline started up her Thursday "at homes" once more. These gatherings had always been somewhat out of tune with what the rest of the world was doing, but now the difference became almost grotesque. While the battle of Ypres raged in northern France, Ottoline and her friends dressed up; played charades; and danced abandonedly to noisy tunes pumped out by Philip on the pianola he had bought back in 1913. As the guests gathered round to sing and dance, Philip treadled out such tunes as "If You Were the Only Girl in the World" and other popular songs of the day. One evening Hilaire Belloc came round to Bedford Square to see Ottoline; but he could not make his knocks heard because of the noise of the gaiety inside, and had to go away.

Later Ottoline asked herself why they had all been so cheerful when they should have been sad. It wasn't that they were heartless about the death and suffering across the Channel; rather their unhappiness was so great that any diversion was welcome, especially in the company of those who were sympathetic. That company now included some recent additions. Several came from the Bloomsbury sphere: an economist Gerald Shove, Francis Birrell (Augustine's son), and David Garnett. Another three came from the Slade School, and were brought to Bedford Square – wearing masks – by Mark Gertler, a young Jewish painter Ottoline had taken under her wing. The trio trooped into Ottoline's drawing-rooms, unmasked, and were identified as Dora Carrington, Barbara Hiles, and the Hon. Dorothy Brett. Carrington was Gertler's great love, and Brett, who was almost deaf, was the daughter of Lord Esher, one of the Empire's most powerful political figures. All three wore corduroy trousers and had their hair cut short in the Slade-style, which was why Virginia Woolf called them "cropheads". They were a liberated trio, and Carrington and Brett (they preferred to be addressed that way) were to become close friends of Ottoline. Other young people came and went, some of them not personally invited by Ottoline. Sometimes these rowdy invaders left behind cigarette butts and empty bottles strewn around Ottoline's elegant drawing-rooms, to her chagrin.

Meanwhile the war had at least one happy consequence: it forged a bond of friendship between Russell and Philip; and now Bertie could come and go at Bedford Square as he pleased. The cheerful goings-on there were for Russell a blessed relief from the tragic events in France. He even joined awkwardly in the jollifications. While Philip provided the accompaniment, the various guests would step out as the spirit moved them. Duncan Grant bounded around like Nijinsky. Russell pumped his legs up and down "with an expression," noted Ottoline, "of surprised delight at finding himself doing such an ordinary human thing as dancing". Lytton stepped out in a courtly minuet with his brother James and sister Marjorie.[16] Ottoline herself would put on her lace mantilla and do wild gypsy dances with Augustus John. On other occasions Ottoline would give over her drawing-rooms to concerts by two talented Hungarian sisters, the D'Aranyis, who played the violin.

And so 1914 drew to a close. It had not been a happy year for Ottoline and some of her friends, especially in the Bloomsbury purlieu. She had lost many who used to be regulars at 44 Bedford Square. But there were also some gains. She and Philip were happier together; and her friendship with Bertie was on a more equable basis. Russell felt this too. "I *do* feel the difference in you," he told her. "And in me there is a *great* difference. I have a really firm resolve to avoid philandering in future."[17] In October he had returned to Cambridge for the new academic year, yet found lecturing on mathematical logic a futile occupation, and so devoted most of his time to non-war or anti-war causes.

At Christmas he visited destitute German aliens with

Ottoline. On December 26 he told her he was still firmly resisting the temptation to philander. He had had a visit from the D'Aranyi sisters, who invited themselves to dinner and only left at 10.30, when he put them out. He told Ottoline that Titi D'Aranyi had been particularly flirtatious, and it had taken all his resolve to deflect her resolute assault. But Ottoline suspected it was only a matter of time before he would succumb to philandering. She herself was now almost 42, and beginning to feel, if not old, certainly weary. The move to Garsington was drawing near and the future seemed uncertain. Yet just around the corner was a meeting with a man who was to assume an importance in her life, at least for a brief period, subsidiary perhaps only to that of Russell and Lytton Strachey (as the three most-important men in her life – see Interlude below).

INTERLUDE
Lunch with Duncan Grant

A rare snapshot of a young Duncan Grant (taken at Charleston), when he was the cynosure of so many Bloomsbury eyes

IT WAS David Garnett who arranged for me to meet (himself apart) the last of the Bloomsburies, the painter Duncan Grant, who had played such a central role in the lives of so many of Ottoline's fellow guests at Bedford Square, Garsington, and finally at Gower Street.

A highly-talented post-impressionist painter, print-maker, textile designer, and set-designer, Duncan Grant was inducted into Bloomsbury by his cousin, Lytton Strachey, and he became a major figure in the Group after befriending Vanessa and Clive Bell.

Despite Grant's homosexuality, Vanessa Bell and Duncan Grant had an affair, and in 1918 she bore him a daughter Angelica (whom, as mentioned above, David Garnett was to marry). Vanessa continued to live and work with Grant for the rest of her life, although he had returned to his homosexual ways.

I took the train down to Firle in Sussex, where I had been invited by Grant to have lunch with him at his home, Charleston, the country retreat where he and Vanessa Bell had based the famous Omega Workshop, painting furniture and designing fabrics in a distinctive and ultra-modern, post-impressionist style.

Charleston, the home of Duncan Grant in Sussex, and once a major Bloomsbury rural retreat

By the time I met him, Duncan Grant was in his mid-eighties. He greeted me at the door clad in a white artist's smock, with grey curls under a white straw hat. We sat down to lunch at a wooden table still covered with the vestiges of an Omega pattern, and talked about Ottoline.

Because of his long-standing friendship with Roger Fry, who had had a serious split with Ottoline, he and Vanessa Bell had been especially caustic about Ottoline. But, like David Garnett, he now stressed the positive side of her, talking about her championing of modern art and the way she had helped so many young artists, like himself.

Then he asked if I would like to see his latest paintings. They were vivid and vibrant pictures, mainly of a handsome young black man, who suddenly appeared in person in the doorway leading from the kitchen. Duncan was obviously very fond of him. After lunch, Duncan offered me a cigarette, and although I had given up smoking, I accepted. Who could refuse such an offer from this great old Bloomsburian?

CHAPTER 15
The Working-class Lad from Nottingham

Ottoline – Lawrence's "Great Lady in Bedford Square"

OTTOLINE probably first heard Lawrence's name before October 1914, when Gilbert Cannan lent her Lawrence's first and third novels, *The White Peacock* and *Sons and Lovers*. However, they may in fact have met earlier, at a Thursday-evening gathering in Bedford Square perhaps around August 13, soon after Lawrence returned to England from Italy.[1] His books, with their vivid descriptions of the Midlands countryside, made a deep impression on her, reviving memories of her own childhood at Welbeck, in the heart of Nottinghamshire. But it was not just nostalgia that attracted her to Lawrence. She discerned in his writing an insight and empathy that intrigued her, and touched her artistic sensibilities.

In 1914 Lawrence was 29, and had recently married Frieda, Baroness von Richthofen, a member of a German aristocratic family. Two years earlier, in May 1912, she had deserted her English husband Ernest Weekley (who was Lawrence's Professor of French at Nottingham University College), abandoning her three children in order to run off, almost-literally (they in effect eloped), with this penniless, working-class miner's son. That provenance alone would have attracted Ottoline's interest. Frieda, who before marrying Weekley had moved in progressive German intellectual circles, had found herself bored in suburban Nottingham, and her husband more than usually dull. (On their wedding night she perched naked on top of the wardrobe in their bridal suite in order to surprise him when he came through the door. Ernest Weekley, a paragon of Victorian virtues, neither appreciated the gesture, nor responded to its promise.) Frieda found domestic life in Nottingham so tedious she would run up-and-down the street; after dark, and in her nightgown. In the event Frieda was to prove more than a handful for the sensitive Nottinghamshire miner's son, who was destined to become one of literature's greatest figures. Now Lawrence and his new wife (they had been married only a few months before in early 1914, after Frieda's divorce came through) were living at Chesham in Buckinghamshire.

As soon as Lawrence arrived at Bedford Square, Ottoline decided he was someone she could, and should, help. Well aware that the support and appreciation of a someone like her would mean a lot to him. she resolved to become his patron. He himself was becoming known as an up-and-coming writer (having been earlier "discovered" by Ford Maddox Ford, the editor of a London literary magazine). He already knew Ottoline's friends Gilbert Cannan, David Garnett, and Mark Gertler, and in August that year he had made his first sortie into "the dress-suit world" at a dinner party at the H. G. Wells's. After also reading Lawrence's book of short stories, *The Prussian Officer*, Ottoline was determined to meet him, and she asked Gilbert Cannan to bring him to dinner at Bedford Square in late December. Her impression was of...

> *...a slight man, lithe and delicately-built, his pale face rather overshadowed by his beard and his red hair falling over his forehead, his eyes blue and his hands delicate and very competent. He gave one the impression of someone who had been undernourished in youth, making his body fragile and his mind too active.*[2]

They took to each other immediately. Ottoline was just the type of woman who fascinated Lawrence. All his life he had an obsession with the idea of a relationship between a man of the people and a woman of rank; the *Lady Chatterley* theme. His marriage to Frieda had fed this obsession, without satisfying it. Now, here was an aristocrat on an even grander scale: the sister of a duke, no less; and a patron of the arts as well. Lawrence was bedazzled, and Ottoline no less impressed with him.

For many years she had been seeking someone who had the sort of intuitive feel of life she had always hoped existed; a prophet, a messiah in direct touch with the true essence of the universe. For a time she believed that Bertie might have been such a prophet. Instead, he seemed more interested in sex; and his god – reason – was to her just a graven image. Lawrence, the working-class lad from Eastwood, was much-more promising material. Moreover, he was a genuine man of the people, someone in the mould of Burns and Blake; a mind with fresh, virile ideas – better ideas than those others of her own class.

After their first dinner, Ottoline wrote to him, telling him how much she enjoyed his stories, and inviting him to come and see her again when next he was in London. He replied, saying he should like to come; but poverty precluded regular trips to the capital. "I shake down the thermometer of my wealth and find it just nearly at zero," he told her.[2] In this first letter he began to expound his beliefs.

> *One wants the appreciation of the few. And it isn't faute de mieux either. I am no democrat, save in politics. I think the state is a vulgar institution. But life itself is an affair of aristocrats. In my soul, I'd be as proud as hell. In the state, let there be the Liberte Egalite business. In so far as I am one of many, Liberte, Egalite – I won't have the Fraternite. The State is an arrangement for myriads of peoples' living together. And one doesn't have brothers by arrangement.- In so far as I am myself, Fierte, inegalite, Hostilite. It doesn't sound very French, but never mind.* [3]

He couldn't respond to an invitation to lunch at Bedford Square on January 14, but he managed dinner on the 25th, when he came with Frieda and was seated next to E.M. Forster. After dinner more people arrived, and there was dancing (it was one of Ottoline's Thursdays). His hostess, wearing her lace mantilla, pranced around with Duncan Grant until he caught his toe in her train, and both crashed to the floor. Undeterred, she left the bruised and shaken Duncan to recover and took Gertler as her next partner. Later she talked to Lawrence about Duncan Grant's paintings, and he expressed a wish to see some. So Grant invited Lawrence, Frieda, Gertler, and Forster to tea in his studio the following afternoon. There Lawrence took it upon himself to lecture Grant on what was wrong with his work; an intimation that Lawrence and Bloomsbury were not going to get on. Lawrence told Ottoline about the afternoon:

> *I have burnt your letter about Duncan Grant. (He looks as if he dissipates, and certainly he doesn't enjoy it. Tell him to stop.) We liked him very much. I really liked him. Tell him not to make silly experiments in the futuristic line with bits of colour on a moving paper. Other Johnnies can do that. Neither to bother making marionettes – even titanic ones. But to seek out the terms in which he shall state his whole.* [43]

Lawrence invited Ottoline down to Sussex to see his new accommodation at Greatham. On January 27 she arrived and sat at the long refectory table while he cooked lunch and poured out a torrent of talk. "It was impossible not to feel expanded and stimulated by the companionship of anyone so alive,"[5] Ottoline wrote later. "Indeed he seemed to possess a magnetic gift of quickening those he talked to and of making them blossom with new ideas, new enthusiasm, new hopes." In spite of his vehemence, she found him gentle and tender. "I felt when I was with him as if I had really at last found a friend," she wrote. Each of them saw in the other possibilities of a new and better world. Lawrence's intuitive philosophy appealed to Ottoline: "He seemed to open up the way into a Holy Land." Lawrence told her he wanted her to be the hub of this new world.

> *I want you to form the nucleus of a new community which shall start a new life amongst us – a life in which the only riches is integrity of character. So that each one may fulfil his own nature and deep desires to the utmost, but wherein the ultimate satisfaction and joy is in the completeness of us all as one. Let us be good altogether, instead of just in the privacy of our chambers, let us know that the intrinsic part of all of us is the best part, the believing part, the passionate, generous part. We can all come croppers, but what does it matter.*[6]

He hoped that his utopia – what he later called his "Rananim" (the name was derived from a Russian lullaby sung by his friend Koteliansky ["Kot"]) – would be the new hope of the common people. It would be based "not on poverty, but on riches, not on humility, but on pride, not on sacrifice but upon complete fulfillment in the flesh of all strong desire". This sort of talk struck a chord with Ottoline. In fact, it was just the sort of thing that Bertie seemed to be looking for. So she decided to take the first opportunity to bring the two of them together.

Russell had certainly been a worry to her lately. The war was eating into his soul and he was extremely melancholy. In addition he had fallen from his high resolve not to philander and had embarked on a half-hearted affair with his new secretary, Irene Cooper-Willis. When Ottoline, who had earlier encouraged Irene to work with Bertie, discovered what he was up to she confronted him and he tried to explain the situation: "I think I may easily come to have a *very* great affection for Irene – not a very passionate feeling, but one which might give happiness and be free from pain of passion."[7] At first she encouraged him in this dalliance, but in the end she couldn't bear to see him slip away to a rival, and decided to rein him in. As usual he responded immediately, and they spent several happy days (and nights) together, after which he wrote to her: "Last night had *everything* – there was a note of wildness of Hey nonny no, men are fools that wish to die."[8] By now Russell probably realised that the one certain way to engage Ottoline's attention was to make her jealous; so, unconsciously or not, this was the ploy he was to often adopt over the next year or so.

In February Ottoline took him down to Sussex to meet Lawrence, who had professed trepidation at meeting the great philosopher, telling her: "I am a bit scared of Mr Russell – I feel as if I should stutter."[9] However, Ottoline's hopes that they would get on well together were soon justified. Yet, once they got talking and arguing, it was Lawrence who had the upper hand. He had the convictions; while Russell was rudderless. Soon Lawrence began to feel that in Russell he might have found the perfect male friend he had always sought. Russell, in turn, was awestruck by Lawrence. As he and Ottoline drove back to London, he said to her: "He is amazing, he sees through and through one...He is infallible...He sees everything and is always right."[10] The friendship that flared between these two passionate, rebellious men was like a firework, intense and bright; but liable to burn out suddenly. But while it lasted, it served as an outlet for Russell's pent-up-passion and mental frustration. "He can give me a vivifying dose of unreason,"[11] he told Ottoline. Early in March Lawrence wrote to Ottoline confessing a hastening of love for Russell. He told her he felt they were all young and that a great cause lay ahead of them.

Around February 11, Lawrence wrote to enlist Ottoline's aid in persuading Frieda's former husband to bring her children to Bedford Square to see their mother. He told her: "I wish you could tell him you are Lady Ottoline – the sister of the Duke of Portland." Again and again he harked back to this theme, telling her:

> It **is** rather splendid that you are a great lady. Don't abrogate one jot or tittle of your high birth: it is too valuable in this commercially-minded mean world...I really do honour your birth. Let us do justice to its nobility: it is not mere accident. I would have given a great deal to have been born an aristocrat.[12]

Ottoline did her best to get Earnest Weekley to bring his children to meet their mother; but Weekley was impervious to her blandishments, and he declined to come to 44 Bedford Square. For her part, Frieda was not as enthusiastic as her husband about his new friendships with Russell and Ottoline. She went along with the relationship with Ottoline only because she thought the contact would be useful in helping her to see her children. In February she wrote to Koteliansky: "The Ottoline is a nice simple person."[13] This misjudgement was indicative of her lack of perception about Ottoline and her friendship with Lawrence. Ottoline, too, tended to dismiss Frieda as unworthy of a mind such as Lawrence's. To her, a Bentinck, Frieda seemed a rather blousy hausfrau. Meanwhile Ottoline and Lawrence exchanged gifts. She sent him an opal pin and he gave her a box he had painted himself, and adorned with a phoenix, the symbol of his new society which was to arise from the ashes of the old world.

Ottoline had told Lawrence that when she and Philip took over Garsington in a month or so, one of the outbuildings might be set aside as a cottage for Frieda and him. Lawrence readily accepted this offer. Garsington would be the headquarters of his Rananim; a bucolic haven where there each member of the new utopia would live a communal life, and fulfil their natural and deep desires. On February 22 he wrote telling her he wanted to hear about "the cottage, the cottage, the cottage."[14] On March 6 Russell took Lawrence up to Cambridge to show him off to the other dons; but the visit was not a success, by any means. Russell reported to Ottoline: "He hates everybody here, as was to be expected."[15] He took Lawrence along to see Keynes, whom Russell regarded (Wittgenstein apart) as the finest mind in Cambridge. Although it was 11am, Keynes was still in his pyjamas; which, Lawrence thought, was corrupt and unclean. "Lawrence has quick, sensitive impressions which I don't understand, tho' they would seem quite natural to you," Russell told Ottoline. "I love him more and more."[16] Lawrence was particularly put off by the atmosphere of sodomy he discerned among some of the dons. In this Russell agreed with him: "Lawrence has the same feeling against sodomy as I have; you had nearly made me believe there is no great harm in it, but I have reverted; and all the examples I know confirm me in thinking it is sterilising," he told Ottoline.[17] Keynes, however, thought Lawrence's antipathy was due to his jealousy of Bloomsbury; Ottoline's "other world". Lawrence wrote to Ottoline about his visit:

To hear these young people talk really fills me with black fury...There is never for one second any outgoing of feeling and no reverence...I will not have people like this – I had rather be alone. They made me dream of a beetle that bites like a scorpion. But I killed it – a very large beetle."[18]

Lawrence's instinctive reactions nevertheless contained a kernel of truth. Russell agreed with him about Bloomsbury. Underneath, there was something slightly creepy about them. Yet Lawrence's hyper-sensitivity could cut both way; and when he took his knife and began to dissect Ottoline, she wasn't quite sure how to react. He wrote to her:

Why don't you have the pride in your own intrinsic self? Why must you tamper with the idea of being an ordinary physical woman – wife, mother, mistress? Primarily you belong to a special type, a special race of women: like Cassandra, and some of the great women saints. They were the great media of truth, of the deepest truth: through them...the truth came – as through a fissure from the depths and the burning darkness that lies out of the depth of time. It is necessary for this great type to re-assert itself on the face of the earth. It is not the salon lady and the bluestocking...but the priestess, the medium, the prophetess. Do you know Cassandra in Aeschylus and Homer? She is one of the world's great figures, and what the Greeks and Agamemnon did to her is symbolic of what mankind has done to her since – raped and despoiled and mocked her, to their own ruin.[19]

All through March Lawrence was eager to move to Garsington. Later that month he wrote to Ottoline full of enthusiasm over the plans for his cottage: "And we cuckoos, we shall plume ourselves, in such a nest of a fine bird."[20] He protested that the rent Philip had suggested for the cottage was far too low. In the same letter he refuted her fear that she wrote dull things, telling her: "They are not dull. The feeling that comes out of your letters is like the scent of flowers, so generous and reassuring." Frieda by now was beginning to get annoyed at the amount of time Lawrence was spending with Ottoline. Nor was she excited about the idea of being Ottoline's tenant at Garsington in a converted cottage in what was called the "monastic building". To Frieda this smacked of serfdom. She and Lawrence were poor, Ottoline was rich; and to a woman with as fiery a temper as Frieda, and a fellow aristocrat to boot, this rankled. Ottoline's attitude towards her didn't help. Lawrence had already begun to suggest he should come to see Ottoline without Frieda. "There is no reason why we should always be a triangle,"[21] he told her.

Lawrence sent a letter to Ottoline full of ideas for how to further renovate the cottage.[22] But soon Ottoline and Philip too began to have second thoughts. Philip wrote to Lawrence in mid-April telling him that the cost of converting the suggested "monastic" cottage would be high. Shocked, Lawrence replied to

Philip saying: "My dear Morrell, Of course the costs for the monastic house are impossible beyond all consideration."[23] He went on to mention that Ottoline had told him that there were three rooms in the gardener's cottage which would be available, and perhaps he and Frieda could rent them for a while. "*Please* don't think any more about *any* alterations or hired workmen on our account — a little furniture in the three rooms is more than enough," he concluded. The same day he wrote to Kot: "Probably we shall not have the Lady Ottoline cottage. In my soul I shall be glad. I would rather take some little place and be by myself. We will look out for some tiny place on the sea."[24] He added: "Thank heaven I shall get out of the Lady Ottoline cottage. I cannot have such a place like a log on my ankle. God protects me and keeps me free."

The preparations for moving to Garsington had exhausted Ottoline, and in May she decided to take a few days' holiday at Buxton in Derbyshire. However, before leaving Bedford Square a disturbing incident occurred. Returning one day from a walk, she was sitting at her dressing-table when the Belgian refugee girl Maria walked into the bedroom, looked at Ottoline reproachfully, and murmured: "*J'ai pris du sublime.*"[25] Then she started to sway alarmingly. It seems that she had been looking forward to going to Garsington, but Ottoline, feeling oppressed by the girl's devotion, had grasped the opportunity to deposit her with some friends in London. Maria had reacted by swallowing some mercuric poison. Ottoline ran to the door and called her maids, Millie and Edith, who tickled Maria's throat while Ottoline telephoned for a doctor. After Maria recovered it was agreed that she should go to Garsington after all. When Lawrence heard of the suicide attempt, he placed the blame on Ottoline:

We were shocked about Maria: it really is rather horrible. I'm not sure whether you aren't really more wicked than I had at first thought you. I think you can't help torturing a bit. But I think it has shown something – as if you, with a strong, old-developed will *had enveloped the girl, in this will, so that she lived under the dominance of your will: and then you want to put her away from you, eject her from your will. So that was why she says it was because she couldn't bear being left, that she took the poison, and it is a great deal true.*[26]

He concluded: "Why must you always use your *will* so much, why can't you let things be, without always grasping and trying to know and to dominate." This upset Ottoline very much and was to have a much more serious echo subsequently. She told Russell about Lawrence's outburst, and he tried to soothe her, saying that although she had a strong will, she didn't use it tyrannously. He told her that Lawrence too had a strong will, adding perceptively: "It is only that his theory doesn't recognise will, because like most tyrants, he dislikes will in others."[27]

So Ottoline departed for Buxton in a sad mood, mulling over the changes in her life, and the uncertainties before her at Garsington. Lawrence, realising he had hurt her, tried to patch things up. "Don't take any notice of my extravagant talk – one must say something," he said. He then upbraided both her and Russell for being unhappy:

Why, then are you both so downcast, both you and Russell? What ails Russell is, in matters of life and emotion, the inexperience of youth. He is, vitally, emotionally, much too inexperienced in personal contact and conflict for a man of his age and calibre... Tell him he is not to write lachrymose letters to me of disillusion and disappointment and age: that sounds like 19, almost like David Garnett. Tell him he is to get up and clench his fist in the face of the world.[28]

Lawrence told her that he was looking forward to a "council of war" with Russell and the Cannans at Garsington. "Don't be melancholy," he told Ottoline, "there isn't time."

INTERLUDE
"Why don't you look into Lawrence?"

AS WE WERE about to leave Austin, the director of the HRC, Dr Warren Roberts, called us in to his office and asked what we planned to do after Ottoline. At this very early stage in my research – assisted by my husband Rob – I had no further plans. Warren Roberts, a distinguished Lawrence scholar (he was Lawrence's bibliographer), had recently been chosen as the joint-editor of a projected complete edition of Lawrence's works to be published by the Cambridge University Press (Lawrence was due to come out of copyright in 1980). He was also to co-edit the first volume of Lawrence's letters (Lawrence was a prolific letter-writer, and the CUP edition of his letters was to run into eight volumes).

Roberts was casting around for possible candidates to edit some of Lawrence's works for the CUP edition. Having two Australians working at the HRC "under his nose", he had called us in to suggest that, when Ottoline was finished – and we presumably returned to Australia – we might look into the novel Lawrence wrote there in 1922, *Kangaroo*. (The HRC was about to acquire the holograph manuscript of *Kangaroo*.) What we might find could also help other putative editors, should *Kangaroo* or Lawrence's time in Australia impinge on their work.

When in 1975 my biography of Ottoline went off to the publishers to be printed, we took up Warren Roberts' suggestion and began to look into Lawrence's time in Australia. In November 1975, after we returned to Sydney, our Lawrence research started in earnest. (The fact that we had read Lawrence's letters to Ottoline helped our research.) Now, however, our roles were reversed. Rob undertook the main research and ultimate writing, while I took on the subsidiary assistance-and-research-role. Little did either of us anticipate, however, that this project was to take more than a further four decades to complete. It started, however, with Ottoline in Texas in 1972. (*D.H. Lawrence's 99 Days in Australia,* by Robert Darroch, was published in 2016.)

CHAPTER 16
Escape to the Country

Ottoline starts her new life at Garsington

DESPITE Lawrence's pep talk, Ottoline was still feeling low as she travelled down from Buxton on May 17, 1915, to start a new era in her life. Philip had been living at Garsington for several months, managing the farm and overseeing the renovations to the main house. He met Ottoline at the local station, and as they drove the few miles to Garsington, Ottoline looked around at the countryside that was to be her home for the next 14 years.

It could almost have been a Constable landscape...tall elms;

drowsy cows munching the spring grass; fields dotted with wildflowers; and, nearby, a rise around which a small village and an old church nestled. As they neared the house, the church broke out into a peal of bells. The high-gabled manor, two storeys plus attics, was built of grey Cotswold stone, with mullioned windows, and surrounded by 200 acres of garden and farmland. Double wrought-iron gates opened straight off the road into a small gravelled courtyard leading to the front door. But the real front of the house was around the other side, looking across the Berkshire Downs. A large garden sloped away through a group of ponds to an orchard, beyond which were open fields and an unobstructed view to Wittenham Clumps.

It was one of the most beautiful houses in Oxfordshire, built originally in the reign of James 1 for some monastic order. However, it was said that its ponds were mentioned in the Doomsday Book, and that the land on which it was built had belonged to the son of the poet Geoffrey Chaucer. For some years the house had been decaying. Inside, the wooden floors were rotten, the window-frames loose, with some panes broken. The whole house was in desperate need of repair. But as Ottoline eyed the oak panelling on the walls, she knew the house would respond to sympathetic renovation and restoration. After tea, in the warm twilight, Ottoline and the gardener wandered around the grounds discussing what needed to be done to the neglected garden. Ottoline, with her innate artistic sense and her long delight in Italian formal gardens (such as her Aunt Louise's garden in Florence), suggested which trees would be planted and where new terraces could be constructed. The church bells were still carolling, so she asked the gardener if they practised every day at this time. He looked at her curiously, then said: "Why, they're ringing to welcome you and Mr. Morrell, My Lady."[1]

The first few weeks slipped quickly by. Each morning Ottoline would get up early; don overalls; breakfast off toast and coffee; then set to work around the house. A team of builders under the direction of a Mr. Davis arrived; and while Philip made himself useful on the farm, Ottoline, Mr. Davis and his workmen, assisted by Ottoline's maids, gradually transformed the old house into something both exotic and comfortable. Ottoline's vision now flew beyond the unorthodox decor of Bedford Square into a new realm of Bakst and Beardsley. The centrepieces were to be the two large drawing-rooms on the ground floor. Though the rooms were beautifully panelled in oak, Ottoline decided to defy tradition and paint one room a vivid Venetian red and the other sea-green. For the hall she devised a colour scheme of dove-grey overlaid with varnish to reflect the red curtains, in imitation of a winter sunset. Then the furniture and furnishings started arriving from Bedford Square…Chinese boxes and cabinets; Philip's blue-and-white china; Chelsea and Worcester porcelain; Samarkand oriental rugs; silk hangings and cushions; lacquered screens; and Philip's pianola. These were distributed round the house while Ottoline decided where to hang her Gertlers, Johns, Conders, Lambs, and Duncan Grants. The overall effect was one of opulence; though Ottoline and Philip, lacking abundant funds, were obliged to scrimp on certain things, having to put linoleum on the bathroom floor instead of the more-expensive ceramic tiles.

Ottoline reserved her most ambitious plans for the grounds. A series of terraces would descend to the main pond, thence to a series of smaller ones below it. Ottoline had the biggest of the ponds enlarged into a small, rectangular lake; round which yew hedges were planted. Putti lined its perimeter and a larger statue of a cherub was erected on an artificial island in the centre of the lake. After the hedges grew, Gothic arches were cut through so people swimming or punting or just strolling could look out and see the blossoming trees in the orchard beyond. New flower beds were built and planted with stocks, zinnias, sunflowers, phlox, and snapdragons; while the herbaceous borders were decked out with poppies, foxgloves, roses, and lilies; and a rambling rose climbed over a stone wall. Into this arcadian setting Ottoline, with a final flourish, planned to introduce some peacocks to strut and preen, much as Lawrence had imagined he and Frieda might have done had they been installed in the cottage in the grounds.

Shortly after Ottoline moved to Garsington, Julian, aged nine, joined her parents. She had a governess now, a young Swiss girl named Juliette Baillot (called Mademoiselle). As May lengthened into June, Ottoline found herself drifting languidly through her rooms; trailing her long fingers through the bowls of potpourri; swirling her taffeta skirts across the now-polished floorboards; merging into dappled shadows; then walking out into the sudden sunlight of the lawn, over which a huge ilex tree leaned; while a latch-gate in a stone wall led to the (projected) large flower-and-vegetable garden.

When most of the work was in hand, all her friends were clamouring to visit her and see her new home. Yet she felt strangely paralysed. She thought Garsington wasn't ready to receive guests, and she found excuses not to invite them. There was only one bathroom, although a second one was added later at the top of the house. What would Lytton's critical eye make of the house? Would anyone want to come all the way from London to see her? And what was she creating at Garsington – was it a home for Philip, herself and Julian? Or was it something more; an oasis perhaps, isolated not only from war, but from all material values; a place where artists, writers and other sensitive people might relax and express themselves in a congenial atmosphere. This was what she was hoping for; what she had been striving for. Yet still she was assailed by doubts and uncertainties. Meanwhile, her friends were missing her. Desmond MacCarthy wrote: "1 passed your home in Bedford Square the other day & plumbed the hole your absence makes in London."[2]

It was Lawrence who shook her out of her lethargy. He was still bubbling over with plans for the utopia that he and Ottoline and their friends might establish at Garsington. He wrote to her, impatiently demanding to know when he could come down and see the house for himself. Though he had turned down the offer of the cottage, he still had hopes of some other, cheaper accommodation, as Ottoline had dropped vague hints that there might be a gardener's cottage or something similar for them. Russell was also anxious to come. It had been almost a month since he had seen her, and he was feeling lonely.

To satisfy them both, Ottoline decided that her first event at Garsington would be a house-warming party, timed to coincide with her 42nd birthday on June 16. She invited not only Bertie and the Lawrences, but Mark Gertler and the Cannans too. At first everything went smoothly. Lawrence was charming and sympathetic, and Frieda behaved herself. Everyone put on overalls and helped put the finishing touches to the red drawing-room, Russell being sent up a ladder to paint the ceiling beams; while Lawrence, who had a bent for decorative work, outlined the red panels with the straightest and finest of gilt lines. But while everyone else mucked in, Frieda sat on a table swinging her legs, mocking the others' efforts, and offering advice on what curtains Ottoline should hang. "She has a terrible irritant quality," Ottoline said later, "and enjoys tormenting, and she liked to torment me because I was taking trouble to make the house nice."[3] Little wonder Frieda was jealous. She had no home; Ottoline's was magnificent. Also Frieda harboured an active fear that Lawrence, for whom she had thrown up everything, might yet leave her, perhaps for Ottoline. After all, Ottoline had attracted a man like Russell; and Lawrence seemed a much weaker reed. Ottoline herself thought that Frieda was envious of the admiration Lawrence attracted. She once overheard Frieda say, "I am just as remarkable as Lorenzo."[4] On the last night of the Lawrences' stay, Frieda's insecurity boiled over, and she and Lawrence had a violent quarrel in their room, with objects heard being thrown around. In the morning Lawrence came downstairs looking whipped; and Frieda stomped off in a temper back to London alone.

After she had gone, Lawrence stood in the hall, pathetic and cowed, his thin frame stooped, unable to decide whether to follow or not. Ottoline and Philip advised him not to; but in the end he capitulated and went off to return to Hampstead, where he and Frieda had recently taken a flat. Frieda told everyone she was "having ructions" with "the old Ottoline", and to one friend she wrote: "She will say such *vile* things about me – and I think it's so mean, when she is rich and I am poor and people will take such a mean advantage of one's poverty." She said that at Garsington she had felt an outsider; "a Hun and a nobody."[5] But such outbursts from Frieda were not uncommon, and Ottoline had not seen the last of them. Lawrence certainly had no wish to terminate their friendship, and the day after his return from Garsington he wrote to Cynthia Asquith: "I want you to know Lady Ottoline. So few women – or men – have any real sense of absolute truth irregardless of circumstance."[6]

Meanwhile Lawrence and Russell were still cooperating, despite the fact that Frieda believed – quite rightly – that Russell's opinion of her was not high. While Lawrence was working on the final draft of *The Rainbow*, he and Russell argued over their personal philosophies, trying to come to an agreement on some mutual plan for helping mankind. One day in July Lawrence took Russell to Holborn to meet some of his closest friends – Koteliansky, John Middleton Murry, and the New Zealand-born writer Katherine Mansfield. Lawrence and "the Murrys" had first met in 1913 when Murry was editing a small literary magazine. The two couples had found they had much in common. Both Katherine and Frieda were foreigners; neither couple were married at that time; and they all four harboured a desire to make a mark in the world. At Lawrence and Frieda's wedding in 1914, Katherine was bridesmaid and Murry best-man. But Russell's reaction to Lawrence's friends was almost identical to Lawrence's reaction on meeting Russell's Cambridge friends. "I thought Murry *beastly*," he reported to Ottoline, "and the whole atmosphere dead and putrefying."[7] Later the same day Russell and Lawrence went to the zoo, then on to Hampstead, where they argued into the night, Russell doing his best to hammer some logic into Lawrence's wild theories about blood consciousness. At last his superior debating technique prevailed, and Lawrence became discouraged, and said he would go off to the South Seas to bask in the sun with six native wives. When next Russell called, Lawrence was writing a long letter to Ottoline, and when Frieda saw what he was doing, she snatched it from him and ripped it up. Undeterred, Lawrence sat down again and wrote another, and this one he managed to get it safely to the post-box. Russell told Ottoline that Lawrence had been *very* angry and had said to Frieda: "Come off that, lass, or I'll hit thee in the mouth."[8]

Throughout the summer Russell and Lawrence held regular conferences to thrash out a series of lectures on human relations. Full of enthusiasm, Lawrence wrote to Ottoline, asking her to preside at their joint lectures, telling her: "You must be the centre-pin that holds us together, and the needle which keeps our direction constant."[9] Garsington would be their headquarters, and there they could meet – himself, Ottoline, Russell, Katherine, Middleton Murry, the Cannans – and knit themselves together. It would be like something out of Boccaccio…"That wonderful lawn, under the ilex trees, with the old house and its exquisite old front – it is *so* remote, so perfectly a small world to itself."[10]

As yet, Lytton hadn't been invited to Garsington, an intimation perhaps that he had slipped slightly in Ottoline's order of precedence. Throughout May and June she put him off, saying that the renovations were incomplete. All the while Lytton was agog with her descriptions of the new house. On June 8 he wrote: "I imagine wonder – ponds, statues, yew hedges, gold paint."[11] At last, in the second week in July, he arrived to see for himself, accompanied by Duncan Grant and Vanessa Bell. Vanessa had recently split up from her husband Clive and gone off to live with Duncan; while Clive had struck up a friendship with Lytton's cousin Mary Hutchinson.

Lytton seemed to be impressed, and afterwards sent Ottoline an enthusiastic letter telling her how much he had enjoyed his stay, and inviting himself back a fortnight later. But in another letter posted the same day, this one to David Garnett, he was less enthusiastic, saying: "The house is a regular galanty-show…very like Ottoline herself, in fact – very remarkable, very impressive, patched, gilded and preposterous."[12] The contrast between the two reactions was an indication that Lytton's attitude to Ottoline was also changing. That he liked Garsington there is no doubt, yet he felt he should be more cynical about it to others, particularly his Bloomsbury friends. On Lytton's second visit later in July he found more things to complain about. Ottoline was fond of lapdogs, and these apparently made a special point of pestering him. This time he had come with Clive Bell and Mary Hutchinson, together with two of the Slade cropheads, Barbara Hiles and Faith Bagenal. While the cropheads joined Maria, Juliette, and Julian scampering around the lawn, Lytton, Clive, Mary Hutchinson, and Ottoline sat under the ilex tree discussing life and art. Though to Lytton's mind it was like a scene from Watteau or Fragonard, the cursed pugs spoilt it. In a letter to David Garnett he wrote: "Since beginning this [letter] I've already had three visitations from the pug world."[13] He had felt horribly lonely, he told Garnett, and usually sat apart from the rest, dozing over Swift's correspondence. But his thank-you letter to Ottoline was in a different vein. He didn't know if it had been the air, or the vegetables, or her conversation, but his visit had done wonders. "I find even my vigorous health taking on new forces, so that I am seen bounding along the glades of Hampstead like a gazelle or a Special Constable."[14] In September he returned again, spending a pleasant week; though, as he reported to his sister Pippa, there were still too many pugs for comfort, plus the added hazard of being waylaid by some budding poetess, and forced to listen to her verse. But to Ottoline he wrote saying that not even angels were equal to the task of describing how much he had enjoyed himself. Should she hear a faint sigh among the bushes, she would know it was his departed spirit, still fluttering about.

Later that summer, Lawrence, anxious to re-establish friendly relations after his last departure from Garsington, invited Ottoline up to London to see the Hampstead flat. Frieda was obviously regretting her outburst at Garsington, and was trying to make amends. Lawrence at Hampstead was as friendly as ever, if rather depressed. He walked with Ottoline on the Heath and told her he needed to escape, to get out of England and go somewhere clean and new. He had decided to travel to the United States to write for Americans. He would go to Florida where his health would improve, and where he could set up his Rananim. He begged Ottoline to go with him. If, however, she didn't fancy Florida, then to some Pacific isle, where he would be king and she could be queen. Ottoline didn't warm to this proposal. "He rushes about with one idea after another like an excited dog, barking and barking at an imaginary enemy," she wrote in her *Memoirs*.[15] So she returned to Garsington, thankful her own utopia was nearer at hand.

Throughout 1915 the war seeped deeper and deeper into Ottoline's existence. In April 1915 a combined British, French and Australasian force had landed in the Dardanelles in Turkey, and with it were two of Ottoline's brothers, Lord Charles Bentinck and Lord Henry Bentinck. Their presence there gave Ottoline's anti-war feelings a personal edge, for although she had drifted away somewhat from her family, she nevertheless felt anxious about them, particularly 52-year-old Henry who, unlike Charlie, was not a professional soldier, and had only joined up in a fit of quixotic patriotism. Henry contracted dysentery and, after almost dying, was invalided back to England. Charlie also returned wounded to England, but later went back to continue fighting. He was wounded again and sent home to recuperate in a nursing home, where in 1917 he and Ottoline had an unexpected reunion.

Most of the latter half of 1915 Ottoline spent relatively quietly at Garsington, mainly overseeing the final renovations to the house, and getting the garden in order. Visitors came only occasionally; and when they did, they were mostly old friends like Lytton and Augustine Birrell. Cambridge came in the person of Maynard Keynes, who wanted somewhere to convalesce after an appendix operation. The Sangers, also devoted pacifists, also came.

Meanwhile relations between Lawrence and Russell were again showing signs of strain. Mainly to blame was Lawrence's habit of telling truths that were too close to home. Like Ottoline, Russell felt guilty about his lack of patriotism, and Lawrence concentrated his arguments on this weak spot. In midsummer Russell wrote to Ottoline: "I am depressed partly by Lawrence's criticisms. I feel a worm, a useless creature."[16] Lawrence continued to bore in. The plan for a series of joint lectures foundered for want of an agreed prospectus. Then there was an argument over a co-authored (with Lawrence) book Russell planned to publish in conjunction with his own social reconstruction lectures. Finally, in September, Lawrence wrote Russell a scorching letter that broke the spell. Ottoline reported that, after reading it, Russell was stunned, and sat without moving for a whole day. In the letter Lawrence accused Russell of being a super-war-spirit. "What you want," he wrote,' "is to jab and strike, like the soldier with the bayonet, only you are sublimated into words." He also alleged that Russell "was full of repressed desires which paraded themselves in the sheep's clothing of peace propaganda." He told him:

> *I would rather have the German soldiers with rapine and cruelty, than with your words of goodness...The enemy of all mankind, you are, full of the lust of enmity. It is not the hatred of falsehood which inspires you. It is the hatred of people, of flesh and blood. It is a perverted mental bloodlust. Why don't you own to it.*[17]

And he concluded: "Let us become strangers again, I think it is better." Russell recalled later that for some time after receiving the letter he contemplated suicide. He recovered, however, and though he and Lawrence resumed their correspondence, their friendship was to all intents over.

One reason for Lawrence's rabid attack was his own insecurity. In October *The Rainbow* was published, and instead of meeting with acclaim, it was universally reviled. Ottoline was almost the only person to write to him praising it. A Sunday newspaper critic took it into his head that it was obscene and urged its suppression. Within days of publication a magistrate had banned it and copies were seized by the police and burned. Philip Morrell tried to get the ban lifted and asked several questions in Parliament about the matter, but to no effect. This blow reinforced Lawrence's desire to quit England; and while he explored possible travel arrangements, he worked with Middleton Murry on a new magazine, which he pressed on Ottoline at 2/6 a copy.[18]

That autumn she again invited Lawrence to Garsington and he came several times, at least once accompanied by Frieda. On one visit he helped Ottoline plant iris bulbs around the pond. He also built a small summer-house for the garden, cutting and nailing the wood with his deft fingers, and planting climbing roses around it. When it was finished he stood back and exhorted the roses to grow with their "essential and primitive rose-force."[19] Later some of Ottoline's guests mocked the rustic structure, calling it "suburban"; but she always saw that it was propped up and preserved, long after her friendship with Lawrence had faded. In the evenings at Garsington Lawrence read poetry by the fire and told stories about his early life. On one occasion he decided they would all act in a version of *Othello* he adapted for the occasion. Inspired by his enthusiasm, Ottoline, the Cannans, Julian, and Maria all dressed up and once more played out Lawrence's obsession of the affair between a noble lady and an outcast male. (Lawrence, decked out in an Arabian coat and large straw hat, characteristically took the part of the tragic Moor.)

In mid-November Lawrence was still planning to go to Florida (on a cotton boat), and he repeated his invitation to Ottoline to join him. Again she declined, sending him instead £30 to help with expenses. She also wrote to George Bernard Shaw asking him for £5 for the same purpose. Shaw complied, though reluctantly. "I suppose I cannot refuse," he said, "but as the love of money grows on me you cannot imagine what a pang it costs me."[20] Ottoline also wrote to Eddie Marsh saying: "I wonder if you would help me in an effort I am making to collect a sum of money for Lawrence – to enable him to go to Florida. Poor fellow, he is miserably depressed and hopeless and he feels that there is no opening for his work here and that he must go forth to new fields. It seems an awful pity that we should lose him as he is a real genius – isn't he? – but I don't think he would live through the winter if he remained."[21] The week before Lawrence was due to depart he went to a farewell party given by Dorothy Brett and several more of his disciples. Ottoline wasn't present, but she did crop up as a topic of conversation. They pulled her to pieces, Brett recorded – so much so that she cried out, "Stop! We must leave her just one feather!" But Lawrence, again according to Brett, was more malicious, saying: "We will leave her just one draggled feather in her tail, the poor plucked hen!"[22] The next day Lawrence wrote to Ottoline: "Don't trust Brett very much: I think she doesn't quite tell the truth about you."[23]

But Lawrence didn't go to America; the Home Office denied him the necessary clearance; and late in November he was back at Garsington again. Two other guests were a tall young man from Oxford, Aldous Huxley, and a young musician, Philip Heseltine. Ottoline was busy getting the house ready for a big Christmas party for the village children. Lawrence found piles of "exquisite rags" heaped everywhere, waiting to be transformed into party outfits. It was like some Eastern bazaar, he decided.[24] Lawrence had bought a new suit, and Frieda had on a new coat and a hat which Lawrence had created from bits of fur. Both Ottoline and Lawrence enjoyed these visits; and even Frieda was feeling less out of things now. Ottoline still fascinated Lawrence. "She is a big woman," he told Cynthia Asquith, "her whole effort has been spent in getting away from her tradition, etc. Now she is exhausted."[25] He felt Ottoline was like an old tragic queen.

Some odd people were to be found at Garsington in 1915, usually as a result of a casually dropped invitation from Ottoline. A Japanese dancer called Itow came for a week in summer. He spent his time fishing in the pond while Maria stood nearby watching him with big eyes. Later a Chilean painter named Guevara, a friend of Duncan Grant, came; but all he could be induced to talk about was boxing – not one of Ottoline's favourite subjects. A more interesting guest was Charles Gore, the Bishop of Oxford. Ottoline had a way with prelates; and Gore, who was a trifle fey, began to make regular calls. He even helped bring in the harvest, and the sight of Ottoline, clad in a large hat and flowing skirts, and the local bishop, plus England's greatest philosopher (Bertie also helped) bringing in the sheaves, caused some amusement among the local villagers. An old lady, a regular churchgoer, felt it her duty to warn Gore of the company he was keeping. Wasn't he in danger of compromising himself, being seen with such controversial people? "Oh, but I like her so much," the bishop replied.[26]

During most of autumn Russell was almost a permanent guest. Ottoline prepared a small flat for him in Home Close, a large cottage across the road from the manor house, furnishing it for him and filling it with flowers. Between his lecturing commitments, he would travel up to Garsington and spend several days, or several weeks, resting and writing his latest book. It was a restful existence, but one still fraught with traumas. The Lawrence business still disturbed him; the war was a constant nagging worry; and his relationship with Ottoline remained unsettled. He still hungered after her, but mostly she was cool to him. With him in permanent residence, she didn't need to bestir herself to keep his interest. He, on the other hand, felt frustrated having Ottoline so close and yet so distant. But at least he could talk to her and get some of his troubles out of his system. Ordinary mortals he couldn't talk to, he told her, because "I feel I am talking baby language, and it makes me very lonely".[27] Before Christmas he left to return to Cambridge, where his antiwar views were causing increasing disquiet.

Ottoline was almost glad of Bertie's absence at her Christmas festivities. She convened her biggest house-party yet, and almost every bedroom was full. There was Clive Bell; Lytton; Keynes; the philosopher George Santayana; Middleton Murry; Lord Henry Bentinck; Vanessa Bell (and two of her children),; plus Marjorie and James Strachey. Ottoline was determined to make this Christmas the brightest and best ever. The entertainments included games of backgammon; a charade entitled Life and Death of Lytton; and a large tree hung with gifts. The crowning event was a party in the large barn for the villagers and their children. Ottoline conducted proceedings with effortless style. To break the ice, she grabbed a kitchen-maid and twirled spiritedly round the floor with her. Then everyone joined in the dancing and games. "I suppose it's her aristocratic tradition that makes her able to do it,"[28] Vanessa in a letter to Roger Fry commented, adding that in contrast Philip had made a rather stingy spectacle of himself by dividing up one and a quarter chickens among nine adults and three children. Lytton was also impressed with Ottoline's performance: "It takes a daughter of a thousand earls to carry things off in that manner," he told his mother.[29]

The Lawrences were also absent from Garsington that Christmas. They had decamped for remote Cornwall, where they had taken a cottage in the village of Higher Tregerthen near Zennor, where the cost of living was much cheaper than in Hampstead. They invited Ottoline to Cornwall. She had been planning to go in January, but another row between Frieda and Lawrence intervened. It seems that Heseltine, the young musician acquaintance of Lawrence, was to blame. He had been at Garsington when Frieda and Lawrence were not, and, as at the Brett party, the topic of absent friends came up, with Ottoline apparently airing her views about Frieda. Heseltine later went to visit Lawrence at Higher Tregerthen and let something drop, and Frieda dragged the rest out of him. She was livid and wrote a most abusive letter to Ottoline. Ottoline in turn wrote to Heseltine reprimanding him. He replied ingenuously that he had merely been truthful, telling Ottoline: "After living with the Lawrences for several weeks, I have come to the very definite conclusion that Mrs. Lawrence has been most unjustly maligned behind her back. She has known this for some time past and, very naturally, she is unhappy about it. Am I, therefore, to blame for trying to help her mend matters?"[30]

Ottoline thought he was. At any rate the visit to Cornwall was off, and the atmosphere between Cornwall and Oxfordshire was cool for several weeks. Before long, however, relations were restored; and Ottoline resumed her flow of gifts to Lawrence; books, a counterpane she herself had embroidered, and (more usefully) cheques. For, since the suppression of *The Rainbow* and the subsequent obloquy it engendered, Lawrence's financial problems had been worsening. He was also suffering recurrent ill-health, the early symptoms of the tuberculosis that would eventually kill him. Ottoline renewed her previous offer of accommodation at Garsington, and sent him boxes of food. In return he sent her a green bowl and a copy of part of his new philosophical treatise (which became his *Study of Thomas Hardy*). He told her he particularly liked the embroidered counterpane, though, unable to decipher her handwriting, he called it "the countrypair". He told Ottoline that Frieda and he would often lie on it and discuss its colourful design.[31] Little did Ottoline realise, however, that as Lawrence lay on her "countrypair", what in fact he and Frieda were discussing was his new novel, in which Ottoline would feature as a hideous caricature of herself; the bitter snake-goddess, Hermione Roddice.

AT GARSINGTON

D.H. Lawrence at Garsington

(l to r) Dorothy Brett, Lytton Strachey, Ottoline, Bertrand Russell at Garsington

Virginia Woolf in the garden at Garsington

Lytton Strachey and Virginia Woolf in the garden at Garsington

Garsington viewed from the pond

Ottoline with the 6th Duke of Portland

A sylvan dance at Garsington

Ottoline inspecting her flower-beds

Bertrand Russell, Maynard Keynes and Lytton Strachey share a joke in the sun

CHAPTER 17
Sticking Pins Into Ottoline

Alas, everything in Ottoline's garden wasn't lovely

RUSSELL's love for Ottoline cooled further during the winter of 1915-1916. He hadn't enjoyed his stay at Garsington in autumn, and his absence at Christmas was not surprising. At an unhappy meeting in November bitter words were exchanged, mainly about faults each saw in the other's character. The real trouble was that Russell was not prepared to be a kept-poodle at Garsington; while Ottoline would not agree to come and see him regularly in London. On November 10 he wrote: "It will be some time before I can make myself believe that you do not hate me – please don't be *froissee* if I am a little shy for some time."[1] Later in the month he threatened suicide again. Russell also had other emotional problems on his mind. His former student T.S. Eliot had recently arrived from America, and Russell put him up in his Russell Chambers flat. Eliot was now married and scratching a precarious living teaching. His young wife Vivienne (she had changed her name from Vivien) was a flighty creature with a tendency towards instability, and already the marriage was showing signs of strain. An inveterate fisher in other people's troubled waters, Russell decided to take them under his wing, providing both accommodation and financial support. He told Ottoline: "I am every day getting things more right between them."[2] But, almost inevitably, he was becoming emotionally involved with Vivienne, and in January he broke the news that the pair of them would be going away for a week's holiday together, although he assured Ottoline his motives were entirely honourable; he was merely giving the woman a holiday away from her husband, who had been ill. It would all be "quite proper". What Ottoline thought of this idea isn't recorded; but she was probably quite pleased. It would keep Bertie occupied.

But Russell's conscience continued to nag him. From the holiday resort he had chosen he wrote to explain further. It was merely a question of health, he assured Ottoline. He himself detested the place. Vivienne appealed to him as a child in pain would, and so on. The holiday had even helped him understand why he was oppressive and tiring. "It is really a clash between artistic and inartistic," he ventured. Vivienne, like Ottoline, was artistic, and she too found him oppressive.[3] For the next few months matters drifted along. Russell spent quite a lot of time with Vivienne, and wrote Ottoline only a few scrappy notes. In March he declined her invitation to come to Garsington, pleading a previous engagement. He also tried to explain what attracted him to Vivienne. It wasn't lust, he said, she merely brought out his latent paternalism. There had been, he conceded, moments when he had been tempted to make love to her, but these had passed. In any case, Vivienne did not want it. He assured Ottoline that it was she whom he really wanted: "My whole soul cries out for you, but I must not listen."[4] Ottoline wrote back sympathising. By now she knew these introspective moods of Bertie. On her part she assured him she loved him, and that he could be confident of that, for she wasn't perfect either. He replied: "You are nearer to perfect goodness than anyone I have ever known."[5]

But the problem of Vivienne Eliot was not at the forefront of either Ottoline's or Russell's thoughts in the early months of 1916. That place was reserved for the question of conscription. If Ottoline, Philip, and Russell had been opposed to events in 1914, they were even more averse to the thought of forcing people against their will to go out to France to be thrown against German machine-guns. Philip and Russell actively opposed conscription, as did most of Bloomsbury, many of whom would be liable for call-up. But it was no use. Under the threat of another khaki election, Asquith was compelled in January 1916 to put through the first Conscription Bill; making all unmarried men liable for compulsory service. But no sooner was the Bill enacted, than the militarists were demanding universal conscription. A few months later, Asquith caved in again, and a second Bill was passed conscripting married men too. From then on opposition to conscription by Ottoline and her friends took the form of aiding conscientious objectors. Philip, still a solicitor, offered to appear at the tribunals set up to hear their cases. Russell became a leading member of an anti-conscription organisation called the No-Conscription Fellowship, and Lytton, Clive Bell, and several others of the Bloomsbury Group were also active in it. Ironically it was Philip – safely above call-up age – who was first to suffer for his stand. He voted against the January legislation, and this landed him in serious trouble with his "supporters" in Burnley. On February 8 he went up to defend himself. At a meeting of the Liberal Association he began on a personal note: he could have wished for a happier circumstance to remind him the date was his 14th wedding anniversary. He said he understood the political problems in Burnley, but he could not put party before principle. Conscription was what you would expect of the Prussians, not Liberal Englishmen. The Association decided to do nothing at present; but Philip was warned that if feeling in Burnley hardened further, his position would be precarious.

Ottoline felt helpless in all this. She gave moral support to Philip and Russell and anyone she knew to be in trouble, and she used her friendship with Asquith to try to influence him. Also she took any opportunity that came her way to seek out and foster those examples of sensitivity and culture which had gone by the board with the declaration of war. One morning in January 1916 she found, in an unlikely place – among the war news and propaganda in *The Times* – a small poem entitled "To Victory (By a Private Soldier at the Front)." It began:

> *Return to greet me, colours that were my joy*
> *not in the woeful crimson of men slain,*
> *But shining as a garden…*

In these lines, signed "S.S.", Ottoline found an echo of her own feelings, and she decided to discover whom this young poet was. She wrote to *The Times* asking whom "S.S." might be. Edmund Gosse, the paper's literary critic and erstwhile dinner guest of Ottoline's, replied that "S.S." was a charming, simple, and enthusiastic young man named Siegfried Sassoon, who was not a private soldier, but a lieutenant in the 1st Battalion Royal Welsh Fusiliers, and who had sent Gosse several poems composed in the trenches in Flanders. Gosse urged Ottoline to write directly to Sassoon, which she did. Several weeks later Sassoon wrote back thanking her for her letter. He told her that the battlefield was not the harsh landscape she and others imagined; but that it could be beautiful, if one had the eyes to see it. He spoke also of the English countryside he loved, and where he used to ride and hunt. He promised to send her a book of his verses. In due course Ottoline received the small volume, together with a photograph of a handsome young officer. She wondered if she would ever see him in person, or whether he too would be blown to pieces.

At the beginning of March Ottoline travelled up to London to attend one of Bertie's lectures, and to give Lytton moral support at his forthcoming conscientious-objector tribunal appearance. She stayed with Philip (who was now living separately in London) at Bedford Square, part of which they had sublet, and part retained for their occasional visits. Lytton was delighted that his chief patron and confidante was back in residence. "I shall fall on the green door's neck like a long-lost friend," he told her. On March 7 he appeared at a pre-tribunal hearing, which recommended to the full tribunal that he be conscripted. While waiting for the final tribunal verdict, Lytton accompanied Ottoline to a range of events and functions in the capital, as Lytton reported to Duncan Grant:

> *Yesterday there was a curious little party at Maynard's, consisting of her ladyship, Duncan with a cold, Sheppard with a beard, James and me. There she sat, thickly encrusted with pearls and diamonds, crocheting a pseudo-Omega quilt and murmuring on buggery.*[6]

Many of Ottoline's friends came to visit her in her improvised boudoir at Bedford Square. Lytton observed with awe the constant stream of visitors received by Ottoline in "exactly-timed *tête-à-têtes* – like a dentist." The principal event of the week was Bertie's anti-war lecture, which was attended by an odd assortment of people: Ottoline and Philip; the Sangers; Clive Bell; Gertler; Vernon Lee; various other pacifists; and – to everyone's surprise – Ottoline's brother Lord Henry, who turned up in military uniform. Despite Lord Henry's valour in going off to fight, his views on many things were similar to Ottoline's. He was the brother most close to her and he enjoyed visiting her, especially from 1916 onwards. Usually he had to confine his visits to occasions when his wife was away, for she was hostile to

Ottoline – perhaps she still resented Ottoline's "stealing" Axel Munthe away from her at Grosvenor Place. The speeches were equally odd – Vernon Lee gave a discourse about a cigarette case; and someone else talked about arts and crafts being a cure for war. Eventually Russell had to call a halt and deliver his own speech, after which he joined Ottoline and Philip at Clive Bell's for dinner. The next evening Ottoline and Philip dined at a Soho restaurant with Russell and the Eliots. It was Ottoline's first meeting with Vivienne Eliot, and (predictably) she was not impressed. As they walked away from the restaurant, Vivienne headed Bertie off, linked arms with him, and generally made a display of their intimacy. Ottoline was not amused.

Ottoline didn't wait for Lytton's tribunal appearance – it was thought its unfavourable verdict was a foregone conclusion – but returned to Garsington, taking Bertie and Lord Henry with her. Philip stayed up in London to attend the hearing as chief character witness for Lytton, and there heard Lytton deliver his celebrated reply to the question of what he would do if he saw a German soldier trying to rape his sister ("I should try and come between them").[7] The case was adjourned for a medical examination, which was held a few days later and which declared Lytton medically unfit for any sort of war activity. The whole thing had been a grave strain on him, and he hastened down to Garsington to recover. Ottoline was most solicitous, and Lytton reported back to Virginia: "I lie about in a limp state, reading the [Plato's] Republic, which I find a surprisingly interesting work. I should like to have a chat with the author."[8]

On Sunday March 20 Henry Lamb's friend Anrep turned up at Garsington, dressed in the uniform of a Russian army captain, accompanied by two fellow officers. The once gentle and naive Anrep had turned into a great red-faced, brutish fellow, puffed up with pride over his glittering uniform. He had left his wife Junia, who had returned to Russia, and now he was fancy-free. He spent most of the day strutting around Garsington trying to impress Maria, and jumping over stiles to show off his legs. As Anrep left, Sir John Simon and two of his daughters arrived.

Simon was a lawyer and a leading Liberal minister who had recently spoken out against conscription. Despite the views they shared, Ottoline considered him insincere, and consequently failed to turn her full charm on him; a failure made more embarrassing by the fact that she was suffering from temporary loss of hearing. All through afternoon tea Maynard Keynes kept poking her in the ribs and saying: "Sir John is talking to you Ottoline."[9]

At Easter, Ottoline invited a large number of people to Garsington, and several more dropped in uninvited. Bloomsbury was particularly well-represented, with Molly MacCarthy, Clive Bell, Mary Hutchinson, Norton and – of all people – her old friend and sometime-lover Roger Fry. Obviously Ottoline's wartime friendship with Bloomsbury was helping to thaw old feuds. The weather was lovely and there were picnics in the wood; long walks in the countryside; and prolonged conversations under the ilex tree. On Easter Monday a large car arrived and Ottoline suddenly realised the Prime Minister had descended on them. While Philip showed Asquith's wife Margot and daughter Violet over the house, Ottoline took the opportunity to buttonhole Asquith in her boudoir and talk to him about conscientious objectors. She described the scene in her *Memoirs*:

> *I started by saying, "You know I am a rebel! I am passionately in sympathy with the conscientious objectors."...He asked many questions and seemed impressed and sympathetic. I was very frank and "explicit"...He on his side abused Military People. After this rather nerve-racking conversation was over, we relapsed into sentimentality, and talking over old days, when he used to come and see me in "My Tower" in Grosvenor Place.*[10]

Yet in a letter to Lytton (who had spent Easter with the Woolfs) Ottoline gave a rather different account of the occasion: "It was indeed a hurly-burly I made prostitute love with PM after having made *a hard clear* serious concise statement of my C.O. case."[11] An even more lurid version came from Vanessa Bell: "According to Mary [Hutchinson] there was love-making everywhere from the pugs and the peacocks to Ott and the Prime-minister – everyone except Philip."[12] Roger Fry reported to Vanessa that the weekend had been amusing, and Ottoline had been very nice to him. He added:

> *There was no chance for me to do any lovemaking, so I had to listen all night long to doors opening and shutting in the long passage, though in common decency I suppose I ought to have gone out to the WC once or twice to keep up appearances."*[13]

After Easter life at Garsington began to quicken; so much so that the house that summer seemed at times more like a popular guesthouse than a private home. Indeed, Ottoline needn't have feared that in removing herself to the country she was isolating herself from her friends, or from meeting new people. Now her problem had become one of trying to manage the almost ceaseless flow of visitors. Lytton remarked:

> *Mon Dieu! There are now no intervals between week-ends – the flux and reflux is endless – and I sit quivering among a surging mesh of pugs, peacocks, pianolas, and humans – if human they can be called – inhabitants of this Circe's cave.*[14]

Of these inhabitants there were three categories: the permanent, the floating, and the casual. Permanent residents, apart from Circe herself, were Philip, Julian, Juliette, Maria, the maids, cook, and other staff, together with long-term guests like Mark Gertler and Dorothy Brett (who had studios in the Monk's building adjacent to the house); and, from August onwards, Aldous Huxley. The floating population – those constantly toing and froing, staying a weekend here and a fortnight there – included

Lytton, Russell, Slade girls such as Carrington and Barbara Hiles, elements of Bloomsbury such as Maynard Keynes and Desmond MacCarthy, and other regular guests such as Ottoline's brother Henry (in uniform) and Carrington's friend Alix Sargant-Florence. Heterogeneous as these inhabitants were, the casual callers were even more diverse. So wide had Ottoline spread her circle that literally anyone could turn up at Garsington; from the Prime Minister down.

In addition, there was another group connected with, but set apart, from Garsington. These were the conscientious objectors, a detachment of whom lived across the road at Home Close. Their presence was due to the habit of tribunals of exempting pacifists from military duty on condition they did non-combatant work. Of such work, farm labouring was probably the most congenial; so Philip and Ottoline took in a number of COs as part-workers, part-guests. The first was the young Cambridge economist Gerald Shove, who moved into Home Close around the middle of 1916, and was later joined by his wife Fredegond, Virginia Woolf's cousin. Soon there was quite a little colony of these agricultural dilettantes. They were of various ages and included for a time (incongruously) Clive Bell who, naturally enough, tended to spend more time chatting with Ottoline and her guests than toiling in the fields. Some of the COs worked hard, but others, especially the younger ones, were less industrious, attracting unflattering comment from the villagers and the attentions of reporters who lurked behind the bushes trying to spot signs of "slacking".

Ottoline and Philip were to have cause to regret their generosity to these pacifists; not the least because of the numerous friends the COs themselves would invite to Garsington, as if it were their own house. At weekends crowds of young people would descend on Garsington; arriving by motorcycle, taxi, bicycle, and on foot; their footsteps crunching on the gravel; their voices clamouring for towels, bathing costumes, and food. Ottoline, observing a particularly frenetic group, remarked to Gilbert Cannan, himself not an infrequent guest: "They regard me merely as a kind manageress of a hotel." To which Cannan replied: "Of course we do."[15]

Putting up – and putting up with – all these guests and visitors was no easy task, and inevitably there were strains. Also, Ottoline was still enough of an aristocrat not to care particularly if she appeared occasionally at a disadvantage before her guests. Soon stories began to circulate, especially around Bloomsbury and its rural retreats, about odd goings-on at Garsington. Ottoline, it was said, was stingy with the food. At breakfast she would get up dreamily from the table and go over to a cupboard and spoon out a mouthful of jam for herself without offering her guests any. Lytton, it was said, complained of the spartan nature of his breakfast, and Ottoline had retaliated by each morning sending up to his bedroom trays groaning with eggs, toast, and sausages; which, to her chagrin, (so said the gossip) he demolished. Another story concerned Ottoline's habit of dropping into bedrooms clad in an enormously-long nightgown that trailed several feet behind her to chat with her female guests as they brushed their hair. Other stories were about her matchmaking and meddling in her guests' love lives; others about the insufficiency of bathrooms at Garsington. Carrington heard some of the gossip and complained to Mark Gertler: "What traitors all these people are! They ridicule Ottoline!...I think it's beastly of them to enjoy Ottoline's kindness and then laugh at her."[16]

Undoubtedly there was an element of truth in some of these derogatory tales. Ottoline was often vague and sometimes eccentric. It is true she tried to economise at times. But with so many mouths to feed, who could blame her? And she *was* an inveterate gossip and an incorrigible matchmaker. Carrington recorded that Ottoline once sent Russell and Brett out to walk together on the downs *three times* in the one morning. Also she did make a habit of summoning her guests up to her boudoir, where she would pump them for details of their private lives, much (it was said) to the embarrassment of some of them.

Often, however, the tales people spread about Ottoline were

cruelly exaggerated, or often completely fabricated. It is here, it seems, the legend – or rather the myth – of Ottoline originates, and the more the myth developed and was embellished, the greater it diverged from the truth. Why this distortion should have occurred is not difficult to see. Many of the people who came to Garsington had reason to be grateful to Ottoline; and, human nature being what it is, they couldn't bear to be beholden to her. The spreading of malicious stories which pulled her down helped them reassert their independence. Another factor that encouraged gossip was Ottoline's reluctance to talk about herself. To the younger generation she was, at 43, very much a mystery woman; and it was inevitable this mystery would inspire rumours about her past life and loves.

Probably the person most to blame for propagating a false picture of Ottoline was her most favoured friend, Lytton. Virginia Woolf said she couldn't understand why Lytton continued to spend so much time at Garsington if he found Ottoline and the house so annoying. To those unused to Lytton's mode of writing, the double standard of his behaviour – accepting Ottoline's hospitality and denigrating her behind her back – might seem mean and petty. But the fact is that Lytton was incurably addicted to exaggeration; about everything and everyone, and particularly about those he was fond of. He was just as mischievous about people even closer to him than Ottoline, and once described Clive Bell as "a corpse puffed up with worms and gasses" and Virginia as "some strange amphibious monster."[17] Nor was Lytton the only one in Bloomsbury prone to hyperbole. Virginia, Clive, Vanessa – in fact all of them – indulged in amusing exaggeration. This tendency was also copied by the younger people in the Bloomsbury sphere like David Garnett and Dora Carrington. In fact at this very moment it was said that Garnett was writing a play lampooning Ottoline and her friends, entitled *The Hue and Cry After Genius*.

Today it is hard to visualise what life was actually like at Garsington in 1916. But some idea can be gained from snapshots taken at the time. Ottoline was a keen photographer and took hundreds of pictures, which she had developed and printed at one of London's leading photographic shops, and preserved in albums. These faded snapshots record still moments; vignettes on the Garsington lawn. There is Lytton, his long frame lounging in a deckchair on the lawn, a straw hat shading his glasses. He leans over occasionally to instruct Maria, who is learning Latin at his knee. There is Bertie, smiling a little primly, on a rug with T. S. Eliot. The tea bell has rung, but one group is still on the pond in the punt. Asquith, white-haired, strolls on the terrace. Augustine Birrell, in a canvas hat, wanders under the ilex tree. Now and then somebody else clicks the shutter and Ottoline joins the group in her flowing garments, buckled shoes, and large hat tied under her chin or a scarf knotted gypsy-style around her head. Philip is also there, a somewhat lonely and misunderstood figure. Many of Ottoline's friends tended to dismiss him as inferior and scoff at what they regarded as his pomposity. David Garnett recalled Philip clad in riding boots, jodhpurs, double-breasted waistcoat, and high stiff collars that caused his nose to incline parallel to his forehead. Garnett said:

> *He was awfully nice to one, but instead of handing information to the younger men, which is what one would have expected, it was more the other way round – he seemed to be looking for something from them. He was profoundly uneasy, always.*[18]

Philip certainly tried to join in the fun. He treadled out ragtime on the pianola; cut the girls' hair into Slade bobs; did his utmost to be a good host. But he suffered failure after failure in his dealings with the clever, sharp-tongued guests of his wife. He meant well, and he undoubtedly worked hard – attending the tribunals of COs all around the country – but there was, it seemed, a bumbling quality about him.

An example of his good intentions was his attempt at persuading Carrington to give up her notorious virginity. One evening after dinner he invited her to go for a walk with him around the pond, and without any preface he launched into the subject, saying how disappointed he had been to hear she was a virgin; and how wrong she was in her attitude to Mark Gertler, whom everyone presumed she was destined to marry. He lectured her for a quarter of an hour, ending up with a gloomy story about his brother Hugh, who had committed suicide. When Carrington escaped back to the house Ottoline took over, lecturing her for another hour and a half in the asparagus patch on the same subject. Carrington said later she preferred Ottoline's approach. "And also she suddenly forgot herself, and told me truthfully about herself and Bertie. But this attack on the virgins is like the worst Verdun onslaught and really I do not see why it matters so much to them all."[19]

Actually, had Ottoline and Philip had their ears to the ground, they would not have been so concerned. For, unbeknown to them, Carrington was developing an affection for – of all men – Lytton Strachey! Ottoline can be excused for not suspecting anything in that direction, as she had long ago given up hope that Lytton might be rescued for the female sex. In November 1915 Carrington – who admittedly was rather boyish – and Lytton were out walking when Lytton suddenly stopped and kissed her. Later the same day, as Michael Holroyd describes in his biography of Lytton, Carrington sought to pay back "that horrid old man with a beard" by snipping off his whiskers while he lay dozing. However, just as the scissors were poised, Lytton awoke and looked into her eyes. "The effect was instantaneous," says Holroyd. "She seemed to become hypnotised, and fell, there and then for the rest of her life, violently in love with him."[20] Carrington's "great love," Mark Gertler, was equally ignorant of this unexpected volte-face. He was conducting what he thought were the final stages in his campaign to induce Carrington to come to bed with him, and believed his cause would be advanced if she were to have a higher opinion of him and his art. Lytton, who had made unsuccessful homosexual advances to Gertler, and apparently appreciated his painting, seemed to Gertler to be just the person to influence Carrington in this regard, So he took every opportunity to bring Lytton and Carrington together, even encouraging Ottoline to invite them both to Garsington so that they might be left alone to discuss his (Gertler's) work. Instead the unlikely twosome Lytton and Carrington spent most of the summer going off for long walks and holding cosy *tête-à-têtes* falling, in their own ways, in love with each other.

Another couple who were to be seen quite often at Garsington in 1916 were Katherine Mansfield and John Middleton Murry. Ottoline had first met them in February 1915, when Lawrence brought them to Bedford Square. She did not taken immediately to Katherine, though this may have been because, on that occasion, Lawrence had made a violent political speech, which so embarrassed Katherine that she froze into silence. Ottoline described her on a sofa as "very silent and Buddha-like – she might almost have held in her hand a lotus-flower!"[21] Later Ottoline, after reading some of Katherine's short stories, revised her opinion, starting up a correspondence with her. And when, around Christmas 1915, Katherine was in France convalescing from an attack of "lung trouble", Ottoline insisted on contributing towards Murry's fare so he could go and join her.

One thing that puzzled many of Ottoline's pacifist friends was why Asquith was made so welcome at Garsington. If Ottoline so despised the war and all its works, why did she entertain, not only its chief architect, but his whole family as well? However, they did not realise how deep the friendship between Ottoline and the Prime Minister had once been; nor the fact that Ottoline and Violet Asquith had also once been close friends. And there was also the consideration that, while Asquith continued to come freely to Garsington, Ottoline and Philip and their friends at least had some access to government thinking. Even so, there were occasional embarrassing moments at Garsington. One weekend Ottoline invited Violet to join a house party at Garsington, but almost as soon as she issued the invitation she regretted it, and wrote to Maynard Keynes: "I beg and entreat you to come then. Only you can save me! – what shall we do for a bath for them – could we hire one – you must bring bath salts –

brilliant talk…pate de foie gras – caviare."[22] Keynes turned up and joined Lytton and Desmond MacCarthy in trying to keep conversation in safe channels, for Violet was much more a militarist than her father. But on Sunday afternoon, while Ottoline was saying goodbye to her brother Henry at the door, an uncomfortable incident occurred. Ottoline returned to the tea table to find Violet had vanished. Jokingly she looked under the table and asked Lytton: "Where have you hidden Violet?" In a high, strangled voice he whispered: "She has fled upstairs to her room."[23] While Ottoline was absent Violet had abused Lytton about conscientious objection, saying the COs had disgraced England and ought to be deported to a desert island. Lytton retorted that if this was the government's view he didn't see much difference between them and the Prussians. Violet, red-faced, had picked up her hat and bag and stamped up to her room, and it took the combined efforts of Ottoline and Desmond MacCarthy to get her into a good temper again. (It did not pay to bandy words with Lytton.)

The following Sunday another embarrassing – though more amusing – Asquith incident occurred. As it was a lovely hot day, Ottoline took Lytton, Carrington, Clive Bell, and some others for a walk, and while they were having tea in the wood a maid ran up and mumbled breathlessly: "The Prime Minister arriving…Lucy drowning…and a gentleman plunging into the pond."[24] Ottoline ran back to the house to find the Prime Minister and his party had already left, but was told by another maid what had happened. Several girls from the house had been bathing in the pond when they saw Asquith arriving with some friends. Either as a joke or to avoid reprimand, one of them, a maid named Lucy, called out that she was drowning, whereupon one of Asquith's party, Robbie Ross, divesting himself only of a pocket-watch that had been presented to him by Lord Alfred Douglas after Oscar Wilde's trial, dived fully clothed into the pond to rescue her – only to discover the water was just four feet deep. Everyone except Ottoline enjoyed the joke, yet within days the story of how the Prime Minister had saved a girl's life at

GARSINGTON REVISITED

Garsington was spreading like wildfire round London. Asquith took it with his characteristic good grace. Yet for years afterwards, his first question when he met Ottoline was "How's Lucy?" Another pond incident involved Asquith and Russell. One day, imagining no one was about, Russell decided to take a dip in the pond. He dived in and surfaced to find Asquith standing on the edge looking at him. As Russell was naked at the time, he felt that the quality of dignity which should have characterised a meeting between the Prime Minister and the nation's leading pacifist was lacking.

Russell had recently written a pamphlet about a young man called Everett who had been gaoled for refusing military orders. Several people were arrested for distributing this pamphlet and Russell wrote to *The Times* demanding that if anyone were to be arrested, it should be he. Nothing happened for several weeks and Russell filled in this time by lunching regularly with Vivienne Eliot. Finally, at the end of May, two detectives served a summons on him and in June he appeared before the chief magistrate in London. Ottoline and Lytton went to the hearing and made a dramatic entrance together, Lytton's stork like figure and red beard providing a foil for Ottoline's spectacular hat and cashmere coat of many colours. Russell was convicted and fined £110, but he refused to pay. Instead of gaoling him the authorities seized his books and put them up for auction. Russell, determined to be a martyr, refused to save them. Finally Ottoline and some of his friends clubbed together to buy them back; which rather incensed Ottoline as she disliked having to pay out money for Russell when he himself was spending money for Vivienne Eliot's dancing lessons.

Ottoline in fact was becoming annoyed with Russell. She realised she should not mind his leading a double life with his lady friends (after all she had led a double life in the past), nevertheless she did. And despite the still-intimate tone of his letters to her, he was obviously beginning to move away from her. In June he forgot her birthday, a sure sign his mind was on other things. Ottoline warned him he was being a fool over

Vivienne Eliot who, Ottoline thought, was frivolous to the point of stupidity. Russell retorted that his interest in Mrs. Eliot was superficial and waning. Besides, he had other matters on his mind. His anti-conscription work was attracting a lot of publicity, and a proposed lecturing trip to America had to be cancelled because of it. Next his fellowship at his beloved Trinity College was withdrawn because his colleagues there disapproved of his "unpatriotic" activities. At the beginning of August he came up to Garsington to stay a few days, and Ottoline took the opportunity to discuss his philandering. She told him he was being ingenuous in giving Vivienne Eliot money, as consciously or unconsciously he was in fact buying her affection, and forcing her to rely on him more and more. Russell told Ottoline he wanted to put an end to the relationship, but was afraid of what might happen if he did. What he didn't reveal, however, was that he had already found another woman friend in whom he was taking a deep interest. Her name was Lady Constance Malleson who was married to the actor Miles Malleson, and was herself an actress, appearing under the stage name of Colette O'Niel. The Mallesons had been helping the anti-conscription cause, and it was through this that Russell met Colette, who was young, very beautiful, and dedicated. Throughout the rest of 1916 he gradually transferred to her much of his affection.

The picture many people have of Ottoline is of a rare and beautifully-marked butterfly flitting from one genius to the next. But behind the flightiness was concealed a considerable strength of will and profound concern for humanity, as both Russell and Crompton Davies had discovered. When Ottoline was up in London attending one of Bertie's court hearings, she met Eva Gore-Booth, the sister of Constance Markiewicz, who had been one of the leaders of the Easter Uprising in Dublin. Eva was trying to get up a petition to save the life of Sir Roger Casement, sentenced to death for treason for his part in the uprising, and Ottoline agreed to help. She was outraged that Casement, who had helped fight slavery in the Congo, could be put to death by the British for trying to obtain Home Rule for Ireland – a cause which Gladstone had espoused. Besides, Ottoline always looked on Ireland with special sympathy, partly because of the Irish blood on her mother's side. Philip too was active on Casement's behalf and even tried to see the King to plead for him, but was thwarted by the King's private secretary, Lord Stamfordham.

Ottoline soon discovered, however, that many of her friends were not as passionate about Casement as she was. Russell offered little more than sympathy, and Lytton was quite cold, telling her: "Casement I don't take much stock of...Of course, I should be very glad if they didn't hang him, but I can't believe there's much chance of that."[25] Ottoline also pleaded with Keynes, who worked in the Treasury, telling him:

> *I know you are awfully reasonable and Anti Irish – but if you can say anything to McKenna or Morgan? or anyone of influence I beg of you to do so. It would be beastly to hang him. After all, he has done good work and is fine – and it is silly as regards Ireland to kill him. I have written to P. M.*[26]

But Keynes could do nothing. She also wrote to Conrad, who had known Casement in the Congo, but he replied that he did not agree with Casement, adding that for himself he wished he could get on to a minesweeper. Any hope that Casement might be saved was dashed when someone in the government "leaked" Casement's diary which exposed him as a homosexual. In a letter marked "strictly private" Asquith told Ottoline that Casement was "a depraved and perverted man" and he refused to intervene. Casement was hanged on August 3.[27]

Towards the end of August Ottoline was back at Garsington and sitting – or rather standing – for a portrait by Dorothy Brett. It was an early venture into portraiture for Brett, and she was having trouble fitting all of Ottoline on to a standard-sized canvas. So rather than start the portrait again, she tacked on a few feet of extra canvas, making the picture over nine feet high, and necessitating the use of a stepladder, which Brett climbed up and down murmuring "Marmalade". On one particular day Ottoline was posing in Brett's studio in a loft of the Monks' building (adjacent to Garsington) when one of the maids knocked on the trapdoor in the ceiling and announced that Robbie Ross, the hero of the pond incident, had arrived with a friend. As Ottoline climbed down the ladder she saw, standing next to Ross in the doorway, a handsome young man in khaki. "This," said Ross, "is Siegfried Sassoon."[28]

For months now Ottoline had been looking forward to this meeting, as indeed had Siegfried. For almost a year he had been in the front line, becoming more disillusioned with war (though he had won a military cross for bravery), and for much of that time he had been building up a mental picture of the titled lady who wrote such nice letters to him. He imagined her as some over-intense aristocratic dilettante. Now, as he looked up at the long pair of legs encased in voluminous pale-pink Turkish trousers descending backwards down the ladder, his illusions fell apart. After introductions, the three of them climbed back up the ladder to inspect Brett's painting. Ross, a colleague of Ottoline's in the Contemporary Art Society, pointed to the tacked-on canvas and commented that it wasn't every portrait that went into a second edition. Siegfried didn't think much of the picture, and he wasn't much impressed by Ottoline either. She had dignity and was charming and amusing, but her appearance was ludicrous. After tea, Siegfried and Ross drove off in a taxi, each clutching a peacock feather Ottoline had presented to them. Ross urged Siegfried to be nice to Ottoline, as she could help when his poems were published. "But you really must not try and look so much like a shy and offended deerhound next time you are talking to her," he told him. Siegfried replied that it had been those Turkish trousers – they were too much for him.[29]

A few days later Ottoline and Brett cycled into Oxford to meet Siegfried and show him around the Ashmolean Museum; but he didn't turn up. The two of them wandered around dejectedly and were just about to leave when they heard footsteps behind them. It was Siegfried. Fearing Ottoline would turn up in her Turkish trousers, he had hidden behind a column to check on her outfit before revealing himself. Ottoline returned to Garsington feeling that in Siegfried she had found an almost perfect example of that romantic and sensitive spirit she had been searching for all her life; and that in John, Lamb, Lytton, Bertie, and Lawrence she had found it only in imperfect proportions. Actually she was beginning to fall in love with Siegfried; and she invited him to come and stay at Garsington as often as he liked, before he returned to France.

Before the end of August Ottoline went off to spend a weekend at Wisset, Vanessa Bell's and Duncan Grant's Suffolk cottage, and where David Garnett and Duncan cultivated vegetables as their contribution to the war effort. Vanessa had invited Ottoline in a moment of weakness, but as the date of her arrival approached, Vanessa was having doubts. She told Roger Fry: "Next week I rather fear we shall have Ottoline on us, which I dread." She said she was worried that her young son Quentin might pinch Ottoline's bottom.[30] Ottoline duly arrived, and Garnett wrote this account of how it went off:

The weather was wet. The low-ceilinged little rooms would scarcely contain our magnificent visitor, who I think was uncomfortable. Duncan and I went out most of the day – working, and Heaven knows how Vanessa kept her entertained. Blanche reported that when she went into Ottoline's bedroom with a tray of tea in the morning, Ottoline was lying in bed with her face already completely made up. I remember the feeling of relief when Monday morning came and Cutts drove his dogcart up to the door. Ottoline, who retired after breakfast, suddenly appeared in a dress which she had not worn before during her visit. It might have been designed by Bakst for a Russian ballet on a Circassian folktale theme. Russian boots of red morocco were revealed under a full, light-blue silk tunic, over which she wore a white kaftan with embroidered cartridge pouches on the chest, on which fell the ropes of Portland pearls. On her head was a tall Astrakhan fez. As we gathered around, with Julian [Vanessa's elder son] and Quentin there to say goodbye...She went down to kiss Quentin, [and] the little boy flinched and asked: 'Why have you got all that on?' There was a moment's silence after this unanswerable question; then a deep gurgle...from Ottoline, which passed itself off as a laugh – a rush of farewells from Vanessa, Duncan handed Ottoline up beside Cutts, she seated herself and waved and off they drove looking exactly like the advertisement for a circus.[31]

Vanessa told Roger Fry she didn't think the visit had been a success. (This time Quentin behaved himself.) She decided she really couldn't stand Ottoline for very long. She couldn't relax in her presence. Ottoline, however, enjoyed the weekend, though she thought the house damp and exceedingly untidy. She wrote: "It is difficult to get one's eye used to untidiness if it has been trained to care for order, but with practice I expect one could probably do it."[32] It also upset her that Duncan, who should be painting lovely pictures, was forced to do hard manual work to save himself from being sent to France.

Back at Garsington, Carrington, in spite of her growing interest in Lytton (and reluctance to break away from Gertler), was conducting a mild flirtation with Aldous Huxley, who had recently finished at Oxford and accepted Ottoline's invitation to stay at Garsington. One night when the weather was hot, Carrington and Huxley took their mattresses up on to the roof and slept under the stars, to be awakened in the morning by the swish of trailing peacock tails on their faces. Carrington reported the incident to Lytton: "Strange adventures with birds and peacocks & hordes of bees. Shooting stars, other things."[33] Carrington at this time was still well-disposed to Ottoline, though she did feel a little guilty about having to hide from Ottoline Lytton's letters to her. She complained: "She makes me steeped in debt by giving me all her letters to read. And then has long jabberfications about people deceiving her!" By September, however, her tone was decidedly critical:

> *A concert is in preparation for this evening. Great confusion. Like Clapham Junction, chairs and tables being shunted about everywhere and Pipsey at the Pianola! What an evening last night. Philip reading Boswell's life of Johnson with his own remarks freely strewn between the passages. "That's good excellent, all this part is very dull and I'll leave it out." Clive cackling in the comfortable chair, your chair, pugs snoring, Ottoline yawning, Maria, Mademoiselle and even Katherine knitting woolen counterpanes. What a scene!"*[34]

Carrington asked Lytton to contribute something to a journal she and Ottoline were thinking of getting out for the amusement of the inhabitants of Garsington and its regular visitors. To be called *The Garsington Chronicle*, it was heralded by a prospectus that Carrington got out in a parody of Ottoline's literary style:

> *In this dark and monotonous land these days at Garsington seem to the humble inhabitants precious and varied and perhaps they may have a thread of eternity in them. To test this we the dwellers in this small island of freedom wish to weave a chronicle of the days as they pass. We ask you to stretch forth your skill and coloured fantasy to aid us weave this tapestry which will hang we hope before us in the future.*[35]

But Lytton declined to contribute anything.

In the autumn Philip's troubles at Burnley flared up again. His opposition to the two conscription bills had hardened feelings against him. He realised that his support had been so eroded that he would have to announce that he would not stand again at the next election. In September he wrote a long letter telling the local Liberals of this decision and the reasons for it. "I have been guided always by the same principles – mainly, that it is our sacred duty even in time of war to preserve the liberties that have come down to us, so far as they are not incompatible with military efficiency."[36] The Burnley Liberals accepted his decision with undisguised relief.

In October Ottoline fell ill and went off to a spa at Harrogate to undertake one of her periodic cures. It was while undergoing a starvation regime at the spa that she met her brother Charles, whom she had not seen for several years. Writing to Maynard Keynes, Ottoline reported that she found she had little in common with her brother, apart from their childhood at Welbeck. His views on the war were "even further to the right of those of the *Morning Post*". Conversation had to be limited to the subject of fox-hunting. "What he would think of me if he knew what I really thought, I tremble to think," she told Keynes. "I fear he would hurry me off to the nearest asylum."[37] This letter sparked a rumour that swept Bloomsbury that Ottoline's brothers were trying to get her certified. Clive Bell, himself ill at Garsington, wrote to Ottoline asking if there was any substance to the rumour. Aldous Huxley also wrote telling her the house was made miserable by her absence. "Everything crumbles, footsteps echo hollowly," he wrote. "It is like walking through the deserted palaces of Nineveh."[38] He spent his days discussing Life with Juliette and pining for Maria, who had gone to London to stay with Brett.

Ottoline returned to Garsington in November to discover that one of the workmen on the farm, an aged cowman, had drowned in the pond. This melancholy news was lightened by the prospect of another visit from Siegfried, on whom Ottoline was beginning to pin more and more hopes. She set aside a room for him in which she placed a copy of the *Oxford Book of English Verse* next to his four-poster bed. The book was covered in pale green vellum – "so civilised but so vulnerable," thought Siegfried. He had come to the conclusion that Ottoline was an idealist with a deficient understanding of how to deal with the problems she contemplated with such intensity. He wrote: "She had yet to learn that the writers and artists whom she befriended were capable of proving ungrateful."[39]

INTERLUDE
MY FIRST GLIMPSE OF GARSINGTON

The front gate at Garsington - the entrance to Ottoline's magical world

MY FIRST visit to Garsington in 1972 enabled me to see, touch, smell, and experience Ottoline's magical world, at first-hand. At that time, it was owned by historian Sir John Wheeler-Bennett and his American wife. He had inherited it from his relations who in turn had bought it from the Morrells in 1928. I was picked up at Wheatley station by Lady Wheeler-Bennett, a pretty blonde woman with a pronounced American accent. We drove back to Garsington, through the country lanes, and entered the manor gates through which Ottoline used to whip her phaeton. After the car was parked, we crunched across the gravel courtyard to the entrance.

I looked up and saw the mullioned windows of what had once been Ottoline's guest bedrooms and, above that, the roof where Aldous Huxley and Dora Carrington used to sit and talk on hot summer nights. Inside the house the panelling, which Ottoline had painted vivid red and sea-green (with individual panels meticulously outlined with gilt by Lawrence), was now restored to its original oak. The rooms were dark and cool, a retreat from the summer heat outside

Over a salad lunch - made I was assured from produce grown in the Garsington vegetable garden - the Wheeler-Bennetts told me that they had wanted to restore Garsington to its pre-Ottoline condition, because they wanted to take the house back to its original Jacobean state. Besides, I was told, Ottoline's paint had faded beyond repair anyway.

The Garsington pond

After lunch I wandered out to the terrace with its distant views of the Downs shimmering in a blue haze of summer heat. I looked down towards the ponds and the yew hedges and imagined Ottoline darting amongst her guests with her German Rolleiflex camera, snapping Lytton and Bertie and Katherine Mansfield reclining in deckchairs; or Eliot and Yeats wandering among the yew hedges chatting about poetry. I could also imagine Lawrence, hammer in hand, nailing the lattice to the little summerhouse by the lake. I recalled Katherine's poem "Night Scented Stocks", about an evening when the guests swam naked in the pond (see below)

Finally it was time to go. The hospitable Wheeler-Bennetts told me they were more than happy for me to come as often as I liked to sit in the garden and absorb the atmosphere – which I was to do on several future occasions.

Sir John Wheeler-Bennett died in 1975 and Garsington was bought in 1989 by Leonard Ingrams, the brother of Richard "Private Eye" Ingrams, when the manor house and garden became the site for their open-air Garsington Operas until 2011.

CHAPTER 18
Biting the Hand That Fed Him

Ottoline – or is it Hermione?

AFTER LAWRENCE took himself and Frieda off to Cornwall in December 1915, he and Ottoline wrote to each other almost every week over the next two or three months. He sent her drafts of various things he was working on. The trouble over Heseltine that had caused Ottoline to cancel her trip to Cornwall seems to have blown over fairly quickly, and on January 24, 2016, he wrote to her, saying:

Frieda was sorry she sent you a disagreeable letter when you were ill. But Heseltine and Kouyoumdjian had been telling her the things you said about her – and her and me – so she was cross. But she is not really cross. Perhaps the way we behave to one another she and I makes everybody believe that there is real incompatibility between us. But you know that really we are married to each other – I know you know it.[1]

Throughout February, Lawrence received regular parcels of books, medicines, knick-knacks, and anything else that might make his stay in Cornwall more comfortable. He was grateful and told her he was dedicating his new book of poems, *Amores,* to her. Then, after a flurry of letters in February,[2] he sent her the first part of his "philosophy", which he initially called *"The Signal"*. Having read it, Ottoline reported to Russell: "It is dreadful stuff – bad in *every* way. I feel so sorry & miserable about it. It is rubbish. A child of Frieda's."[3]

There was a hiatus before his next letter, dated March 9,[4] in which he told her that they were moving to a smaller and cheaper cottage at Higher Tregerthen. He asked about Bertie and told Ottoline that there was a farm near their new cottage where she could stay if she came down to visit them. Lawrence's next letter, over a month later, was still friendly, though he was rather sour about the prospect of general conscription. By now Katherine Mansfield and Middleton Murry[5] had joined them at Higher Tregerthen, taking a nearby cottage; all four settling down to a simple rural life in their pocket-sized Rananim.[6] Around May 5 Lawrence wrote Ottoline a long letter containing a tirade against the war. Then he told her: "I have begun a new novel: a thing that is a stranger to me even as I write it. I don't know what the end will be." This was to be what is today regarded as his greatest novel, *Women in Love.*

Actually, this "new novel" had been gestating for some time; beginning in March-April 1913 after *Sons and Lovers* was accepted for publication. This "new" novel was initially called

'The Sisters'. By August 1916 he was rewriting the text, having changed its name to 'The Wedding Ring'. However, this was merely the beginning of a long process of re-writing and re-naming the manuscript, which was eventually divided into two parts, the first becoming *The Rainbow* and the second *Women in Love*. So impoverished was Lawrence down in Cornwall that he had to type the novel himself. But he hated typing, and was soon to forsake the typewriter and return to pen and paper.

Then there is a gap of several weeks in their correspondence. His next letter was dated May 24 and in it he told Ottoline that he had had a visit from Meyrick Cramb, who told him about the novels his father J.A. Cramb had written (including, presumably, *Cuthbert Learmont,* in which Ottoline was portrayed as Mary Fotheringham – see above). It could well be that Katherine Mansfield, who studied under Cramb at Queens College, facilitated this meeting. Yet the Cramb novel Lawrence chose to read was not that, but rather another one, *Hester Rainsbrook* (in which Ottoline did not figure). Lawrence said he had found it "rather good". Interestingly, Lawrence does not appear to have been aware how closely Cramb and Ottoline were acquainted; and indeed probably lovers (see *The Men in Ottoline's Life* below). Lawrence told Ottoline that Meyrick wanted to send her a novel he himself had written (so Meyrick may have said something about the relationship between his father and Ottoline). In the same letter Lawrence told her that he had altered the dedication in *Amores* to read simply "To Ottoline Morrell". He thought she would prefer that, as "it was best, seeing people are as they are, so jeering and shallow".[7] He concluded by informing her, somewhat enigmatically:

> *I have got a long way with my novel. It comes rapidly, and is very good. When one is shaken to the very depths, one finds reality in the unreal world. At present my real world is the world of my inner soul, which reflects on to the novel. The outer world is there to be endured, it is not real – neither the outer life.*

After this letter there is a (perhaps ominous) silence. A little earlier, however, there had been a brief exchange of letters between Ottoline and Frieda. The two had apparently quarrelled again, although what the argument was about isn't known, Nevertheless, the upshot was that Frieda fired off an angry letter accusing Ottoline of being arrogant and vulgar. Frieda reported to Cynthia Asquith:

> *I had a great "rumpus" with dear Lady Ottoline, finally; I told her what I thought of her. All her "spirituality" is false, her democracy is an autocrat turned sour, inside those wonderful shawls there is cheapness and vulgarity.*[8]

A little later, in an undated later, Frieda changed and was all sweetness and light. She said she hoped Ottoline had forgiven her nasty letter of the spring, adding: "Few people I have met have moved me so deeply." She begged Ottoline to come down to Cornwall and visit them.[9] This was followed by another undated letter in which Frieda said she wanted to "start afresh" and added: "My quarrel with you was never that you were fond of Lawrence but that you seemed to underrate *me*. And what you wanted Lawrence to be, and his work to represent, was not my idea of him."[10]

Although Lawrence, in exile in remote Cornwall, no longer figured prominently in her life, Ottoline was nevertheless interested to learn more about her errant genius's next literary work. What was it about? Lawrence himself was not sure. He told E.M. Forster:

> *I am writing another novel, sequel to* The Rainbow, *but quite different. Here in this book I am free at last, thank God, and can move without effort or excitement, naturally. I feel rather triumphant in myself, really. I feel that I have conquered: what I don't know, but everything. Nearly everybody has dropped off from me – even Ottoline is very*

cool. It is better to be alone in the world, planté by oneself."[11]

On September 26 Lawrence wrote to Ottoline telling her:

Now I think I should like to see you again…when this novel is done. Will you come here, or shall we come to Garsington for a little while? – to stay in the bailiff's house, if nobody is wanting the rooms. I only want to finish this novel, which is like a malady or a madness while it lasts, It will only take a week or two.[12]

On October 3 he wrote again to Ottoline, asking solicitously after her health, then returning to the topic of his novel, saying:

As for my novel, I don't know if I hate it or not. I think everybody else will hate it. But this cannot be helped. I know it is true, the book. And it is another world, in which I can live apart from this foul world which I will not accept or acknowledge or even enter. The world of my novel is big and fearless – yes, I love it, and love it passionately. It only seems to me horrible to have to publish it.[13]

Although it took a little longer than "a week or two", Lawrence finished the first draft of the new novel, which he had retitled *Women in Love*, in November 1916. The text then underwent numerous changes and re-writes, with various different versions circulating among Lawrence's friends. Finally two settled typescript texts emerged (today dubbed TS1a and TS1b).

Meanwhile, Lawrence was having a major quarrel with "the Murries", the upshot of which was Katherine stalking off to a more congenial cottage in southern Cornwall, taking Murry with her. On November 7 Lawrence wrote to Koteliansky saying: "I have done with the Murries both, for ever – so help me God. So I have with Lady Ottoline and all the rest. And now I am glad and free."[14] There is no evidence that Lawrence had quarrelled with

Ottoline. However, around this time she heard (from perhaps several of their mutual friends who had read one of the circulating manuscripts) that she had been portrayed in his new novel in an unflattering light. On November 27 Lawrence wrote from Cornwall to his friend Catherine Carswell, whose barrister husband Donald was checking through the text for possible libel. In a previous letter Lawrence had told Catherine: "Halliday is Heseltine, The Pussum is a model called the Puma, and they are taken from life – nobody else at all lifelike." He now added:

> *I heard from Ottoline Morrell this morning, saying she hears she is the villainess of the new book. It is very strange, how rumours go round – So I have offered to send her the MS – so don't send it to Pinker [Lawrence's literary agent] until I let you know…Don't talk much about my novel, will you? And above all, don't give it to anybody to read, but Don. I feel it won't be published yet, so I would rather nobody read it. I hope Ottoline Morrell won't want the MS.*[15]

However, it was the American poet Hilda Doolittle, who had one of the texts, who sent her copy of the MS to Ottoline. By January 20 Ottoline had read it, and she was, to put it mildly, outraged. Turning the pages, she had been on the lookout for a character that might resemble her. She did not have far to look. Early in the first chapter Lawrence describes a wedding at which the two main female characters in the book, Ursula and Gudrun Brangwen, watch a bridal procession. The text read:

> *The chief bridesmaids had arrived. Ursula watched them come up the steps. One of them she knew, a tall, slow, reluctant woman with a weight of fair hair and a pale, long, face. This was Hermione Roddice.*[16]

Lawrence's description of Hermione shows how closely he had observed Ottoline. Hermione "drifted forward as if scarcely conscious, her long blanched face lifted up, not to see the world...she drifted along with a peculiar fixity of the hips, a strange unwilling motion." Physically there were differences; Hermione's hair was not Ottoline's dark-auburn, but fair; she was in her 20s not her 40s; and there were other dissimilarities. Nevertheless, Ottoline could hardly have avoided seeing herself in Lawrence's verbal portrait. Lawrence had written: "People were silent when she passed, impressed, roused, wanting to jeer, yet for some reason silenced." Hermione was a woman of the "new school," full of intellectuality, passionately interested in reform, the daughter of a Derbyshire baronet. She moved in the world of culture and of intellect; she was a medium for the culture of ideas. She speaks in long slow murmurings full of emphasis and pregnant pauses:

> *"Well –"* rumbled Hermione. *"I don't know. To me the pleasure of knowing is so great, so wonderful – nothing has meant so much to me in all life, as certain knowledge – no, I am sure – nothing."*
>
> *"What knowledge, for example, Hermione?"* asked Alexander.
>
> *Hermione lifted her face and rumbled –* "M - m - m - I *don't know. But one thing was the stars, when I really understood some-thing about the stars. One feels* **uplifted,** *so* **unbounded...**"

Also it would have been obvious, not only to Ottoline and Philip, but all their friends and acquaintances, that "Alexander" was also partly based on her husband, Philip Morrell. (Lawrence's choice of "fictional" names almost always had a connection to the real person they were based on – the link here being via Alexander the Great's father Philip of Macedon. Needless to say, the name Hermione was derived from Ottoline's Dutch/Germanic first name [Herman=Otto].) Lawrence gave Hermione Ottoline's bizarre taste in clothes. Hermione wears ostrich feather hats, cloaks of greenish cloth lined with fur, dresses of prune-coloured silk, and shawls "blotched with great embroidered flowers". Few people who knew Ottoline would have been in much doubt where Lawrence got the inspiration for the physical shell of Hermione.

Yet, if this were all he had done, Ottoline might not have minded so much. What roused her to a fever-pitch of anger and indignation was the character Lawrence chose to put into that shell (and thus by association imposed on Ottoline). In the paragraph where Hermione is first introduced, Lawrence set the tone, describing her as "macabre...repulsive". She "seemed almost drugged, as if a strange mass of thoughts coiled in the darkness within her, and she was never allowed to escape." With what seemed to Ottoline almost fiendish relish, Lawrence proceeded to build up Hermione's tormented, twisted character. She was a demonic woman, possessed by hatred and envy; a thwarted high priestess over whom a mantle of death and poison hung. She hurled a lapis lazuli paper-weight ball at Birkin (this was a reference to some lapis lazuli Ottoline had once given Lawrence, and which was now being fictionally hurled back). And to cap this malign portrait, Lawrence portrayed Hermione as being crazed with lust for Birkin, the chief character in the book, who forsakes Hermione to fall in love with the heroine, Ursula. And just as it was obvious to Ottoline that she was Hermione, it was equally clear to her that Birkin was a self-portrait of Lawrence – and Ursula was Frieda!

As Ottoline sat in her boudoir at Garsington reading the manuscript, it seemed to her the full weight of Lawrence's vituperation was being heaped on her. Her dresses were described as "shabby and soiled, even rather dirty"; another outfit made her look "tall and rather terrible, ghastly"; she was incapable of decent passion and instincts. And if for a moment she attempted to seek refuge from the terrible caricature in some dissimilarity; Lawrence rudely dragged her back. In one particularly telling scene he harkened back to the letter he wrote to her in April, 1915,[17] after Maria took poison at Bedford Square in 1915. Birkin is arguing with Hermione:

> *"You want a life of pure sensation and 'passion'." He quoted the last word satirically against her. She sat convulsed with fury and violation, speechless, like a stricken pythoness of the Greek oracle. "But your passion is a lie," he went on violently. "It isn't passion at all, it is your will. It's your bullying will. You want to clutch things and have them in your power. You want to have things in your power, and why? Because you haven't got any real body, any dark sensual body of life. You have no sensuality. You have only your will and your conceit of consciousness, and your lust for power, to **know**.*

The words of that April 1915 letter must have rung in Ottoline's ears, for in it Lawrence had written: "Why must you always use your *will* so much, why can't you let things be, without always grasping and trying to know and to dominate?"

Early in February 1917, Clive Bell, who was then living at Garsington, mentioned in a letter to Vanessa that Ottoline had "calmed down a little now."[18] Indeed, her anger and outrage must have been palpable to everyone around her. In her *Memoirs* she recalled her feelings at the time. "I read it and found myself going pale with horror, for nothing could have been more vile and obviously spiteful and contemptuous…I was called every name from an 'old hag' obsessed with sex mania, to a corrupt Sapphist…In another scene I had attempted to make indecent advances to the Heroine, who was a glorified Frieda. My dresses were dirty and I was rude and insolent to my guests."[19] What particularly upset her was that Lawrence had satirised not only her but Philip, Julian, Juliette, Maria, Bertie Russell, her house and garden, and many more of her friends as well. "Oh, I read, chapter after chapter, scene after scene all written, as far as I could tell, in order to humiliate me."[20] She showed the manuscript to Aldous Huxley, who was also at Garsington at the time, and he was "equally horrified" and thought it "very very bad."[21] She added: "for many months the ghastly portrait of myself written by someone whom I had trusted and liked haunted my thoughts and horrified me."[22]

Why did Lawrence turn on his first major patron and benefactor, twisting her into a character apparently so venomously drawn that even people with little sympathy for Ottoline felt sorry for her? The short answer is that Lawrence probably had no intention of doing anything of the sort. Incredible as it may seem, it did not occur to him that Ottoline would take Hermione as a violent attack on her personally; indeed, that she would see much of herself in Hermione. It seems that – on the surface at least – all he intended to do was to use certain aspects of Ottoline's appearance and character to make a point about a certain type of woman: the civilised, unspontaneous, "sex-in-the-head" priestess archetype which Lawrence regarded as the opposite to the earthy, intuitive, "mother goddess" archetype. In *Women in Love* and other of his works he argues that it would be better for everyone if the goddess should prevail. When he began rewriting "The Sisters" in late 1915, the representative of the "priestess" archetype is called Ethel, and was probably based on Jessie Chambers, Lawrence's first love, whom he had portrayed as Miriam in *Sons and Lovers*. In his first rewrite of "The Sisters", Ethel becomes Hermione, but this early Hermione still bears more relation to Jessie Chambers than to Ottoline. It is only when Lawrence starts his third rewrite, around March 1916, that Hermione becomes more overtly based on Ottoline. Perhaps Lawrence decided Ottoline was a far more vivid example of this type of woman.

What Ottoline did not comprehend (nor have very few others since) was that Lawrence was almost incapable of inventing things. He wrote from real-life, from reality; or at least a version of reality he wanted to focus on. (One of the most perceptive books written about Lawrence and his "fiction " is *The Betrayal*, by his childhood friend George Neville [CUP 1981]. Neville, whom Lawrence portrayed no less than four times in his novels, pointed out that the characters, their backgrounds – and even their names – had been expropriated by Lawrence from real life and converted, by various transformation techniques, into substantial elements of his subsequent writing.) Ottoline, however, was ignorant of Lawrence's compositional habits and quirks, and she took what he wrote (apparently about her) at its face-value. So when Ottoline read Lawrence's fourth novel she had no way of knowing how Hermione had evolved through the various texts. She was not in a position to make the distinctions and reservations Lawrence retained in his own mind between the earlier character-type based on Jessie Chambers and the later physical shell of Ottoline.

Yet it was not Lawrence whom Ottoline initially blamed for the Hermione caricature, but Frieda. After she finished reading the MS, Ottoline said in her *Memoirs*: "The only assuagement to the shock was that all the worst parts were written in Frieda's handwriting." She seems to be implying here that Frieda either composed these sections, or inspired them. When later Ottoline read a published copy of *Women in Love* [23] she wrote in the margin against those sections such comments as: "Frieda!" "Surely Frieda," and "Frieda again!" Most Lawrence scholars today reject the idea that Frieda wrote any part of Lawrence's *oeuvre*. It seems the most likely explanation for Ottoline's misapprehension is that Frieda helped transcribe and correct the MS [TS1b] that Hilda Doolittle sent Ottoline to read. Indeed, Lawrence is unlikely to have been influenced by any other human being when he was writing. He himself appeared to believe (see his *Fantasia of the Unconscious*) that when he was writing his creative works he was "possessed" by a *daemon* who guided his pen.

To Ottoline, however, the depiction of Hermione Roddice seemed nothing but cruel and vicious. On the other hand, with Hermione in *Women in Love* Lawrence created a memorable character. Ottoline, admittedly unwillingly, had participated in the creation of a major work of art. And though Lawrence was creating a figure of fiction, in choosing Ottoline for part of his inspiration he was saying something significant about her. The portrait contains some truth (Lawrence was a superb observer). Hermione is possessive; so, to some extent, was Ottoline.

Hermione is not earthy; neither was Ottoline. Hermione overflows with almost electrical energy; as did Ottoline. Hermione disdained the vulgarity of sex and regarded it as a weapon to be used to ensnare Birkin; Ottoline's view of sex was not dissimilar. In the novel – as in Ottoline – there is a tension between sensuous, intuitive experience on the one hand, and cerebral, conscious knowledge on the other. It is a constant lament in Ottoline's *Memoirs* that she can never find anyone to close up this "deficiency of being" within her. Lawrence had latched on to the facet of Ottoline's persona that was one of the main causes of her unhappiness in life. Lawrence describes Hermione as

> ...*knowing perfectly that her appearance was complete and perfect, according to the first standards, yet she suffered torture, under her confidence and her pride, feeling herself exposed to wounds and to mockery and to spite. She always felt vulnerable, vulnerable, there was always a secret chink in her armour. She did not know herself what it was. It was a lack of robust self, she had no natural sufficiency, there was a terrible void, a lack, a deficiency of being within her. And she wanted someone to close up this deficiency. To close it up forever*

Perhaps this is why Ottoline reacted so strongly to *Women in Love*. Lawrence had discovered her Achilles' heel.

Yet there is no mystery about Ottoline's response once she read the novel. She reacted like a scalded cat. First of all she showed it round the Garsington household where, it appears, no one, apart from possibly Philip, got anywhere near as angry as she did. A day or so after Clive Bell read the MS he wrote to Ottoline, playfully chiding her for not turning up at Home Farm, where she had been asked to tea.

> *"No you don't Hermione" as I dare say you remember Lawrence's hero says when he has had a smart clip with a*

lapis-lazuli ball over one ear and looks for no less over the other. No, my dear Ottoline, you don't put the blame off onto me. I remembered quite well that I had asked you to tea and I still hoped at four o'clock that you would still come.[24]

But Ottoline was so beside herself with anger that forgotten tea appointments were as nothing. The next thing she did was to despatch a furious letter to Lawrence. Precisely what she said is not known, as Lawrence seldom kept his correspondence; but Clive Bell knew something of its contents, for he reported to Vanessa:

Ottoline returned Lawrence his MS with an incredibly foolish reply, in spite of excellent counsel from me, and some desperate admonitions from Philip against falling into the depths of folly. Every line of her letter that I was allowed to hear revealed a wound: Lawrence must have rejoiced. She, also, it seems, commanded him to return a rather expensive pearl pin that she had given him. But he, very sensibly, having sold it or pawned it, declined to do anything of the sort.[25]

Bell is wrong here: it wasn't a pearl pin but the opal one Ottoline had given Lawrence in happier days. Ottoline herself says in her *Memoirs* that she wrote to Lawrence to protest about Hermione, but his only answer was that Hermione was a "very fine woman."[26] She goes on to say that Desmond MacCarthy was asked if it should be published and that he had replied that it was a very poor book and advised against it. Ottoline then says that Philip took up the matter of the libellous aspects of the portrait with Lawrence's literary agents. She says Philip told them that if the novel were published he would sue for libel. Although in fact Lawrence did not find anyone to publish it for several years, whether this was due to Ottoline's threatened writs, or because it was unmarketable until the war was over, is an open question.

Biting the Hand That Fed Him

Ottoline claims that when *Women in Love* was eventually published Lawrence had expunged from it – presumably because of her threats – "some of the worst scenes."[27] But evidence that Lawrence did alter the manuscript in this way has yet to be found.

Ottoline's reaction to *Women in Love* killed off her friendship with Lawrence (at least for some considerable time). For several months her efforts to have the book suppressed were the main talking-point of Bloomsbury and Lawrence's circle. In February Frieda wrote to Koteliansky: "Campbell will tell you about L's quarrel with the Ott. She played Salome to L's John the Baptist!"[28] Frieda also wrote to Campbell (Gordon Campbell, Lord Glenavy, a friend of Lawrence's) telling him about the book:

> *You must read the novel, it will be sardonic enough for you even – the 'Ott' read it – was furious, wrote as a vulgar cook who writes to her young man. She asked for an opal pin back she had given him!! Lawrence wrote and said that he had given it to me, I keep it, be more careful another time to whom you give your friendship so freely!"*[29]

Ottoline, Frieda added, was "just a flapper full of cheap spirituality and adoration of young geniuses." Anyway, Frieda concluded smugly, she and Lawrence were really happy now.

Lawrence's own reaction was anger. After his agents told him about Ottoline's libel threat, he wrote back to them on February: 20:

> *Really, the world has gone completely dotty! Hermione is not much more like Ottoline Morrell than Queen Victoria, the house they claim as theirs is a Georgian house in Derbyshire I know very well – etc. Ottoline flatters herself. There is a hint of her in the character of Hermione: but so there is a hint of a million women, if it comes to that. Anyway, they could make libel cases for ever, they haven't half a leg to stand on. But it doesn't matter. It is no use trying to publish the novel in England in this state of*

affairs. There must come a change first. So it can all lie by. The world is mad, and has got a violent rabies that makes it turn on anything true, with frenzy. The novel can lie by till there is an end of the war and a change of feeling over the world.[30]

On March 19 Lawrence wrote to his agent Pinker again, asking if he might have a copy of the MS, now that it had been typed: "I would like to look at Ottoline Morrells [sic] imaginary portrait again."[31] After this, a feeling of bewilderment came over him, and he wrote to Mark Gertler, as he was close to Ottoline, asking him for his opinion: "*please* tell me how much likeness you can see between Hermione and the Ott."[32] Three days later Lawrence again wrote to Kot, concerned that Carrington had sent a telegram asking to see the MS Lawrence said he hadn't wanted Carrington to see it, but Frieda had opened the telegram and had wired "yes". Lawrence cautioned Kot to make sure Carrington showed the MS to no-one else. He added that if however Gertler and Campbell had seen it, he was not to let it go any further. Lawrence went on:

You know that the Ottoline threatens me with law-suits...I feel that she would go to any lengths to do me damage in this affair. I feel that these people, all the Ott. crowd, are full of malice against me. Altogether I feel bad about that novel, and I will not publish it now. I know it is a good book. But my god, to have all these canaille, already grunting over it is more than I can bear.[33]

To Cynthia Asquith Lawrence denied that Hermione was meant to be a portrait of Ottoline. Hermione, he insisted, was infinitely superior. Cynthia wrote that Philip had asked Lawrence's publisher to come down to Garsington and compare the fiction of Hermione to the reality of his wife. "Fancy calling in that worm of a publisher as detective," Cynthia commented.[34] On March 5 Cynthia recorded in her diary that Lawrence had "*said* Ottoline no longer minded about the book (I wonder if this can be true) and that she was anxious to see him again, but that he was unwilling."[35]

Over the next 18 months Lawrence and Frieda, having been expelled from Cornwall for allegedly spying for the Germans, went from friend-to-friend and house-to-house, virtually living on charity. Despite Lawrence managing to have some articles, essays and other minor works published, his finances were in a desperate state. He toyed with having *Women in Love* published privately.[36] Gertler asked him how Ottoline would take this. Lawrence replied: "As for the Ott – why should I bother about the old carrion? If I can publish, I shall publish. But ten to one I can't, and I don't care a straw either way."[37] By this time, however, Lawrence had been reduced to such a state that Koteliansky had suggested some of his troubles might be relieved if he tried to make it up with Ottoline. Lawrence replied:

> *I got your letter. Yes, I know the Ot. is very nice, somewhere. I once was very fond of her – and I am still, in a way. But she is like someone who has died: and I cannot wish to call her from the grave.*[38]

And a few days later he warned Mark Gertler: "I should beware of Garsington. I believe there is something exhaustive in the air there, not so very restful."[39]

On 20 March[40] Lawrence asked Kot if he would ask Ottoline to return the bundle of manuscripts she had been minding for him over the years. Did he really want his old manuscripts? Or was this a tentative effort to make a rapprochement with Ottoline? After Ottoline obliged and sent the manuscripts, Lawrence wrote to thank her:

> *My Dear Ottoline, Thank you for the two bundles of MS which came this morning. I am sorry to have troubled you – but I wanted to hunt up a few old things that might possibly meet a publisher in these days of leanness. I am*

awfully sick of the world that is. I wish to heaven there would be an end of it. Meanwhile one persists in one's way against it all. Perhaps we shall meet in some sort of Afterwards when the laugh is on a new side. – D. H. Lawrence [41]

In June Lawrence was begging Gertler to see if Ottoline would accept him and Frieda back at Garsington: "How is Ottoline now," he wrote, "do you think she would like to see us again? Do you think we might be happy if we saw her again – or we went to Garsington? I feel, somehow, that perhaps we might. But tell me how it is – what you think."[42] On July 2 he wrote to Kot:

I wrote to Gertler thinking we might see the Ott. again – then we should have come to London for a bit. But I got such a stupid answer from him – vague and conditional like Mr Balfour discussing peace terms. To hell with the Ott. – the whole Ottlerie – what am I doing temporising with them?[43]

In January 1919 Lawrence learned that Cynthia Asquith had sent a copy of the MS of *Women in Love* to Ottoline's friend Prince Bibesco in the hope he might help finance the publication of *Women in Love*. But this had been thwarted by Desmond MacCarthy who advised the Prince that publication of the novel would cause Ottoline pain. Lawrence's reaction was contemptuous:

I knew that it was Desmond Macarthy [sic] who had put a stopper on Prince Bibesco, moaning on Ottoline's outraged behalf. I knew that. And I knew that Prince B. had not the courage to say a word either to me or to Cynthia Asquith, but returned the MS wordless. And I knew that Desmond Maccarthy was quite pleased with himself for having arse-licked Ottoline and the Prince, both at once, both of them being pretty sound benefactors of Desmond, who rather enjoys his arse-licking turns.[44]

In a later letter to Cynthia Asquith, Lawrence wrote of Ottoline "stinking in Garsington."

Women in Love was finally published in America in 1921 and was an almost instant success for its publisher, Seltzer. It was not long before the American royalties started to flow, and while Lawrence was in Australia a year later his financial future was assured (though he did not realise this for some time later). Lawrence had deeply offended probably his greatest patron, and she never forgave him for the injury he had inflicted on her; she thought gratuitously. They were never to meet again. However, a year before his death, some sort of rapprochement took place, and they corresponded until his demise in Vence, France, on March 2, 1930. Ottoline wrote in her *Memoirs*: "The hurt that he had done me made a very great mark in my life. The wound took many years to heal."[45] Even as late as 1932 she was describing *Women in Love* as "that wicked, spiteful book". She had opened her heart and mind (and purse) to Lawrence as she had to no other person, apart perhaps from Bertie. She vowed that never again would she leave herself so vulnerable.

INTERLUDE
I SEE A GHOST

(from left) Igor Vinogradoff, W.J. Turner, James Redfern, and Mark Gertler, photographed by Ottoline at Garsington

AS MY RESEARCH into Ottoline's life widened, I returned several times to Broughton Grange to discuss with Ottoline's daughter Julian Vinogradoff what I was finding about her mother. Usually we would have lunch or tea. On this final occasion, instead of travelling to Banbury by train, Rob drove me up in our old Rover. While I was having tea with Julian, Rob sat in our car parked outside on the gravel driveway and listened to the cricket (1972 was an Ashes year, and the Australian team was playing Test matches on the various English cricket grounds). Igor, Julian's husband, was also a keen cricket fan, so came out and asked Rob if he could sit and listen to the cricket too. Rob suspected he was lonely.

Inside the house, Julian was being evasive. On a previous visit, shortly after we returned from Texas, Julian had revealed to me that Ottoline had kept a Diary (of which there was no sign in her papers lodged in the HRC in Austin). Obviously, I asked to see it. She told me, on that occasion, that it had been "lost in a

I SEE A GHOST

fire at the bank" where it had been kept. At a later meeting she changed the fire to a flood at the bank. (Yet it turned out, years later, that all the while it was in a cupboard under a seat in the very room where I was chatting with her!) The "missing" diary had been used by Ottoline to compose her *Memoirs*, which had recently been typed. Julian gave me access to the typescript, which had yet to be edited by an acquaintance of Ottoline, Robert Gathorne-Hardy (thus I had "second-hand" access to the Diary)..

On this particular visit to Broughton Grange, Julian and I were sitting at the dining table when she suddenly got up and left the room, to return with a large hat-box which she plumped down on the table. Then, with a flourish, she took off its lid and drew out a long hank of dark auburn hair. "This was my mother's hair," she told me, passing it to me to feel. "I sold the other half to a wig-maker," she said.

It was on this visit that I met a ghost. As I was walking down the hall back to the dining-room from the bathroom, I suddenly encountered a tall, slender, youngish-looking woman in a white dress. She had a pale face, blazing blue eyes, a long nose and a strong chin. Her hair caught a ray of sunlight which lit up its auburn-gold colour. I stopped and looked at her. She gazed back at me, then went into a side room. It was Ottoline ! Stunned, I went into the dining-room and slumped into my chair. "Who was that woman?" I asked Julian. "Oh, that's my daughter, Anne," she said. "She suffers from a nervous condition."

Soon I went out to the car, where Rob and Igor were still sitting listening to the cricket. Igor thanked Rob, and said goodbye, then returned indoors. As we drove back to London Rob told me that Igor had been rather distressed when the Australian bowler Bob Massie destroyed England's first innings, taking eight wickets.

This visit was the last occasion that I saw Julian in person.

273

CHAPTER 19
The Worst Year of Her Life

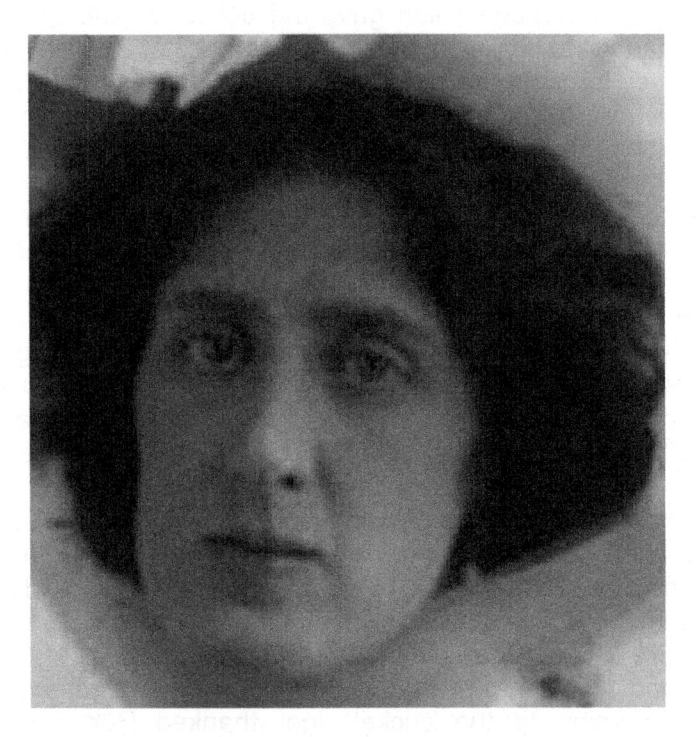

Ottoline's world is in disarray

THE YEAR 1917 had started badly for Ottoline. The discovery of Lawrence's *Women in Love* "treachery" still hung over her. Yet far worse was to follow. At her otherwise pleasant party at Garsington at Christmas 1916 she had detected undercurrents that did not please her. From Carrington's behaviour it seemed obvious she had gained some hold over Lytton, confirming the rumours about them. Also other rumours that had been eddying around London for some time began lapping at her doorstep. In Chelsea, it was said, a group was putting on a play featuring an eccentric character called Lady

The Worst Year of Her Life

Omega Muddle. Slowly it began to dawn on Ottoline, now 44, that many people – some of them her close friends – regarded her as a figure of fun. Another disturbing undercurrent was the interest Russell was taking in, of all people, Katherine Mansfield (what an old roué he was).

For more than a year now Ottoline's relationship with Russell had been losing its intensity. At first he had resented this, but as he found other women friends it became a blessing. Ottoline suspected something of what was going on with Bertie's flirting and, as we have seen, was not too unhappy; it saved her from having to take the brunt of his affections, and allowed her to keep things to the more spiritual level she preferred. All the same, she didn't like to see Bertie drifting too far. It had been the inelegance rather than the seriousness of his affair with Vivienne Eliot that had annoyed her, so she had been content to let it run its course without too much interference. Now that Mrs. Eliot was out of the way she waited to see where his fancy would take him next. But she had underestimated Bertie's flirtatious activities. Almost as soon as he had disengaged himself from Vivienne Eliot, he had launched into a far more serious liaison with Constance Malleson (an actress whom he preferred to call Colette, her stage-name). Writing of this period in his autobiography, Russell says: "I used to go down to Garsington fairly frequently but found [Ottoline] comparatively indifferent to me. I sought about for some other woman to relieve my unhappiness, but without success until I met Colette."[1] He said that what most impressed him about Colette was that, like Ottoline, she was very courageous.

After their first meeting in mid-1916, Russell and Colette saw each other casually several times Then, one evening, Russell escorted her back to her house after one of his lectures. It was a situation similar to that evening in Ottoline's Bedford Square drawing-room back in March 1911. "We talked half the night," Russell says, "and in the middle of the talk became lovers."[2] He did not go to bed with Colette that night, as there was too much to say, but from that moment it was Colette, not Ottoline, who became central to his life, at least for the time being.

It took him some time, however, to break this news to Ottoline. In September 1916 he was still writing affectionately: "I yearn for you terribly. The rest of the world fades away in comparison. Dearest I hardly knew before how profoundly I love you."[3] He told her that he was trying to disentangle himself from Vivienne Eliot, and as soon as he had, he would come to Garsington. He added however that unless he could overcome his feeling that he had failed with her, he would go on looking for stimulus elsewhere. Ottoline recognised this as a danger signal and early in November invited him to visit her at Harrogate, where she was taking the waters, and they had a happy reunion. Russell wrote to her afterwards: "Yes, it was a very happy time. I felt we were *very* much one – I loved it."[4]

It was not until December that he first let slip some hint of his involvement with Colette. In between professions of devotion, he wrote: "In a gay boyish mood I got intimate with Constance Malleson, but she doesn't suit serious moods."[5] He ended this letter by reiterating how much he was longing to see Ottoline: "I want your spirit, my dearest." Ottoline told him that she couldn't see him until Christmas. Russell wrote back: "I am sorry to lose the time with you and sorry you have so many worries." When Russell did come to Garsington at Christmas he spent most of his time talking to Katherine Mansfield. He had previously dined with her at least once. At such meetings they discussed Ottoline, apparently to her detriment. During the Christmas festivities at Garsington Katherine and Bertie sat up one night in the room beneath Ottoline's bedroom talking about their hostess into the early hours. Next morning Ottoline – as a joke – said she had heard what they had said about her, and the guilty look on their faces showed her remark had struck home. A little later Russell told Ottoline to beware of Katherine "as she had a vicious tongue". In his autobiography he says: "It had become clear to me that I must get over the feeling that I had had for Ottoline, as she no longer returned it sufficiently to give me any happiness. I listened to all that Katherine had to say against her."[6] Although much of this tittle-tattle he later rejected, at the time it helped him to rationalise his need to free himself from Ottoline, and by January he had made up his mind to do to Ottoline what he had done to Alys: kill her love.

He decided a clean break, a quick amputation, was the best and possibly the kindest method. Precisely how he set about this is not known, as his letters to Ottoline of this period have been mostly lost or destroyed. In their absence we have to rely on what Ottoline says in her *Memoirs*, together with other references in letters from other people. In her *Memoirs* Ottoline said that, about a month after Christmas 1916, Russell wrote to her saying he must "shake her off".[7] She wrote:

> *It is a sort of garden party parting, polite and formal, unexpected and casual...He has hurt me so much by this way of parting that I feel I can never get over it or be frank with him again...My rapier is out. I will elude him in future and defend myself from him and be free; free for my own flights, unimpeded by him. Cut all that binds me to him, my soul must be free, and rise above it all, free to embrace trees, clouds, sunsets, and far distances, to brush away all these dead thoughts and grievances.*[8]

She refers to long walks with Russell in April 1917, during which he told her some "truths" about herself. Here Ottoline's dating is probably incorrect and it seems (from cross-referencing with Brett's letters) that these conversations belong to a period beginning January 15. It was around this date that Russell told her that he had decided to break with her. Yet, as he had said this several times before over the past four or more years, she didn't take his words too seriously. Almost certainly he did not tell her the real reason for his wanting to break; Colette. Nor did he tell her that he planned to spend a three-day "honeymoon" with Colette at a hotel near Buxton.

Ottoline was not prepared for Russell's defection, and she reacted unsympathetically. Harsh letters (now lost) must have been exchanged, and a meeting followed at which harsher things were apparently said. Neither was in a conciliatory mood and Ottoline, still recoiling from Lawrence, was at a low ebb. Her account of the meeting is bleak. Russell told her she was uninstinctive and lacking in the qualities that would make her a comfortable companion. She was too like Blake and not enough like Shakespeare. She was too fastidious and aloof, always wanting the transcendental and not content with ordinary companionship. Ottoline was stunned by his words, but had no wish to argue or retaliate. A day or so later they had another meeting at which Russell at last told her of his involvement with Colette. Ottoline now realised the real reason behind his hurtful words. As they parted he delivered an exceptionally cruel thrust, saying to her: "What a pity your hair is going grey."[9] That Ottoline was upset by Russell's onslaught is understandable, yet her erratic behaviour in early 1917 cannot be attributed solely to the breakdown of her relationship with Russell. There was something else; far worse. Meanwhile she retired to her nursing home in Maida Vale.

Russell and Ottoline continued to exchange letters full of accusations and recriminations. On one of his envelopes Ottoline jotted distractedly: "Don't let me go…The end of intimacy…All is in the past…You have lost me…Don't you see I can never be friends with you again…I am *gone* [underlined three times]."[10] Brett, for one, warned Ottoline not to do anything irrevocable. "Don't be hard on Bertie," she told her, "I mean don't misinterpret him. Be awfully sure you are right in what you think. I am not very sure myself that you are."[11] Bertie's cry for freedom, said Brett, was the cry of help creative people gave to keep from losing their individuality. It was the same sort of thing that had caused Henry Lamb to "turn on you & stamp on you", she added.

In February Ottoline's gloom was lifted by a telegram from Siegfried Sassoon asking her up to London to lunch with him. She took a room in a Bloomsbury hotel and waited for him to arrive. But he was late, and when he did come her pleasure at seeing him was marred by the news that he had been ordered to return to

The Worst Year of Her Life

France, and was to leave the next day. He told her he wanted to take her to the Ritz for lunch, but the thought of trying to converse accompanied by a jazz band put Ottoline off, and instead she suggested a quieter restaurant in Fitzrovia's Percy Street, after which they went on to the National Gallery. Lytton happened to be at the gallery that day and derived some amusement from the sight of Ottoline gliding through the rooms, her long dress sweeping the floor, followed by a pale and worried-looking Siegfried. Afterwards Ottoline and Siegfried walked to Tower Bridge where they stood looking at the grey river, with Ottoline murmuring that there was "something so moving about it – so mysterious and immense."[12] Siegfried agreed, but wished she wouldn't go about looking quite so extraordinary. Then they went back to Ottoline's hotel room for tea where they sat by the fire while he confessed to her that he was afraid he would be killed. She tried to lift his spirits, telling him he must remain alive to write poetry. As he left she gave him a piece of opal. Now feeling even lower, Ottoline caught the train back to Garsington. Lytton came down at the end of February and was genuinely shocked by Ottoline's condition. Disguising his concern in flippancy, he told Virginia Woolf:

> Lady Omega Muddle is now I think almost at the last gasp – sink into a nursing-home, where she will be fed on nuts, and allowed to receive visitors (in bed).[13]

It was while she was in the nursing home - where Lytton came to see her - that Ottoline learnt something that relegated all her earlier blows to comparative insignificance.[14] It concerned Philip, Ottoline's long-suffering husband on whom she relied for stability. He had been absent from Garsington for much of the summer and autumn of 1916, having explained to Ottoline that his political work required him to remain in London. When he did eventually come up to Garsington he was accompanied by his secretary, an attractive young auburn-haired woman called Alice Jones (whose daytime job was assisting the editor of The

Nation, H.W. Massingham). Alice also did some secretarial work for Philip and Ottoline, which was why she had come up to Garsington. Ottoline did not pay much attention to Miss Jones as she was far too involved in other events happening around her. Nor had she taken much notice of the decision of her maid, Evelyn Merrifield, to leave around the same time. Ottoline had never been fond of Evelyn, whose tawny yellow eyes unsettled her. Again, she noticed nothing amiss.

Some weeks later Aldous Huxley caught sight of Philip at the Palladium in London in the company of a young woman. He accosted him, but Philip was evasive as to the identity of his female companion. Philip now realised that once Aldous started gossiping, the several secrets he was trying to keep would inevitably come out. Ottoline was still in the nursing home, but Philip felt he must tell her about what he had been hiding, which was that he had not only one but two mistresses: Alice Jones and Ottoline's former maid, Evelyn. And both of them were pregnant! Evelyn's child was due in June and Alice's in August. Rather than being concerned about how Ottoline would feel about his revelation, Philip was far more concerned about Evelyn's threat that, if she were not adequately provided for, she would spread the news about his promiscuity, and its consequences. He knew that this would destroy his political career. What effect it would have on Ottoline was secondary. It would have been little relief to him that Alice Jones, who was further up the social scale than the maid Evelyn, was planning to do all she could herself to support herself and her child, and was not threatening a scandal.

Having broken the shocking news to Ottoline, Philip dashed straight off to the House of Commons, where he was due to speak. But there he spoke so incoherently, and behaved so erratically, that he had to be escorted home to Bedford Square; after which he hurried back to Ottoline's nursing-home to try to do something to salvage the situation. But the establishment had closed for the night, so he left a note to Ottoline begging forgiveness and declaring that he loved only her. Next day, while Ottoline was still at the nursing-home, he went up to Garsington

The Worst Year of Her Life

where he summoned Gerald and Friedegond Shove into his room and informed them (they reported to Bloomsbury) that he was more intelligent than Ottoline, asking Shove to take down in writing what he was saying. He had created Ottoline, he said. Gerald, suspecting that Philip was suffering some form of mental breakdown, contacted Ottoline, who left her nursing home and raced up to Garsington with her brother, Lord Henry, who arranged for Philip to be put into an institution in south London. Meanwhile Clive Bell passed on news these goings on to Lytton and Carrington, and thus to all of Bloomsbury. In the event, Philip, who had suffered an earlier breakdown in his youth, quickly recovered his senses, though thereafter he would succumb to occasional "nerve attacks", some of them severe.

Ottoline tried to put a brave face – at least in public – on this, but she was now in a trough of deep depression, one which lasted for several months. Indeed, she never fully recovered from this crushing blow. Her whole world seemed to have collapsed. She had lost Bertie; Lawrence had pilloried her; now Philip had gravely deceived her. That the two women were to bear sons added to her anguish; as memories of the loss of her own baby son haunted her. She sent the babies christening presents; but was mortified by the knowledge that the two women had produced healthy sons for Philip. Now Ottoline herself started behaving erratically, making pathetic efforts to hide her years. She dyed her hair in an effort to rid it of the grey Bertie had observed. She smothered her face in make-up and smeared black kohl around her eyes. Her appearance verged on the bizarre, to the consternation of her friends.

The discovery of Philip's infidelity had been all the more devastating because of its total unexpectedness. Philip – that foundation on which her whole life was built, the cornerstone of her sanity – had been unfaithful to her. That she had been unfaithful to Philip, many times over, did not seem to enter her thoughts. Now she would wander off into the woods below Garsington, distraught, talking aloud to the trees in her black despair. The entries in her Diary at this time were, apparently, wild and chaotic. She envisaged Furies coming down to mock her; she felt she was at the bottom of a deep pit; and that light and sunshine had left her. Her life had become a mockery; all her foolish dreams and ideals were in tatters. The whole fantastic edifice she had built around herself had collapsed. During this difficult time Philip stayed aloof, distant, and unfeeling. Only two people came to her aid. The first was Millie Ellis, who had first been Ottoline's maid in 1914 and was now the housekeeper at Garsington. She became Ottoline's loyal companion and adviser during this difficult time. Millie also kept a close eye on Philip, whom she feared might try to commit suicide during one of his nervous episodes. Ottoline's second supporter was her other former maid, Brenty, who had warned Evelyn against the threatening course of action she was pursuing against Philip. Brenty advised Ottoline that she had to take on the task of supplying Evelyn and her child with financial support. This Ottoline did until Evelyn married in 1922.

Only gradually did Ottoline recover from this catastrophe. Looking back from 1936, she said in her *Memoirs* that the anguished things she wrote in her diary were but faint cries compared to her real feelings. "The potter's thumb-marks are still there," she wrote, "but as life has baked me and made me firm, and age has made me wiser and experience has helped me to lose more of self, so I hope I may never feel again those agonies."[15] She added that from then on she formed the habit of pulling down a curtain between herself and the outside world.

Philip, needless to say, was going through his own private hell. For years he had played second, or even third fiddle to Ottoline and her frenzied guests. He had been derided and ignored. His efforts to mix in and to help people met with constant rebuffs. So over the years he had retired behind his own stolid facade and led a private life of his own, and he had a place up in London he could escape to. The ingratitude of the conscientious objectors, together with what happened in Burnley and the way his colleagues in the Liberal Party had treated him over his anti-war sentiments, had left him little to feel proud of.

Now there was the additional burden of Ottoline's discovery of his infidelity and her subsequent breakdown.

During this fraught period Ottoline spent some of her time sitting – or more often stranding – for the portrait that Brett was labouring over, which had grown so tall it could only be accessed via a ladder. Clive Bell gleefully spread a rumour that Brett's "Colossus" had turned out to be a cruel caricature *"au Lawrence."* And though Brett strove long and hard with ladder and paintbrush, it soon became clear to everyone that the picture was not a success. Julian told her: "It's no good your painting Mummy, you can't ever make her as beautiful as she is."[16] When the work was eventually finished, Ottoline accused Brett of making her look like a prostitute, an accusation Brett denied vehemently.

Brett, like Maria, had developed a sort of schoolgirl crush on Ottoline. Early in 1917 someone cast doubts on the health of Brett's affection, for around this time Brett wrote to assure Ottoline that her love was "entirely pure." She had no physical feeling for her, she said, beyond the "intense enjoyment a beautifully shaped head and beautiful form give to anyone who loves forms and shapes. I have no real perversion. My love for you is as clean and clear as Crystal & fresh as the Wind".[17] Nevertheless, sometimes Ottoline found Brett's adoration as irritating as her deafness. At other times her sympathy was helpful, and they would spend hours closeted together discussing Ottoline's various emotional problems. Apart from Philip's infidelities and the drama surrounding them, Ottoline was concerned about Siegfried's attitude towards her. Did his aloofness mean he rejected her friendship? Or was it just shyness and diffidence? Brett was doubtful, and advised Ottoline to give up any idea of having a close emotional relationship with Siegfried; and instead concentrate on helping him as a poet.

By May Ottoline had recovered sufficiently to venture down to London, where she stayed in Gower Street where Brett had rooms. The city seemed to her lonely, arid and empty. She saw few soldiers; only women, children, and old men. The only pleasant memory was of an afternoon with Virginia Woolf, who herself was recovering from a mental breakdown, and was about to launch into the publishing business. Virginia seems to have been as pleased with the meeting as Ottoline was, as she reported to her sister Vanessa:

> *I was so much overcome by her beauty that I really felt as if I'd suddenly got into the sea, & heard the mermaids fluting on their rocks. How it was done I can't think; but she had red-gold hair in masses, cheeks as soft as cushions with a lovely deep crimson on the crest of them & a body really shaped more after my notion of a mermaid's than I've ever seen; not a wrinkle or blemish, swelling, but smooth. Our conversation was rather on those lines, so I'm not surprised that I made a good impression. She didn't seem so much of a fool as I'd been led to think; she was quite shrewd, though vapid in the intervals. I begged her to revive Bedford Sqre. & the salon, which she said she would, if anyone missed her. Then came protestations, invitations – in fact I don't see how we can get out of going there, though Leonard says he won't, & I know it will be a disillusionment. However, my tack is to tell her she is nothing but an illusion, which is true & then perhaps she'll live up to it.* [18]

Had Ottoline given up her futile attempts to ring her eyes with kohl and to plaster her face with heavy make-up? It would certainly seem so from Virginia's description of her. Virginia appreciated Ottoline's extraordinary qualities, despite often satirising her. She accepted an invitation to come to Garsington later in the year. Ottoline also spent an evening with Katherine Mansfield; they went to a balalaika concert at the Grafton Galleries. For an hour or so the music swept them both away from the drabness of London and the depression of war. Afterwards, as they walked arm-in-arm to the tube station, Katherine turned to Ottoline and said: "My corns are hurting, I must go to my old corn cutter tomorrow. Good night darling."[19]

The Worst Year of Her Life

Meanwhile, Ottoline's relations with Russell had recovered a little. With Siegfried absent and Philip a doubtful quantity, Ottoline turned back to Bertie for comfort and reassurance. He welcomed the reconciliation. He was finding he could not let Ottoline go as easily as he had thought. If he were to break away, the process would have to be more gradual. By Easter 1917 their letters had resumed an affectionate tone; and that summer he was a frequent guest at Garsington. Early in May he told Ottoline that he was tired and depressed, and couldn't prove to her how much he wanted her. Yet the thought of him seeing Colette continued to annoy Ottoline; and she told him so. He replied: "You mustn't imagine that I see C.M. constantly – only now and then when I happen to have nothing to do."[20] Ottoline replied in friendly terms and he wrote back gratefully: "My Darling, Thank you, thank you for your letter – it gave me very great happiness."[21] He said he was looking forward to coming to Garsington and saying lots more things to her – "all nice things".

Lytton was another visitor in May. He noted that Ottoline had improved greatly and had returned to her old self, though "still overwrought". He told Carrington:

> *Her ladyship is more fevered, jumpy and neurasthenic than ever, though as usual there have been moments (especially at first) when my heart melted towards her. She seems to me to be steadily progressing down to the depths of ruin. Perhaps the whole thing is simply the result of physical causes, perhaps if she could really rest and eat and be alone for a month or two we should see wonders, but I can hardly believe that now she ever will.*[22]

At Garsington Lytton sat out on the terrace in a deck-chair listening to Russell, "Old Birrell," and Clive Bell; while observing in a bemused fashion Ottoline's "new love", Siegfried; who had come back from France. Ottoline was overjoyed to have him safely back – the more so because he was now totally opposed to the war. His months in the trenches had shattered his nerves and he had written no more poetry. Siegfried felt he should make some public statement protesting at the slaughter, and was encouraged in this by Ottoline. Philip was less keen, pointing out the absurdity of a solitary second lieutenant raising his voice. Siegfried thought Philip's attitude was weak-kneed. He remembered one talk he had with Philip: "Staring at the sunset he leant on a farm gate, he himself – in his wide-brimmed hat – looked somehow defeated and ineffective, a compromising pacifist who had lost hope of dissuading mankind from its madness."[23] But Philip had been fighting for his beliefs far longer than Siegfried. Soon the poet had to return to his camp near Liverpool where he was pursued by a constant stream of gifts, including a large rug Ottoline had crocheted and doused with scent, the smell of which caused much ribaldry among his fellow officers. Finally in July he sent to a newspaper his "Soldier's Declaration" against the war and waited for the storm to break. When nothing happened, he flung his MC ribbon into the Mersey.

Two of his friends, Robert Graves and Eddie Marsh, fearing Siegfried might do something to get himself into even deeper trouble, mounted a campaign to have him declared mentally overwrought, and soon afterwards Siegfried was sent to a convalescent hospital near Edinburgh. Graves in particular thought that Ottoline and her fellow pacifists were a disruptive influence on Sassoon, and one reason he wanted to get him certified was to rescue him from their clutches. Ottoline's infatuation with Siegfried was a topic of much amusement in Bloomsbury, and even Philip was guilty of a little wry humour; remarking one day when an airman flew over Garsington and dropped a billet-doux to one of the lady guests: "Siegfried is Ottoline's airman."[24] Whether Ottoline was aware that Sassoon was primarily homosexual is not known. Over the years he had affairs with such notables as the actors Ivor Novello and Glyn Byam Shaw; Prince Philip of Hesse; the writer Beverley Nichols; and the Hon. Stephen Tenant. Perhaps she thought she could convert him. And indeed in 1933 he married an old friend, Hester

The Worst Year of Her Life

Gatty, and had a son, George. The marriage ended in 1945 when Sassoon returned to the company of his male friends.

Despite her unhappiness, Ottoline did her best to keep up appearances; and that summer of 1917 Garsington, more than ever before, seemed like some tableau transplanted out of the France of Louis XV, with Ottoline playing the part of Madame du Deffand. No wonder Lytton, a determined Francophile, relished it so. Brittle though its surface was, Ottoline clutched at the outward gaiety to prevent her inward troubles from rising up and overwhelming her. Yet things continued to turn against her. Even Siegfried was proving a disappointment. One day Middleton Murry, who had helped Siegfried draft his Soldier's Declaration, showed Ottoline a letter in which Siegfried thanked him warmly for his help and support. Ottoline wrote in her Diary: "He has never once said a word of thanks to me, and after all I have done a good deal for him."[25]

In June she went down to London where she met Russell and they had yet another quarrel over Colette; whom Ottoline had conceived a dislike for, describing her as "beautiful in rather a vulgar, stagy manner…too assured and self-confident, too much the attitude of the duchess."[26] She made no secret of her opinion and this – Russell explained to her – was why he had been so cruel to her in January. "It was practically the first time I had deliberately disagreed with your judgment of anyone," he told her.[27] He admitted that his relationship with Colette was not as casual as he had earlier implied; but, he assured Ottoline, this made not the shadow of a difference to what he felt for her. "Nearly a year and a half ago now I realised once and for all that I must detach my instinct from you because otherwise life was too painful to be borne ["instinct" was one of Russell's euphemisms for sexual relations]. That left me with a feeling of grudge, unless I could let my instinct go to someone else."[28] For a while this satisfied Ottoline, and for the time being she and Russell were back on pre-January terms. "I got your dear letter yesterday," he wrote later in June, "I *will* hold on to you. My Darling, I love you always, always. I mustn't look to you for a sort of mundane every-day happiness, but you hold my inmost being...my love, my dear one."[29] But it was a reconciliation built on shifting sand, and a month later the more usual on-again, off-again pattern was resumed. "There are times when I am *absolutely* in tune with you," he wrote to her in July, "but they would not be quite genuine unless they were interspersed with moods of a different kind."[30]

Early in the same month Ottoline caught the measles from Julian and was laid low for several weeks; afterwards going off to convalesce on the Isle of Wight, accompanied by Philip. In the train down they sat opposite each other and Ottoline saw Philip's lips moving in silent conversation. *How inaccessible we all are,* she thought, *so apart and alone.* On the Isle of Wight they joined Julian, who was already holidaying there with several young friends. Ottoline swam and sunbathed; and, although she got sunburned, her strength began to return. When she got back to Garsington she found a letter from Middleton Murry asking her to take in as a boarder his brother Arthur, who was about 15. "Dear Ottoline," Murry wrote, "shape my brother. I would have him in no other hands."[31] After her experiences of the past 12 months Ottoline doubted her ability to shape anyone, but she agreed to take Arthur, who was put to work on the farm.

Around the middle of August Katherine also came to stay for a few weeks. The weather was warm and she and Ottoline spent many happy hours pottering around the garden, cutting lavender and other aromatic plants. She told Ottoline: "I positively lead another life with you there, bending over the flowers, sitting under the trees, feeling the delights of the heat and the shade."[32] It was on a late summer's evening that Garsington was at its most magical. Katherine would watch Ottoline come out on to the lawn swinging a Chinese lantern while the moon shone down illuminating the grey stone house and the silver pond below. On one such balmy evening Mark Gertler, David Garnett, Carrington, Murry, and several others dressed up in fancy costume and danced an improvised ballet on the lawn as Katherine wandered the paths, her senses alive to the sights and smells of the night. She wrote a poem about that scene, entitled "Night-scented Stocks," the first two verses of which went:

> *White, white in the milky night The*
> *moon danced over a tree.*
> *"Wouldn't it be lovely to swim in the lake!"*
> *Somebody whispered to me.*
>
> *"Oh, do-do-do!" cooed someone else,*
> *And clasped her hands to her chin.*
> *"I should so love to see the white bodies –*
> *All the white bodies jump in!"*

Katherine returned to London, leaving Murry behind to spend hours talking with Ottoline about life and literature. Ottoline thought the relationship between Murry and Katherine rather curious. When Katherine was around, Murry acted like a devoted spaniel. Yet Katherine, she noted, sometimes treated him very offhandedly; once calling him "a little mole hung out on a string to dry."[33] Ottoline herself liked Murry, and regarded him as just as poetical and idealistic as Katherine. One evening, after a long discussion about Lawrence, Murry and Ottoline were standing alone in the red room when Murry suddenly asked her if "he might come into her heart."[34] He went on to say how wonderful it was that he and Katherine had found someone whom they could love and trust. He was implying, thought Ottoline, that he wanted to demonstrate his love in a more concrete way. "My answer," said Ottoline, "was rather vague, as I was quite unprepared for any emotional intimacy with him." After they had retired to their respective rooms, Ottoline found she couldn't sleep, and went out into the garden to think over what had happened. "After wandering about for some time," she recalled, "I couldn't resist calling up to Murry in his room, as I saw his light was still burning. 'You must come down, Murry. It is wicked to miss this lovely night.'" They walked together round the garden talking "very openly, very intimately, not of love but of life."[35] Later Ottoline went to bed happy in the belief that in Murry and Katherine she had found two close friends. Murry returned to London next morning to re-join Katherine, and Ottoline was surprised not to hear from either of them for some time. At last came a polite letter from Murry refusing Ottoline's offer of a cottage at Garsington. This abrupt change of tone hurt Ottoline and she wrote in her Diary: "Why did he ask to come into my life and push against the door as he did, and then run away?"[36] Ottoline's account of this incident, however, could be suspect. It may be that she read into Murry's behaviour more than was actually there. She wrote in her Diary: "Why am I tormented by the desire of companionship? I am too easily hurt, too fastidious and proud, too sensitive. But now I must put all these desires away and be happy alone."[37]

And indeed, they may have had a physical relationship at some time. A letter Murry wrote Ottoline a little before this implies that there was a reciprocal affection between them. He had said: "But when I try to find a name for my feeling towards you, then it is that I begin to suspect that I am in love with you."[38] After Murry returned to London, Katherine's letters to Ottoline were distinctly cooler. Brett said Katherine told her she was bitter and angry about Ottoline. The next time Ottoline was in London she went to see Katherine. At first Katherine was "formal and haughty", but then she told Ottoline why she had changed. She said that Murry had come back from Garsington "exceedingly distraught" and had collapsed on a sofa groaning and sighing. When Katherine asked him what was wrong he told her that a "dreadful thing" had happened. Ottoline, he said, had fallen "deeply and passionately" in love with him.[39] Katherine accused Ottoline of treachery, saying that she was trying to take Murry away from her. Ottoline laughed, so she recorded; but to Katherine it was no laughing matter, and it brought to a premature end the budding intimacy between her and Ottoline. Yet it did not end Murry's friendship with Ottoline, though henceforth it resumed a strictly platonic tone.

More disillusioned than ever, Ottoline now pinned her

The Worst Year of Her Life

hopes for finding the sympathetic soul she had always been searching for entirely on Siegfried. Even though he too had disappointed her, he remained her symbol of how the Moloch of War was devouring England's youth and creativity. Long intimate letters, interspersed with gifts of books and quilts, continued to follow him to his military hospital in Scotland. In November he told her that since his protest had failed, the only way he could help his fellow soldiers was to go back to the trenches in France. Horrified, Ottoline wrote begging him to change his mind. She even offered to send Bertie up to dissuade him. Siegfried responded: "I don't think there is any doubt about my going back to the war as I've dreamt that something burst and it smashed me up. But it doesn't matter does it?"[40] Ottoline decided to go up and see Siegfried in person. She had expected him to meet her train, but he wasn't there because he had been playing golf and couldn't get to the station on time. So she hired a taxi and went off to wait for him at her hotel. Finally he arrived and they had dinner together. He poured out his problems and doubts, interspersing them with comments about some of the other female guests in the dining-room whom he criticised for wearing furs "like primitive savages."[41] (For a former fox-hunter this was indeed strong talk.) Next morning she waited for him to come and pick her up, but he was late again. In the afternoon they went for a walk and Siegfried told her he found her very complicated and artificial. That night Ottoline went back to her room feeling chilled and rejected. The next day she left. Siegfried didn't see her off; he was playing golf again. In the train she broke down and wept. In her *Memoirs*, Ottoline, describing this visit, said: 'It is exhausting to give and give...without any return. One deludes oneself with the belief that by giving one will receive something, but it isn't true."[42] Back at Garsington she didn't parade her disappointment, and in fact her friends thought she and Siegfried were still on the best of terms. Hearing about her visit to Edinburgh, Mark Gertler wrote to her playfully: "I wonder...'Not a word, Ah! Hah! Hem! Hem!' as George Robey would say'."[43] On February 12, 1918, Siegfried, now recovered, was ordered out to Egypt to continue his war service.

Throughout the autumn of 1917 Ottoline's relations with Russell went from crisis to crisis. One Friday she returned to Garsington from seeing a film in Oxford to find that a very unhappy Bertie had turned up wanting to stay the weekend. "He flattened me out at once and extinguished all my sparkle," Ottoline wrote. "He is always depressed when I have had a happy time that he hasn't shared in."[44] On the Sunday they had a long talk in Ottoline's boudoir. Ottoline recorded in her Diary that Russell had said "his usual unkind things" about her, accusing her of living in a state of high tension and of tiring everyone.[45] But the real point of disagreement was Colette. Ottoline wrote: "He isn't able to manage a friendship. I thought now that he is happy, in love with someone else, it would be easier and that we could be good friends; but he is so very reserved about that side of his life, which makes it awkward and then my pride is hurt and I am reserved too, so the residue is small."[46] She believed that Russell's protestations of unhappiness were a sham and she suspected that he spent most of his time gallivanting around London with Colette. On one of his letters she wrote: "He was really very happy at this time with C. M.!"[47] She accused him of "enjoying life up to the hilt" and told him she would have no further truck with him; and that they would have to end their friendship. Russell replied: "I can only accept what you say – but I am profoundly unhappy that things should end in such a spirit." He finished his letter with a curt "Goodbye."[48] Yet within a week both were regretting what they had said, and on September 20 he wrote saying he wanted "to start afresh". They should put aside mutual criticism, and he added: "I do want to get back to a sense of union, not division."[49] Ottoline, too, was tired of bickering and from now on relations between them began to improve.

Her emotional fingers by now well and truly singed, Ottoline began to turn for companionship and sympathy to the younger people who were beginning to come to Garsington. For them, Bedford Square meant nothing. Most came, not from

Cambridge, but Oxford. Perhaps because of this, they did not bring with them the atmosphere of gossip and intrigue that Bloomsbury generated. She had already met one of the first of this new breed. This was Aldous Huxley, and for over a year now he had been an almost permanent guest at Garsington; and Ottoline was beginning to regard him as one of her dwindling band of intimate friends. Lytton didn't like him; "too Oxfordy", he said.[50] But Aldous was the shape of things to come at Garsington. In fact he was the first of a new generation who mostly came not to talk with Ottoline on equal terms, but to sit instead at her feet – or at the feet of her illustrious guests – and listen. Aldous, however, like one or two there such as Robert Gathorne-Hardy and David Cecil, broke through the age barrier, and became close friends on an equal footing with Ottoline

At Garsington Aldous worked at what odd jobs he could manage around the farm (he was almost blind) and spent the rest of his time peering through a magnifying glass at a book, or just sitting in a chair; his long body coiled up, observing the crazy and fascinating things that went on around him. Many people, including Ottoline at first, took his long silences as aloofness, but it was only a device he used to disconcert people. Aldous found it easy to talk with Ottoline; for though she often disclaimed any conversational or intellectual skills, she was nevertheless able to sustain the interest of people with minds of the quality of Huxley's and Russell's for long periods; and over many years. Sometimes Aldous and Ottoline would talk most of the day and late into the night. Then he would follow her up the stairs, pausing on each step to continue the discussion, talking all the way down the corridor and into her bedroom where Ottoline would undress unselfconsciously while he sat on the floor talking on and on past midnight. In letters he was always telling her how much he appreciated her and Garsington. "After all, Ottoline," he wrote to her once, "you and I are some of the few people who feel life is real, life is earnest."[51]

In September 1917 Aldous left Garsington to take up a teaching post at Eton. But he returned regularly for visits, despite his father's disapproval of his son visiting Garsington, "Where all the cranks are."[51] Aldous came back to Garsington particularly to hear news of Maria Nys, of whom he had grown very fond. She had been packed off first to stay with Brett in London, then to her family's villa in Florence, where Ottoline hoped she would settle down happily and lose some of her childish ways. Ottoline believed Aldous' friendship with Maria to be ill-starred: "He so intellectual and so highly cultivated and self-absorbed; she so very passive and yet like all foreign girls, expecting so much attention."[52] In November 1917, in response to the invitation Ottoline had issued earlier in the year, Virginia and Leonard Woolf paid a visit to Garsington. There Virginia observed people strewn about in a "sealingwax coloured room" and Aldous Huxley toying with great discs of ivory and marble; "the Garsington draughts". She saw Philip "tremendously encased in the best leather," and Ottoline in velvet and pearls. Brett and Gertler were there, together with Lytton, who was "semi-recumbent in a vast chair". Droves of guests moved from room to room and up to Ottoline's boudoir for private chats. The day drifted on. Fredegond Shove was admitted to the inner-sanctum in the morning; and after tea Virginia herself was granted an audience for an hour or so's chat over a log fire. Virginia found Ottoline more likable than she had anticipated: "Her vitality seemed to be a credit to her and in private talk her vapours give way to some quite clear bursts of shrewdness."[53] Virginia felt that, as an artist, she ought really to quarrel with Ottoline because she was an aristocrat. She was sure that was why so many of Ottoline's artist friends were so disagreeable. Yet she felt Garsington was quite enough of a work of art to excuse the comings and goings into Ottoline's boudoir (a perceptive point, which is also discussed below). She told Ottoline that when she wrote her "great Garsington novel" there would be a streak of white lightning, and that would be Ottoline. Virginia saw Garsington not as a house but a caravan, a floating palace, and she noted in her Diary:

> *The horror of the Garsington situation is great of course, but to the outsider the obvious view is that O. and P. and the house provide a good deal, which isn't accepted very graciously. However to deal blame rightly in such a situation is beyond the wit of a human being: they've brought themselves to such a pass of intrigue and general intricacy of relationship that they're hardly sane about each other. In such conditions I think Ott. deserves some credit for keeping her ship in full sail, as she certainly does.*[54]

The high-priest of Bloomsbury described the "horror of Garsington" in slightly different terms. Lytton observed a Virginia "in high feather". She dominated the gathering, very different, he remarked, from her demeanour ten years ago at Peppard; when she crouched before Ottoline "like a suppliant kitten".[55] He himself described Ottoline as being "worm-eaten with envy & malevolence". He went on:

> *...one hardly knows where to tread – very unfortunate. I thought, too, (after 24 hours of tete-a-tete) that I detected something like a sense of guilt, and perhaps if one got hold of her, isolated from Philip and the rest of the horrors, she might take on a new lease of life. The worst of it is that she shows no symptoms of liking anybody – it is all either underhand cat's-clawing or vague romantic flummery: decidedly most unfortunate.*

Ottoline's ship might have appeared to Virginia to be in full sail that November 1917; but it was still an unhappy vessel. "I feel as if some black evil cloud has descended onto this place," wrote Ottoline, "and has blackened all the happiness and joy, eclipsing colour and sunshine."[56] Keats was the only soul she could commune with, she told Vanessa Bell. Vanessa commented to Roger Fry: "Did you ever hear such twaddle? Think of poor Keats as Ottoline's latest poet at Garsington!"[57] Ottoline even considered leaving Garsington, of escaping somewhere and becoming purged and renewed. She discussed the idea with Brett, who offered to go with her. Finally she decided to stay and keep going through the motions. "Everything I lived for seems to be knocked over," she wrote in her Diary. "Everyone that I thought was a friend has shrivelled up, faded away...I have a feeling that I am in a long dark tunnel – calling, calling for help – but no answer comes."[58]

And so 1917, the worst year in Ottoline's life, drew to a close. It had begun badly and it finished badly. Christmas that year at Garsington was a pale spectre of the festivities of the two previous years. Mark Gertler hardly improved the day by repeating some of the gossip that was currently circulating around Bloomsbury about Ottoline. Then matters were made even worse when a turkey served up for Christmas dinner proved to be suspect. There are several (malicious) accounts of this incident. David Garnett said it was one of the peacocks, called Argos, whose feathers had fallen out and whose skin had broken out in green carbuncles. Clive Bell was horrified to see the bird on the table, and refused to take a helping. But the rest of the guests tucked in and almost immediately were stricken with violent stomach pains. Ottoline, said Garnett, insisted it was a mass outbreak of appendicitis. But this unlikely explanation was rendered even more suspect by the fact that Brett, one of the worst-stricken, had had her appendix removed years before. Clive, who had to go to London unexpectedly, had written an amusing letter about the disaster and left it on the hall table ready for the post the next day. Gertler and Carrington suggested steaming open his letter and reading it to the company. Ottoline no doubt had no part in this, but she certainly got to hear its contents. Again, she was not amused.

INTERLUDE
A BRIEF MOMENT IN THE LIMELIGHT

Olga Deterding - perhaps the last of the great London literary hostesses

WHEN NEWS that I was writing the biography of Lady Ottoline Morrell began to circulate around London's literary circles, I started to get invitations to the city's various literary salons. One salon was run by Jean Gimpel, of the Paris art firm, Gimpel et Fils. Gimpel's salon was held on regular Sunday afternoons in his house in Fulham.

His was a relatively low-key affair, although the guests were leading authors and other literary identities. The conversation was seriously literary, and the guests suitably well-known. Another smaller salon was held in a basement in Chelsea where all the women guests seemed to have very long chins and earnest looks on their bespectacled faces.

Another very different literary salon was run by Dutch-born Olga Deterding, the Shell Oil heiress, who (it was rumoured) had inherited £50 million from her father, Sir Henri Deterding, the founder of Royal Dutch Petroleum.

Olga's salon was very glamorous indeed, held in her three-storey apartment above a bank in Piccadilly, overlooking Green Park. An Oxford graduate, Olga had worked in Albert Schweitzer's leper colony in West Africa, before returning to live in London in 1957. Later she had a romance with the TV presenter Alan Whicker.

She was a down-to-earth, intelligent woman, who enjoyed talking about Ottoline, and we got on well. At that time she was living with Jonathan Routh, the prankster presenter of the *Candid Camera* television show. Jonathan had created a rural tableau on one floor of Olga's apartment, putting a flock of life-size model sheep on a fake-turf meadow.

Each floor of the apartment was connected by a spiral staircase, and the accepted practice was to climb up and down the stairs to join and re-join the various groups gathered on each floor. As the biographer of Ottoline, I was the latest biographer on the block, and much in demand for snippets of gossip gleaned from my research.

Alan Riddell, who also had a literary "salon" in the 1970s

It was Alan Riddell, a Scots-born Australian whose concrete poetry, or typewriter art, was then in the vanguard of literary endeavour, who had introduced me to Olga. Alan was a gentle, quiet, unassuming man who wore socks and sandals whom we had previously known as a journalist in Sydney. He had returned to England where he lived in a mews house off Queensway where he held his own much-more-modest salon at irregular intervals.

One we attended in 1972 was graced with the presence of Susan George, who regaled us with stories of the behaviour of director Sam Peckinpah during the filming of *Straw Dogs*, in which she starred.

Some years later Alan Riddell died from an aneurism of the brain. All of his friends, including Olga Deterding, attended his funeral, some bringing hors d'oevres for a wake held in the garden of his mews house.

Olga herself died not long after from a freak accident caused by choking on a chop bone at a New Year's Eve party. I believe that was the end of the era of great London literary salons.

CHAPTER 20
Bertie Goes to Gaol

Ottoline in a pensive mood – she had much on her mind

ACTUALLY the incident of the carbuncular turkey (or peacock) might have been an echo of another event at Garsington around the end of 1917. This was the infamous workers' revolt, and its aftermath. The Wat Tyler of this insurrection was the future left-wing economist Gerald Shove; who had assumed moral leadership of the conscientious objectors who worked on the farm ("worked" is perhaps overstating it, for, according to Ottoline, almost all of them were bone-lazy, and Shove the laziest of the lot). A practising socialist, he saw it as his duty to expose capitalistic oppression wherever he found it – even in the house where he was a non-paying guest – and one of the first things he did at Garsington was form a union. Most of his fellow COs signed up; but the farm workers from the village proved less militant, and the uprising collapsed. Next, Shove decided to direct his collectivisation skills to reorganising the fowl-house. He convinced Philip – the chief plutocrat on the farm – that egg production could be boosted if a special feed were purchased. But, instead of improving, the egg-yield dropped; moreover, the hens became increasingly prone to illness (which may well have spread to the peacocks). Yet Shove's socialistic ambitions still simmered, and – so one story went – he decided on a grand stroke. At the head of a group of COs he stormed the manor house shouting: "Down with capitalist exploitation!" The revolution was short-lived and soon afterwards its leader decamped in a taxi, taking with him a number of the Garsington laying hens. When Philip went down to the fowl-house to count the loss he discovered why the hens had been producing so poorly lately. Shove had failed entirely to attend to their material well-being. The roosts hadn't been cleaned for weeks, and the unfortunate occupants were sitting on mounds of accumulated droppings and rotting grain. So the presence of a sick fowl at the Christmas dinner-table would not have been altogether surprising.

From this it might be thought that Philip was not a competent farmer; but this isn't so. His personnel policy may have been faulty – though there were reasons for this – but in other respects he was both conscientious and knowledgeable in matters agricultural. Farming had interested him long before he bought Garsington; and in Parliament he was a frequent speaker on land reform issues and the plight of agricultural workers. During the war he had made Garsington virtually self-sufficient in food; and he was always going off to sales to buy new equipment and stock. In every way he was the very model of the gentleman farmer; a career he was to concentrate on more and more as his political star waned. After the end of the war his biggest problem on the farm was that he no longer had access to the free labour of the COs; and was obliged (Gerald Shove or not) to pay full farm-wages, which began to undermine his rural enterprises.

By early 1918 Ottoline had begun to recover from the blows of the previous terrible year. In January she wrote: "I think I am emerging...as I look back on the past year it seems as if I had traversed a land of swamps and mire and jungle and fever and horrors. Now I am in a canoe alone, pushing off from that unhappy country."[1] Though she was much more cynical now, she still needed human company and sympathy. To her they were as essential as light and oxygen; so she had to force herself to overlook the slings and arrows of her outrageous fortune. Thus in January, when Katherine asked if Murry, who was ill, could come to convalesce at Garsington; Ottoline welcomed him. Yet after he arrived, he spent most of his time with Brett; and Ottoline suspected they were talking about her behind her back. Katherine also came for a weekend, and her attitude filled Ottoline with mistrust. 'She is too dreadfully lacking in human kindness," she wrote in her *Memoirs*. "I was relieved when they left."[2]

But if it was so unpleasant to have Katherine at Garsington, why did Ottoline ask her to come in the first place? And why did she invite her back later in 1918? The answer is that Ottoline was not consistent, by any means. At times she liked Katherine, at others she didn't; and this applied to other friends too. In fact, Ottoline's *Memoirs* cannot be taken as always reflecting her considered opinion. Compiled from her Diaries, from which she transferred large hunks without much revision, they were, as Ottoline herself said, her "only outlet"; and into them she poured all her private thoughts, grievances, and fears.[3] Moreover, these she usually expressed in a style that today is regarded as sentimental and Victorian; what Vanessa Bell called her twaddle. But behind this "twaddle" was a keen mind and perceptive eye, as Virginia Woolf recognised when she observed that, once Ottoline banished her "vapours", she could be sensible and acute.

In February 1918 Ottoline spent several days in London, staying at the Kenilworth Hotel in Bloomsbury (44 Bedford Square was now fully let, and its lease was soon to be sold to Margot Asquith). There she witnessed an air raid by German dirigibles. She also went for a long walk, observing how much the war had changed London since the start of the war. Later, after she returned to Garsington, she composed a short sketch which she called "Shadows", describing her visit to London. She recounted how she had met several old friends whom she expected would help lift her depression; but their self-centred interests merely increased her loneliness, and when the air-raid siren sounded, they scuttled off without saying goodbye. The following day she went out into the streets of the city searching for human contact. In Whitehall she saw office girls flowing out of the War Office "fluttering off like a flight of birds, shaking their feathers in the air".[4] Where did they come from? she asked herself. Did they realise as they tripped from one office to another that they were frail little shuttles in a vast mill of destruction? She was swept along with them into the Strand, where she saw group after group of men in uniform, mainly from the colonies. On the corner of Waterloo Bridge she saw a young soldier, standing on the edge of the pavement; mud-stained, weather-beaten, and just back from the front. It began to dawn on her it was these young soldiers – not her cynical London acquaintances – who were the real, substantial people she was looking for.

With this discovery, Ottoline's pacifist attitude began to change. The hatred she felt for the war and all its works was gradually replaced by a sense of helpless compassion for those caught up in its machinery. To her, this suffering was all the more real because her young poet Siegfried had gone back to the front to face the guns again. From the Middle East he wrote to her: "The whole thing is too mad. Why should I be in *Palestine,* and being paid 15/- a day, to *kill Turks?*[5] She sent him books and other gifts to keep up his morale. He himself had started writing again, and a book of his poems was about to be published. His bitterness for the war spilled over into his letters. He told Ottoline he had seen a line of Turkish prisoners at work: "One was shot the other day for striking an officer – so he has escaped."[6] In May he was sent back to France. Ottoline sent him chocolates and he thanked "Lady Bountiful." He wrote: "The gas is awful bad out here and now our gallant fellas take every opportunity of availing themselves of it to get away from the line – small blame to them."[7]

Up at Garsington, Ottoline had befriended two young Royal Flying Corps pilots; and one day in March, in return for hospitality at Garsington, they invited her and Brett to watch a flying display at their airfield. The two women stared skywards as daring young men in their flying machines looped-the-loop and showed off their flying skills. Then, as they watched, the wings of one plane crumpled and the aircraft crashed, killing the pilot. Ottoline assumed that this would put an end to the day's aerobatics. But no; within a few minutes the other aircraft resumed the display. Such demonstrations of reckless bravery increased her feeling of helplessness. But what could she do? She couldn't bring herself to "help the war"; and she didn't believe that taking up lorry-driving or nursing would make her feel less guilty. Later in the summer she assuaged her guilt a little by inviting groups of wounded soldiers from Oxford to come out to Garsington to sit in the garden on Sunday afternoons; mixing incongruously with conscientious objector Lytton Strachey and former Prime Minister Asquith. The wounded soldiers' clerklike signatures appear on successive pages of Ottoline's green visitor's book...S.S. Thornton (Sherwood Foresters); James Graham (Royal N. Lancs); D. Thomas (13 Batt. Tanks). But they remained symbols of the horror of the war, rather than individuals.

At th end of March Clive Bell wrote saying he had heard Ottoline had been in the thick of "the most surprising adventures".[8] What tale had reached into the wilds of Sussex to titillate Clive's ears? Maybe it was the aerobatics display, maybe something else. His enigmatic letter gave no further clue. Certainly March was a particularly worrying month for Ottoline. One concern stemmed from a meeting Philip and probably Ottoline attended early in the month at which the future Soviet Foreign Minister Litvinov spoke in praise of the Bolshevik revolution that had broken out in Russia. Philip also spoke, and the following day the newspapers reported that he said it would be a good thing if there were a revolution in England too. This report caused a furore; and in Parliament the Home Secretary, Sir George Cave, made a virulent attack on Philip, almost branding him a traitor. Philip wasn't in the House to answer the attack and, the next day, he got leave to make a personal explanation. He complained about Sir George's gross impoliteness in attacking a fellow MP without notice, and without checking the facts. Then Philip explained that, far from advocating revolution, he had said the exact opposite; that a revolution like the Bolsheviks' could not happen in Britain, and that the only revolution the British people would accept was a revolution of opinion. Philip's reply did not attract the same publicity that his original misrepresentation had done; yet the episode turned respectable opinion further against the "pacifist" Morrells.

It is significant that Ottoline and Philip should have been seen flirting with socialist ideas; if not its ideals. As the war went into its fourth year, many radical Liberals had begun to turn further to the left. For a while Philip and Ottoline harboured the hope that socialism might be the answer to Britain's and the world's problems. Several of their friends joined the emerging Labour Party whose leaders, including Ramsay MacDonald and Philip Snowden, were welcome guests at Garsington. Here, MacDonald was often prevailed upon to do his famous impersonation of George V (who had a very high regard for the future Labour Prime Minister). Later in 1918 Ottoline and Philip attended a national conference of the new party and where Ottoline met Kerensky, the former Prime Minister of an interim government in Russia. But their flirtation with socialism was short-lived. Ottoline and Philip soon decided it was politics itself, rather than its particular varieties, that was at fault. The subsequent election in 1918 produced a coalition of Liberals and Conservatives (forming a "National" Government). With only 133 Liberals left standing, Philip lost his seat in Burnley (to the Labour candidate). With that, Philip's and Ottoline's involvement in active politics ended; and after the war ended he and Ottoline had little to do with the Liberal (or any other) political party.

Another worry for Ottoline was Bertie, whose increasingly-overt anti-war activities were starting to get him into trouble. Despite her annoyance over his infatuation with Colette, she agreed to go up to London to discuss his problems and see what she could do to help him. Yet Russell was not the only man in her life causing her concern. In France Siegfried was facing death daily, while at home Lytton and Gertler had again been threatened with conscription; as the government sifted through the residue of cripples and COs in a final effort to provide more fodder for the Western Front. Again Lytton's "Mahomet's coffin" came to his rescue; but Gertler had to wait for the decision on his appeal. Ottoline's women friends were not much consolation to her. Katherine wrote apologising for her silence, and Brett, moping round Garsington with her ear-trumpet, was getting on Ottoline's nerves. By April Ottoline's headaches had reached such a pitch that she consulted a woman doctor, who told her that catarrh was causing her migraines; and prescribed daily gargling. The gurgles didn't help; so Ottoline and Philip went off on a driving-tour around Oxfordshire and Berkshire. As they drove through the spring countryside, the beauty of the fields and flowers slowly restored her spirit. Also the tour did a lot to knit up Ottoline's much-ravelled marriage. "Philip was happy," she wrote in her *Memoirs*, "and I loved being alone with him."[9] They drove back by way of Sutton Courtenay, where they dropped in on Asquith; Ottoline noting that her old admirer was declining into a rather boring anecdotage. "It shows such an arrested lazy mind," she wrote in her *Memoirs*.[10] Asquith did, however, reveal a glimmer of interest in the current scene, evincing a marked dislike of Clive Bell, whom he described as "that fat little yellow-haired bounder".

When she returned to Garsington, Ottoline found Mark Gertler waiting for her. Poor Gertler had been having a rough time of it lately. Only a handful of friends and critics had appreciated his work; and since 1916, (when he finished "The Merry-Go-Round", which Lawrence praised as "the best *modern* picture I have ever seen"), Gertler had hardly sold a thing. His health wasn't good – soon tuberculosis was to be diagnosed –

and, worst of all, he had at last realised that he had lost his boyhood love Carrington to Bloomsbury's leading homosexual. He and Lytton had actually come to blows recently; the following day Gertler apologised, thereafter confining his aggression to the composition of obscene stanzas addressed to Lytton, but which he never dared to send. At the end of March Gertler's call-up appeal was finally granted and he fled down to Garsington; where he knew he would find sympathy for his many troubles. Gertler was a particular favourite of Ottoline's. He had been a welcome guest both at Bedford Square and Garsington ever since the day four years earlier he saw the tip of the ostrich feather of Ottoline's hat emerge up the stairs of his East End garret. In a way, Ottoline discovered Gertler, introducing him into the smart world and hanging his paintings for her Thursday guests to see. Later, at Garsington, she set aside a studio for him; and offered him employment on the farm, should the tribunal force him to do agricultural work. But, most of all, she had been his staunchest ally in his pursuit of Carrington. He told Brett: "You have no idea how comforting it feels to have a sort of family and home now at Garsington. There have been moments [in London] when I sunk to the lowest pit of depression. At such moments the thought of Garsington was my only consolation."[11]

There was an element of maternalism in Ottoline's fondness for Gertler; but this was only part of their relationship. She found him an amusing and delightful companion whose swarthy good looks ("like a young Corsair") and sensitive mind stimulated her. Often they would go off alone together to galleries and theatres. "She is better to meet in the evenings than most people," he said. At Garsington, Ottoline and Gertler spent many hours mulling over the turns of fate that had deprived them each of the companions of their heart (that is, Carrington for Gertler and Siegfried for Ottoline). At dinner Brett would join them (Julian, now 12, was away at boarding school, and Juliette, her governess, had gone off to work for Brett's sister, the Ranee of Sarawak) and the talk would turn to that odd household over at Tidmarsh; where they imagined Lytton and Carrington were wallowing in domesticity; as peculiar a spectacle as Lytton playing tennis with Nijinsky in Bedford Square.

Meanwhile, at Tidmarsh, over similar lunches and dinners attended by the Shoves, Clive Bell, Mary Hutchinson, and other elements of Bloomsbury, the motherly attentions Gertler was getting at Garsington caused just as much comment and amusement. Carrington suspected that Ottoline's current concern for Gertler's well-being was influenced not a little by a sense of rivalry: Carrington had "got" Lytton; so Ottoline would lavish her attentions on Gertler. To all this Lytton affected indifference; though he did remark that he was puzzled at what Ottoline and Gertler saw in each other, concluding that the clue to their relationship was that they were so different that neither personality ever impinged on the other. The rift between Tidmarsh and Garsington widened only gradually; with Lytton and Ottoline continuing to exchange friendly letters; while Ottoline still wrote to Carrington. In one letter Ottoline told her "Give my love to the Eminent One...I hope he won't become quite like Maynard – whom I find too far gone into the land of...???"[12]

As a result of his anti-war campaigning, Bertie went to prison. For a long time his activities had been threatening to land him there; but the way it happened was something of a surprise. The immediate cause was a fairly innocuous article he wrote for *The Tribunal*, a weekly newspaper issued by an anti-conscription group, in which he predicted that American troops would be used to intimidate strikers in England. Apparently this struck a sore spot somewhere, and Russell, despite his eminence and background – his grandfather had been Prime Minister of England – was arraigned and sentenced to six months' solitary confinement in Brixton Prison. Lytton, who attended the hearing, wrote to Ottoline: "It was really infamous...the spectacle of a louse like Sir John Dickinson [the magistrate] rating Bertie for immorality and sending him to prison!...James and I came away with our teeth chattering with fury."[13]

Actually Russell wasn't too perturbed about going to gaol. It would be a fitting climax to his anti-war work, and would focus even more attention on the stupidity of the authorities. However, he did take precautions; writing to his friends asking them to use whatever influence they had to get him classified as a First Division prisoner, which would allow him comforts like special food and plenty of books (which was granted). Ottoline was very upset by this new example of war hysteria, and did her best to relieve the austerity of Bertie's incarceration. Although their love affair had by now virtually flickered out; there remained between them a tie of loyalty and understanding that went beyond mere friendship. Moreover, whenever one of Russell's new loves (such as Colette) impinged on this friendship, some of the old possessiveness would come back, and she would reel him in again.

When he went into gaol, Russell was very much in love with Colette; but soon she became involved with another man, causing him acute pangs of jealousy. In this situation Ottoline and Colette came to an agreement about visiting rights to Bertie. They would go to see him at Brixton prison on alternate visiting days, following a schedule drawn up by Ottoline and Russell's elder brother, Frank (whom he was to succeed as the Third Earl Russell). In her *Memoirs* Ottoline describes how Frank would meet her and accompany her to Brixton. The second Earl Russell had himself been imprisoned in Brixton for bigamy; and at the gate the warders would welcome him as an old habitué. "How are you my Lord?" "Quite well, thank you, Jackson, how is my brother getting on?"[14]

Ottoline would take along large bunches of flowers from the garden at Garsington, together with lavender bags, scented soap, and toilet water – to make his cell smell sweet – and quantities of books. All these had to be first handed to a warder who presided over the visit to ensure nothing improper occurred. Ottoline would also bring a little bunch of sweet-smelling herbs which she would hold out across the table, glancing first at the warder for his permission, then handing them to Russell and saying: "I think you will find *this* bunch *very* sweet."[15] What warder could deny these unworldly descendants of two of England's greatest families this little breach of prison discipline? Rolled up inside the posy, however, was an illicit note from Ottoline. Bertie, too, soon found a way of evading prison censorship. One day Ottoline was puzzled to receive from him a weighty volume entitled *The Proceedings of the London Mathematical Society*, with a note saying she might find it "more interesting than it seemed". Ottoline examined the book from every angle, holding its pages to the light to see if it contained writing in invisible ink and feeling the pages for a message pricked out with a pin. Finally she found a letter that Bertie had tucked between uncut pages in the book. Russell was quite happy during the first months of his imprisonment. He enjoyed the seclusion and was able to do a great deal of thinking and writing. But as time went on worry over Colette and her lover drove him almost mad. On one visit Ottoline was annoyed by Russell's obvious desire to see her leave so he could read a letter from Colette that Ottoline had brought him hidden in a book. He kept holding the book in his hands and fingering it impatiently.

One of the high spots of Russell's time in gaol was reading *Eminent Victorians*, the book that Lytton had been working on for several years; and which had finally been published. Russell found Lytton's sacrilegious treatment of such Victorian demigods as Florence Nightingale and General Gordon so amusing that he burst out laughing in his cell; causing one of the warders to admonish him for unprisonly behaviour. It was a major departure from Lytton's earlier specialisation in French literature, and before its publication his Bloomsbury friends had not been confident of his wisdom in undertaking it. Even Lytton seemed diffident about its chances. In March he had written to Ottoline:

> *My life passes almost entirely among proof sheets, which now flow in upon me daily. It is rather exciting, but also rather harassing. All sorts of tiresome details, and minor crises...but my hope is that in about six weeks or so Eminent Victorians will burst upon an astonished world.*[16]

He had no need for concern. The book became a best-seller almost overnight; and no one was more astonished than Lytton and his Bloomsbury friends. Virginia and Vanessa, while accepting the brilliance of the book, felt it wasn't quite worthy of Lytton; but Clive was more enthusiastic, and said Virginia was jealous. Ottoline herself was delighted that the writer whom she regarded as her major protégé had at last achieved success; and, though she and Lytton were drifting apart, she could lay claim to having had a hand in the book's success. She gave a copy to Asquith and later reported to Lytton that "old Squith" was very enthusiastic; and was going to mention it in an important lecture he was to deliver at Oxford in June. Lytton and Ottoline drove into Oxford to hear the lecture and sat in the front row of a very colourful and distinguished audience. Asquith, who looked particularly robust and Roman, opened his lecture (which was on the Victorian Age) with a discussion of Lytton's book, praising it to the skies. The former Prime Minister's public endorsement gave a distinct fillip to its sales, and within a month it had gone into its third edition. Now Lytton was lionised by the very people who eight years before had scoffed at Ottoline for having such a scruffy and odd young man in her drawing room. Lytton was asked to stay with the Asquiths and was feted by Ottoline's rivals, Lady Colefax and Lady Cunard.

At Garsington that summer *Eminent Victorians* was required reading. Lytton himself made several visits, and seemed more urbane as the book went into each subsequent edition. The house appeared much the same as it had in previous summers – the crowd of friends sitting out on the lawn, the conversation, the pond – but there was still that feeling of unreality about it, a feeling even the presence of Ottoline's wounded soldiers from Oxford could not dispel. Bloomsbury was not much in evidence now, but there was an increasing number of younger guests, including T.S. Eliot and Siegfried Sassoon's friend, the poet Robert Graves. Aldous Huxley came down regularly from Eton for weekends; and Mark Gertler was in almost permanent residence in his studio next to Brett's.

Lytton was not the only one of Ottoline's friends to be publishing a book that summer. Katherine's collection of short stories, *Preludes*, also appeared and was read with critical interest at Garsington. Gertler didn't think much of it himself, but he said that others felt that after reading it through it somehow stuck in the mind "and then one suddenly realises that it *is* rather exquisite."[17] Siegfried Sassoon also published his book of poems, and Ottoline was keen that Murry should review them in the *Nation*. But when she read what Murry wrote about Siegfried's poems, she exploded. Gertler reported to Kot: "Murry wrote a scathing criticism of Sassoon's poems – Ottoline furious."[18] Russell wrote to Ottoline from Brixton agreeing with her that the review was unkind: "The reviewer's safe smugness made me angry – what business has he to feel superior to one who has suffered?"[19] Russell himself was feeling restless in prison and beginning to think about his future. "The position I want for *myself* after the war is with young intellectuals – if I have that I shall be quite satisfied."[20] He saw himself as a latter-day Socrates; a role Ottoline playfully recognised when she named a puppy sired by her favourite pug Socrates after Bertie. He was amused, and wrote: "Give my love to my pug namesake! I feel it an honour to become a son of Socrates."

Ottoline's growing impatience with Brett finally boiled over in August. "I had it out with Brett about staying at Garsington for ever," Ottoline told Carrington.[21] Brett retreated to London like a hurt puppy. Ottoline soon regretted her outburst and a reconciliation followed, with Brett once again making regular visits to Garsington, where she even began another portrait of Ottoline; this one proving more successful than the Colossus. What it was about Brett, ear-trumpet-apart, that annoyed Ottoline isn't too clear. In her unpublished memoirs she wrote: "I give and give to Brett, all my ideas about life and literature and religion and she gives me nothing, only a clinging devotion. But I want more than that."[22] Yet Brett was still probably Ottoline's closest confidante; and it was her sympathy that had helped

Ottoline over a time of transition from intimate friendships with men like Russell and Lamb to the more platonic relationships of her later years. Ottoline was depressed and tetchy; and Brett did her best to get her out of one dark mood by pressing on her a new book about married love. Its revelations could explain all of her problems, Brett assured Ottoline. "Go forward, and find a lover. S.S. is alas of no use in that way," she advised.[23] What Brett may have been hinting at here was their mutual concern that Siegfried was trespassing into that land Ottoline had referred to in her letter to Carrington about Lytton and Maynard Keynes. Certainly, by the time Siegfried was again wounded and invalided back from France, Ottoline had given up any thought of an intimate (*ie*, sexual) relationship with him.

In September Russell came out of prison, enriched mentally, but both emotionally and financially broke. Colette's infidelity had caused him to denounce her "with great violence", the result being that her feelings towards him were "considerably chilled".[24] Into this emotional vacuum came, almost inevitably, Ottoline. The day he was released she took him to the Wigmore Hall to hear a Bach concert. On other days they went for long walks in Richmond Park (where Russell had grown up in a grace-and-favour residence granted to the widow of the first Earl Russell). Bertie told her that he felt they had come back to the intimacy of long ago: "I think that what we have now ought to last as long as we live."[25] Ottoline, too, was happier with him than for a long time. Towards the end of his prison term he had written her some particularly nice letters; some of the best he ever wrote, she thought, and she felt that their friendship was now established on a new basis. "He is franker too, which is a great comfort," she said.[26] But, as usual, Bertie wasn't being frank at all. In August he had told her: 'I *must* have *some* complete holiday when I first come out of prison,"[27] but it turned out that this was so he could go away and patch up his affair with Colette. While his mind was filled with thoughts of Colette, Ottoline and several other of his friends were busy organising a fund to support his future work. Since he had lost his fellowship at Trinity (and bestowed gifts on the Eliots and other deserving causes), his income had been so eroded that he was on the verge of penury. Ottoline went to see one prospective donor, an old philosopher, but was embarrassed by the quite reasonable question: "Why is Mr. Russell so poor? What has he done with his money?"[28] Ottoline could hardly tell him. Eventually some money was raised and Russell was very grateful: "I am wonderfully touched by what all of you have done."[29]

That autumn Ottoline's spirits were also raised when Diaghilev's Russian Ballet returned to London. One night she went along to see Massine dance in *The Good Humoured Ladies*, and after the performance she spied David Garnett in the foyer and bore him off backstage to meet Massine and his co-star Lydia Lopokova, the future wife of Maynard Keynes. Garnett stared at Lopokova in dumb worship, and wondered if he had been "wafted into heaven by Ottoline".[30] Two tall young officers named Osbert and Sacheverell Sitwell joined them, and they all went off to supper. At another performance Osbert Sitwell saw Ottoline wearing a yellow Spanish gown and looking like "an oversized Infanta of Spain". For the Ballet's visit, Ottoline had taken rooms at Garland's Hotel in Suffolk Street, where, in an old-fashioned sitting-room furnished in plush with a marble clock on the mantelpiece, she entertained the dancers to tea; the Russians eating strawberry and raspberry jam out of silver spoons which they dipped in their tea. Osbert admired Ottoline's masterly handling of the temperamental Diaghilev. One day he was at Garsington when Diaghilev, "a born snob" according to Osbert, was displeased to find nobody of particular genius or fame there; but Ottoline saved the situation by pointing at Brett and murmuring to Diaghilev: "That woman is sister to a Queen."[31] No matter that Brett's sister was not actual royalty, but only the Ranee of Sarawak, it was sufficient to appease the snooty Diaghilev.

In the autumn of 1918 the end of the war came where it had begun; in the Balkans. In September an Allied army broke through on the Macedonian Front, and Bulgaria, Germany's ally, collapsed. On October 27 Austria also collapsed, and Germany sought an armistice; which was signed in Foch's railway carriage. At 11am on November 11 a salvo of guns in London told the somewhat surprised populace that the Great War was over. That afternoon in the House of Commons Lloyd George read out the Armistice terms and concluded: "I hope we may say that thus, this fateful morning, came to an end all wars."[32] Then he and Asquith walked side-by-side to a nearby church to give thanks to the Almighty.

Throughout the rest of London there was rejoicing. When Carrington heard the guns, she thought it was a joke; or some new German terror weapon. "But it soon turned out to be Peace with a big P," she said.[33] She travelled down from Hampstead and as she got closer to the city the scenes became more wild. Slum girls and coster people danced in the streets: "…as one [approached] Trafalgar Square office boys and girls, officers, Majors, WAACS all leaped on taxis, and army vans driving around the place waving flags. In the Strand the uproar was appalling."[34] As soon as Katherine heard the guns, she sat down and wrote to Ottoline, telling her that her thoughts at that moment flew to her. Siegfried was at Garsington and all he noticed was a little peal of bells from the village church; and a flutter of flags from the windows of the thatched cottages. At Richmond when the guns went off, Virginia Woolf looked out of the window and saw the man painting their house give one look at the sky; then go on with his job. "The rooks wheeled round and wore for a moment the symbolic look of creatures performing some ceremony, partly of thanksgiving, partly of valediction over the grave," she wrote in her Diary.[35] Bertie was in Tottenham Court Road at 11am and noticed that within seconds people were pouring out on to the streets. "I saw a man and woman, complete strangers to each other meet in the middle of the road and kiss as they passed."

As evening came on, the madness increased. Girls from the Woolwich arsenal, their bodies stained yellow from picric acid fumes, danced in the streets and embraced passers-by. Ottoline, who was still in London, celebrated by going to the Adelphi flat of Montague Sherman, friend and patron of Gertler. "Everyone was there," wrote Carrington, "the halt, the sick and the lame."[36] Even an ailing Lytton came up from Sussex to join in the merriment. The flat was filled with a constantly changing company – Clive Bell, Diaghilev, Massine, Augustus John, Roger Fry, Duncan Grant, Keynes, the Sitwells, David Garnett, and a host of others. Even Lawrence and Frieda had turned up earlier in the day.

It was a strange, almost ritual occasion. While outside in the Strand people danced on the tops of automobiles and kissed in doorways; inside Sherman's flat England's intellectual elite celebrated in its own way. Lytton, looking like "a benevolent but irritable pelican," jigged about.[37] Ottoline chatted with Massine, while Garnett and Carrington pranced around amid the jostling guests. Russell stayed out in the streets[38], picking his way through the mass of people; observing their behaviour, as he had done the day war was declared four years earlier. He noted that they had learned nothing from the period of horror; except to snatch at pleasure more recklessly than before. He could find nothing in common between his happiness and the crowd's; and he felt even more alone than he had in August 1914.

INTERLUDE
The Men in Her Life

Lytton Strachey  *Bertrand Russell*  *D.H. Lawrence*

THREE GREAT friendships, Ottoline believed, dominated her life – those with Lytton Strachey, Bertrand Russell, and D.H. Lawrence. Although there were other friendships and love affairs, the high intellectual and spiritual moments of her life centred on those three men. Each gave her something unique. With Russell she had access to a great mind and an intense passion. With Lawrence she had a genius who shared her intuitive love of life and nature. But it was Lytton who had given her the most fun.

Men played a prominent role in Ottoline's life – socially, sexually and emotionally. "She had a heart of gold and a yen for men" is how Dorothy Brett described her, and from an early age she showed an insatiable desire to move in the world of men. And what men! How many other women could claim to have had deep, and sometimes sexual, relationships with not only such intelligent (not to mention famous) men as Russell, Strachey, and Lawrence but also Augustus John, Henry Lamb, Roger Fry, Mark Gertler, Henry James, Charles Conder, T.S. Eliot, Prime Minister Asquith, Aldous Huxley, L.P. Hartley, Diaghilev, Nijinsky, Yeats, Conrad, Shaw, John Middleton Murry, etc, etc, etc.

Ottoline's lineage and her outstanding – often outrageous – appearance and aristocratic style added to her appeal. She provided a sympathy and understanding of masculine needs and insecurities which attracted men like a magnet. She possessed a unique kind of intelligence, too, which led to many friendships with men who enjoyed talking about art and literature. On the one hand, she herself desperately needed to *know* a man, to get inside him, to commune with him. On the other, she gave men much-needed self-confidence and inspiration. She helped them make the fullest use of their talents. That she saw as her role in life. In other words, she acted as their Muse.

With some of her relationships, sexual drive was indeed an important element. But it wasn't paramount. Ottoline deployed her sexual allure to achieve her aim: to reach into a man's deepest self. Although she had friendships with women, she devoted her life primarily to seeking out interesting and intelligent (but not necessarily young or handsome) men. She began with older men, of the ilk of Archbishop William Maclagan of York, flattering and pandering to their masculinity by playing the role of the winsome young girl in need of fatherly attention. Unsurprisingly, she found that many older men were lonely, and had unhappy marriages. They were grateful to find somebody to listen to them and to show an interest – sometimes a romantic interest - in them. She filled that need with style and intelligence, for Ottoline possessed a unique form of intellect, coupled with an innate artistic sense.

Then Axel Munthe sailed into her life. I believe I can say with something close to certainty that she lost her virginity to Munthe, that fascinating satyr from Capri. From then on, her interaction with the male sex fell into two categories: those where physical sex was involved; and those where her sexual allure was subsumed by strong and usually enduring friendships. In fact, of all the close relationships she had with men, only a select few involved actual sex. After Munthe, there was, from the older brigade, H.H. Asquith and John Adam Cramb. (Although there is scant evidence that Ottoline was involved sexually with either of these two men, there is sufficient subsidiary tinder to suggest more than a flicker.) Then came the younger division, represented by Augustus John, Henry Lamb (and, yes, Bertie, who was close to Ottoline's age), and probably Middleton Murry too. Finally came the youngest set in the improbable person of the young stonemason at Garsington, Lionel Gomme (see "Tiger, Tiger" below).

She had a particular rapport with artists, and her innate artistic sensibilities and intuitive mind could relax and luxuriate in their presence. Ottoline fell for Lamb at first sight, and when she was with him she didn't have to try to think rationally, as she did with Russell. She wanted to help artists in their careers, and they needed her help. She not only inspired them to paint her but also provided studios for several artists: Lamb, Gertler, Stanley Spencer ...where they produced some of their finest work, such as Gertler's "Merry-Go-Round.

Her relationship with the homosexual, mordantly witty Lytton Strachey is a fascinating one which brought out a new side in Ottoline: that of the worldly Elizabethan-style sophisticate. Their tete-a-tetes in her boudoir, with Lytton mincing about in her shoes; their hilarious games of tennis in Bedford Square; and Lytton's confidences about his affairs produced a special rapport.

With D.H. Lawrence, the attraction was intuitive. Lawrence had a unique ability to relate very directly to another person. He began his friendship with Ottoline as the fawning game-keeper yearning to be an aristocrat, but soon their relationship stabilised as Lawrence found himself on an equal footing with her – to the point where finally he bored so deeply into her that she became his Hermione Roddice. Hermione is possessive; so, to some extent, was Ottoline. Hermione is not earthy, neither was Ottoline. Hermione overflows with almost electrical energy, as did Ottoline. Hermione disdained the vulgarity of sex and regarded it as a weapon to be used to ensnare Birkin. Ottoline's view of sex was not dissimilar. Lawrence pinned her down like a netted butterfly.

As for Bertrand Russell. Ottoline's long affair with Russell must rank as one of the great love-affairs in history. That he wrote over 2,500 letters to her is proof enough of his devotion to her during the five years they were romantically involved. Interestingly, she didn't regard him as being particularly sexually attractive, but the two of them had an affinity that went far beyond mere sex. She would, however, play the sex card with him when she feared he was straying, exerting her sexual powers beyond their normal level until she had him safely back in her arms. That they were both of aristocratic stock was a vital ingredient in their relationship; they could understand one another's values and beliefs on an equal footing. He would have married her if she had been willing to divorce Philip, and none of his future liaisons and marriages reached the heights of his affair with Ottoline. That they continued to be friends for the rest of her life is testimony to that.

There is little doubt where Ottoline's main interests lay. Her relationships with so many men of the highest intellectual calibre singles her out as one of the world's great goddesses of inspiration. As D.H. Lawrence said in a letter to her after they had reconciled their differences over *Women in Love*: "After all, there's only one Ottoline. And she has moved one's imagination"

CHAPTER 21
Tiger, Tiger

Ottoline at a crossroads

WHEN THE war ended Ottoline was 45; no longer young. Indeed, she often seemed older than she really was. Her contemporaries – those who had shared her great days at Bedford Square – were drifting away. Her post-war friendships were to be less passionate and intense. Also, the element of sex had largely gone out of her life. Bertie, however. was just the opposite. He seemed to be getting younger and more frisky with every passing year. The loneliness he had felt on Armistice night had been partly a feeling of alienation from the common people; but also the lack of a satisfactory love-life. On November 20 he pleaded to be allowed to come to Garsington. It was, he said, "a cry of distress & an appeal for help."[1] He was still seeing Colette – he had a duty towards her – but if Ottoline would let him come he would put himself in her hands. But that November Ottoline wasn't feeling gregarious; and the prospect of having Bertie's long face at Garsington did not attract her, so she put him off. He replied sadly that her shrinking away from intimacy would cause him to retire into his shell. "But I am ready to come out at any time," he added brightly.[2]

The anticlimax of the end of the war had left many people feeling let down. It seemed that everyone had expected the pre-war world to open up again; as if August 1914 had been put into cold storage, and could be taken out and warmed up, now that the nightmare was over. But the world went on from 1918; not 1914. What the Twenties would bring no one really knew; but Ottoline echoed Bertie's hope: "What is wanted is to carry over into the new time something of the gaiety and civilised outlook and general expansive love that was growing when the war came."[3] For her part she did her best to carry on; and at Christmas she organised a big house-party at Garsington, inviting Bishop Gore, Asquith, Violet Asquith, Gertler, Clive Bell, Aldous, and a number of others. But it wasn't as happy even as 1916; much less 1914 (though it was certainly happier than 1917). "What an appalling tale of disasters you had at Christmas," wrote Bertie early in January.[4] These disasters, according to Ottoline's next letter, included: Cook ill, Julian and Ottoline colds, Millie flu, Philip toothache, and various other retainers ill. Another shadow over the festivities was the recent "coupon" election, which had shrunk Lloyd George's supporters in the House of Commons to a handful. Though Philip didn't stand for re-election, he shared the general gloom. Not only did the election mark the end of his own political career; but also the beginning of the collapse of the cause – liberalism – into which he and Ottoline had put so much over the past ten years or more.

Lytton was not among the guests at Garsington that Christmas. Instead, Ottoline sent him a volume of Cowper's poems; and he in return described his own quiet Christmas at Tidmarsh. "We eat large chickens which pretend to be turkeys, not very effectively,"[5] he reported. For the past year he had been dipping into Queen Victoria's voluminous correspondence, and now he had decided to follow up *Eminent Victorians* with "the Life of Her Late Majesty".[6] We do not know whether this new project was the subject of the gossip at Garsington that Christmas; or whether the much more exciting news about the latest turn of events in the Lytton household had worked its way through via Gertler or Clive Bell. Certainly within a short time it became common knowledge that the ménage at Tidmarsh had become a triangle; and an isosceles one at that. In August 1918 Ralph Partridge, a handsome young infantry officer, turned up at the Mill House and within a few months had become established there. Carrington was mildly attracted to him – but Lytton was swept off his feet. For his part Partridge was not sexually attracted to Lytton. He had fallen in love with Carrington, whose interest in him, however, was directly proportional to her fear that unless she encouraged him he would leave; thus weakening her own position in Lytton's life. This convoluted reasoning washed over Lytton. His mind was on other things. "Why am I not a rowing blue, with eyes to match, and 24? It's really dreadful not to be," he asked himself.[7]

Russell, who also hadn't been at Garsington that Christmas, went off in January for a holiday in the country with his friend Clifford Allen. But Ottoline suspected he was hiding something, and put the question to him directly; also complaining about the scrappy notes he had been sending. "I am very sorry my letters have been short," he replied. "A holiday existence leaves one so little to tell: walks, meals, sleep and a blessed cessation of the grinding wheels of one's mind. Yes, C.M. is here."[8] On January 14 he returned to Garsington and spent several days discussing his future plans with Ottoline. What he needed, they both agreed, was a wife; or rather a new wife, as officially he was still married to Alys. However, for this role Colette was not a candidate. For one thing she was married to someone else; for another she had specifically ruled out the idea of having children, and Russell was becoming almost obsessed with the thought that he should start a family before it was too late. Neither Alys nor Ottoline had been able to fulfil this need. Indeed, he believed that this had been the main reason why his relationships with them had failed. Sometime earlier he had met someone else who had a different outlook. Her name was Dora Black; a young university student who surprised Russell by showing a preference, not for academic pursuits, but for family life (which presumably involved children). But they hadn't met again until the summer of 1919, when Russell, after an argument with Colette, asked Dora to replace her as his holiday companion at a resort in Dorset. Later Colette, regretting the tiff, also turned up; placing Russell in a similar position to that of Ottoline back in 1911 at Studland, juggling two lovers and trying to keep them from meeting each other. Gradually, however, Dora, due to her willingness "not to take precautions", gained the ascendancy; and Colette gave up the field to her more compliant rival. Bertie, who had accepted Ottoline's offer to live in a cottage at Garsington for the time being, did not break the news of his newest entanglement to Ottoline until September 4; when he mentioned in passing that he had been staying in Dorset "with a Miss Black".[9]

At the beginning of 1919 Ottoline was just as unsure of the future as Bertie. The end of the war and Philip's exit from politics had robbed her of one of the main causes in her life. Russell was occupied elsewhere, and Siegfried was proving less and less of a replacement. This left her with the role of salonniere. Yet how could she hope to rekindle the success of Bedford Square and the early days of Garsington? Now it was the platinum-plated London salons of Lady Cunard and Lady Colefax to which people like Lytton were drawn. ("Lady Cunard is rather a sport, with her frankly lower-class bounce," Lytton wrote in May, "she makes the rest of 'em look like the withered leaves of Autumn, poor things."[10])

Also, now that Garsington's unique wartime function as a refuge was ended, Ottoline would have to compete with the other country establishments; like the Bloomsbury ones presided over by Virginia at Rodmell and Vanessa at Charleston. For the time being however she didn't have a great deal of trouble keeping her guest rooms well-stocked. Even Lytton found time to fit her in between sorties up to the glitter of London, although, like Lawrence, he found Garsington "exhaustive," as he told Virginia:

> *I was often on the point of screaming from sheer despair, and the beauty of the surroundings only intensified the agony. Ott I really think is in the last stages – infinitely antique, racked in every joint, hobbling through the buttercups in cheap shoes...She is rongee, too, by malevolence; every tea party in London to which she hasn't been invited is wormwood, wormwood.*[11]

As usual, Lytton was exaggerating. Ottoline was far from antique, and she never much enjoyed tea parties in London. Yet no doubt there was a scintilla of truth in his observations: Ottoline's appearance around this time did cause some comment; as it had back in 1917, when she tried to improve her appearance after Bertie had made the remark about her hair going grey. In 1919 she bobbed her hair and initially dyed it an improbable shade of orange. She refused, however, to go flapper and clung steadfastly to styles reminiscent of Beardsley that for many years had been her trademark. And though she never could have competed with the bounce of Lady Cunard, there were in 1919 extenuating circumstances for her hobbling through the buttercups; the principal of these being her almost habitual ill-health. One evening at the opera she nearly fainted; later, tonsillitis was diagnosed, and in June she went into a nursing home for an operation. There she was visited by Augustine Birrell and they discussed her forthcoming trip to Ireland. After the war the cause of Irish nationalism was almost the only political activity which Ottoline supported; and she looked forward to her holiday as something of a pilgrimage (her mother had been Irish). She was also hoping to meet some of the people she had worked with on Casement's behalf. Birrell, who had resigned as Irish Secretary after the 1916 Uprising, was concerned for Ottoline's safety; and warned her that parts of the countryside were dangerous, even for the native Irish to travel in. This didn't deter

Ottoline. Indeee, it gave added spice to her trip.

In Ireland she and her maid travelled around Galway and Donegal – strongholds of the Irish nationalists – in a pony trap; and far from avoiding contact with Republicans, Ottoline made efforts to seek them out, attending their meetings and dressing up in Sinn Fein colours and singing IRA songs[!]. Though the holiday restored to her life some of the colour and romance that had been recently lacking; it had a painful and premature end. During one excursion Ottoline fell, hurting her leg, and despite the ministrations of a charming Irish doctor-poet named Oliver St. John Gogarty, complications set in. To add worry to injury Brett wrote from Garsington telling her Julian was unhappy at school and recounting excursions she had organised to London with the aim of making Julian happier. As Ottoline read about Brett's mothering activities, she grew increasingly annoyed, finally despatching a stiff letter of reprimand that so shook Brett she replied by telegram: SO VERY SORRY HAVING HURT YOU. QUITE A MISTAKE. MUCH LOVE. PLEASE DON'T BE UNHAPPY. BRETTIE.[12] Another point of friction between the two women was a consumptive part-Sioux Canadian poet named Frank Prewitt, whom Siegfried Sassoon had befriended and brought back to Garsington with him. Ottoline took quite a fancy to Prewitt (whom everybody called "Toronto") and invited him to stay at Garsington while he waited to be repatriated to Canada. During Ottoline's absence in Ireland Brett had been clucking over him and trying to matchmake, to Ottoline's further chagrin, and she wrote another letter to Brett saying: "Amused at the way you have annexed Toronto & intend to organise him."[13] Toronto remained at Garsington much of 1919, revelling in the illustrious company that came and went with each passing weekend.

Later that summer the Russian Ballet returned to London, and when Ottoline got back from Ireland she invited its reigning stars, Picasso and Massine, to Garsington. She made regular trips up to London to see Diaghilev's new ballets and Picasso's sets. On one occasion she was unable to find a seat, and an usher was just about to move her on when Diaghilev spotted her. Grandly he strode up and instructed the usher: "This lady may sit wherever she wishes", and conducted Ottoline to a special seat in the front row. When Siegfried was discharged from the army in early 1919 he hastened down to Garsington. Later he decided that he would like to take up residence in one of the cottages, which she decorated herself with multi-coloured curtains. That summer the two of them spent a lot of time in each other's company; often going off to point-to-point races and other sporting events, where Ottoline's presence earned for Siegfried the title "The Dowagers' Delight". Any hopes, however, Ottoline may have entertained that the end of the war would change Siegfried's apparent uninterest in her were soon dashed. She told Lytton: "I evidently do not magnetise him."[14]

The reason why Ottoline went to so much trouble to seek out people like Sassoon and Toronto was her love of poetry. Throughout the Twenties and Thirties any promising poet, old or young, homegrown or foreign, was assured of a warm welcome at Ottoline's gatherings. And though Ottoline's taste in poetry was broad; it could also be discriminating, and the two figures who dominated her post-war salons were the poets W. B. Yeats and T. S. Eliot. That Yeats should have swung into her orbit is not surprising. He was Irish, romantic, and plainly a major figure in contemporary literature; besides, he had been a frequent guest at Bedford Square before the war, and felt quite at home in Ottoline's drawing-room. Their friendship however had an unfortunate beginning, and an even more unfortunate ending. The former can be described here. When they first met, Ottoline remarked to him: "It's wonderful how the Irish have got so much more sensible now – none of that Celtic Twilight stuff any more."[15] Yeats had to confess that he wrote *The Celtic Twilight*. But after this initial setback, their relationship blossome, and Yeats was to become, especially in the Thirties, the leading VIP (Very Important Poet) at Ottoline's gatherings.

That Eliot and Ottoline should have got on well together is more surprising. His poetry was very complex; not the sort of romantic verse Ottoline usually liked. Also, Eliot himself was a pretty dry stick. Yet of all Ottoline's post-war literary friendships, the one with Eliot was probably the closest and most genuine. Between 1919 and her death in 1938 he wrote over a hundred letters to her, all of them couched in affectionate and grateful terms. And she helped him in both his career and his personal life. He once said she was one of the few friends he had in England. After *The Waste Land* was published he told her she had been the only person to write to him praising it. However, Ottoline and Eliot did have another thing in common; religion. Despite Ottoline's partial conversion to scepticism under Russell's influence, she remained devoutly spiritual; and in 1919, free now from Russell, she reconverted back to religion, while still eschewing any established orthodoxy. Her return to religion did not create much of a stir among her friends; they had tended to take her brand of mystical romanticism for religion anyway. When informed by Ottoline of her new frame of mind, Desmond MacCarthy told her: "I think it will suit you."[16]

Concurrent with her new interest in verse was Ottoline's decision to take up her *Memoirs* again. Several times in the past she had begun to convert her Diary into a more formal account of her life. Now she began to think seriously of preparing a text for eventual publication. When Virginia heard of the project she told Ottoline:

> *Please do it, I think it is one of the things you owe the world. Pick us all to pieces. Throw us to the dogs. It is high time you came off your heights & did a little dusting in a high-minded manner.*[17]

Although Ottoline didn't really follow Virginia's advice about throwing people to the dogs, she did permit herself a little dusting. In writing her *Memoirs* (in progressive volumes) she consulted not only her daily entries, but her growing collection of letters, which she had assiduously preserved, and which her maid Millie tended in their neat piles tied with ribbon. And though it was some time before Ottoline had any MS to show anyone, she was rather proud of the fact that she had taken up writing again. It had always been a deep regret of hers that she could not be a writer or a poet.

In the autumn of 1919 Bertie returned to London from Dorset and, despite his discovery of Miss Black's childbearing proclivities, he was feeling rather sour. He told Ottoline that Wittgenstein had written to him from Vienna saying the city was starving and that he himself was taking up school-teaching. Russell added: "Einstein, a German Jew, has invented a new theory of gravitation [but] our object [is] to cause these people to die of hunger, because we are afraid they will compete with our trade. It is glorious to be an Englishman, isn't it?"[18] In December Bertie went off for a reunion with Wittgenstein in Holland, where, he reported to Ottoline, he was astonished to find that his former pupil in logic had turned to religion.

While in Holland Bertie decided to make a clean breast to Ottoline about the recent changes in his personal life:

> *Now I come to my own affairs, which I wanted to speak of sooner but on the whole decided not to. I made friends last summer with a Miss Black (I regret to say her Christian name is Dora) whom I had known for a year...she was at Lulworth during a great part of the summer and was the cause of my being so exceedingly happy there.*[19]

He added that the present intention was to begin a common life, with the hope of children. "I believe (tho' it is rash to prophesy) that you would like her very much." Ottoline replied in favourable terms, for which Bertie was almost pathetically grateful. "Thank you, thank you my dearest O."[20] A few days later he had an afterthought: "My dearest O – I forgot to say in so many words that *of course* anything that happens with regard to Dora Black will not interfere with our friendship in any way whatsoever."[21] He was planning to get a divorce from Alys, though not necessarily to marry Dora, who didn't think much of matrimony. He told Ottoline that his relations with Colette could continue, "tho' in the nature of things they will grow less intimate with time."[22] And while Ottoline made plans to go to London for a few weeks, Russell and Dora went off to Spain together.

In London Ottoline stayed with Ethel Sands in Chelsea, where she staged a busy series of parties and receptions. A long line of guests came to the house in the Vale – including Ezra Pound, Edith Sitwell, Murry, Keynes, Clive Bell, Vanessa, Duncan, Aldous, and Augustus John. John was about to put on a major exhibition in London which was to prove controversial, mainly because of a portrait of Ottoline. John's biographer Michael Holroyd described the picture as

> ...a high-voltage oil portrait...he depicts her as some splendid galleon in full sail, triumphantly breasting the high seas. Her head, under its flamboyant topsail of a hat, is held at a proud angle and she wears, like rigging, several strings of pearls (painted with the aid of tooth powder) above a bottle-green velvet dress. Her eyes are rolled sideways in their sockets like those of a runaway horse and her mouth bared soundlessly.[23]

The painting caused a furore. When the Press saw the picture they took it to be a cruel attack on Ottoline. On March 2 the *Daily News* said: "The portrait of Lady Ottoline Morrell is an unmistakable presentment, but she is not flattered."[24] *Truth* said he had made her look "rather witchlike."[25] *The Tatler* on March 10 said of it: "Not a very kind picture – in fact he's been rather hard on all women. It was Lady Ottoline's house in Bedford Square, you know, that the Asquiths took not long ago."[26] *Everyman* said: "That curiously Elizabethan Lady Ottoline Morrell is even more unpleasantly snake-like and snarling. It may puzzle one to imagine why society women should like to see themselves painted like this, even by Mr. John."[27] The *Weekly Dispatch* sent a reporter to see Ottoline and ask her what she thought. "I regret to say I have not yet seen the portrait,"[28] she told them, coldly. They then interviewed John, who said he had not been intentionally cruel, but it was "the aspect he had been unfortunate enough to get". The picture dated from well before the war. When Philip went to see it at the Alpine Club Gallery, he decided to write to John to tell him what he thought:

> *I feel I must write and tell you how greatly moved I was by that wonderful show of yours which I saw for the first time the other day – and not the least by Ottoline's portrait, which seemed to me one of the finest things there. I see that the journalists are very anxious to assure us that it is a "cruel" presentment of her, that she looks like a witch, and a snake, and an insolent aristocrat and I don't know what else besides; but whether kind or cruel it is a wonderful piece of work, and I think Ottoline (who by the way has not yet seen it) ought to feel proud to be the subject of it. She says she rather dreads going to see it, but I tell her to cheer up and not be frightened, for after all it is better any day to look wicked than feeble or commonplace.*[29]

Ottoline did eventually see the picture and, while she may not have thought it flattering, she did think enough of it to eventually acquire it from John and hang it over her fireplace in her future home in Gower Street.

In June 1920 a young man from the Garsington village came to work on some stone plinths in the Garsington garden. His name was Lionel Gomm, and he was to play an extraordinary role in Ottoline's complicated life.[30] Ottoline was aware people would laugh about her involvement with a young stonemason, whom she called "Tiger ", and what she recounts must be taken with a grain of salt. Nevertheless, the phenomenon of upper-class women having affairs with working-class men – the "Lady Chatterley Syndrome" – is well-known. It was rumoured that Ottoline's own mother, Lady Bolsover, was very fond of a young gamekeeper from Bolsover Castle, who allegedly came to visit her in her sitting-room. Lawrence knew from Ottoline about this upstairs-downstairs friendship and tucked the gamekeeper's name – Mellors – away for future use in *Lady Chatterley's Lover*. (There is, however, a competing theory that the name Mellors came from a name – Dame Agnes Mellers – on a book which Lawrence won as a schoolboy at Nottingham Grammar School.) It must be remembered, too, that Ottoline, at 45, was in a fragile emotional state, still recoiling from Philip's infidelities and the depiction of herself as Hermione Roddice in *Women in Love*.

Apparently[30] when Ottoline first set eyes on the young Lionel Gomme working in the garden on the stone plinths she thought she was seeing a ghost: the ghost of her baby son, Hugh, who had died from a cerebral haemorrhage a few days after his birth. For several days she made excuses to potter in the garden near the young stonemason. Finally, she opened a conversation with him about stone-masonry while he worked on the plinths. She invited him to join her on a trip into Oxford to inspect some of the stonework in the colleges. They finished their expedition by having tea together. Not long after this, Gomme, whom she was now calling "Tiger", knocked on her study door and asked if he could might come in. Ottoline records in her Diary that they then "became friends". As the summer of 1920 wore on, again according to Ottoline's Diary, they became lovers and, she recorded, she experienced "a physical happiness" with him equalled only by one other man in her life: her first lover, Axel Munthe. (And we know what Ottoline meant by "physical".) She seems not to have minded that Tiger had little to talk about apart from cars; although he did, she also recorded, know a great deal about insects. (Ottoline's interst in gardens might have kicked in here.)

Meanwhile, in May 1920 Russell went off to Russia, there to acquire an instant dislike of Communism and all its works. He went with a group of socialists bent on seeing the good things the Russian revolutionaries had achieved. But despite his efforts to summon up all he knew about the knoutings and pogroms of the old regime (so as to have a favourable view of the new regime); it was no use. This almost caused a rift with Dora Black. She had followed him to Russia, and, said Russell, came back "loving the

Bolshies". This difference of opinion was, however, patched up, and he and Dora began preparing to go to China; where Russell had been appointed to a lectureship. He sent £10 to Ottoline and asked her to choose some books on China he could take with him. "You are so very good at choosing," he said.[31] Ottoline consulted all her friends, including Lytton, and eventually compiled an interesting selection. Russell was now planning to marry Dora as soon as his divorce from Alys came through, and he took his wife-to-be up to Garsington to be inspected by Ottoline. It seems she approved; though later on she came to refer to the second Mrs. Russell as "that Dora". Before he set sail for the Orient, Bertie wrote Ottoline a farewell note, saying: "What you and I have in common is indestructible, and what you did for me in bringing it out was a very great thing. Goodbye my Dearest O. Your B."[32] In her next letter to Lytton, thanking him for suggesting some books on China that Russell might read, Ottoline said: "Bertie went off in fine feather. He is accompanied by a lady sect.! He is an old rep!"[33]

Ottoline next had to make a trip to the Continent with Julian who, at 14, was proving to be a very temperamental young teenager. Ottoline regretted having to make this trip and leave Tiger, but she had arranged it long before her encounter with him. In her Diary she said he often wrote "delightful letters" to her while she was away. (No letters from him seem to have survived, however – which is odd.) So in November 1920 Ottoline and Julian set off, first to Marseilles and then on to Paris, where Philip joined them for Christmas before returning to Garsington; where the farm was causing him concern – so much so that he feared they would soon be ruined. Ottoline, however, was apparently thoroughly enjoying the trip, and showed no sign of pining for Tiger. In Paris she and Julian went to the theatre with Andre Gide, and visited Picasso in his studio. In Monte Carlo they attended a performance of the Ballet Russe and caught up with Diaghilev. There they met Mary Cannan, now divorced from Gilbert, who inducted Julian into the mysteries of gambling. Julian began to enjoy herself for the first time on the trip. Ottoline had already realised that Julian's interest in cultural matters was limited. She did not want to join Ottoline on a visit to Katherine Mansfield, and she showed no interest in ancient frescoes. Dancing and frivolity were what she wanted. While in Rome Ottoline had an audience with the Pope. Of this meeting Philip wrote to his mother: "Ottoline is nothing if not courageous. She asked his Holiness in her best Italian for a special blessing for 'Poor Ireland!'"[34] Among the many old friends of Ottoline's who were also holidaying in Rome, Julian found some convivial companions in the Huxleys, particularly her childhood confidante Maria; and when Ottoline and Julian moved on to Florence, the Huxleys were there too, making them welcome. By April 1921 Ottoline was beginning to feel so ill that she booked herself into a nursing home at Lausanne; whose doctors she trusted. Back at Garsington Ottoline soon regained her health, and spent the rest of the summer of 1921 enjoying her friendship with Tiger, their liaison being known (according to Miranda Seymour) only to a small handful of her closest friends; such as Gertler.

Before this, in early 1921, Ottoline had been horrified to read in the newspapers that Bertie had died in China. Her distress at this report can be imagined. Even though they had had times of trouble and disagreement, Bertie to her was still one of the greatest and most sympathetic minds she had ever come in contact with; and her lover. At one point she had almost left Philip and gone off to live with him. For weeks she read obituaries in the papers enumerating Russell's qualities and achievements. Then it was announced that the whole thing had been a mistake: Russell had indeed been critically ill; but was recovering. The mistake had occurred because Dora, exasperated with journalists asking about his condition, told them he was dead; and it was this report that had reached England. Eventually Russell was able to write to say he had recovered; that Dora was pregnant; and they planned to return home as soon as possible. Dora, who was still not married to Russell because his divorce from Alys had not yet become absolute, was very worried lest none of Bertie's friends would like her. But Ottoline wrote and reassured her, for which Russell was very grateful. In October 1921, after Bertie and Dora had returned home, Ottoline was invited to visit the cottage in Sussex that they were renting in order for her to meet Dora; who was by then eight months pregnant. After the visit Ottoline wrote to Bertie full of praise for Dora, and on November 16 their son John Conrad was born. In his autobiography Russell says: "...and from that moment my children were for many years my main interest in life."[35] For the next several years Bertie drifted out of Ottoline's life; and they corresponded only irregularly. Ottoline, however, still continued to receive some of the backwash of his life; and in late November 1921 Colette wrote asking if she could come to visit Garsington. Ottoline commented: "I'll be comforting another of Bertie's cast-offs."[36]

In November 1921 Ottoline received from Aldous Huxley an advance copy of his first novel, *Crome Yellow*. She was looking forward to reading it; for in her estimate Aldous was the cleverest of the young men who had been at Garsington during the war. So although she had seen him only infrequently since he went off to teach at Eton in 1917; she retained a warm regard for him. As she opened the book she saw that he had written an inscription to her: "Ottoline Morrell with apologies for having borrowed some of her architecture and trees."[37] Ottoline's instincts were alerted. Surely; no, he wouldn't...after all, he had been just as horrified as she had been at what Lawrence did to her in *Women in Love*. But, as she read, the old hurts from 1917 came flooding back. For page after page her family; her guests; everything that she held precious were caricatured. In many ways it was worse than Lawrence. The whole novel was devoted to it, not merely a few chapters. There were scenes on the lawn with guests in deck-chairs under an ilex tree; people dancing to ragtime pumped out on a pianola; an almost libellous portrait of Asquith "with a face like a Roman bust" chasing young girls across the lawn.[38] There was an artist who was deaf and enigmatic; obviously Brett. There was a resident painter; Gertler. A girl whose hair hung "in a bell of elastic gold about her cheeks"; clearly Carrington.[39] And there was Priscilla Wimbush's pianola-playing husband Henry, whose face resembled "a grey bowler hat"; a maliciously unflattering portrait of Philip.[40] There was even an incident where two of the characters slept out on the roof, to be wakened in the morning by a peacock; just as Aldous and Carrington were in 1916.

Stunned, Ottoline sent off an angry letter to Aldous. He wrote back to "Dearest Ottoline":

> *Your letter bewildered me. I cannot understand how anyone could suppose that this little marionette performance of mine was the picture of a real **milieu** – it so obviously isn't. You might as justifiably accuse Shaw of turning Garsington into Heartbreak House or Peacock of prophesying it in Nightmare Abbey and Gryll Grange. I have made use of the country house convention because it provides a simple device for getting together a fantastic symposium.*[41]

He conceded he had erred in using some of Garsington's physical details; he should have set the book in China. But, he insisted, characters are nothing more than marionettes with voices, designed to express ideas and the parody of ideas:

> *My mistake, I repeat, was to have borrowed the stage setting from Garsington. I am sorry – but it never for a moment occurred to me that anyone would have so little imagination – or perhaps so much [he added tactfully] – as to read into a comedy of ideas a portrait of the life of the place in which it is laid.*

But Aldous's explanation did little to mollify Ottoline. Virginia Woolf, who had been at Garsington when Ottoline received Aldous's letter, said that his protestations that his characters were just marionette would not save his friendship with Ottoline. As she remarked in her Diary, his "marionettes" had destroyed it.

To Ottoline, his action was a gross betrayal. She recalled: "I was filled with dismay. I felt somehow that having given Aldous opportunities of meeting these people, I was responsible for these cruel caricatures, and that not only had he behaved dishonourably but that he had involved me in his dishonour and it might be thought that I had acquiesced in his mocking." Ottoline couldn't get over the fact that Aldous could have done to her the same hurtful thing as Lawrence had: "He already knew how much I had suffered by Lawrence having written of me and Garsington in *Women in Love,* and he had seemed to share my indignation about it, but here he had done almost the same thing. And in one way it was worse, for he had lived with us so long and had become almost one of the family, and he was quite aware that both Philip and myself were not people who were insensitive to the actions of our friends."[42] The publication of *Crome Yellow* caused a rift between Ottoline and Huxley which lasted for several years. When they finally met again it was at a party in London. Ottoline recalls: "He sat down by me and said with eagerness, 'I hear you've been seeing the Kaiser in Holland. What was he like?' I began to tell him, but after a few sentences I heard myself saying, 'No, no Aldous, I can't tell you about him, for you would write about it'."[43] Ottoline added, however, that later on they patched up their friendship and spent many happy days together, especially in Italy.

Why did Huxley write what he did in *Crome Yellow*? In her biography of Aldous Huxley, Sybille Bedford says that Aldous was irritated by the practice of people trying to work out who might be who in his novels. "He felt that this whole process of writing, this process of transposing life and fiction is far from wholly conscious and a good deal more obscure and complex than putting Jack Robinson or D.H. Lawrence into a book."[44] She says Aldous did not so much put real characters into his books as use aspects of them as a starting-point for his own creations. "He had a habit," says Sybille Bedford, "of mixing up his starting points – one man's philosophy, another's sexual tastes, one trait from a member of his family, another from a character in history

– and as he did not like to stop and think that any particular person might recognise fragments of himself in an otherwise outrageous context, he took little trouble to cover up his traces."[45] She explains that Huxley thought he was, if anything, complimenting his friends by putting them, or aspects of them, into his books.

The letters Huxley wrote to Ottoline after *Crome Yellow* tend to support this theory of surprised innocence. We know Ottoline was hypersensitive in such matters, and it was probably unrealistic of her to expect not to be portrayed in the novels of her friends; after all, Ottoline and Garsington were far and away the most extraordinary experiences they had had in their young lives. On the other hand, she did have a point. Huxley need not have been as cruel and specific in his descriptions of his characters in portraying her and her milieu in *Crome Yellow*. After all, as she rightly said, he could hardly plead ignorance in the matter of her feelings about this sort of thing.

A point that should be borne in mind, however, is that over four years had passed since Aldous had been living at Garsington as one of the family. In that time much had happened in his life. In 1919 he resigned from Eton; started work on Middleton Murry's *Athenaeum*; and finally married Maria. In 1920 they went to live in London and, after their son Matthew was born, they came to stay at Garsington. In her *Memoirs* Ottoline says: "I was not very well and was not able to put them all up in the house, but I found them lodgings in the village and they came to meals with us...but somehow it was not a great success. Maria was not happy in the lodgings; she may have resented not staying with us in the house...I have a feeling they were not contented."[46] And if Ottoline says they were not contented, it is likely that there were some difficulties between her and the Huxleys on that visit.

In addition there was an embarrassing incident the following year in Rome. Clifford Allen mentioned in Maria's presence that Ottoline had said that "Maria was a liar and could not speak the truth."[47] The relationship between Ottoline and Maria had always been extremely close. On the other hand,

Ottoline did not approve of the marriage between Maria and Aldous. Although we cannot be sure, it is not inconceivable that a certain coolness developed between Ottoline and the Huxleys after 1919 and before the publication of *Crome Yellow* in late 1921. This may have blunted Aldous's sensitivity to Ottoline's feelings. There is also another possibility. It may well be that Aldous felt he had to break the spell that Ottoline had cast on him when he was young. Lytton had done something similar by indulging in catty letters about her. Lamb quarrelled violently with her, and Russell deliberately hurt her so as to escape her thrall. Lawrence, too, may have unconsciously cut himself loose from Ottoline and his debt to her by "writing her out of his system" in *Women in Love*.

If this is true, then by writing *Crome Yellow* Aldous did not free himself completely from Ottoline's apron strings; for, several years later, he wrote another novel, *Those Barren Leaves*. in which he did it again! In this novel he invented an Ottoline-like character in the glittering Mrs. Lilian Aldwinkle, mistress of an Italian palace in which there is a congregation of writers, poets, and hangers-on. Ottoline's reaction to this novel is not recorded; but if she recognised some aspects of herself in *Crome Yellow*, there is little question she would have seen even more of herself in the character of Mrs. Aldwinkle. She has sagging cheeks and a prominent chin; her lips are of a rather vague contour whose indefiniteness is enhanced by her carelessness in reddening them; her clothes are sometimes dirty; she believes in passion, passionately; she has lots of doctors and illnesses; and she has a weakness for great men. It is her greatest regret that she herself has no aptitude for any of the arts.

> *Nature had endowed her with no power of self-expression; even in ordinary conversation she found it difficult to give utterance to what she wanted to say. Her letters were made up of the fragments of sentences: it was as though her thoughts had been blown to ungrammatical pieces by a bomb and scattered themselves on the page.*[48]

Again there are scenes Ottoline could not but trace back to those evenings at Garsington when Aldous would put on a friendly face while absorbing detail for future use:

> *For on the threshold of her bed-chamber she would halt, desperately renewing the conversation with whichever of her guests had happened to light her upstairs. Who knew? Perhaps in these last five minutes, in the intimacy, in the nocturnal silence, the important thing would really be said.*[49]

Mrs. Aldwinkle also has a peculiar genius for breaking with her friends and lovers, and an almost indecent interest in other people's love lives. "She liked to bring people together, to foster tender feelings, to watch the development of passion."[50]

Mrs. Aldwinkle was certainly a crueller caricature than Priscilla Wimbush. But then Ottoline never admitted she was Priscilla Wimbush. The thing that she objected to most in *Crome Yellow* was the caricature it contained of the way of life at Garsington, and, more particularly, Huxley's mockery of Philip as Henry Wimbush, and Asquith as Mr. Calamy. But the fact that she did not avoid all contact with Aldous after *Those Barren Leaves* was published suggests that she may have become more reconciled to such portrayals; at least by people as talented as Aldous. Another novel *Pugs and Peacocks* which featured a caricature of Ottoline was published in 1921 by another of Ottoline's favourites: Gilbert Cannan It was no match for *Crome Yellow*, and though she was mildly hurt by it, Cannan's novel did not inflame Ottoline in the way *Crome Yellow* had.

By the winter of 1921 Ottoline's health began to deteriorate yet again and she was soon to go into a nursing home for further treatment. Aldous's "betrayal" of her trust and friendship with *Crome Yellow* had upset her greatly. Nevertheless, she looked back on the events of the past year with a certain degree of satisfaction, particularly in regard to her relationship with Tiger.

INTERLUDE
My Visit to Hatfield House

Lord David Cecil (Professor of English Literature at Oxford from 1947 to 1970) in his study next to Hatfield House, where I interviewed him in 1972

LORD DAVID CECIL invited me to tea in his mews house next door to Hatfield House, the great Elizabethan mansion in Hertfordshire which had been built by his ancestor Robert Cecil, 1st Earl of Salisbury, who had been Queen Elizabeth's first advisor and confidant.

Aged about 70, he was wearing a neat grey suit and spectacles, and at first I found it difficult to envisage him as one of Ottoline's "pink-and-white undergraduates". But when he started reminiscing about his visits to Garsington in the 1920s, his eyes suddenly sparkled as the memories started to flow.

At the time of my visit, he was writing the Introduction to a volume of photographs, most of them taken by Ottoline, of the people who came to Garsington, and much of what he told me that afternoon over tea is in his book, *Lady Ottoline's Album*, which was published not long after my biography.

He described his first sighting of Ottoline. "It was in the Oxford High Street and I saw her come sailing through a crowd of people who were staring at her and whispering. She was very stately and upright and she was wearing a dress of canary-coloured silk with a long skirt that swept the pavement. She had a wide-brimmed royal-blue hat trimmed with royal-blue ostrich feathers. Her face was powdered and she was looking up as if walking in a dream."

Not long after this Cecil was introduced to Ottoline by her nephew Morven Bentinck in his rooms at Oxford, and soon after she invited him to Garsington. He was fascinated by her. "Lady Ottoline was the only person I have ever seen who could look, at the one moment, beautiful and grotesque," he recalled. She had deep-set eyes and jutting chin with square teeth, which he described as "equine" (an echo of Bertrand Russell's description of Ottoline having a face "something like a horse"). Her voice flowed up and down the scale from treble to base, and she exuded a musky scent.

Lord David thought that Garsington was the most beautiful house he had even seen (and he would have seen a lot of them). Although it was a little shabby in places, "the shabbiness enhanced its beauty".

Our tea finished, and it being time for me to leave, I got up to go. But Lord David wanted me to stay a little longer so he could make two further points about Ottoline. He wanted to emphasise that, while she was deeply romantic, she could have a sharp and occasionally satiric sense of humour. Nor was she a "lion hunter", as some people had labelled her. She was as equally welcoming of people who would never be famous as she was of Prime Ministers and famous authors like Yeats, Lawrence and Eliot. The impression Cecil wanted me to leave with was of an Ottoline who could achieve with her gatherings at Garsington an ambiance on the same level as poetry and music.

CHAPTER 22
The Younger Brigade

Ottoline, by Cecil Beaton

IN OXFORD in the early 1920s a not infrequent sight, arousing a good deal of comment, was a well-turned-out phaeton drawn by two horses trotting splendidly up the High. At the reins was a tall, impressive, large-featured man; and next to him an equally tall, impressive, and large-featured woman: Philip and Ottoline out shopping. Often Ottoline would drive in alone, or perhaps with Julian. She was an excellent "whip" – a legacy of her Rotten Row and Sherwood Forest days – and was one of the few people who dared take the narrow turning through the gates of Garsington at speed.

Sometimes she left the phaeton behind and rode into Oxford on her bicycle; leading a little crocodile procession with Brett and Gertler, and whoever else wanted to go. David Cecil, a young undergraduate, recalled her distinctive figure, sailing along the pavement, shrouded in billowing shawls and flowing dresses, darting into Hall's to buy a silk scarf or into Blackwell's to buy a book.[1] She frequently patronised the shoe shop, Ducker & Son, a shop also patronised over the years by J.R.R. Tolkien, H.H. Asquith and many other luminaries, whose names were entered into the shop's ledger now housed in the Bodleian Library. On one occasion Ottoline had three pairs of boots re-soled, re-heeled and the uppers repaired at a cost of £1.8/4 (which in today's money is about £80 or so). Some of the young men who were at Oxford during those years regarded her as a comic figure; but to a handful, the sight of Ottoline aroused very different sentiments. To them she represented one of the most desirable of all undergraduate goals; an entree into the magic world of Garsington.

One of those who watched enviously her progress up the High was Robert Gathorne-Hardy, then a second-year student reading English literature; and who was to become one of Ottoline's closest friends, and later editor of her *Memoirs*. For months he tried to find some way to wangle an invitation to Garsington. Then one day he was browsing in Blackwell's when Ottoline suddenly appeared beside him. Phrases of introduction formed in his mind, but he was too shy to utter them. At last another friend got permission to bring him along to one of Ottoline's Sunday afternoon-teas. Millie, who took it upon herself to vet prospective guests, met them at the door. Once inside there was a blur of impressions; the cluster of pugs and pekes, the panelling, the startling colours, the paintings, and, permeating everything, the heavy sweet smell of potpourri. Then the grand lady herself; long skirts, many pearls, short auburn hair and a friendly smile on the already-known, distinctive face. Then, for the first time, her unique voice.

Another undergraduate, L.A.G. Strong, also remembered what it was like to go to Garsington:

> *First of all…one would go into the drawing room. The guest of honour would be still upstairs. There would be one or two people in the drawing room, Julian, the daughter of the house, rousing herself from a book, or Philip rising hospitably from a chair beside the fire. I remember winter afternoons, when, just in time for tea, Yeats would descend, flushed and ruffled like an eagle that had been to sleep and omitted to preen its feathers. Tea soon woke him up and set him talking. One week-end he and Bertrand Russell were there together. Doubt had been expressed beforehand as to how the two would get on, but each treated the other with the utmost respect and courtesy, the eagle speaking for a while, and then inclining his head in polite silence while the secretary-bird took up the tale.*[2]

Occasionally Ottoline's efforts to bring people into the conversation were accompanied by an element of teasing. One Sunday the Asquiths turned up unexpectedly to tea. "The Asquiths! How *inconsiderate* of them!" said Ottoline.[3] There was a quick reshuffling of places at the tea table and Strong was placed next to Asquith's daughter Elizabeth. After the Asquiths left Ottoline turned to Strong and asked: "Does she attract you *physically*, Strong?"[4] Then there was the ritual of the invitation to a chat in Ottoline's private sitting-room; where guests would be quizzed about their personal and literary progress. This could be sometimes a bit of an ordeal. Peter Quennell recalled one such interview: "M-m-m – Are you writing much poetry nowadays? *M-m-m-m* – Do you often fall in love?"[5] At times the undergraduates would not know how seriously to take Ottoline's questioning. C.M. Bowra recalls her saying to Anthony Powell: "Mr. Powell, do you prefer spring or autumn?" He thought for a moment and then replied that he preferred autumn, to which Ottoline responded: "At my age, Mr Powell, you'll prefer spring."[6]

Invitations to Garsington were highly prized; and the degree of familiarity that did away with the need for one even more so. Yet Ottoline bestowed such treasures with a carelessness that was sometimes disconcerting. Peter Quenell remembered the first time he went. After finally managing to get invited, he was in a line of young men whom Ottoline was saying goodbye to at the door. To the person in front of him she extended a cordial invitation to return, "Come back next week, *do*." But to Quennell she said a curt "Goodbye", before resuming her fulsome invitations, "Come again".[7] Yet any slight was imaginary or unintended, and Quennell was welcomed back to Garsington many times. Robert Gathorne-Hardy described another occasion when Ottoline visited his rooms in Oxford, and found a relative of his there. She couldn't stay, Ottoline said, and only came to issue an invitation to come to Garsington on such-and-such a day. 'Perhaps," she droned benevolently at the relative, "you would care to come too?" The young man looked up at the apparition, his mouth opening and shutting uselessly. Ottoline smiled sweetly, then said to him: "Well don't trouble if you can't manage it."[8]

If Ottoline really took to someone, he – or less often she – was privileged with a personal brand of intimacy quite different from her public manner.[9] Gathorne-Hardy was one of these fortunates, and he would often accompany Ottoline to Charlie Chaplin films, art galleries, and concerts. Another was the future historian A.L. Rowse. He was taken to dinner at Garsington by David Cecil, by then one of Ottoline's favourites; and evidently made something of a hit with his hostess. He was invited alone to lunch and she took him to meet Siegfried Sassoon, who was one of his heroes. Later, however, Rowse looked back on those visits with a tinge of regret. He remembered having made a bit of a fool of himself one day by pacing up and down the yew hedge walks haranguing Desmond MacCarthy on the Marxist approach to history (of which Rowse approved).

Not all the young men who went to Garsington were homosexuals, but quite a number were. It might seem poor taste to remark on this; nevertheless it is an undeniable fact of Ottoline's life in the 1920s; and one that reflects a good deal of credit on her. To their delight, these young men discovered that Ottoline not only had no objection to what most of society regarded as their perversion; but often she would enter into spirited discussions about their love lives; or, more usually, their lack of love life. She was, it must be admitted, not unlettered in such matters; she was after all an old friend of Lytton's. And, as with Lytton, she would first make efforts to bring them around to more conventional ways. One of her favourite post-war doctors was a German physician-cum-psychoanalyst named Dr Marten, who claimed he could be of some help to these young men. Ottoline took several parties across to Freiburg, where the doctor had a clinic, to see what could be done. The answer was very little, and if there were any conversions, they were of brief duration.

Lytton was somewhat caustic about these conversion forays, and when he finally met Dr Marten at Garsington in 1923; he was not impressed. "Psychoanalysis is a ludicrous fraud," he told Carrington, "the Sackville-West youth was there [at Freiburg] to be cured of homosexuality. After 4 months and an expenditure of £200, he found he could just bear the thought of going to bed with a woman."[10] Lytton observed several undergraduates at Garsington who had been through the Marten treatment wandering around the lawn looking haggard, or so he said. After a while Ottoline gave up these well-meaning efforts and resumed her more natural role of den-mother; discussing love affairs; suggesting liaisons; and generally being of what assistance she could. There are even hints that she may have provided Garsington as a discreet rendezvous for certain of her friends. In return they kept her informed of their goings-on; and

The Younger Brigade

their grateful letters are some of the liveliest in her correspondence.

In befriending these young men and treating them in a civilised manner, Ottoline was performing a useful social service. As a sister of a duke and a friend and patroness of the great, she provided them with a feeling of acceptability that otherwise they would not have received; and it is no exaggeration to say she saved many of them from some of the misery they might otherwise have been condemned to. In return she reaped many rewards. Not only did such guests add a lightness and brightness to her drawing-room; they also attracted more famous guests like E.M. Forster, Lowes Dickinson, and Maynard Keynes. Yet this aspect of Ottoline's life should not be exaggerated; it was a minor undercurrent, invisible to all except those with specially acute antennae.

In another field Ottoline endeavoured to do some equally sterling work; though here she achieved less success and no reward. This involved her attempts to help some of her slightly older men friends with their matrimonial difficulties. The trouble was that some of the bright young men who had earlier come to Garsington had a habit of going off and marrying the most unsuitable women; which later led to problems. One of these marital imbroglios that Ottoline got mixed up in was between the poet Edmund Blunden and his wife Mary. At Garsington one day Blunden was looking sad and preoccupied; Ottoline asked him what was the matter. He told her that his wife didn't understand him; and so Ottoline volunteered to write to her. After this she did not hear from him for several months. Finally in September 1921 he wrote apologising for his silence and explaining that he had in fact written a long letter; but his wife Mary had not allowed him to send it. He explained, however, that Ottoline's earlier letter had helped "reform" Mary; she had dropped the pursuing, hectoring tactics that had so worried him before. He apologised for having mentioned the matter to her and said that nothing now could be "sweeter and more helpful than Mary's ways to me for weeks past."[11] Alas, the effect was short-lived, and soon Blunden was miserable again. Over the next few years Ottoline continued to try to help, inviting them, separately and together, to Garsington; liaising between them and offering advice; but to limited effect.

Just as unsuccessful were Ottoline's ongoing efforts to help T.S. Eliot. In July 1922 she was to be one of the prime movers, with Virginia Woolf, in organising a fund to subsidise Eliot so he would not have to do boring work in a bank. She wrote to many leading literary figures seeking donations. Some obliged; others declined. Arnold Bennett replied: "It irks me to refuse an appeal from you; but I do not think that this kind of an appeal can be logically justified. According to my gospel the first duty of a man is to earn his living; he must be an artist afterwards."[12] Eliot thought the same way and, though tempted, he finally turned down the idea of a subsidy; although the organisers had already sent him £50 for Christmas (which he later repaid). A year or so later Eliot freed himself from the trammels of his bank by other means. However, in addition to his financial troubles, Eliot was having marital problems. Despite the fact that Ottoline had never had a high opinion of his wife Vivienne (whom Bertie had latched on to); she had invited her to Garsington for long talks, and kept up a regular correspondence with her. At first her efforts did some good, and Eliot asked her to keep them up. Vivienne's irritability with Eliot seemed to have some connection with her health; and Ottoline recommended that Vivienne should go and see the ubiquitous Dr Marten. This advice was disastrous. Eliot told Ottoline that Marten, who prescribed Draconian starvation courses and injections of animal glands, had made Vivienne even worse. Now it was Vivienne's deteriorating mental condition that gave Eliot most concern, and for this he partly blamed Russell for having over-excited her mind "with ideas and books".

By comparison, in 1922 Bertie's domestic life, post-Mrs Eliot, was less eventful. In January Ottoline played an unaccustomed grand-motherly role by sending Bertie's young son Conrad a present. His father replied:

The Younger Brigade

The beast you sent to John Conrad is a great joy to his parents – he will have to be a little older before he can quite appreciate him. He flourishes and I have discovered that his eyes and forehead are exactly like those of Immanuel Kant, which is a great blow, as we both regard Kant as an arch reactionary.[13]

Russell told her that he spent most of his time watching John Conrad playing. Later, after he and Dora bought a cottage in Cornwall ("to be near moving water"), he tried to entice Ottoline down with utopian pictures of the sea, the rocks, the bluebells, and details of John Conrad's activities. "He is full of fun and very roguish, with bright eyes which notice everything. He is altogether lovely, and I love him beyond measure."[14] Ottoline declined, sending instead a book to Bertie for his 59th birthday. In September he and Dora came to visit Garsington, after which Russell went to see his aged Aunt Agatha; who, he reported back to Ottoline, told him that it had been all very well for him to have kicked up a fuss about the war, but that the pain he had caused various women was greater than all the harm wrought by the war.

Ottoline's own parental responsibilities were now giving her some concern. Julian had been at boarding school for three years; but in 1920 she had to leave after developing whooping cough. She stayed at Garsington for almost a year; after which Ottoline declared her formal education at an end. "You'll learn much more by sitting by the fire listening to Bertie Russell talk," she told her.[15] Nevertheless, to supplement such fireside schooling, a governess was engaged; a dumpy little German woman whom Gathorne-Hardy described as "insipid and unalluring."[16] She didn't last long and was succeeded by a tall sinister foreign lady who got off to a bad start by remarking loudly to Ottoline at the dinner-table, in front of Gertler, that she couldn't understand how Ottoline could bring herself to have Jews to dinner. However, Gertler got his own back when later playing cards by coining a nickname for her, saying: "It's Miss

Hunka's turn."[17] After that she became known as Hunker Munker Gabber Gabber. Hunka Munka (about whom, Gathorne-Hardy felt, there was something which "faintly, horribly, suggested an evil caricature of Ottoline") would join in the games of croquet, at which, if she thought she wasn't being observed, she would kick her ball into a more convenient position.[18]

When Ottoline took her daughter to the Continent in 1920-21, the 14-year-old Julian had won the hearts of a number of young officers, and on her return from Europe, fearing her daughter might become too precocious, Ottoline, on the advice of her mother-in-law Mrs Morrell, had her packed off to a convent at Roehampton; where Julian was thoroughly miserable. Dorothy Brett became so incensed at the way Julian was being treated, that she decided to kidnap her. She sent her a rope ladder in a parcel and outlined an escape route for her, arranging to wait for her outside the school in her car ready to whisk her away. But the nuns opened Brett's suspicious-looking parcel and the plan was foiled. The incident did little to improve relations between Ottoline and Brett; and not long after this they parted company permanently. In December Brett, who apparently had been performing some sort of postal duty, wrote her a bitter note, starting "Ottoline Dear..."

> *...You have the most strange ideas of friendship. Anyhow I post your letters regularly, I've no doubt it is something to be useful! but I feel a line or two at the same time thanking one for one's small services might be more polite or even friendly. I had thought of suggesting myself for a weekend but think perhaps it would be better for me to wait for you to ask me? Yrs. Brett* [19]

Soon after this the two women had a row during which Ottoline apparently threw a brooch at Brett. The evidence of this incident comes from a letter written two years later by Lawrence to Mark Gertler in which he said he had seen Brett wearing "a little blue chalcedony stone brooch" which he had given Ottoline years

The Younger Brigade

before. Brett, Lawrence said, told him that "Ottoline flung it at her at the time of the row."[20] This suggests the cause of the break between Brett and Ottoline might have been an argument over Lawrence. (Brett had fallen under Lawrence's influence during the war, and in 1924 she joined him and Frieda to go off and establish Lawrence's Rananim in a log cabin outside Taos in New Mexico.)

At the start of 1922 Ottoline was once again in the hands of specialists; as ill-health continued to plague her. There was also trouble on the farm. Philip had not yet learned his lesson about employing Ottoline's gilded amateurs; and when Toronto returned from Canada, Philip offered him a job at Garsington. Later an argument arose over accounting for milk receipts and, whatever the truth of the matter, it led to Toronto being given his marching orders.

Another slightly worrying matter was a begging letter Ottoline received from Warsaw from a friend of Boris Anrep's former wife Junia, informing Ottoline that Junia was on the verge of starvation. For several years after this Ottoline sent to Warsaw regular parcels of books and clothes and gifts of money. She kept such philanthropies; and, like Russell, she had more than one of them, to herself.

In July 1922 Virginia Woolf paid another visit to Garsington. Ottoline had just returned from her nursing home and Virginia noted that she seemed unnaturally subdued. Nevertheless, Virginia enjoyed her visit. Her pen, in describing it, was not dipped in too much vitriol. It was during this visit that Ottoline had brought up the idea of setting up a fund to free Eliot from the drudgery of working in a bank. What Virginia did not deduce, however – despite her acute observational abilities – was the real cause for Ottoline's subdued manner during her visit. While she had been in the nursing home the previous week,[21] Ottoline had received a telegram from Tiger's foster-mother telling her that Tiger was gravely ill. Ottoline caught the next train back and rushed to Garsington where she found Tiger lying in the stable-yard, having just suffered a second cerebral haemorrhage. He died (records Miranda Seymour in her biography of Ottoline) in her arms. Distraught, Ottoline fled to the seclusion of her bedroom where (Seymour further reports) she wept heart-rending tears. Ottoline apparently did not say much in her Diary about Tiger, and she did not reveal what Philip might have thought of the affair. Perhaps he had not been fully aware of his wife's latest dalliance; for he had been spending so much time away from Garsington. After this tragedy Ottoline strove to hold her head high in public; and to carry on as if nothing untoward had occurred. Only her few confidantes knew what had happened. Mark Gertler and Yeats, in particular, showed their sympathy. Indeed, Yeats and his wife held a series of séances which Ottoline attended where, she later claimed, she had made contact with Tiger "in the other world".

Another matrimonial tangle Ottoline became involved in was between a talented young Australian poet and critic W.J. Turner and his wife Delphine. Turner was a fairly regular visitor to Garsington from about 1919 onwards, having been introduced to Ottoline by Siegfried Sassoon. How highly Ottoline came to regard Turner is shown by the fact that in September 1922 she asked Lytton, probably her most prized guest, to come and spend a weekend at Garsington, specifically to meet Turner. Lytton described the weekend to Virginia Woolf as "pretty grim" and Turner as...

> ...*a very small bird-like man with a desolating accent, and a good deal to say for himself – but punctuated by strange hesitations – impediments – rather distressing; but really a nice fellow, when one has got over the way in which he says "count."*[22]

(What a wonderful letter-writer Lytton was.) Ottoline continued to promote Turner and to help him with his wife; who was suspicious of the time Turner spent out of her company, particularly at Garsington. Ottoline had several long talks with Delphine; and once travelled up to London to meet her on

Westminster Bridge "for a discussion". Turner was extremely grateful for Ottoline's interest and help; or so it seemed to her at the time.

Lytton's visit to Garsington in September was his first after a year's absence, even though Ottoline had done everything she could to lure him back. In February 1922 she had written to him: "I hear you have a beautiful motor bed (Lytton apparently was getting about in a car). I'm wondering if your Eminence could be conveyed here on the aforesaid motor bed on Sunday in time for luncheon bringing with you your Lords and Ladies in waiting."[23] But his Eminence had not turned up for seven months; and when he did come to stay, his letter to Virginia describing the visit indicated that such calls were becoming increasingly painful. After mentioning how bored he had been with Turner, he moved on to the subject of his hostess, whom he described in the cruellest possible terms, dwelling with relish on her bodily malfunctions. (Later in September, Ottoline went into hospital for an operation, possibly to put right the trouble that Lytton had hinted at so indelicately in his letter to Virginia.) On the same day that he wrote that letter, however, he wrote to Ottoline herself in a different vein:

> *It was a great pleasure to see you and to have some talks – I only wish there could have been more of them. Needless to say that I enjoyed my week-end very much. It was delightful to find Philip in such good trim, and I liked making the acquaintance of Turner. I hope your health is really taking a turn for the better at last. What a disgusting arrangement one's body does become when its machinery goes out of order.*[24]

Lytton's disinclination to go to Garsington may have had something to do with the fact that his own ménage at Tidmarsh was demanding more and more of his attention. The previous year Carrington had married Partridge, and the three of them had settled down at Tidmarsh; Carrington sleeping with Partridge, and Lytton occasionally sleeping with Partridge (but not, needless to say, with Carrington). Ottoline's comment on Carrington's marriage was: "I think this is very clever of Lytton for he will still retain his maid & attendant & he will also have a manservant too – 'Married Couple' in fact!"[25] Later in 1921 Carrington had fallen in (actual) love with Partridge's best friend, Gerald Brenan. Then, early in 1922, while holidaying on the Continent, Partridge fell in love with their hostess, a passionate woman named Clare Bollard. A little later Partridge found out about Brenan, and had a furious argument with Carrington, threatening to leave Tidmarsh. Throughout that summer Lytton had to use all his diplomatic skill to keep Carrington and Partridge together. Later Clare turned up at Tidmarsh only to forsake Partridge and fall in love; with, of all people, Carrington's old lover, Mark Gertler. And if this wasn't complication enough, Carrington later conceived a Lesbian affection for Clare. No wonder Lytton was feeling harassed domestically.

Next year 1923 also did not start well for Ottoline. She had sent Bertie a Christmas present, and it took him some time to write to thank her. Next she received a postcard from France from Middleton Murry. It said:

> MY DEAR OTTOLINE, *Katherine died suddenly on Tuesday night: she was buried yesterday in the cemetery here at Avin. J.M.M.*[26]

It was no surprise that Katherine had died. She had been suffering from tuberculosis for a long time. Murry now resolved to devote the rest of his life to her memory. He told Ottoline: "the only thing that matters to me is that she should have her rightful place as the most wonderful writer and most beautiful spirit of our time."[27] Ottoline, too, did her best to perpetuate Katherine's memory, and composed an essay about her which she read out to a group of friends one evening. David Cecil, who was there, recalls Ottoline's voice purring and dipping over her words; and as night fell Philip lighting a candle and holding it over her so she could read on. It was Ottoline's opinion that Katherine was a clever writer who struggled constantly to escape her colonial background. Her taste, Ottoline said once, was "Swan & Edgars" (by which she meant rather lower-middle-class), and in her *Memoirs* she recalled a telling incident concerning Katherine:

> *We were playing a game after dinner when she was here, describing people by symbols, such as pictures and flowers and scents; unfortunately Katherine was described by some rather exotic scent such as Stephanotis or Patchouli, and although her name was not mentioned, we all knew and she knew who was meant. It was dreadful. The spite that was in the company maliciously flared out against her and hurt her. We all filed out of the drawing-room to bed very silently.*[28]

After Brett's defection and Katherine's death, Ottoline's closest female friend was Virginia Woolf; and from 1923 onwards their relationship grew from cordiality into warm friendship. Virginia's chronic mental instability was for the time being more or less under control; and now her novels were beginning to attract attention. In 1924 she felt well enough to move to Tavistock Square in Bloomsbury; and when Ottoline returned to London to Gower Street a few years later, they visited each other frequently, and meanwhile corresponded regularly. To most of Virginia's Bloomsbury friends, her consorting with Ottoline was something of a mystery. What did Virginia see in her? Probably the same things Lytton did; gossip, and a sympathetic ear. But there was much more to their friendship. They discussed poetry together, Ottoline appreciating the way Virginia read the words of poets such as Donne. Nevertheless, like Lytton, Virginia did not let her friendship stand in the way of lampooning what she regarded as some of Ottoline's more eccentric aspects. After a visit to Garsington in 1923, Virginia described the experience to Barbara Bagenal (one of the Slade cropheads who was in hospital recovering from scarlet fever):

I have often thought of you in hospital, as I take my way about the streets in comparative freedom. Yet I would have changed places with you last Sunday fortnight, when Ottoline completely drew the veils of illusion from me, and left me Monday morning to face a world from which all heart, charity, kindness and worth had vanished. How she does this, in ten minutes, between twelve and one, in the best spare bedroom, with the scent of dried roseleaves about, and a little powder falling on the floor, Heaven knows. Perhaps after 37 undergraduates, mostly the sons of Marquises, one's physical life is reduced, and one receives impressions merely from her drawl and crawl and smell which might be harmless in the stir of normal sunlight. Only is the sunlight ever normal at Garsington ? No, I think even the sky is done up in pale yellow silk, and certainly the cabbages are scented.[29]

For a time Virginia toyed with the idea of incorporating Ottoline into one of her novels; but it seems that she eventually decided not to, perhaps because she was aware of Ottoline's hostility to such things. (That did not stop her, however, portraying Philip as Hugh Whitbread in Mrs. Dalloway; the name is something of a pun; both Whitbread and Morrell are English brewers.) Virginia quite often had sat and chatted with Philip and analysed his character, saying in her Diary on Monday 19, February 1923, that...

...he wished to be an actor, & suffers from dual personality. He sees himself, & seldom unifies – sees himself farmer, host, speaker, & so on. But talking to us he felt himself single, so he said, & there is something diluted in the quality of his emotions. He is an amorous man, a man of different generation & tradition, in cross-over waistcoat & jewels, half man of the world, half aesthete, appreciating furniture that is, but living my word! Among what

> *humbugs, & palming them off on us plausibly enough – Ottoline &c. Layers of shifting vapours trail over him perpetually, keep him restless, chattering uneasy.*

Lytton was at Garsington at least three times in 1923, torn between his dislike of being a trophy on display, and the prospect of seeing the latest crop of pink-and-white undergraduates from Oxford. Even so, his patience was sorely tried at times. After one visit in June (during which he was introduced to Dr Marten, who happened to be in town) he reported to Carrington: "Appalling! A fatal error to have come. I see now only too clearly...The boredom has been indescribable. Most of the conversation is directed towards the dog when the doctor is not holding forth."[30]

Dr Marten may have been a bit of a bore, but he gave Ottoline some excellent advice; counselling her to eat plain foods and lead a simple life. Her regard for him was very high and for a time she acted as a sort of unpaid publicity agent for him; while, however, retaining a certain scepticism about his treatment, especially the amateur psychoanalysis he threw in with his more orthodox physicking. Once, when Robert Gathorne-Hardy asked what Marten had discovered about her, Ottoline replied (only half-jokingly): "I find that my brothers play an undue part in my life."[31]

In the summer of 1923 Gathorne-Hardy and his companion Kyrle accompanied Ottoline to Germany for what was now almost her annual pilgrimage to Dr Marten's clinic at Freiburg. Even there, in a town noted for its odd visitors, Ottoline stood out. "*Die komische Englanderin*" was what the townspeople called her. Gathorne-Hardy noted that, although far away from Garsington, Ottoline managed to convert her hotel room into a travelling boudoir, displaying around the room pretty little boxes and other knickknacks, some brought with her, some bought on the trip, and infusing the room with her distinctive personal scent. Ottoline also managed to continue talent-spotting. She learned that the Russian writer Maxim Gorki was in the same hotel and, despite the language barrier, she arranged to meet him and somehow communicate her admiration, which he rewarded with his autograph. It was on a similar trip to France several years later, again accompanied by Gathorne-Hardy, that the opportunity arose for Ottoline to meet the aged impressionist Monet at his home at Giverny. An efficient housekeeper refused to allow Ottoline in; so she had to content herself with looking at the garden with its pond, bridges and waterlilies. (Subsequently, however, she managed to get in and see some of Monet's water-lily canvasses.)

The following year 1924 was when Ottoline returned to the fold. Although she was now on good terms with all her brothers (and had lent one of her cats to the Duchess of Marlborough for stud purposes), she had not had any direct contact with the fashionable world since 1914. Now she had come to the conclusion that, although the Bohemian life might be all right for her, it was not necessarily the life that Julian would be suited to. Her brother Charlie's two daughters were to be debutantes that year; and so Ottoline felt that Julian should share their London experiences. So she decided that Julian should "Come Out" – officially – into Society. In that cause she rented Ethel Sand's house in Chelsea as their headquarters for the 1924 summer Season.

Presenting a debutante at Court, and participating in the round of dances and other entertainments associated with Coming Out, was a costly affair. Ottoline, after a failed attempt to get financial assistance from her brothers, was grateful for the generosity of her cousin Lord Howard de Walden (who had inherited the London estate of the Fifth Duke of Portland, and had attended her wedding). Toning down her eccentric attire, she made contact again with the grand houses in Mayfair and Belgravia that she had known in her girlhood. She found that many of the dowagers and matrons now chaperoning their daughters were the same young girls she had met at balls and receptions back in the 1890s. She was invited to tea-parties given by Ettie Desborough and the Duchess of Devonshire and other aristocratic ladies; all of whom welcomed her back, as if nothing

The Younger Brigade

had happened in between. Ottoline decided that Julian should have a lady's maid for the Season; so she engaged for that purpose a girl named Ivy Green, whose father was the gardener at one of the big Oxfordshire houses. During the Season, Julian and Ivy did the rounds of the great Home County houses. "There was no limit to the sport and shooting and they'd talk about nothing else than what had been shot and what had been caught," Ivy remembered.[32]

Ivy was to stay on at Garsington after Julian Came Out to become Ottoline's personal maid and dressmaker. The latter was an important position, as the sort of clothes Ottoline liked weren't to be found in ordinary shops. Once Ivy was sent all the way to Kenwood House in Hampstead to inspect a portrait of Nelson's Lady Hamilton; and copy details of her pink silk taffeta dress. Another time Ottoline, who had been up in London, returned to Garsington in great excitement, exclaiming: "Ivy, I've seen a coat! It was running along the street on a person, so I jumped off the bus and stopped her and asked if she would send it to us to copy it."[33] The woman obliged. Ivy (whom I interviewed) recalled that Ottoline preferred very bright colours; that her shoes were bought in Bond Street; and her hats from Mrs. Wilson's in Mayfair. Ottoline herself shopped at the big stores like Marshall and Snelgrove, where she would make friends with the shop-assistants, asking the girls about their lives; and on several occasions inviting them to Garsington (where they had tea in the servants' quarters).

It was Ottoline's hope that Julian would marry some well-set-up young man; and so to expedite this she made a practice of inviting presentable young gentlemen to Garsington. The historian C.M. Bowra was present one day when the main guest was a young Spanish Duke, whom Ottoline had summed up shrewdly, suggesting a charade in which the Duke would play Napoleon. Bowra recalled: "It happened that at this moment Philip's mother was dying, and he came into the room at intervals with increasingly bad news." Ottoline would stop the charades for a moment to console Philip with a few words, then turn back to the guests; crying gaily: "Go on! Go on!"[34] On another occasion Leslie Hartley, the future author of *The Go-Between*, had come to lunch with several more eligible young men. After Ottoline carefully placed the others round the table, she waved a hand at Hartley and said: "Anywhere, Mr. Hartley."[35] In August 1925 Ottoline took Julian to Holland where they attended a Bentinck family dinner at which Ottoline was placed next to the exiled Kaiser, who expressed pleasure at seeing her again (apparently the two had met in Germany before the war).

After supervising Julian's Coming Out, Ottoline divided her time between London, where she arranged *the dansants* for Julian, and Garsington, where life went on more or less as always; with the usual influx of guests arriving every Friday evening, and many staying on till Monday morning. At other times Ottoline would merely follow her daily routine, which consisted of rising early; ordering the day's meals; attending to the household arrangements; then writing letters in her boudoir until lunch. In the afternoon she would relax and read; or go into Oxford. In the evening a local village woman came to light the oil lamps (Garsington still hadn't electricity) and Mrs. Sue Wain would come over from a nearby village to take up the jugs of water and turn the beds down in the guest rooms. After dinner Ottoline did her embroidery, while Julian, Philip, the painter Gilbert Spencer, and Gertler, or whoever else was staying, would play bridge. Gilbert, who was now a particular friend, had come from his home in Cookham to stay at one of the cottages at Garsington and help Philip on the farm. He was very grateful for Ottoline and Philip's friendship, and once told Ottoline: "Without in any way wishing to compliment myself I think you have both helped me turn my brain into something tolerably intelligent."[36] (He would continue his painting when he returned to back his home at Cookham.)

While the opportunities Garsington offered a young man of literary ambition were rich; they could also be daunting. L.A.G. Strong recalled going there one spring; wandering around the garden with Yeats in the morning; then sitting by the pond with

E.M. Forster in the afternoon. On another day Strong joined a group under the ilex tree.[37] A few people were playing tennis while the rest talked. Ottoline introduced him to Eliot and the Woolfs. "A rarefied silence resulted," Strong recalled, "and after five minutes Eliot excused himself. Leonard Woolf presently made a polite remark about the peacock, while Virginia gave her gentle, tortured smile. I was relieved when the party reshaped itself."[38] Ottoline was a scrupulously conscientious hostess, yet such was the constant stream of comings and goings that slights and omissions inevitably occurred. Once, when Virginia Woolf had been staying, Robert Gathorne-Hardy, who was particularly anxious to meet her, found himself left out of the group she was in, and wandered about the house looking forlorn, before departing. Next day, after Virginia had gone, he got an urgent invitation from Ottoline to back come to Garsington. She told him she was sorry he had been neglected, and from that day forward she tried to place him next to Virginia whenever she was at Garsington.

In such illustrious company, many of Garsington's young guests were, not unexpectedly, shy and reticent. Nevertheless, Ottoline did her best to bring them out and look after them. Gathorne-Hardy said that she orchestrated the conversation, drawing out the principal guest, whether it was Yeats, Strachey, Birrell, Asquith, or Virginia Woolf. "But," he added, "there was no question of a monologue, and no breaking-up of the talk as at a formal dinner party."[39]

She would induce a shy undergraduate to say something, then cunningly lead him on with questions and comments; finally linking the boy's remarks into the general conversation. Such talk was, to the initial shock of many undergraduates, allowed to drift to topics not normally broached in polite company. "It ranged far and wide," recalled Gathorne-Hardy. But if it ranged too far, Ottoline was there to smooth over any awkward moments that resulted. Gathorne-Hardy told how once he annoyed Lytton Strachey with a priggish remark:

A friend of mine was travelling with a character alleged to be not very reputable in his behaviour. I said that I thought this was degrading – a silly word to use. "I don't see why," piped Strachey sharply; "all I've heard about him is that he has a penchant for…it was a penchant that a great many people would have though it very shocking indeed.[40]

Ottoline intervened: "Not for people like you and me, Lytton. Not for older people like us. But for a much younger, unformed person, perhaps…"[41] And the meal became easy again. On December 29, 1924, one of her young protégé's wrote to her:

Christmas was pretty depressing, but tonight there seems to be fair prospect of entertainment of a sort. Did you know that a new beauty has arisen in the midst of our small circle? He pulls down the blinds in the office scene of "Old English," and is beautiful and tiresome, about fifty-fifty; but then he's only 17. "Is there such a place as the Zoo?" is a fairly representative remark of his! Eardley is stricken unto death. Kyrle is interested, and even Bob "sees something in him." He was produced by Rawley Leigh at a bridge party, and only appears at these functions. The formula of conduct is always the same. Whoever is dummy sits on the arm of his chair and kisses him, – and if he is dummy he selects one of the three players on whose chair to sit etc., great excitement![42]

Philip's mother had died in November 1924, and he was keen to move to Black Hall, the Morrell family home. In January 1925 Ottoline reluctantly agreed to a trial three-month period of residence there. But she hated it. Its stuffy Victorian atmosphere stifled her; as it did Julian. For Ottoline, Julian's distaste for anything associated with the late Mrs Morrel (who had been the cause of her incarceration in the Roehampton convent) was sufficient for her to convince Philip that Black Hall was not the solution to their mounting financial problems; and they soon retreated back to Garsington, where Ottoline busied herself with renovating the house, using some of the money Philip had inherited from his mother to, for example, at last replacing the oil-lamps with electric light. Other necessary repairs were also made. Yet, despite the Morrell inheritance, the cost of the renovations ran up a large overdraft. The house's upkeep was a constant drain on their finances. Already Ottoline had had to sell her Marie Antoinette pearls, replacing them with paste (though that raised £1,300). They had sold off some of their land; but the farm was still not paying its way. Ottoline's mind was turning to other ways of balancing their budget. She began to entertain the possibility of selling Garsington.

By 1926 Julian was 20, and many of the young men who now came to Garsington were there to see Julian, not her mother; something Ottoline would not have relished. She also suspected Mark Gertler was becoming over-fond of Julian, and that fondness was being reciprocated. However, far more serious was the growing attraction between Julian and one of the Oxford undergraduates. He was Igor Vinogradoff, a tall and brilliant Oxford young man (see his photo above) whose father was a Russian emigre and a distinguished jurist. In the ensuing months he became very fond of Julian, and finally proposed to her. Ottoline was strongly against such a match; partly because she did not feel that Julian, who was used to living comfortably, would enjoy having to economise, as Igor was virtually penniless. So she went to considerable lengths to put a damper on the romance; extracting a promise from Igor that any engagement would be postponed for a year. Although Philip and Gertler sided with Julian over this matter, Siegfried supported Ottoline, and suggested Julian should be taken on excursions to meet other people. Thus a visit to Ettie Desborough at Panshanger was arranged, where Ottoline (and perhaps Julian) enjoyed a number of elegant receptions. Shortly after returning to Garsington, to Ottoline's surprise and no doubt gratification, Julian came into her bedroom and said she no longer wanted to marry Igor; and that she would welcome a trip away in Europe "to clear her mind".

What was to prove to be an eventful journey started in late July. Departing in the Morrell's old Overland car, the party consisted of Ottoline, Philip, and Siegfried; while Robert Gathorne-Hardy and his lover Kyrle Leng and Julian followed in a Buick. It began happily enough with a visit to Monet's garden at Giverny; followed by an inspection of Chartres Cathedral; and then a tour of the gardens at Versailles. But after four days of travelling, discontent broke out. Robert Gathorne-Hardy and Kyrle decided to drop out and return to England, because they didn't like having to sleep separately. Sassoon, pining for his current lover, the actor Glen Byam Shaw, then switched to the Buick where his passenger Julian was grumpy. Not only that, but the Overland kept breaking down. They travelled on and on through Italy; with Ottoline wanting to visit art galleries and Julian wanting to find places where she could dance the Charleston. Finally, they drove back over the Alps with the Overland belching steam and requiring top-ups of water every 25 miles; while Julian and Ottoline squabbled and Philip tried to keep the peace.

On their return to England, tension between mother and daughter became so fraught that Ottoline decided to send Julian up to London to stay with Juliette Huxley for three months, and study home-science. This time away gave Julian a much-needed break from Ottoline and time to make new friends, whom she started to bring back for weekend visits to Garsington. Two of her new friends, the brothers David and Stephen Tennant, particularly amused her, and she decided she would like to marry David. However, he was shortly to marry the actress Hermione Baddeley. Finally, in the summer of 1927, while travelling in Austria, Julian met another young man, Victor Goodman, who was a clerk in the House of Lords, and later became Clerk of the Parliaments. Victor (later Sir Victor) proposed; Julian accepted; and they planned to be married in early 1928, and set up house in Chelsea.

Ottoline began to feel, if not redundant, then progressively relegated to the sideline. She and Philip also began to think that Garsington was becoming too big and too expensive to manage at their stage in life. Ottoline felt that people could come to visit more easily if she were in London, rather than away at Oxford. One incident reflected this growing disillusionment with where they had lived for more than a decade. In March 1925 Lytton paid one of his rare visits. On the day he was to leave, Carrington and Partridge arrived in their car to pick him up, and Ottoline, who hadn't seen Carrington for a long time, took her reappearance as a gesture of reconciliation. She called out her name joyfully and asked her in. But Carrington did not budg; and said coldly: "No thank you, Ottoline."[43] An expression of grief came over Ottoline's face; then, pulling herself together, she managed to get out some trivial conversation about the tyres on the car. Lytton then came out, said goodbye, and drove off. That was his last visit to Garsington.

Julian's impending marriage was yet another factor in Ottoline's decision to contemplate giving up Garsington and returning to London. At first, Ottoline and Philip looked for a house near Ethel Sands in Chelsea. They found one in St. Leonards Terrace that suited them perfectly. But once again the past cast a pall over their plans. Logan Pearsall Smith also happened to live in St. Leonards Terrace, and when he heard that Ottoline was planning to take a house in the same street, he circulated a letter to the other residents telling them that the Morrells were not reputable people, and shouldn't be allowed to live near them. Ottoline was cut to the quick, and so began looking around Bloomsbury instead. She found a four-storey house around the corner from Bedford Square at 10 Gower Street, and took a lease on it.

As Gower Street was a dull, undistinguished street compared with other parts of Bloomsbury (let alone Bedford Square), many of Ottoline's friends, unaware of the Morrell's financial and other predicaments, were surprised when they heard she wanted to live there. After 44 Bedford Square, it was a definite "come down". But perhaps Ottoline felt it was time to give up trying to carry out her life on an elaborate stage. After moving to Gower Street she was to go out of her way to "mute herself down", and live like an ordinary person; not the grand hostess. When she came back to Garsington and announced she had discovered somewhere for them to live, she told Ivy Green: "I've found the dearest little doll's house!"[44] Later, when in the summer of 1928 the Morrells finally sold Garsington, the new owners asked Ottoline about the local shops; and where they could buy meat and fish. Ottoline replied: "Don't talk to me of fish. You may talk to me about poetry and literature, but not fish."[45]

10 GOWER STREET

T.S. Eliot, in the garden at Gower Street

Bertrand Russell dined around Bloomsbury with Ottoline after she moved to Gower Street

Virginia Woolf and Ottoline became firm friends as they both grew older

W.B. Yeats in the garden at 10 Gower Street

The front door of No. 10 Gower Street with Ottoline's blue plaque

Aldous Huxley and Ottoline became close friends once more

Charlie Chaplin was in his 40s when he visited 10 Gower Street

Margot Asquith, who took over 44 Bedford Square and lived around the corner from Ottoline

Robert Gathorne-Hardy and his friend Kyrle Leng were regular visitors at 10 Gower Street

CHAPTER 23
The Dearest Little Doll's House

Ottoline in her declining years

WHY DID Ottoline and Philip sell Garsington? Their shaky financial position was certainly a factor in what must have been the painful decision to give up that idyllic sanctuary and return to the bustling, crasser world. Yet they could have sold some of their valuable farmland while still retaining the house and garden, and living more frugally. Julian's impending marriage was certainly a factor in the decision to sell;

as was the feeling that a whole new generation of bright young things had started to invade Garsington, dancing to ragtime and heedless of such matters as art or poetry. Moreover, Ottoline was beginning to feel burdened by the memories of so many friends who had turned against her, particularly those who had made use of her and the house and her guests for their satirical literary portrayals. But none of these factors would seem a sufficient explanation for the decision to sell Garsington. So what was the real reason?

A possible, if not probable, answer to this question has remained a secret until now. When I visited David Garnett on his houseboat in the Thames in 1972 he told me what he believed was, if not the main reason, then a powerful factor in the Morrell's decision to give up Garsington. However, I could not reveal this when I first wrote *Ottoline*. It had to be embargoed until now because it could have adversely impacted on the lives of two men who, at that time, had young families to bring up; and whose lives might be affected, even blighted, by the revelation. But with the passing of time, the truth can at last be told.

Around 1927 Alice Jones and Evelyn Merrifield, the two mothers of Philip's illegitimate sons, joined forces (according to David Garnett) to approach Philip to insist he and Ottoline must pay for the education and upkeep of their now 10-year-old sons. This, said Garnett, meant sending the boys to good schools and supporting them through university, if they were that way inclined. That the two sons did indeed do well at school and university is partly the legacy of the sale of Garsington; which supplied Philip and Ottoline with sufficient money to pay for the two boys' schooling and their mothers' livelihoods over the next 12 or more years. So it proved a worthwhile outlay of funds. One son became a leading London surgeon and the other a senior British diplomat, and each of whom went on to have families of their own (who also had to be shielded from the truth, and source of their family finances). Nevertheless, it came at a heavy cost to Philip and Ottoline.

That is not to say that there weren't (as mentioned above)

other reasons. Robert Gathorne-Hardy mentioned one in his Introduction to Ottoline's *Memoirs*.

> *One day I was lunching with* [Ottoline and Philip at Gower Street when] *Ottoline opened a letter and as she read it gave out a cry of the utmost distress. A massive limb had fallen off the great ilex tree at Garsington. I cannot recall her exact words, but she cried out that the place was ruined – that she would hardly endure to look at it again so dreadfully disfigured. And then for the only time in my life, I saw her lose her temper. Philip had been calmly sympathetic. "You drive me mad," she said suddenly and fiercely, "taking it so calmly."*[1]

Other less serious but worrying matters were weighing on Ottoline's mind at that time. In April 1927 the Australian poet J.W. Turner wrote to Ottoline asking if he could dedicate a book to her. She had not seen much of Turner recently (perhaps as a result of her unsuccessful endeavours to sort out his marital difficulties) and she received this request with mixed feelings. The last person to ask if he could do this was Lawrence (for his book of poems, *Amores*), and what happened after that was still painfully fresh in her memory. She liked Turner, but she suspected there might be more to his request than met her eye. She had heard rumours about the book he was writing, and didn't like what she had heard. She sent a letter back to him, asking for more information:

> *It is very nice of you to suggest dedicating your book to me but I feel it is rather difficult to give my consent unless I see the book first or know a little what it's all about. At present you see I really know nothing, I merely heard a kind of rumour which I hope is untrue that there was a character in it that might easily be mistaken for me.*[2]

But Turner was persistent. For some reason he was particularly anxious to obtain Ottoline's name on the book; and he pressed her further. Far from linking her with the book's contents, he told her, it would do the opposite. Ottoline was unimpressed:

> ...but as to that I am afraid I don't agree. On the contrary it might put the idea into people's heads. It would certainly lead people to suppose that the book was being published with my approval and consent, which of course is not true.[3]

She concluded with the hope that Turner would leave her name out of his proposed work and wait until another time to dedicate one of his books to her, "if you really want to do so". Turner replied rather sadly that he greatly regretted her decision. The book, entitled *The Aesthetes,* was published later that year. It was dedicated not to Ottoline but "To Cynthia", and although it did not create much of a stir – only a handful of people could have read it – it is quite easy to see why Ottoline would have objected to it; and did. *The Aesthetes*[4] is a dialogue carried on by a group of guests at a country house called Wrexham over a period of three days. Their conversation centres on a well-known literary hostess, Lady Virginia Caraway, who, it is said, killed the first American poet that ever came to England. "He came to me a genius, he left me a man," she writes in the little orange book in which she records her daily struggles among the arts. Lady Caraway's taste in poetry is highly coloured. She likes poets of "passion". Two of the guests, one named Esmond Darthy, the other called Dytton, give long, malicious descriptions of Lady Virginia, dwelling on her "crimson-lake" hair, her strange hats and her made-up face. Dytton refers to her collected novels of Henry James; her portraits by John and Conder; and her love of needlework. There is no question Turner meant Lady Virginia to be taken for a depiction of Ottoline. One day Virginia Caraway comes down to lunch with her head swathed in bandages (because of her neuralgia), followed by 15 pugs whose pantings and gurglings so annoy one guest that he exclaims: "Virginia, I shall throw all of those horrible animals out of the window if you won't have them sent away." Virginia replies: "The darlings! They're only dreaming! aren't you Necropolis?" One of the little horrors spits at her. While Virginia works at her embroidery, spasms of neuralgia and exultation struggling across her face, the conversation ebbs and flows around her. Occasionally she speaks, once venturing the theory that a landscape is "a state of mind". At this an artist called Radenlac asks sarcastically whether this didn't mean just as much as saying that a soul was a state of the landscape. Virginia replies coldly: "I don't think you care much for nature, Mr. Radenlac."

The Aesthetes was as harsh an attack on Ottoline as Lawrence's had been; just as vicious and, at times, just as cruelly accurate, although crudely-written by comparison with Lawrence's superior prose. Ottoline's only consolation would have been that, while *Women in Love* was by 1927 quite widely-read, Turner's had little hope of being so; until, that is, a curious event resurrected it more than ten years later (and we will come to that). But although it was not a best-seller, in one respect Turner's caricature of Ottoline is more perceptive than those of Lawrence and Huxley. In *The Aesthetes* Turner made a significant point about Ottoline. Virginia Caraway's guests are talking about art and what it is. After conjuring up his parody of Virginia, Dytton says:

> ...*if we look upon Lady Caraway merely as a freak, a psychological sport, we are being extraordinarily superficial, because those terms don't express Lady Caraway, but only a conception of Lady Caraway. In short, we have made a mere intellectual construction which we call Lady Caraway, whereas Lady Caraway is a work of art.*[5]

Dytton goes on to argue that it is possible to look at the whole of Lady Caraway – and, for the sake of argument, let's replace Virginia Caraway with Ottoline Morrell – that it is possible to look at Ottoline as being a collection of impressions, memoirs, gossip; everything known about her; all combined in the one object, or at one point. Turner employs the simile of a painting, which is not merely canvas and dried paint, but a focus; its reputation; people's impressions of it; how it evokes memories; and so on. Turner says that Virginia (*ie*, Ottoline):

> ...is not the physical construction we may shake hands with or photograph, nor the intellectual or conceptual construction Darthy may present to us as a psychological fiction, nor the intuition-image each one of us may have, nor the work of art each one of us may experience, but the indiscernible, where all these meet.[6]

Another of Turner's puppets goes on to say that Lady Caraway is like Switzerland; or the Russian Ballet; or the Tower of Pisa: "She is known only to tourists or sight-seers. They look at her and go away – and write books about her."[7]

Although Turner's book dealt yet another cruel blow[8] to Ottoline – and indeed was possibly the cruellest book written about her – he made an important point about her. Ottoline was not merely a person. She is in a sense a combination of everyone's image of her. Any attempt to reconstruct what Ottoline was like in fiction or legend is not a matter of attempting to winkle out from the morass of truth, half-truth, and fiction the supposedly "real" figure. It is more a matter of trying to catch all the diverse and scattered images of her at one focal point.

Both Virginia Woolf and Lytton Strachey had observed that, with Garsington, Ottoline had created her own, unique work of art. Yet neither took the next step and described Ottoline as a work of art herself. Virginia almost did when she imagined Ottoline as something rich and wonderful, like "a Spanish galleon, hung with golden coins & lovely silken sails". Other writers' descriptions of her – an oversized Infanta of Spain; an enormous bird; a lion-hunting hostess – are equally picturesque. But they are just as false and inaccurate as Hermione Roddice,

Priscilla Wimbush, or Lilian Aldwinkle were. Ottoline in her Diary, letters, and *Memoirs* promoted a self-image – a legend – which ranged from what might be close to the truth, to what is wildly fanciful.

After she moved to Gower Street, the legendary side of her image developed and expanded. Stephen Spender saw on her walls a misty spiritualist painting by the Irish poet, AE; yet Gathome-Hardy said Ottoline never owned such a painting; it merely fitted in with the image Spender was trying to create. Spender also describes her going out with two or three pekinese dogs tied by ribbons to a shepherdess's crook. But they were almost certainly pugs; the ribbons were leather leashes; and she never possessed a crook. How important are such errors? Spender's image is a vivid one and has come down to us today woven inextricably into the composite image of Ottoline. And, as such – as Turner implied – it is as good as any other part of the legend. However, Ottoline never spoke to Turner again.

In August 1927 Ottoline, having made one of her regular late-summer trips to Italy, returned to supervising the renovations at Gower Street, and organising Julian's wedding to Victor Goodman, scheduled for the New Year. The wedding took place at St Martins-in-the Fields on January 24 the following year. After their honeymoon, the Goodmans went to live in Chelsea (a year later, Julian gave birth to their daughter Anne Arianna). Julian remained married to Victor until 1942 when she divorced him and married her old flame, Igor Vinogradoff.

The burst of activity leading up to the wedding exhausted Ottoline, and, coming on top of the wrench of giving up Garsington, it was no surprise when she fell ill again. This time, however, it turned out to be something more serious than her chronic migraines and stomach disorders. First she complained of neuralgia of the jaw; then abscesses appeared. Several doctors were consulted, without much effect, until Juliette Huxley recommended an expert on tropical medicine named Dr. Rau. He diagnosed necrosis of the jaw; a disease in which part of the bone-marrow dies. (Apparently Ottoline had been infected during her trip to Italy.) She was admitted to a nursing home in Fitzroy Square where an operation was performed to remove the diseased part of the bone; after which she had to remain in bed in a darkened room with tubes draining her jaw. (There had been some suspicion that it was cancer, but the need to drain the jaw points to an infection.) For several weeks she was in almost constant pain. She told Juliette Huxley, who came to visit her: "At times it is so bad I just growl like a tiger."[9]

The seriousness of the illness jolted all Ottoline's friends, many of whom realised how much they might miss her were she not to recover. Lytton was very worried and asked Gathorne-Hardy in hushed tones: "What is the matter with Ottoline?" When told what it was he breathed a sigh of relief: "I thought it must be cancer."[10] Her old antagonist Roger Fry felt concerned enough to visit her in hospital, while Portland himself insisted she convalesce at Welbeck, where he set aside a suite of rooms for her. There she slowly recovered, but the operation had taken its toll, and left the lower part of her face badly scarred. She did little to hide this disfigurement, however, only occasionally wearing a scarf to shield her pitted jawline.

Yet there was one outcome of this ordeal that Ottoline welcomed: after 12 years she and Lawrence made up their quarrel. He had learned of her illness from Aldous Huxley while staying in Italy, and he wrote to her immediately:

My Dear Ottoline,
I was so sorry to hear of you ill and in all that pain – so was Frieda. But now thank goodness you are a lot better, and soon one can think of you nicely going around again and being there in the world. I do hope you'll keep well – I consider people like you and me, we've had our whack of bodily ills, we ought to be let off a bit…I trust we shall meet again one day, you and I, because I'm sure we're quite fond of one another really through all this long lapse. But the chief thing for you at the moment is to get quite well.
from us both,

D. H. LAWRENCE[11]

Ottoline replied in equally friendly terms and told him about giving up Garsington, adding that she felt sad their early hopes for it as a possible Rananim had not been realised. She told him she was feeling depressed and feared that her life had been largely wasted. "Don't feel you're not important," he wrote back. "You've been an important influence in lots of lives, as you have in mine: through being fundamentally generous, and through being Ottoline. After all, there's only one Ottoline. And she has moved one's imagination." He then went on to make what can be interpreted – and what he probably meant Ottoline to take – as an apology for Hermione Roddice:

> *It doesn't matter what sort of vision comes out of a man's imagination, his vision of Ottoline. Any more than a photograph of me is me, or even "like" me. The so-called portraits of Ottoline can't possibly be Ottoline – no one knows that better than an artist.*[12]

He told her that he and Frieda were staying in a villa in Florence and that he was working on the final stages of a new novel (which was to be his last and most controversial work, *Lady Chatterley's Love*). Ottoline welcomed the reconciliation, and thereafter she and Lawrence exchanged regular letters, as he travelled around Italy searching for somewhere to rest between his worsening bouts of tuberculosis. (Earlier, in 1922, he had written to her returning some money she had lent him; and expressing how grateful he had been for her help.)

Towards the end of the summer of 1928 Ottoline felt sufficiently recovered from her jaw operation to think about "officially" opening her new premises in Gower Street to the talent and intellect of London. Garsington by now was just a cluster of memories – good and bad – and a weekly hamper of flowers and vegetables sent up by the gardener; while Bedford Square, where 20 years ago she first launched herself on an

The Dearest Little Doll's House

unsuspecting capital, was distant history. Yet it had partly been the memory of Bedford Square that had lured her back to London and Bloomsbury. So, as she stood on the threshold of another new era in her life, she hoped that Gower Street might help her recapture some of the magic of those pre-war days; while at the same time allowing her to entertain on a less grand scale. She especially hoped that people like Lytton, who had excused themselves from the long journey to Garsington, would feel more inclined to accept invitations to the Thursday "at homes" she now began holding at regular intervals.

In Lytton's case she reinforced her invitation with a bit of nostalgia. She sent him a postcard showing a photograph of the pond at Garsington. On the back of it she told him how much she envied his cottage in the country: "I believe I once had such a place where there was an ilex tree and statues where you used to come and talk to your admirers. But perhaps I am dreaming. It must have been in another existence (a tear!) for it has all vanished now."[13] Whether it was the photograph or the tear, the approach had the desired effect, and that autumn Lytton turned up to one of Ottoline's first Thursday tea-parties. There he met Aldous Huxley, Yeats, and several other old friends. The occasion, however, was considerably spoilt for him by the presence of "a little gnome-like Irishman" named James Stephens, whom Ottoline had acquired somewhere. Though a poet, Stephens was better known as an almost unstoppable chatterbox:

> *On and on he went* [Lytton told his friend Roger Senhouse] *inveighing against "destructive criticism" (that tedious old story), pointing out that no one could write about love, but only about sex, lamenting that there were no epics...Ethel Sands filled up gaps with her appreciative shiny teeth, and Pipsey interrupted and floundered as usual...I was suddenly asked to give my opinion upon some long-winded dictum of Mr. J. S.'s on medieval clothes – the differences between the sexes –*

> *beauty of women – love – and all the rest of it. I was rather at a loss and could only shriek "Armour: I'm in favour of armour!" Mr. J. S. condemned me, of course, as destructive.*[14]

Ottoline must have noted Lytton's unease, for she wrote saying how good it was to see him again: "It was such a real, real, real pleasure! I hope the little Irish gnome didn't weary you – I was afraid he might."[15] Yet it was almost two months before she could lure Lytton back again and this time, despite the gnome, things went off rather better, though, as Lytton again reported to Roger Senhouse, his entrance created more of a stir than he had planned: "I made a pompous entry – late – everyone sitting around the table – a general remuement, etc. and some slightly dazed looks. I didn't know why, but on at last taking my seat found that *all* my front buttons were undone from top to bottom."[16]

Ottoline's hopes for Gower Street had been realised, and soon most of the old Garsington faces – Aldous, Yeats, Siegfried, Eliot, Gilbert Spencer and the rest – were coming regularly. Even Bertie called in occasionally, though like Eliot and Siegfried he preferred tete-a-tetes to the larger, noisier gatherings. To supplement the old faces was a stream of new talent, including a new generation of young poets and writers like Stephen Spender and William Plomer, plus a sprinkling of bright young women such as the poet Ruth Pitter. In the past women had been almost a rarity at Ottoline's gatherings, for she had little patience with the usual female conversation, and only those rare individuals with special gifts – or with special male friends – had found a welcome at Garsington or Bedford Square. But at Gower Street an older, more placid Ottoline began to seek out female companionship, often finding in these easier, shallower friendships more comfort, and fewer problems.

Indeed, the Ottoline who received her guests at Gower Street was altogether a quieter, less hectic figure. She had, as she confessed, deliberately chosen to "mute herself down" in order to survive. This "muting down" was also reflected in the more conventional decor she chose for her new house. Veterans of Garsington recognised the boxes; the familiar knick-knacks; the china, pictures, books, silk cushions; and the all-pervading perfume. But there was no longer anything especially startling or dramatic. The hall was painted plain-white and the reception rooms were exceptional only for the pink and silver curtains that Ottoline's maid Ivy had run up.[17] Now the Gower Street "at homes" were even less formal than before, with everyone sitting round the large first-floor dining-room table tossing conversation and ideas around like ping-pong balls. Portland called in whenever he was in town.

Another reason for Ottoline's more placid aspect was the contentment of her new-found relationship with Philip – a relationship that Juliette Huxley characterised as "Darby and Joan".[18] For though they still led lives that were largely separate – with Philip spending much of his time playing bridge at his clubs – as time went by he took on a more assertive role in their partnership. He advised her with the more complicated areas of her personal affairs; and shielded her from people who might make trouble for her. If there were a difficult letter to write, it was Philip who would draft a tactful reply; and then Ottoline would then copy it out in her inimitable handwriting.

Ottoline's health continued to be poor, and she was afflicted by deafness, which she combatted (like Brett) with the use of a large, black ear-trumpet. Her increasing deafness was another reason for the more subdued character of Gower Street. Also dampening things down was the worsening economic situation in the country. The looming Great Depression did little to engender an atmosphere of gaiety in any part of London. Nevertheless, Ottoline remained very comfortably off – thanks to Portland's allowance – and the "doll's house" in Gower Street ran to a full-time staff of five. Even so, Ottoline's life generally was in keeping with her more modest circumstances. She and Philip did not go out often, and then it was usually to see a film, or more rarely to a play or perhaps an opera. Sometimes she would call on Ethel Sands in Chelsea, or Virginia Woolf in nearby Tavistock Square, or have tea with one of her new friends, such as Dame Ethel Smythe, a voluble ex-suffragette and composer.

Ottoline almost always dined at home – except on Sundays, which was Cook's day off. Then the Morrells would go out to eat at a restaurant, their favourite being the L'Étoile in nearby Charlotte Street, which Ottoline described as "a charming little restaurant – so cheap"[19] (it is no longer cheap). She herself could hardly boil a kettle unaided, and Julian recalls going down to the basement of Gower Street to make a cup of tea and a maid rushing up to stop her, then saying, "Oh, I forgot – you're not as helpless as her Ladyship."[20] Home-science hadn't been one of the courses included in Ottoline's education.

Some time during 1928 Ottoline obtained an illicit copy of Lawrence's new novel *Lady Chatterley's Lover*. She wrote to him praising it and gently taking him to task over his ideas on sex expressed in the work. He told her that he wasn't advocating perpetual sex – nothing nauseated him more than "sex in and out of season" – rather he was trying to promote a healthy attitude to it.

> ...*one of the reasons why the common people often keep – or kept the good natural* **glow** *of life, just warm life, longer than educated people, was because it was still possible for them to say shit! or fuck! without either a shudder or a sensation. If a man had been able to say to you when you were young and in love: an' if tha shits, an' if tha pisses, I'm glad, I shouldna want a woman who couldna shit nor piss – surely it would have been a liberation to you, and it would have helped to keep your heart warm.*[21]

Ottoline showed this letter to Robert Gathorne-Hardy and, with a straight face, waited for his reaction to Lawrence's speculation that a bit of "rough trade" would have brightened her younger years. Gathorne-Hardy was rather at a loss as to what to say, so while he thought about it, she said: "I don't think it would," then, shaking her head and laughing, added: "In fact, I'm quite *sure* it wouldn't."[22]

The letters that Ottoline and Lawrence exchanged at this time have an air of two elderly ladies reminiscing about old friends and acquaintances. Ottoline told him she didn't think much of Aldous Huxley's books, particularly his latest work, *Point Counter Point;* Lawrence agreed, though he had to confess to a grudging admiration for the way Huxley could describe things (one presumes he recognised himself in the character of Mark Rampion). Lawrence and Ottoline exchanged symptoms, and he suggested that perhaps a little burgundy might help her headaches. He told her that all he wanted now was a few people around him that he could really be fond of. He told her he wished he and Frieda could live closer to Ottoline and Philip. He recalled the day in 1915 when Ottoline visited him in Greatham in Sussex, "stepping out of an old four-wheeler in all your pearls, and a purple velvet frock."[23] What a pity, he added, that something had come between them, and prevented them keeping a "nice harmony". In the summer of 1929 he urged Ottoline to go and see an exhibition of his pictures that Dorothy Warren was putting on in London, telling her that "some of them you will surely like – there is a suggestion of Blake sometimes."[24]

Unfortunately there was also a suggestion of something else in the paintings; and after the exhibition opened it was raided by the police and a number of the works seized on grounds of obscenity. In August 1929 a court sat to decide if the seized paintings should be destroyed. The hearing was attended by many luminaries from the artistic and literary world. Lawrence wasn't there. He was ill in Italy (besides, he would have probably been arrested on his arrival for sending copies of *Lady Chatterley* through the post). But Ottoline attended the hearing, and her entrance, not unexpectedly, created a stir in the courtroom. The proceedings halted as her tall resplendent figure wove through the public gallery. The magistrate, determined to get on with the evidence, began to get impatient. At last he said testily: "Can nobody find that lady at the back a seat?" There was a shuffle of chairs and muffled voices said: "Please sit here, Lady Ottoline." But Ottoline had already found a seat and now rose to her full height and, pointing her long forefinger at the Bench, intoned in her best droning voice: "He ought to be burned. He ought to be burned."[25] In the event, the court refused to grant an order for the paintings to be destroyed. Frieda also resumed writing to Ottoline, telling her that she had always appreciated Ottoline's "bigness and real spirit". She added: "I think the tragedy of your life has been that it was a small age you lived in and the men were small beer & the women too."[26]

In 1929 Philip launched into print with a potted version of the diaries of Charles Greville. Ottoline had encouraged him to write the book. Two years earlier she had begun to be concerned that Philip, despite now being a magistrate, had little else to occupy himself with, apart from playing bridge at the Saville Club. Ottoline was very proud of Philip's book – Greville was a remote ancestor of hers – and sent a copy to Lawrence, who told her he enjoyed it. She also sent a copy to Lytton who, however, was rather taken aback; as he was in the process of putting together his own edition of the same diaries. Ottoline assured him that, had Philip known Lytton had embarked on such a project, he wouldn't have undertaken it. Lytton, however, was very understanding and said that Philip's work had underlined the need for a full edition of the diaries; and would spur him and his helpers on to complete their task. Philip then began a more daunting task, researching the life of another of Ottoline's ancestors, Lord William Bentinck. He had been Governor-General of India from 1828 to 1835; and had abolished suttee. This project was to lead Philip and Ottoline to later undertake a trip to India. (Philip, however, died before completing this project.)

In April 1929 Ottoline acquired a new doctor who put her on to a starch diet which, she remarked to Lytton, was probably why she felt so stiff. In May she was feeling no better and was admitted to Preston Deanery Hall, a curious establishment near Northampton which specialised in starvation cures and where silver platters of nuts and caraway seeds were served to patients by footmen. The new doctor responsible for her incarceration there was a society quack called Cameron, who was to become over the next nine years her favourite physician; and the man who eventually, through his ineptitude, killed her.

It was now that three of Ottoline's old lovers drifted back into her life, briefly. The first was Augustus John, who was also an habitué of Preston Deanery Hall, being sent there, Ottoline suspected, to remove him from within reach of too much food and wine. In 1929 John wrote thanking her for buying one of his drawings. He was grateful that she was still collecting him: "I was rather afraid you were beginning to think I was dead."[27] The second old flame was Henry Lamb, whom Ottoline was distressed to hear was having similar dietary trouble to Augustus John. In recent years Lamb had fallen into a state of *degringolade* and Dorelia remarked in a letter to Ottoline that "his case was more serious than John's."[28] The third old flame was the oldest of the lot – Axel Munthe, who arrived in London in May 1929 in a pathetic state. He wrote to Ottoline telling her that he was almost blind and begged her to find him a decent hotel near Hyde Park; and someone who would come and read to him. He signed his letter "Your Old Friend."[29] Ottoline did her best to help, asking him to one of her Thursdays; but when he came it turned out that the old fraud wasn't as decrepit as he made out.

Probably it was Munthe's reappearance that caused Ottoline to start pondering her current beliefs. Late in 1929 she exchanged several letters with Robert Gathorne-Hardy on the subject of religion, explaining to him that she believed the Divine Spirit was at the back of all life. "The best human relationships – indeed all – have something divine in them," she told him, "and that one can possess the spirit of someone by really *understanding* them – as one can possess a poem or flower, or anything beautiful one absorbs and loves."[30] In another letter she harkened back to her disappointment that she herself was not creative. "I wish, I wish, one could *express* some new expression of the Divine. It is so humiliating that one is so uncreative. Perhaps in another existence I may be able to. I don't know quite what I would rather be, a mystic or a poet. In this life I have learned to be content."[31]

In January 1930 Ottoline received her last letter from Lawrence. He told her that he had had a bad winter, and that there was a possibility he might have to go to a sanatorium for a few months. "Perhaps I will," he said. "I am tired of always being defeated by bad health."[32] Two months later Ottoline opened a telegram from Aldous Huxley telling her that Lawrence was dead. She wrote in her *Memoirs*: "I had always thought that we should have a time to laugh over our old quarrels, to disagree and argue, and to plan a new Elysian world."[33] Ottoline later wrote an essay about Lawrence, entitled "Recollections of D. H. Lawrence by O.M.", which was published in *The Athenaeum*. In it she said Lawrence was obsessed with titles; that he was extremely sensitive to women's emotion; that his "dark gods" philosophy was claptrap; and that, despite his rejection of England, he remained until his death profoundly English. She also had something to say about Frieda. She said Frieda was jealous of any other female influence in Lawrence's life; even that of his mother. Ottoline said Frieda was Lawrence's refuge from the rest of the female world. "He had great fear, and like a frightened dog he could dash out from his kennel and bark and bark," she wrote, "and Frieda was his kennel." Ottoline blamed Frieda for turning Lawrence against her, and of having inspired Hermione Roddice. In October 1932 Ottoline told Virginia Woolf: "I am trying to do a sketch of [Lawrence] for my memoirs, but I find my fury against Frieda runs away with me & burns up all else."[34]

Frieda herself sailed back briefly into the Morrells' life in 1931 when she sought Philip's help to sort out the financial mess Lawrence's death had left her in. Lawrence's will, in which he left everything to her, had been mislaid, and his other relations, principally his brother George and sister Ada, were contesting Frieda's claim to be the sole beneficiary of the now growing estate. Philip did his best to help and spent some time straightening out the tangle with agents and lawyers; and negotiating on Frieda's behalf with George and Ada. But his efforts were undone by Frieda's irresponsible behaviour. Philip had been to see George Lawrence and arranged a reasonable settlement. He then wrote to Frieda explaining the arrangement and warning her to restrain her natural inclination to write a "blister" to Lawrence's family. Frieda ignored his advice, and duly wrote a blister; telling George and Ada and all the other Lawrences, not only what she thought of them and this shabby haggling, but also revealing everything Philip had told her in confidence about the tactics he was using in the case. Thereafter Philip washed his hands of the whole business. Frieda eventually succeeded in having her rights confirmed – but only after a court case – and she bore Philip and Ottoline no grudge. (During the hearing Frieda's lawyer had rather over-egged her difficult life with Lawrence...years of poverty, a model of concord, etc, etc. Suddenly Frieda jumped to her feet in court and cried out: "But that's not true – we fought like hell!") Later she wrote to Philip saying: "I wish Lawrence had known you for I believe he only saw a rather swanky, conceited Philip, well I know better!" and she signed it: "Yours, Frieda (the poor widow in distress)."[35] Frieda also wrote to Ottoline telling her not to think that Lawrence had said nasty things about her: "You meant so much to him – and I thought Hermione was such a noble & splendid figure in *Women in Love*, Greek and moving."[36] When Frieda subsequently went off to America and Taos with her Italian lover Ravagli, Ottoline gave her a grudging tribute; "I wish I had her vitality," she said.

In 1928 Ottoline again became embroiled with T.S. Eliot and his wife. Vivienne's frail mental condition had declined further, but Eliot was loyally staying with her, even though he realised she restricted his relationships with other people. He was particularly anxious to remain friends with Ottoline. Some time earlier, when a cloud had passed over their friendship, he had written saying he had a sure conviction that he had offended her; and begging her to write and tell him how he could patch things up. On another occasion he wrote saying he was afraid she was ill and asked if somebody could send him a card to say how she was. "It would be a great relief," he added. Vivienne, too, was writing to Ottoline, and in January 1928 she told her that "Tom hates the sight of me."[37] Later Vivienne conceived a suspicion that Ottoline was seeing too much of her husband, and Eliot was forced to write to Ottoline explaining that, though he wanted to see her, he couldn't because of Vivienne. He suggested that Ottoline write to them both saying that she wasn't well and could only see one at a time; and so would like to see them both separately. The following year matters got even worse. Vivienne, who was coming to Gower Street quite often, told Eliot that Ottoline was upset because she thought Eliot had "dropped" her. Eliot wrote to assure Ottoline that it wasn't so; and begged her to come and dine with them alone. This misunderstanding was ironed out and the following Christmas Eliot wrote thanking Ottoline for the diary she made a practice of giving him each year. Vivienne's condition deteriorated further and in 1932 Eliot thanked Ottoline for her kindness to Vivienne throughout the past year. Not long after this Eliot abandoned Vivienne and went to America, from where he begged Ottoline to keep an eye on his wife. Though Ottoline didn't like this task, she went to see Vivienne and reported back to Eliot on her state, advising him that it might be better if he did not return to her. Eliot had already decided this was the best course anyway. He blamed Russell for a lot of what had happened. He told Ottoline: "He has done Evil."[38] Vivienne continued to write to Ottoline and in March 1933 she told her that she had taken only two or three baths since Eliot had left. Later she was put into an asylum, where she died insane. Eliot returned to England in 1933, and his friendship with Ottoline resumed.

What were Ottoline's motives in helping Vivienne? The answer is that Ottoline was a generous person who put herself out to help people. For many years it was – and still is – fashionable to wax sarcastic about this aspect of her nature. Many writers have put Ottoline's friendships down to "lion hunting". But this epithet is neither subtle nor particularly apt. It is, for instance, understandable (if she were a "lion-hunter") that she should have gone out of her way to befriend, say, Thomas Hardy.

The Dearest Little Doll's House

Yet why did she bother to make friends with his widow, Florence – who had very little greatness in her – and why, long after Hardy's death, did she continue to invite and write to her? This example could be repeated many times. Nor does any simple lion-hunting theory explain why Andre Gide should ask Ottoline to the theatre in Paris; nor why art collector Samuel Courtauld would invite her to dinner and a show at the Golders Green Hippodrome; nor why Lord Beaverbrook, whose views Ottoline could hardly have agreed with, should write to her hoping she was recovering from her jaw operation? One might ask a madwoman to tea once out of pity; but not twice and more. Ottoline once told Virginia Woolf: "Obviously I was endowed with an extra amount of interest in human beings – an absurd overdose of 'kindness' – I suppose a sort of extended maternal instinct."[39] But on an earlier occasion Ottoline told Virginia that she felt "people are just vampires – sucking one's life. I am a magnet for egoists".[40]

Vivienne was not the only person Ottoline helped. Her kindness to her was echoed in another case, this one involving Lawrence's old friend, Koteliansky ("Kot"). Kot – a translator of Tolstoy and a friend not only of Lawrence but of Katherine, Murry, and the Woolfs – was not particularly close to Ottoline. But she was friend enough to have him fairly frequently at both Garsington and later at Gower Street. There his sombre, intense face is sometimes seen in group snapshots taken in the garden. In the early Thirties his mental state began to deteriorate; and he became subject to black depressions. These eventually became so severe that he couldn't leave his house in Swiss Cottage. From there would write sad letters to Ottoline describing his condition. Beatrice Campbell, a friend of both Kot and Ottoline, wrote to Ottoline asking if she could help him. Ottoline visited Kot several times; and kept up a correspondence with him. She would act like a mother to him, and he told her once: "Your severity is very helpful."[41] In 1933 he wrote telling her about arriving at her place and, as soon as he saw her, "her understanding smile" lifted his depression. He said: "It is good to understand and be understood...Ottoline, thank you so much for all your presents; and I do admire you for what you are."[42] Later, when he was sent to a nursing home, Ottoline visited him there. He was very miserable and to brighten him up she conjured up madcap schemes to kidnap him. He could dress up in one of her hats; impersonate her; and walk out of the hospital unaccosted. In 1936 he wrote to Ottoline recalling being photographed in her garden with several of her other guests and said: "I think now that it would be worth my getting well again for one more photograph in your garden."[43]

Ottoline had seen very little of Russell for some time; he was too busy bringing up and educating his two children (Dora had also given birth to a daughter). He and Dora had actually started a school in a disused semaphore station high on the Sussex downs where they instructed their own children and a small group of others "along progressive lines". He was also busy lecturing and writing, and could only infrequently spare time for a visit to Gower Street. Even his letters were few and far between. But he did find time to dictate his memoirs. He entitled the first draft of this, *My First Fifty Years,* and sent a copy of the manuscript to Ottoline for her comments, telling her that it contained some mention of "those apocalyptic events" that had begun in March 1911.

Ottoline reacted to what Russell had written – virtually what was later published in 1968 in his autobiography – in the same way she did the caricatures of Lawrence, Huxley, and Turner. She was irate. On the MS she angrily scratched out several references – in particular his description of her as having "a face rather like a horse" – and was generally unenthusiastic about the whole project, suggesting that it shouldn't be published for many years. There is even a hint that she may have threatened to publish or somehow expose *his* love letters; if he went ahead and brought out his version of their affair. In one way her reaction was understandable. The subsequent publicity would have caused a great deal of fuss and much hurt; particularly to Julian and Philip. In the end Russell concurred. He promised he would not publish until after he and Ottoline were both dead. Meanwhile Russell's second marriage was breaking up. He told Ottoline that he had decided to leave Dora, as she was pregnant by another man.

While checking through Bertie's letters, Ottoline also came across Lytton's old letters, and in April 1931 she wrote to him: "I like occasionally to plunge into the past & to relive it again – to walk in that mysterious wood – but it is fatal to do it often for it fades away. I think really in those days I was too overdone, too worried to appreciate all its delights."[44] She added that she felt steadier and wiser now. Lytton replied with an amount of sentiment suitable for Ottoline's mood:

> *For me, getting to know you was a wonderful experience – ah! those days at Peppard – those evenings in Bedford Square! I cannot help surmising that if H[enry] L[amb] had been a **little** different – things would have been **very** different, but perhaps that is an impossible notion. Perhaps we are all so deeply what we are that the slightest shift is out of the question. I don't think I want to go back. It was thrilling, enchanting, devastating, all at once – one was in a special (a very special) train, tearing along at breakneck speed – where? – one could only dimly guess – one might be off the rails – at any moment. Once is enough! I have been astonishingly happy now for a long time – if only life were a good deal longer – and the sunshine less precarious!*[45]

This was the last letter he wrote to Ottoline. But it was not the last time she saw him. In October or November 1931 he was one of the special guests invited to Gower Street for a tea-party in honour of Charlie Chaplin, Ottoline's favourite screen hero. She regarded his acceptance of her invitation as a great coup; and all her oldest and dearest friends were invited along to meet him, including Russell, Gathorne-Hardy, Duncan Grant, and Augustus John (as well as Lytton). Ottoline also found excuses for Millie, Ivy, and the other servants to come into the room and catch a glimpse of the famous star. The conversation was about Chaplin's East End background and the life of the working-class people who grew up there, and Ottoline told him about her visits to Burnley. Then she startled Chaplin by turning to him and saying intensely: "Those people have no poetry. You don't feel that anyone ever felt ecstasy in Burnley."[46] Augustus John also gave an account of the party in his *Autobiography*, relating:

> *It was at the Morrells that I once met Charlie Chaplin. He found it difficult, I think, to preserve his natural cheerfulness amidst the habitual gloom of the Bloomsburyites who formed the rest of the party, but his spirit was more than equal to these adverse conditions: he was not one to be silenced and he had the hearty backing of his hostess to count on. While he was speaking on social conditions in a strain which seemed to be familiar and sympathetic, I was impelled to slap him on the back, saying, 'Charlie, why, you're nothing but a dear old anarchist!' Recovering, he replied,'Yes, that's about it.' Although he agreed that London was his proper habitat, he admitted to being enticed by the powerful lure of Hollywood. Recalling his early days and the vicissitudes of his family, all rolling stones of the music hall, he mentioned that his mother had been courted by a lord: 'Oh,' drawled Ottoline, much interested, 'Which lord?' 'Ah. I'm not going to tell you,' replied Charlie.*[47]

Soon after this party Lytton became gravely ill, and by early January 1932 it was obvious he would not recover. Ottoline wrote to Carrington advising her to call in a certain eminent specialist, and in turn Carrington kept Ottoline informed of Lytton's weakening condition. Carrington told Ottoline that each time Lytton was washed with the scented water she had sent him, he asked: "Is this Ottoline's?"[48] On January 21 Lytton died and a few days later Carrington wrote to Ottoline saying: "It is to you I owe the happiness, probably of my life with Lytton. I thank you for those days at Garsington where I grew to love him."[49] In March she sent Ottoline a packet of photographs of Lytton taken in Cornwall in 1916. On the envelope Ottoline wrote: "She shot herself two days later."

Not long before Lytton died, another death shocked and saddened Ottoline. This was the death of her favourite brother, Lord Henry, who died on October 6, 1931. After his death Ottoline stayed on to help his widow, Birdie,[50] tidy up his belongings. She was disconcerted to discover that, as a result of his obsession for collecting works of art and other beautiful objects, he was virtually bankrupt. Ottoline had to break the news to Julian that the inheritance from Lord Henry that had been promised would not eventuate. The death of Lord Henry brought Ottoline and her half-brother, Arthur, the Duke, closer. Portland, who had occasionally visited Garsington, had begun in recent times to appreciate Ottoline more; and after losing his best friend, George Baker-Carr, as well as his half-brother, Henry, he turned to Ottoline for affection. He started visiting Ottoline at Gower Street, sometimes coming inside to meet her friends, but often sitting outside in his Rolls-Royce, waiting for her to come out and join him for a visit to the cinema or a play. (David Cecil remembers coming across Portland sitting in his Rolls-Royce outside 10 Gower Street. When he mentioned this to Ottoline, she replied, "Oh yes, Portland's outside, reading."[51]) For the last six years of her life, Ottoline and the Duke wrote to each other constantly; and he often professed his (brotherly) love for her.

Following Lytton's death, Ottoline began to think about polishing up her own memoirs once again. She was also gaining more satisfaction from spiritual reflection, and for a while flirted with Eastern mysticism; once going so far as seeing a swami. Now nearing 60, she felt she was an anachronism, that her day had passed. "I don't suit the modern mind," she had told her young friend Sebastian Sprott a year or so earlier.[52] In another letter she revealed to Sprott her current thoughts on friendship:

Somehow I never feel now that anyone cares to know me. I think it is partly because I have been very ill and have had to live so retired. But it is also my old Inferiority Complex, that crops up in full vigour from time to time. It is depressing reading old letters. It makes one feel that one's life is all over and past – and too that awful realisation of how quickly the sand of friendship and love runs through the hourglass…One may keep a friendship…but it seems a thin little trickle. I am I believe more faithful than most people. Also I am much more interested in other people [her emphasis] *and other lives than anyone else that I know.*[53]

So the search for new minds and fresh talent went on. One day Ottoline read an article on T.S. Eliot which she enjoyed and wrote to its author, a young writer (and later film critic) named Dilys Powell. The two women became friends and often went out to movies together. They also attended the opening night of Eliot's play *Murder in the Cathedral*. Afterwards Ottoline suggested: "Let's go and have a doughnut!"[54] So they adjourned to a Lyon's Corner House, where Ottoline's unusual clothes and manner caused no little consternation.

Another new friend whom Ottoline met through Eliot was the crippled writer and critic John Hayward. Ottoline embarked on a campaign to get the shy Hayward out into society; visiting him; giving him a pheasant for Christmas; and trying to entice him to *Cosi Fan Tutte*. She told him that Philip would come for him in the car; their dining-room was on the ground floor, so there wouldn't be any problem with stairs; and there was a side door at the theatre that didn't involve stairs. Ottoline even tried to marry him off to Frieda's daughter, Barbara Weekley. Hayward responded slowly to Ottoline's blandishments, and his letters to her show both appreciation for her generosity, and an insight into her own situation. In 1933, when Philip was ill and about to have some teeth out, Hayward wrote remarking that Philip had always been her anchor. "Yes," Ottoline replied, "you

The Dearest Little Doll's House

are right. I have had Philip – and whatever the difficulties and complications 'that' entails...It is a rare and wonderful thing and I am *unspeakably grateful*...The inner centre of everyone's life must go on alone, but it is so very very hard to be alone in the other chambers of one's life."[55] By December 1933 Ottoline was on such good terms with Hayward that she was able to reveal her most sensitive thoughts to him; even her regrets about the passing of her looks. She told him that she had been to Elizabeth Arden's to buy a handkerchief, and found herself surrounded by shop assistants, "paroquets," who started pecking at her face, and telling her that her skin was dry. "I came out feeling a hag," she told Hayward.[56]

Another acquaintance who became a regular at Gower Street in the Thirties was the poet Thomas Sturge Moore (the brother of Russell's friend, the Cambridge philosopher G.E. Moore). Ottoline showed him her *Memoirs* for his comments. But she wasn't pleased with the advice he gave her about them. Concerning her version of the troubles with Lawrence and Frieda, he said (perceptively): "I do not doubt your accuracy, but you are up against one of the oldest prejudices which will long outlast any of us. Namely that what two women fond of the same man say of each other must not be believed."[57] He also advised her that the repetition of words like "tigress," "violent," and "jealous" four or five times would tend to impress people in the opposite sense to that intended. He told her that her ideas on modem art would date. He criticised some of the more flowery passages: "Perhaps you indulge a little too much in descriptions of spring and country. Such things have nearly always been done so well in the classics that they can be taken very much for granted."

A new younger friend was Francis Needham, one of Ottoline's Younger Set, whom she helped to get a job at Welbeck Abbey as historian and librarian. Ottoline had had him to dinner several times, and occasionally gave discreet assistance to his love life. In his case, however, her aid did carry a small charge. For some reason around 1931 Ottoline was in need of money, so she asked Needham if he would be interested in buying several Lawrence first editions from her for the Welbeck library. This put poor Needham in rather a difficult position. How could he deal equitably with his friend who was also the half-sister of his employer? He replied doubtfully that the library might not need her Lawrence editions and, seeing she had two copies of *Sons and Lovers,* might not she donate one anyhow? Ottoline was persistent and finally sent him two Lawrence books for appraisal, one of which he kept, returning the other with a rather uncomfortable letter saying that he never thought money would matter to her. She replied that she needed the money to buy a new coat.

Earlier, Ottoline, in an effort to raise money, had been trying to sell off some other books and manuscripts through Gathorne-Hardy. She sold some letters of Katherine's to his firm for £40; only to complain later that they cheated her on the deal. These are not the only instances of what might seem meanness on Ottoline's part. Sometimes she would sell things, then forget she had been paid for them; or demand books back that had been returned already. Much of this can be put down to simple forgetfulness, or an aristocratic inability to be too precise in such mundane matters. Yet put beside all her philanthropies and kindnesses; such incidents are insignificant. The money and other help she lavished on several generations of poets, painters, and writers would add up to uncounted thousands of pounds; not to mention the cost of her hospitality generally. She was always either giving money to, or getting up appeals for, destitute poets, writers, and artists. In 1935, for example, Eliot was getting some money together to help a young poet called George Barker. Not only did Ottoline give generously, she also worked on Barker's behalf for several years.

She had many charities, among them the Women's Public Lodging House Fund, whose secretary wrote gratefully to her after receiving a gift of £20. 5s: "You were the first to give us a hand." For many years, after moving to Gower Street, she volunteered weekly to help the Women's Public Lodging House. Also Ottoline never forgot her old friends at Welbeck. One of them wrote to her from Laundry Lodge, Welbeck, thanking her for some photographs of Julian she had sent him:

> MY LADY,
> I beg to offer my thanks for the charming photographs...I'm afraid your Ladyship would not find many members of your bible class still at Welbeck, they have got scattered about, and I know of two at least who made the great sacrifice in the war. One was poor G. Marples of Holbeck Woodhouse, and the other was Joe Willies of Holbeck. I thank God that I was spared to return to my wife and boys of whom we have been blessed with three, and I was away from the day we mobilised until March, 1919. I was in Gallipoli, Salonica, Palestine and Syria.
> Thanking your Ladyship once again,
> I beg the honour to remain Your Ladyship's humble servant,
> F. HANCOCK[58]

Robert Gathorne-Hardy recalled several other examples of Ottoline's kindness towards former servants. He quotes a letter an old servant wrote to Philip after Ottoline's death: "It's strange how often I think of her. Sometimes at the station when I'm trying to get my change, I put my ticket in my mouth and then I think 'Her Ladyship would not do that,' and I desist."[59] When Virginia Woolf was shown this letter she said it was the most touching tribute she had ever read.

In some quarters, however, Ottoline was still the figure of fun she had become to many of her former friends. In January 1931 Roger Fry wrote to Clive Bell, describing a masked children's party Vanessa had held at which her daughter Angelica gave an "almost alarmingly good" impersonation of Ottoline. Sybille Bedford remembered an incident at the Aldous Huxley s' when Ottoline's string of pearls broke and bounced and rolled over the floor like peas, disappearing under the furniture and carpet. The younger guests went down on their hands and knees scavenging for the pearls, which they placed one by one in a saucer in front of Ottoline. Quite unruffled, she refused to count them (obviously they were some of the paste pearls she bought after having to sell her Marie Antoinette string) and presently took her leave, pearls in a paper bag. Stephen Spender recalled another occasion when, in the middle of a sentence, a large earring fell off Ottoline's ear and dropped into her teacup. Without interrupting what she was saying, she fished it out and attached it to her ear again. "I once saw far worse things happen," he recalled, "but she was not at all embarrassed as with a diving, pulling motion, she set herself to rights."[60]

In her later life, travelling became one of Ottoline's main pleasures and pastimes. She seemed to be off somewhere, almost continuously. She travelled to Germany, Holland, France; and, of course, her beloved Italy. In 1931 it was to the Low Countries, where she toured galleries and was converted to Franz Hals; which pleased Augustus John, as Hals had always been one of his favourite painters. In 1932 it was Freiburg (Dr Marten's haunt) again. Here she didn't like the other tourists: "There are some *awful* people here mostly, smart, rich and insolent...they are the type of people one sees in the stalls at a *silly* play in London."[61] She had also developed a deep antipathy to Hitler and Nazism (and as early as 1933 she was expressing strong anti-fascist views). In 1933 she went to Sicily, reporting back to Robert Gathorne-Hardy: "We went and returned by *sea* – wasn't that *brave of me!* Who do you think got on board at Palma – but Godfrey Winn !! [an actor and newspaper columnist] I did my best to put away prejudice and I liked him *fairly* but got so tired of him and his voice – and ended up by never wishing to see the silly lad again...and to think he makes £2000 writing!"[62] In 1934 it was Athens. Then, in 1935 Ottoline and Philip embarked on a major expedition to India (Philip having started on his book about Ottoline's ancestor William Bentinck). They set out in January by P & O steamer, with Ottoline spending most of the voyage lying in a deck-chair and reading books about India.

When they got there, their progress was like a royal tour in miniature. Indians travelled long distances to see "Lady Ottoline Bentinck", the descendent of the great Governor-General; and Ottoline and Philip were feted by local princelings, governors, and even the Governor-General himself. Oddly enough, Ottoline – stern foe of British Imperialism during the First World War and in Ireland – thought very highly of the Raj and of the hundreds of loyal Englishmen working all their lives out as magistrates and clerks to help "civilise" India.

In 1935 Maynard Keynes wanted to organise a dinner in Ottoline's honour at the Cafe Royal; but Ottoline, though grateful, put the kibosh on the idea. "I'm too shy," she said. She preferred to meet her friends in less formal circumstances. But it should not be thought that all these friends were all present-or-future celebrities. Many of the people she devoted her attention to were anything but celebrities. One was a Frenchman called Jean de Menasce, who sent scores of letters to Ottoline before taking the cloth and immuring himself in a monastery. Another dud-penny was a New Zealand poet, D'Arcy Cresswell. He came over to England on the basis of a book he had published called *The Poet's Progress.* He called Ottoline "Dear Lady Ginger", and after he returned to New Zealand they kept up a correspondence for many years. Unfortunately it was not Cresswell's lot to become internationally famous; and he ended up a radio announcer in windy Wellington.

With others, however, she was more successful. She patronised a young novelist called Graham Green e and helped him get a job in London. Someone else she helped was the poet Stephen Spender, whom William Plomer brought along to one of her Thursdays. Spender made quite a hit with Ottoline, and for some time it was not Yeats nor Virginia Woolf who were dangled as bait for other guests, but the good-looking Spender. Ottoline wrote to one prospective guest: "We have had one or two newcomers...Stephen Spender who is so lovely to look at." Plomer remembered one of the most feudal remarks he had ever heard. It came from an old noblewoman who, hearing Ottoline praised as a patron of the arts, said severely: "But she has betrayed our Order."[63]

From 1935 Ottoline's health declined steadily. For much of the time now she was in nursing homes and clinics; and her letters of the period are filled with discussions of symptoms and doctors. One of her last good doctors had been Dr Rau, who had saved her life with the jaw operation. Later, when she went to him with a whole ragbag of symptoms, he told her bluntly: "Sack your cook."[64] But Ottoline enjoyed her food; and refused to give up the quantities of butter and cream and other rich things she so liked. So instead of sacking her cook, she sacked Rau; and from then on it was Dr. Cameron, with his nice bedside manner and easy cures, who held sway. Ottoline went to his clinic at Tunbridge Wells many times; and no doubt the rest there did her some good. "I had to retire to my clinic at Tunbridge Wells – I had a lovely quiet time there,"[65] she told a friend.

In 1936 she was struck down with a severe illness and was so ill that she decided to compose a last message to all her friends. She recovered however, and what she wrote was later circulated among her friends after she did die:

> *Don't mourn for me, dear friends. When you are quiet and alone remember me kindly, and when you are in lovely country – in England or Italy or Greece – give an affectionate thought to one who drank in the beauty and poetry of the lands that you are gazing at...and when you walk the streets of London, remember one who passed in and out amongst the crowds trying only to understand...I should like to call to my side and wave goodbye to the many friends I had in the shops. I could name them all...and then to those friends who came on Thursdays. Remember I have watched you all and tried to understand what you are like underneath, and when possible I have tried to help you and encourage you to do your best in life.*[66]

After recovering from this latest illness, she resumed her

The Dearest Little Doll's House

Thursdays. Virginia would come round for private chats; what she called their "owling sessions". Both were involved in encouraging younger poets, and one day Virginia asked Ottoline to help a young friend of hers by coming round to one of Virginia's functions and making friends with him. "The world requires the presence of your golden wing,"[67] she said. At this time Ottoline's other main friend was Yeats, but in 1936 their friendship ended abruptly (as mentioned above). Yeats had made friends with W.J. Turner, who prevailed on him to write an introduction to a collection of poems Turner was bringing out. In this introduction Yeats mentioned *The Aesthetes,* praising it highly. When Ottoline learned about this she was outraged; and her actions soon made it clear to Yeats that something was wrong. He wrote to her asking rather bewilderedly what he had done to offend her. She wrote back telling him. In several letters he tried to appease her; but her anger would not be abated. On March 10, 1937, she told him:

> *I am afraid your letter makes matters worse! I had hoped that you had not read through "The Aesthetes" and so were unaware of the repulsive caricature that Turner had drawn of me in it – but obviously you knew all about it and you knew that it was intended to be my portrait...this leaves me all the more astonished that you should have singled it out of all of Turner's prose works to mention in your preface and introduction. In fact you rescued it from oblivion – the oblivion into which I was thankful it had fallen...That Mr. Turner should have written it did not surprise me very much, for though I liked him and found him clever I had never regarded him, to put it plainly, as much of a gentleman...I still cannot understand what induced you to write as you did. The book after all was not poetry. There was no need for you to mention it at all.*[68]

Yeats was dumbfounded, and made vain attempts to make light of the matter. But Ottoline wrote back coldly and on his last letter she scrawled at the bottom: "Yeats fini!"

Yeats' "betrayal" soured Ottoline greatly, and she began to believe that all her efforts at friendship had been wasted. But in 1936 she met two people who were to help her regain her trust. They were Francis Hackett, an Irish historian and novelist, and his Danish wife Signe, also a writer; and from 1936 on they were possibly Ottoline's closest friends. She visited them in Ireland and sent them her *Memoirs* to read, together with her articles on Lawrence and Katherine. Hackett gave her the sort of praise she needed after the split with Yeats: "I liked so much what you said about Henry James," he wrote, "at times I feel he was exactly – well, one of us!"[69] In another letter he said: "You are the most deeply appreciative human being I ever knew. To have been in love with you must have been very dangerous."[70]

At the beginning of 1937 Ottoline went up to Liverpool to have some medical tests, and a few months later entered a clinic with suspected gall-bladder trouble. She continued to correspond with people; but her Thursdays at Gower Street were suspended. She wrote to Gathorne-Hardy asking him to drop the "Lady" when he addressed her; and he in turn told her that at a party he had been at recently there had been a discussion about whether her street was pronounced Gower or Gore, and that Max Beerbohm had said the correct name was "Lady Ottoline Street."

In May she was put on a starvation-cure for a month. Later the same month Philip saw a doctor who told him he had a bad heart. The doctor also told Ottoline, and at this news she apparently suffered a stroke, which partially paralysed her. She was sent to Dr. Cameron's Tunbridge Wells Clinic where a "diseased heart" was diagnosed. Among all this illness she still found time to try to help Russell, whose finances were now in a parlous state. In June she wrote to the philosopher George Santayana asking if he could use his influence to get Russell a post somewhere. She wrote: "For through perhaps his own impetuous altruistic fault he is now very poor and there seems no way here in England for him to get a post as he is over age for a university job...he has to pay a good amount yearly to one of his brother's widows and also a good deal to that dreadful Dora."[71] Santayana replied that he couldn't do much; but Ottoline thanked him anyway: "He perhaps has done foolish things but he has such fine integrity & courage that is rare," she wrote.[72]

By August 1937 Ottoline had partially recovered. She wrote to Dora Sanger: "Yes I was very ill and nearly died. I was paralysed but thanks to my dear Dr. Cameron at Tunbridge Wells in whose clinic I was for nearly 3 months I am alive."[73] Ottoline returned to London and made an attempt to recommence her Thursdays, but she found the effort too much. Nevertheless, she still entertained a few old friends; including Russell (who had by now married his third wife, Patricia Spence), Eliot, Duncan Grant, and one or two others. She also visited Juliette Huxley, who now lived with her zoologist husband at Regents Park Zoo. Juliette noticed how ill Ottoline looked – her skin was not merely white, but grey. "I don't think Philip realises just how ill I am," Ottoline told her.[74] In December Ottoline had some "X-ray treatment" and also had a heavy cold. In January she was making plans for a trip to France; but was too ill to leave. Again Cameron was called in and injected her with a powerful antibiotic called Prontosil. Apparently Cameron had been administering Prontosil to other of his patients, with results that were bringing threats of investigation by the medical authorities. In April Ottoline entered his clinic again and soon after was told that Cameron had committed suicide. A few days later, on April 21, when a nurse was administering her usual Prontosil injection, Ottoline fell back on her pillow. When a doctor was brought in he pronounced her dead. The official cause of her death was given as heart-failure.

Four days later Ottoline was buried at the Portland family chapel on the Welbeck estate. Next day a memorial service was held in St. Martin's-in-the-Fields in Trafalgar Square. Virginia Woolf and Margot Asquith both wrote obituaries, which were published in *The Times* on April 21. Virginia wrote: "A life-long struggle against ill health had impeded the literary productiveness which she desired."[75] She added that Ottoline had held fast to her deeply-rooted Christian mysticism. Margot

Asquith said that Ottoline's appearance was considered eccentric by those who did not know her well, but that she herself was unconscious of this. "We delighted in her distinguished carriage, beautiful countenance and original clothes. In spite of an admirable sense of humour I never heard her utter an unkind word – of how many clever women can we say the same?"[76]

Hundreds of people wrote to Philip expressing their sympathy; and not just the conventional polite note. Some letters were several pages long, extolling Ottoline's virtues with a warmth that reflected genuine fondness. Philip ordered an inscribed slab and a memorial plaque for Ottoline and engaged their friend the sculptor and typographer Eric Gill to inscribe them. When Virginia heard of this plan she said: "How could anyone get Ottoline on to a slab?" When Gill's memorial plaque was ready, Portland – who had been so upset at Ottoline's death that he retired to his bed for three days – refused to allow it to be hung because he didn't approve of its design. Finally it was placed in the parish church at Garsington.

After Ottoline's death Philip continued to live at Gower Street; going to the Saville Club to play bridge, and devoting much of his time to rearranging his collection of blue-and-white china; the hobby he had begun at Eton as a boy. He also decided to edit and rewrite Ottoline's *Memoirs*. Gathorne-Hardy made a point of visiting Philip after Ottoline's death. Sometimes Philip would take him upstairs where Ottoline's clothes still hung in their wardrobes; her unique scent clinging to them. Philip would gently lift the silks and velvets, in an apparent attempt to get in touch with her again.

Soon after the war began, the house at Gower Street was damaged by a bomb; and Philip went to live in various hotels on the south coast, where he whiled away his time playing bridge. He returned to London occasionally, and it was in the Saville Club in February 1943 when he suffered a fatal heart-attack. His last words reportedly were: "Partner, we can't make it. We haven't enough hearts."[77]

He was buried next to Ottoline in the church graveyard at

Welbeck, his simple sanserif gravestone (in Gill Sans type) identical with hers, the two monuments contrasting with the traditional Gothic script on the other Bentinck graves.

INTERLUDE
My Strange Visit to Pamela Diamand

A self-portrait by Roger Fry, Pamela Diamand's illustrious father, and Ottoline's one-time lover (and nemesis)

IN 1975 my UK publisher Chatto & Windus was pressing me to gather the last permissions from the copyright-holders of unpublished letters for quotes that I wanted to cite in my book. Speed in gaining the final copyright permissions was of the essence, if we wanted to reach the very important Christmas book market. (At that time permission to quote even a single word of unpublished material had to be obtained from the copyright-owner of the material, usually a descendant of the author.) After a great deal of effort and perseverance, I had obtained most of the permissions I needed. However, there was one outstanding permission which I was unable to get, no matter how many times my publishers wrote requesting it.

My Strange Visit to Pamela Diamand

In my text I had quoted from three letters from the Bloomsbury art critic Roger Fry to Ottoline. One very brief quote – in itself perhaps insignificant to others – was in one of the three Fry letters to Ottoline. It had been signed: "Your loving friend, Roger". This particular letter, however, formed an important part of my reconstruction (which I had deduced from various sources) of the course of the brief affair – a "one night stand" in fact – between Fry and Ottoline in March 1911. In the letter Fry had written to Ottoline: "*I'm still all amazed and wondering...can't begin to think – I can only know how beautiful it was of you, how splendid...What terrifies me is that you should suffer for it – regret it in any way – you mustn't indeed dear, it was altogether beautiful and right.*" This letter was my primary evidence for the affair, made all the more important by the fact that the Fry liaison, though brief, was concurrent with her separate affairs with both Lamb and Russell. It was vital that I had permission to cite this letter (one of the most significant Ottoline ever received).

Yet it was even more important than that, because (as I relate in my book) it dated the start of Bloomsbury beginning to turn against Ottoline, for when Vanessa - with whom Fry was about to launch into a long-term relationship - learned about it, she began to sully Ottoline's name in Bloomsbury circles.

I decided to go and confront Fry's daughter and copyright-holder Pamela Diamand myself. I found that she was not far from us (we lived in Kensington Park Road, Notting Hill) in a terrace house in a street off nearby Holland Park Avenue. I got on my bicycle and pedalled over to her terrace house, chaining my bike to the railings on her front fence.

A late middle-aged woman with a no-nonsense face, she invited me in. We sat down at her desk where I handed her the letter to sign, granting me permission to use the vital quote. As she picked up her fountain pen, my hopes rose - at long last, I was going to get the crucial permission. But then she stopped, put her pen down, and looked at me with a serious expression.

"Have you ever wondered how the Yom Kippur War was ended?" she asked earnestly. Startled, I stammered: "Nnnno..." She then said: "Have you ever heard of the Etherea Society ?" "No," I replied, wondering what on earth she was getting at.

"We at the Etherea Society work for world peace by sending out messages in capsules into the ocean," she replied. "We sent a capsule into the ocean off Hawaii calling for an end to the Yom Kippur War. It did the trick," she said, a triumphant gleam in her eye. I mumbled something about how wonderful this all was.

Then she asked me if I would like to join the Etherea Society (I'm pretty sure that was its name). By this stage I would have agreed to virtually anything she requested. "It will cost you five pounds," she added.

I pulled out my chequebook and wrote a cheque to the Etherea Society for five pounds and handed it over the desk to her. She then picked up her pen and signed my letter giving permission to publish the quote by her father Roger Fry. With that, we said goodbye, and she escorted me to the door. As I moved to go down to my bike and pedal thankfully away, she suddenly said: "May I see your bicycle? I'm very interested in bicycles." We then went down to her front gate and she inspected the gears on my bike. Satisfied, she bid me farewell, and I cycled off, clutching the letter of permission.

Ottoline was now on the road to publication.

The Lady and the Pug

by Aldous Huxley

There was a Lady loved a Pug
   "Honey," said she
"I long to kiss your ugly
   mug!" "Gr-r-rumph," said
   he.

"I'll give you red morocco shoes,
   "Honey," said she
"And little hats and tartan
   trews." "Gr-r-rumph," said
   he.

"I'll make you pants of purple
   plush, "Honey," said she.
Pug turned aside to hide a
   blush: "Gr-r-rumph," said
   he.

"To make your figure slim and
   svelte, "Honey," said she
"I'll give you an abdominal
   belt," "Gr-r-rumph," said
   he.

"I'll give you sixteen meals a day,
   "Honey," said she.
Pug would have liked to shout
   Hurray But Grumph was all
   that he could say,
   So "Gr-r-rumph, Gr-r-rumph, Gr-
   r-rumph, Gr-r-rumph!!" said he.

ACKNOWLEDGEMENTS

A great number of people helped me with this book. I would like to thank in particular Julian Vinogradoff, Lord David Cecil, David Garnett, Duncan Grant, Ivy Green, Lady Huxley, Lady Pansy Lamb, Dilys Powell, Peter Quennell, and Daphne Sanger. Also I want to thank Sir John and Lady Wheeler-Bennett who invited me to Garsington.

I am especially grateful to Michael Holroyd for his constructive advice and encouragement.

Of the many organisations and institutions that assisted me I would like to thank the Staff of the Humanities Research Centre of the University of Texas at Austin, and their Director, Dr. F. Warren Roberts, and Assistant Director, Dr. David Farmer. The Phoenix Trust provided me with a grant to assist me in the later stages of the book. The Strachey Trust, Dr. Paul Levy and Michael Holroyd provided me with valuable material on Lytton Strachey. Kenneth Blackwell of the Mills Memorial Library, McMaster University, Ontario, helped with information about Bertrand Russell.

I would like to mention the following people and organisations who also helped me: Dr. A.L. Munby and Mrs. Penelope Bullock of King's College Library, Cambridge; the Director and Staff of the University of Sussex Library; the Director and Staff of the British Museum Reading Room and Manuscripts Room; Dr. Neil Radford and the Staff of the University of Sydney Library; the Staff of the (UK) National Register of Archives; the Staff of the Wellcome Museum and Library; Hubert Rigg, Curator of the Towneley Hall Art Gallery and Museum, Burnley; Patricia J. Palmer, Stanford University Library, California. Also these individuals: Quentin Bell; Leo Chapman; Robert Darroch; D.M. Devine (Secretary and Registrar, University of St. Andrews); Edwina Doe; D.J. Enright; Angelica Garnett; G. Gregory (Secretary, Burnley Liberal Association); Peter Grose; D. Keith Hall; Edward Harvane; H. Hughes; Ingrid Ismail; Yusuf Ismail; Peter Jeffery; Roy Jenkins; Barbara Jobson; Mark Kinkead-Weekes; Kenneth A. Lohf; Ree Mantz; Charles Ross; June Sears; Richard Shone; Gilbert Spencer; Marlay Stephen; Stephen Tennant; Tom Thompson; Anne Wilson.

Acknowledgement is gratefully made for permission to include the following works or extracts from them:

Asquith, Lady Cynthia: *Diaries: 1915-1918* (edited by E. M. Horsley. Copyright © 1968 by Michael and Simon Asquith) Hutchinson Publishing Group Ltd., and Alfred A.

ACKNOWLEDGEMENTS

Knopf, Inc.

Asquith, H.H. and Violet: Unpublished letters by permission of the Hon. Mark Bonham Carter.

Bedford, Sybille: *Aldous Huxley: A Biography.* Copyright © 1973, 1974 by Sybille Bedford; Chatto & Windus Ltd., and William Collins Sons & Co., and Alfred A. Knopf, Inc.

Bell, Clive: *Old Friends.* Copyright © 1956 by permission of Chatto & Windus Ltd., and Quentin Bell. Unpublished letters by permission of Quentin Bell.

Bell, Quentin: *Virginia Woolf: A Biography.* Copyright © 1972 by Quentin Bell by permission of The Hogarth Press Ltd., Harcourt Brace Jovanovich, Inc., and the author.

Bell, Vanessa: Unpublished letters by permission of Quentin Bell.

Bennett, Arnold: Unpublished letters by permission of Mrs. Dorothy Cheston Bennett.

Brett, Dorothy: Unpublished letters by permission of International Creative Management.

Carrington, Dora: *Carrington: Letters and Extracts from her Diaries,* chosen and with an introduction by David Garnett. Copyright © 1970 by David Garnett and The Sophie Partridge Trust. Reprinted by permission of Jonathan Cape Ltd., and Holt, Rinehart & Winston, Inc.

Epstein, Jacob: Unpublished letters by permission of Lady Epstein.

Forster, E.M.: Unpublished letter by permission of The Society of Authors as the literary representatives of the E.M. Forster Estate.

Fry, Roger: *Letters of Roger Fry,* Vols. I & II, edited by Denys Sutton. Copyright © 1973 by Mrs. Pamela Diamand, Chatto & Windus Ltd., and Random House, Inc. Unpublished letters by permission of Mrs. Pamela Diamand.

Garnett, David: *The Flowers of the Forest.* Copyright © 1955 by permission of Chatto & Windus Ltd. Harcourt Brace Jovanovich, Inc., and the author.

Gertler, Mark: Unpublished letters by permission of Mrs. Marjorie Kostenz.

Holroyd, Michael: *Lytton Strachey.* Copyright © 1968 by Michael Holroyd. Reprinted by permission of William Heinemann Ltd., Holt, Rinehart & Winston, Inc. and the author.

Huxley, Aldous: *Crome Yellow* Copyright © 1922 by Aldous Huxley. *Those Barren Leaves.* Copyright © 1925 by Aldous Huxley by permission of Chatto & Windus Ltd., Harper & Row, Inc., and Mrs. Laura Huxley. 'The Lady and the Pug' and unpublished letters by permission of Mrs. Laura Huxley. *The Letters of D.H. Lawrence,* W. Heinemann,

Morrell, Lady Ottoline and Morrell, Philip: Unpublished letters, documents, photographs and images of paintings, by permission of **Julian Vinogradoff.**

Every effort has been made to contact the owners of copyright material. If any further acknowledgements are required for photographs in this edition, please contact the publishers.

BIBLIOGRAPHY

Asquith, Cynthia. *Diaries 1915-1918,* E.M. Horsley, editor. London: Hutchinson, 1968. New York: Alfred A. Knopf, Inc., 1968.
Ayer, A. J. *Bertrand Russell,* New York: Viking Press, 1972, reprint ed. London: University of Chicago Press,
Bedford, Sybille. *Aldous Huxley: Vol. I, 1894-1939.* London: Chatto & Windus, 1973. New York: Alfred A. Knopf, Inc., 1974.
Bell, Clive. *Civilization.* London: Chatto & Windus, 1928.
Old Friends: Personal Recollections. London: Chatto & Windus, 1956.
Civilization and *Old Friends.* Chicago: University of Chicago Press, 1974.
Bell, Quentin. *Bloomsbury.* London: Weidenfeld & Nicolson, 1968.
Virginia Woolf: Vol. 1, 1882-1912, Vol. II, 1912-1941. London: The Hogarth Press, 1972.
Virginia Woolf: A Biography (Vols 1 & 2), London: The Hogarth Press, 1982. New York: Harcourt Brace Jovanovich, Inc., 1972.,
Bowra, Cecil M. *Memories: 1898-1939.* London: Weidenfeld & Nicolson, 1966. Cambridge: Harvard University Press, 1966.
Brett, Dorothy. *Lawrence and Brett.* Philadelphia: Lippincott, 1933.
Cecil, David. Entry on Lady Ottoline Morell, *Dictionary of National Biography, 1931-40.* London: Oxford University Press. New York: Oxford University Press, New York.
Clark, Ronald W. *The Life of Bertrand Russell,* London: Jonathan Cape, 1975
Delavenay, Emile. *D.H. Lawrence: The Man and His Work 1885-1919.* London: Heinemann, 1972. Carbondale: Southern Illinois University **Press, 1972.**
Fry, Roger. *Letters,* Denys Sutton, editor. London: Chatto & Windus, 1972. New York: Random House, 1973
Garnett, David, editor. *Carrington: Letters and Extracts from her Diaries.* Introduction by David Garnett. London: Cape, 1970. New York: Holt, Rinehart & Winston, 1970.
Garnett, David. *The Flowers of the Forest.* London: Chatto & Windus, 1955. New York: Harcourt Brace Jovanovich, 1956
Gertler, Mark. *Selected Letters,* Noel Carrington, editor. Introduction by Quentin Bell. London: Hart-Davis, 1965.
Glenavy, Beatrice. *Today We Will Only Gossip.* London: Constable, 1964.
Holroyd, Michael. *Augustus John: Vol. I, The Years of Innocence.* London: Heinemann, 1974. New York: Holt, Rinehart & Winston, 1975.
Augustus John, New York: Farrar, Straus and Giroux 1996.

Lytton Strachey. London: Heinemann, 1967-8. New York: Holt, Rinehart & Winston, 1968.

Huxley, Aldous. *Crome Yellow.* London: Chatto & Windus, 1921.

Those Barren Leaves. London: Chatto & Windus, 1925. *The Letters of D.H. Lawrence,* W. Heinemann, 1956.

Jenkins, Roy. *Asquith.* London: Collins, 1964. New York: Chilmark Press, 1965.

John, Augustus. *Chiaroscuro: Fragments of Autobiography.* London: Cape, 1952. Philadelphia: Richard West, 1952.

Autobiography with Introduction by Michael Holroyd, London: Jonathan Cape,1975.

Lawrence, D.H. *Collected Letters*, 2 vols., Harry T. Moore, editor. London: Heinemann, 1962. New York: Viking Press, 1962.

"I Will Send Address: New Letters of D.H. Lawrence " by Mark Schorer, *The London Magazine,* Vol. 3, No. 2 (February, 1956).

The Quest for Rananim: Letters to S.S. Koteliansky, G.J. Zytaruk, editor. Montreal and London: McGill-Queen's University Press, 1970.

The Rainbow and *Women in Love,* Colin Clarke, editor. Introductory Note by George H. Ford. London: Casebook Series, Macmillan, 1969. Nashville: Aurora, 1970.

The Letters, Aldous Huxley, editor. London: Heinemann, 1932.

Women in Love. London: Martin Seeker, 1921.

The Letters of D.H. Lawrence, Cambridge University Press Edition, Cambridge.

Lawrence, Frieda. *Memoirs and Correspondence,* E.W. Tedlock, Jr., editor. London: Heinemann, 1961. New York: Alfred A. Knopf, Inc., 1964.

Not I, But the Wind... London: Heinemann, 1935. New York: Viking Press, 1934.

Moore, Harry T. **The Intelligent Heart.** London: Heinemann, 1955. New York: Farrar, Straus & Giroux, 1974 (retitled *The Priest of Love: A Life of D.H. Lawrence*).

The Life and Works of D H. Lawrence. London: George Allen & Unwin," 1951. New York: Twayne, 1951.

Morrell, Lady Ottoline. *Ottoline,* Vol. 1, *The Early Memoirs 1873-1915,* Robert Gathorne-Hardy, editor. London: Faber, 1963. New York: Alfred A. Knopf, 1964.

Vol. 2, *Ottoline at Garsington 1915-1918,* Robert Gathorne-Hardy, editor. London: Faber, 1974. New York: Alfred A. Knopf, 1975.

Nehls, Edward H. *D.H. Lawrence: A Composite Biography.* Milwaukee: University of Wisconsin Press, 1957.

Nijinsky, Romola. *Nijinsky.* London: Gollancz, 1933. New York: Simon & Schuster, 1934.

BIBLIOGRAPHY

Plomer, William. *At Home: Memoirs.* London: Cape, 1958.
Portland, Sixth Duke of. *Men, Women and Things.* London: Faber 1937.
Quennell, Peter. *The Sign of the Fish.* London: Collins, 1960.
Revermort, J.A. *Cuthbert Learmont.* London: Constable, 1910.
Rowse, A.L. *A Cornishman at Oxford.* London: Cape, 1965.
Russell, Bertrand. *The Autobiography,* Vols. 1 and 2. London: George Allen & Unwin, 1967-8. Boston: Little, Brown & Company, 1968.
Sassoon, Siegfried. *Siegfried's Journey.* London: Faber, 1945.
Sitwell, Osbert. *Laughter in the Next Room.* London: Macmillan, 1949.Boston: Little, Brown & Company, 1948.
Spender, Stephen. *World Within World.* London: Hamish Hamilton, 1951.Berkeley: University of California Press, 1951.
Stein, Gertrude. *The Autobiography of Alice B. Toklas.* London: John Lane, 1933. New York: Harcourt Brace, 1933.
Strachey, Lytton. Article on H.H. Asquith, Introduction by Michael Holroyd, *The Times,* London, January 1, 1972.
Strong, L.A.G. *Green Memory.* London: Methuen, 1961.
Turberville, Arthur S. *A History of Welbeck Abbey and Its Owners,* 2 vols. London: Faber, 1938-9.
Turner, W.J. *The Aesthetes.* London: Wishart, 1927.
Victoria, Queen. *Letters.* Second Series, 1862-1885. London: John Murray, 1928.
Wilson, Trevor. *The Downfall of the Liberal Party.* London: Collins, 1966. Ithaca: Cornell University Press, 1966.
Woolf, Leonard. *Beginning Again.* London: The Hogarth Press, 1964. New York: Harcourt Brace Jovanovich, 1964.
Downhill All The Way. London: The Hogarth Press, 1967. New York: Harcourt Brace Jovanovich, 1967.
Woolf, Virginia, and Strachey, Lytton. *Virginia Woolf and Lytton Strachey: Letters,* Leonard Woolf and James Strachey, editors. London: The Hogarth Press and Chatto & Windus, 1956. New York: Harcourt Brace Jovanovich, 1956.Wool, Virginia, *The Diary of Virginia Woolf* Edited by Anne Olivier Bell, London: Hogarth Press, 1978.
Zytaruk, George J and Boulton, James T. editors. *The Letters of D.H. Lawrence.* (Cambridge University Press) 1979-2000.

KEY TO ABBREVIATIONS OF SOURCES IN END-NOTES

Charleston: Charleston Papers HRC: Humanities Research Center
CUP: Cambridge University Press *The Letters of D.H. Lawrence*
Huxley: *Letters of D.H. Lawrence*
King's College: King's College Library
McMaster: Bertrand Russell Archives, McMaster University *Memoirs: Memoirs of Lady Ottoline Morrell*, and Unpublished memoirs
Moore: Harry T. Moore's *Collected Letters of Lawrence Memoirs* the two volumes of Ottoline's Memoirs edited by Robeert Gathorne-Hardy
Strachey Trust: Miscellaneous Letters of Lytton Strachey, Dora Carrington, and James Strachey
Sussex: Letters from Ottoline to Virginia Woolf, Sussex University.
Unpublished Memoirs, the unpublished Diaires and Memoirs of Ottoline

AH	Aldous Huxley	JAC	John Adam Cramb
AJ	Augustus John	JV	Julian Vinogradoff
Asquith	H.H. Asquith	Kot	S.S. Koteliansky
BR *Auto*	Bertrand Russell *Autobiography*	LS	Lytton Strachey
		LW	Leonard Woolf
BR	Bertrand Russell	MG	Mark Gertler
Brett	Dorothy Brett	Murry	John Middleton Murry
CB	Clive Bell	OM	Ottoline Morrell
CUP	Cambridge University Press	PM	Philip Morrell
		RF	Roger Fry
DC	Dora Carrington	Seymour	*Ottoline. Life on the Grand scale*
DG	David Garnett		
DHL	D.H. Lawrence	SJD	Sandra Jobson Darroch
FL	Frieda Lawrence	SS	Siegfried Sassoon
GBS	George Bernard Shaw	TSE	T.S. Eliot
GH	Robert Gathorne Hardy	TSM	Thomas Sturge Moore
Hackett	Francis Hackett	VB	Vanessa Bell
HL	Henry Lamb	VW	Virginia Woolf
Holroyd	Michael Holroyd, *Lytton Strachey*	WJT	W.J. Turner
HRC	Humanities Research Center		

END-NOTES

CHAPTER 1
[1] Virginia Woolf (VW)—Ottoline Morrell (OM) (nd) HRC.
[2] D. H. Lawrence (DHL)—Mark Gertler (MG) (24 May 1928) Huxley.
[3] David Cecil, interview with SJD (1973).
[4] Osbert Sitwell, *Laughter in the Next Room*, p. 16.
[5] Dorothy Brett (Brett)—Sybille Bedford, *Aldous Huxley*, vol. 1, p. 71.
[6] Peter Quennell, *Sign of the Fish*, p. 123.
[7] Stephen Spender, *World Within World*, p. 162
[8] Leonard Woolf, *Beginning Again*, p. 199.
[9] Vanessa Bell (VB)—Roger Fry (RF) (October 1917) Charleston.
[10] Lytton Strachey (LS)—VW (27 May 1919) *Lytton Strachey*, p. 771.
[11] David Garnett (DG), *Flowers of the Forest*, pp. 36-39.
[12] DG 1972 interviews with SJD.

CHAPTER 2
[1] Mrs. Bentinck to Henry Bentinck, Julian Vinogradoff (JV).
[2] OM—Lord Henry Bentinck (nd) JV.

CHAPTER 3
[1] *Memoirs*, vol. 1, p. 77.
[2] Unpublished Memoirs.
[3] Unpublished Memoirs.
[4] *Memoirs*, vol. 1, p. 94
[5] *Ibid.* p. 96.

CHAPTER 4
[1] William Maclagan—OM (nd) HRC.
[2] *Memoirs*, vol. 1, p. 98.
[3] Maclagan—OM (3 June 1897) HRC.
[4] Maclagan—OM (9 July 1897) HRC.
[5] *Memoirs*, vol. 1, p. 95.
[6] *Ibid.* p. 99.
[7] *Ibid.*
[8] *Ibid.* p. 101.
[9] *Ibid.* p. 102.
[10] H. H. Asquith—OM (25 August 1898) HRC.
[11] Hilda Douglas-Pennant—OM (1 January 1918) HRC.

[12] *Memoirs,* vol. 1, p. 105.
[13] *Ibid.* p. 106.
[14] *Ibid.* p. 107.
[15] *Ibid.*
[16] *Ibid.,* and Lady Huxley 1972 interview with SJD.
[17] Unpublished Memoirs.
[18] *Memoirs,* vol. 1, p. 113.
[19] *Ibid.* p. 114.
[20] Asquith—OM (Easter 1900) HRC.
[21] Asquith—OM (1 May 1900) HRC.
[22] Asquith—OM (14 June 1900) HRC.
[23] Asquith—OM (21 June 1900) HRC.
[24] Roy Jenkins, letter to SJD (14 November 1973).
[25] *Ibid.*
[26] Essay on Asquith by Lytton Strachey published in *The Times* with Introduction by Michael Holroyd (15 January 1972).
[27] *Ibid.*
[28] *Memoirs,* vol. 1, p. 114.

CHAPTER 5
[1] *Memoirs,* vol. 1, p. 120.
[2] OM—Philip Morrell (PM) (nd) JV.
[3] OM—BR (10 April 1911) McMaster.
[4] *Memoirs,* vol. 1, p. 121.

CHAPTER 6
[1] *Memoirs,* vol. 1, p. 147.
[2] *Cuthbert Learmont,* p. 80.
[3] *Memoirs,* vol. 2, p. 148.
[4] OM—LS (2 November 1913) JV.
[5] J. A. Cramb (JAC)—OM (nd) HRC.
[6] JAC—OM (20 May 1904) HRC.
[7] Cuthbert Learmont, p. 94.
[8] JAC—OM (May 1904) HRC.
[9] JAC—OM (4 June 1904) HRC
[10] JAC—OM (9 June 1904) HRC.
[11] JAC—OM (18 November 1904) HRC.
[12] *Memoirs,* vol. 1, p. 132.
[13] *Ibid.* p. 148.
[14] Unpublished Memoirs.

INTERLUDE
The Centre of the World
[1] Leonard Woolf. *Beginning Again..*

CHAPTER 7
[1] Unpublished Memoirs.
[2] *Memoirs*, vol. 1, p. 155.
[3] William Rothenstein— OM (December 1908) HRC.
[4] *Memoirs*, vol. 1, p. 161.
[5] Michael Holroyd, *Augustus John,* p. 280.
[6] *Memoirs*, vol. 1, p. 141.
[7] *Ibid.* p. 156.
[8] Called Seraphita, inspired by Balzac's novel of the same name, the painting, Ottoline says, depicted "a girl dressed in a tight black dress standing on a mountain top with strange ice-flowers at her feet." (*Memoirs,* vol. 1, p. 157).
[9] Augustus John, *Autobiography,* p. 97.
[10] Augustus John (AJ)—OM (22 April 1908) HRC.
[11] AJ—OM (3 May 1908) HRC.
[12] AJ—OM (30 May 1908) HRC.
[13] *Memoirs*, vol. 1, p. 158.
[14] *Ibid.* p. 159.
[15] Jacob Epstein —OM (22 October 1908) HRC.
[16] AJ—OM (30 November 1908) HRC.
[17] AJ—OM (18 December 1908) HRC.
[18] Dorelia McNeill—OM (nd) HRC.
[19] AJ—OM (18 December 1908) HRC.
[20] AJ—OM (8 January 1909) HRC.
[21] *Memoirs*, vol. 1, p. 163.
[22] AJ—OM (23 July 1909) HRC.

CHAPTER 8
[1] *Virginia Woolf,* vol. 1, p. 144.
[2] *Ibid.* p. 124.
[3] *Ibid.* p. 144.
[4] *Ibid.* p. 145.
[5] *Ibid.*
[6] *Memoirs*, vol. 1, p. 158.
[7] RF—D. S. MacColl (March 1909) *Fry Letters.*
[8] *BR Auto.,* vol. 1, p. 202.
[9] Gertrude Stein, *Autobiography.*
[10] *Memoirs*, vol. 1, p. 186.

[11] HL—OM [March 1910] HRC.
[12] HL—OM [March 1910] HRC.
[13] *Memoirs*, vol. 1, p. 194.
[14] HL—OM (25 April 1910) HRC.
[15] *Memoirs*, vol. 1, p. 195.
[16] HL—OM (26 May 1910) HRC.
[17] HL—OM (14 June 1910) HRC.
[18] HL—OM (18 June 1910) HRC.
[19] HL—OM (7 July 1910) HRC.
[20] Desmond MacCarthy-OM (nd) HRC.
[21] RF—G. L. Dickinson, *Fry Letters*.
[22] *Memoirs*, vol. 1, p. 202.

CHAPTER 9
[1] LS—Leonard Woolf (1910) HRC.
[2] *Memoirs*, vol. 1, p. 202.
[3] OM—LS (16 November 1910) JV.
[4] *Memoirs*, vol. 1, p. 203.
[5] LS—James Strachey (18 November 1910) *Lytton,Strachey*, p. 451.
[6] HL—OM (28 November 1910) HRC.
[7] LS—OM (8 December 1910) HRC.
[8] Seymour, p. 103.
[9] Unpublished Memoirs.
[10] OM jotting on envelope (January 1911) HRC.
[11] Unpublished Memoirs.
[12] HL—OM (25 January 1911) HRC.
[13] HL—OM (8 March 1911) HRC.

CHAPTER 10
[1] *Memoirs*, vol. 2, p. 266.
[2] *BR Auto.*, vol. 1, p. 203.
[3] *BR Auto.*, vol. 1, p. 203.
[4] BR Notebook, HRC.
[5] BR Notebook, HRC.
[6] *Ibid.*
[7] *Ibid.*
[8] *Ibid.*
[9] *Ibid.*
[10] *Ibid.*
[11] *Ibid.*
[12] *Ibid.*

[13] *Ibid.*
[14] *Ibid.*
[15] *Ibid.*
[16] *BR Auto.*, vol. 1, p. 151.
[17] BR—OM [21 March 1911] HRC.
[18] BR—OM [22 March 1911] HRC.
[19] BR—OM [23 March 1911] HRC.
[20] BR—OM [25 March 1911] HRC.
[21] *Memoirs,* vol. 2, p. 267.
[22] BR—OM [28 March 1911] HRC.
[23] BR—OM [28 March 1911] HRC.
[24] BR—OM [29 March 1911] HRC.
[25] BR—OM [31 March 1911] HRC
[26] BR—OM [2 April 1911] HRC.
[27] BR—OM [3 April 1911] HRC.
[28] BR—OM [4 April 1911] HRC.
[29] BR—OM [6 April 1911] HRC.
[30] BR—OM [7 April 1911] HRC.
[31] BR—OM [8 April 1911] HRC.
[32] BR—OM [8 April 1911] HRC.
[33] BR—OM [8 April 1911] HRC.
[34] BR—OM [10 April 1911] HRC.
[35] BR—OM [10 April 1911] HRC.
[36] BR—OM (nd) HRC.
[37] BR—OM [12 April 1911] HRC.
[38] BR—OM [14 April 1911] HRC.
[39] BR—OM [15 April 1911] HRC.
[40] BR *Auto.*, vol. 1, p. 204.

CHAPTER 11
[1] Roger Fry (RF)—OM (nd) HRC.
[2] RF—OM [3 April 191 1] HRC.
[3] RF—OM [4 April 1911] HRC.
[4] *BR Auto.*, vol. 1, p. 204.
[5] *Memoirs,* vol. 2, p. 272.
[6] *Ibid* p. 273.
[7] *BR Auto.* vol. 1, p. 205.
[8] *Memoirs,* vol. 2, p 273.
[9] BR—OM [4 April 1911] HRC.
[10] Unpublished Memoirs (see *Memoirs,* vol. 2, p. 267 for published version).

[11] HL—OM [8 April 1911] HRC.
[12] HL—OM [11 April 1911] HRC.
[13] HL—OM [6 May 1911] HRC.
[14] HL—OM [10 May 1911] HRC.
[15] HL—OM [16 May 1911] HRC.
[16] *Virginia Woolf,* vol. 1, p. 145.
[17] BR—OM [29 May 1911] HRC.
[18] BR—OM [1 June 1911] HRC.
[19] *Memoirs,* vol. 1, p 213.
[20] HL—OM [22 May 1911] HRC.

CHAPTER 12

[1] LS—George Mallory (nd) *Lytton Strachey,* p. 459.
[2] LS—Clive Bell (CB) [21 October 1909] *Lytton Strachey,* p. 454.
[3] *Ibid.*
[4] *Ibid.* p.453.
[5] OM—LS (nd) JV.
[6] *Memoirs,* vol. 1, p. 214 (first sentence from Unpublished Memoirs).
[7] BR—OM [3 June 1911] HRC.
[8] LS—OM (nd) HRC.
[9] LS—OM (28 July 1911) HRC.
[10] VB—RF (28 June 1911) Charleston.
[11] BR—OM (6 June 1911) HRC.
[12] OM—BR, (2 July 1911) McMaster.
[13] HL—OM (22 June 1911) HRC.
[14] *Memoirs,* vol. 1, p. 216 (last sentence from Unpublished Memoirs).
[15] BR—OM (20 June 1911) HRC.
[16] *Memoirs,* vol. 2, p. 278 (last 15 words from Unpublished Memoirs).
[17] BR—OM (9 June 1911) HRC.
[18] BR—OM (17 July 1911) HRC.
[19] BR—OM (16 July 1911) HRC.
[20] BR—OM (9 July 1911) HRC.
[21] OM—BR (9 January 1912) McMaster.
[22] BR—OM (nd) HRC.
[23] BR—OM (September 1911) HRC.
[24] BR—OM (nd) HRC.
[25] VB—RF (15 August 1911) Charleston.
[26] BR—OM (nd) HRC.
[27] BR—OM (August 1911) HRC.
[28] OM—BR (nd) McMaster.

[29] BR—OM (nd) HRC.
[30] *Memoirs,* vol. 2, p. 279 (with corrections from Unpublished Memoirs).
[31] BR—OM (13 November 1911) HRC.
[32] HL—OM (21 November 1911) HRC.
[33] LS—OM (26 December 1911) HRC.
[34] BR—OM (27 December 1911) HRC.
[35] *Ibid.*
[36] BR—OM [29 December 1911] HRC.
[37] HL—OM [23 February 1912] HRC.
[38] BR—OM [18 March 1912] HRC.
[39] HI —OM (March 1912) HRC.
[40] HL—OM [20 March 1912] HRC.
[41] BR—OM [6 April 1912] HRC.
[42] BR—OM (20 April 1912) HRC.
[43] HI—OM (23 April 1912) HRC.
[44] HL—OM [27 May 1912] HRC.
[45] LS—OM (12 June 1912) HRC.
[46] HL—OM (July 1912) HRC.
[47] HL—OM [19 July 1912] HRC.

CHAPTER 13

[1] *Memoirs,* vol. 1, p. 228.
[2] Romola Nijinsky, *Nijinsky,* p. 155.
[3] OM—LS (7 June 1912) JV.
[4] OM—LS (nd) JV.
[5] BR—OM [1 August 1912] HRC.
[6] BR—OM [26 July 1912] HRC.
[7] BR—OM [23 May 1912] HRC.
[8] BR—OM [25 July 1912] HRC.
[9] *Memoirs,* vol. 1, p. 231.
[10] LS—OM (19 August 1912) HRC.
[11] LS—OM (August 1912) HRC.
[12] BR—OM (August 1912) HRC.
[13] LS—OM [25 September 1912] HRC.
[14] LS—OM (27 September 1912) HRC.
[15] LS—OM (October 1912) HRC.
[16] LS—OM (October 1912) HRC.
[17] Molly MacCarthy—CB (23 November 1912) Charleston.
[18] BR—OM (nd) HRC.
[19] Unpublished Memoirs (see *Memoirs,* vol. 2, p. 281 for edited version).
[20] *Memoirs,* vol. 2, p. 281.

[21] LS—OM (October 18, 1912) HRC.
[22] LS—OM (April 4, 1913) HRC.
[23] VB—RF (April 8, 1913) Charleston.
[24] OM—LS (nd) JV.
[25] OM—LS (nd).
[26] BR—OM [4 May 1913] HRC.
[27] BR—OM [23 May 1913] HRC.
[28] BR—OM [28 May 1913] HRC.
[29] BR—OM [17 June 19131 HRC.
[30] BR—OM (June 1913) HRC.
[31] *Memoirs,* vol. 1, p. 240.
[32] BR—OM (10 August 1913) HRC.
[33] Bessie Burrows—OM (9 January 1914) HRC.
[34] LS—OM (21 November 1913) HRC.
[35] LS—OM (21 November 1913) HRC.
[36] *Memoirs,* vol. 1, p. 251.
[37] BR—OM [13 February 1914] HRC.
[38] BR—OM (25 February 1914) HRC.
[39] BR—OM (19 March 1914) HRC.
[40] BR—OM (6 April 1914) HRC.
[41] BR—OM (1 June 1914) HRC.
[42] LS—CB (4 May 1914) Charleston.
[43] *Memoirs,* vol. 1, p. 253.
[44] *Ibid.* p. 254.
[45] LS—OM (19 May 1914) HRC.
[46] E. M. Forster —OM 25 (May 1914) HRC.
[47] *BR Auto.,* vol. 1, p. 213.
[48] Unpublished Memoirs.
[49] BR—OM [3 July 1914] HRC.
[50] *Memoirs,* vol.1, p.258.

CHAPTER 14

[1] BR—OM [1 August 1914] HRC.
[2] *Hansard* (3 August 1914).
[3] BR—OM [1 August 1914] HRC.
[4] BR—OM [5 August 1914] HRC.
[5] *Memoirs,* vol. 1, p. 262.
[6] Max Gieland—OM (nd) HRC.
[7] Violet Asquith—OM (27 May 1914) HRC.
[8] Violet Asquith—OM [29 August 1914] HRC.
[9] Norton—OM (23 August 1914) HRC.

[10] BR—OM (nd, August 1914) HRC.
[11] Unpublished Memoirs (for edited quote see *Memoirs*, vol. 2, p. 286).
[12] BR—OM [29 August 1914] HRC.
[13] Unpublished Memoirs.
[14] Unpublished Memoirs (for edited quote see ***Memoirs***, vol. 2, p. 287).
[15] Masefield—OM (11 May 1915) HRC.
[16] ***Memoirs***, vol. 1, p. 277.
[17] BR—OM (nd) HRC.

CHAPTER 15

[1] *Letters of D.H. Lawrence* (CUP) vol. 2, p. 253 [CUP *Letters*]
[2] *Memoirs*, vol. 1, p. 272.
[3] D. H. Lawrence (DHL)—OM (3 January 1915) Huxley, p. 213. Also CUP *Letters*, vol. 2, #833. (CUP).
[4] DHL—OM (nd) HRC. Huxley, p. 215; CUP Vol. 2 (27 January 1915), #848.
[5] *Memoirs*, vol. 1, p. 272.
[6] DHL—OM Huxley. CUP *Letters*, vol. 2 (1 February 1915) #854.
[7] BR—OM [January 8, 1915] HRC.
[8] BR—OM [January 20, 1915] HRC.
[9] DHL—OM (nd), *London Magazine* (February, 1956) vol. 3, no. 2; CUP *Letters*, vol. 2 [11? February 1915] #864.
[10] *Memoirs*, vol. l, p. 273; CUP *Letters*, vol. 2, #856.
[11] H. T. Moore, *Intelligent* Heart, p. 183.
[12] DHL—OM CUP *Letters*, vol. 2 [11 February 1915] #864.
[13] Frieda Lawrence (FL)—S. S. Koteliansky (Kot) (nd) *M and* **C**, p. 208.
[14] DHL—OM (February 22, 1915) *London Magazine*, vol. 3, no. 2, p. 48; CUP *Letters*, vol. 2 [22 February 1915] #872.
[15] BR—OM (March, 1915) HRC.
[16] BR—OM (March, 1915) HRC.
[17] BR—OM (March, 1915) HRC
[18] DHL—OM CUP *Letters*, vol. 2 [19 April 1915] #900.
[19] DHL—OM (nd) Huxley. CUP *Letters*, vol. 2 (23 April 1915) #905.
[20] DHL—OM (nd) HRC. CUP *Letters*, vol. 2 [24 March 1915] #892.
[21] DHL—OM CUP *Letters*, vol. 2, [1 March 1915] #878.
[22] DHL—OM CUP *Letters*, vol. 2, [15? April 1915] #898.
[23] DHL—PM (April 20, 1915) *London Magazine*, vol. 3, no. 2, p. 51; CUP *Letters*, vol. 2, [20 April 1915] #903.
[24] DHL—Kot (nd) Moore, p. 333; CUP *Letters*, vol. 2, [20 April 1915] #902.
[25] Unpublished Memoirs.
[26] DHL—OM (April 23, 1915) *London Magazine*, vol. 3, no. 2; CUP *Letters*,

vol. 2, (23 April 1915) #905.
[27] BR–OM [1 May 1915] HRC.
[28] DHL–OM [nd] Huxley, p. 228; CUP *Letters*, vol. 2 [19 July 1915] #955.

CHAPTER 16
[1] *Memoirs*, vol. 2, p. 32.
[2] MacCarthy–OM (1 July 1915) HRC.
[3] *Memoirs*, vol. 2, p. 36.
[4] *Ibid*.
[5] *Intelligent Heart*, p. 213.
[6] DHL–Cynthia Asquith (nd) Moore, p. 349; CUP *Letters*, vol. 2 [21 July 1915] #956.
[7] BR–OM (nd) HRC.
[8] BR–OM [19 July, 1915] HRC.
[9] DHL–OM (nd) Moore, p.349.
[10] *Ibid*.
[11] LS–OM (8 June 1915) HRC.
[12] LS–DG (14 July 1915) *Lytton Strachey*, p.599.
[13] LS–DG (25 July 1915) *Lytton Strachey*, p.600.
[14] LS–OM (31 July 1915) HRC.
[15] *Memoirs*, vol. 2, p. 40.
[16] BR–OM (nd) HRC.
[17] DHL–BR (nd) *Memoirs*, vol. 2, p. 67.
[18] DHL–OM CUP *Letters*, vol. 2 (9 September 1915) #983.
[19] . DHL–BR (nd) *Memoirs*, vol. 2, p. 69.
[20] GBS–OM (nd) HRC.
[21] OM–Marsh, 12 November 1915, HRC.
[22] Brett, *Lawrence and Brett*.
[23] DHL–OM (12 December 1915) HRC; CUP *Letters*, vol. 2 (12 December 1915) #1098.
[24] DHL–Cynthia Asquith . Huxley, p. 283; CUP *Letters*, vol. 2 [5 December 1915] #1089.
[25] DHL–Cynthia Asquith (nd) Moore, p. 381.
[26] *Memoirs*, vol. 2, p. 48.
[27] BR–OM (nd) HRC.
[28] VB–RF (nd) Charleston.
[29] LS–Lady Strachey (28 December 1915) *Lytton Strachey*, p. 613.
[30] Philip Heseltine–OM (28 January 1915) HRC.
[31] DHL–OM (25 February 1916) Moore, p. 437; CUP *Letters*, vol. 3 (15 February 1916) #1187.

CHAPTER 17

[1] BR—OM [10 November 1915] HRC.
[2] BR—OM [10 November 1915] HRC.
[3] BR—OM (nd) HRC.
[4] BR—OM [18 March 1916] HRC.
[5] BR—OM (nd) HRC.
[6] LS—DG (10 March 1916) *Lytton Strachey*, p. 629.
[7] *Ibid.*
[8] LS—VW (15 April 1916) *Lytton Strachey*, p.629.
[9] *Memoirs*, vol. 2, p. 98.
[10] *Ibid.* p. 102.
[11] OM—LS (27 April, 1927) JV.
[12] VB—RF (nd) Charleston.
[13] RF—VB (nd) Charleston.
[14] LS—Barbara Hiles (17 July 1916) *Lytton Strachey*, p. 661.
[15] *Memoirs*, vol. 2, p. 84.
[16] Dora Carrington (DC)—MG (nd) *Letters and Extracts*, p. 21.
[17] LS—OM (23 April 1916) *Lytton Strachey*, p.630.
[18] Garnett, interviews with SJD 1972-73.
[19] DC (nd) *Letters and Extracts*, p. 33.
[20] Holroyd, *Lytton Strachey*, p. 635.
[21] *Memoirs*, vol. 1, p. 279.
[22] OM—Maynard Keynes [Keynes] (2 May 1916) Charleston.
[23] *Memoirs*, vol. 2, p. 106.
[24] *Ibid.* p. 107.
[25] LS—OM (3 July 1916) HRC.
[26] OM—Keynes (11 July 1916) Charleston.
[27] Asquith—OM (nd) HRC.
[28] *Memoirs*, vol. 2, p. 121.
[29] *Siegfried's Journey*, p. 11.
[30] VB—RF (nd) Charleston.
[31] *Flowers of the Forest*, p. 116.
[32] *Memoirs*, vol. 2, p. 123.
[33] DC, *Letters and Extracts*, p. 34.
[34] *Ibid.* p.39.
[35] Draft of prospectus, HRC.
[36] PM — Minutes Burnley (5 October 1916).
[37] OM—Keynes (October 5, 1916) Charleston.
[38] Aldous Huxley (AH)—OM (nd) HRC.
[39] *Siegfried's Journey*, p. 22.

CHAPTER 18

[1] DHL—OM CUP *Letters* vol. 2 (24 January 2016) #243.
[2] DHL—OM CUP *Letters* vol. 2 [27? February 1916] #289.
[3] OM—BR [March 1916] McMaster .
[4] DHL—OM CUP *Letters* vol. 2 (9 March 2016) #1204.
[5] DHL—OM CUP *Letters* vol. 2 (7 April 1916) #1227.
[6] DHL—OM CUP *Letters* vol. 2 (7 April 1916) #1227.
[7] DHL—OM CUP *Letters* vol. 2 (24 May 1916) #1242.
[8] FL—Cynthia Asquith (24 May 1916) *M and C,* p. 212.
[9] FL—OM (nd) HRC.
[10] FL—OM (nd) HRC.
[11] DHL—E.M. Forster . CUP *Letters* vol. 2 (30 May 1916) #1244.
[12] DHL—OM CUP *Letters* vol. 2 (26 September 1916) #1286.
[13] DHL—OM CUP *Letters* vol. 2 (3 October 1916) #1280.
[14] DHL—Kot (November 7, 1916). CUP *Letters,* vol. 21 (7 November 1016) #1305.
[15] DHL—Catherine Carswell (27 November 1916) Moore, p. 488; CUP *Letters,* vol. 3 (27 November 2016) #1320.
[16] Note: this quote and the following excerpts are from the first (Secker) edition of *Women in Love,* which Ottoline, having first read the manuscript, was later to re-read and annotate the published novel.
[17] DHL—OM CUP Letters, vol. 2 (23 April 1916) #905.
[18] CB—VB (2 February 1917) Charleston.
[19] *Memoirs,* vol. 2, p. 128.
[20] *Ibid.*
[21] *Ibid.*
[22] *Ibid.*
[23] Marginal comments on Ottoline's copy of *Women in Love* . Report filed at HRC.
[24] CB—OM (nd) HRC.
[25] CB—VB (20 January 1917) Charleston.
[26] *Memoirs,* vol. 2, p. 129.
[27] *Ibid.*
[28] FL—Kot (6 February 1917) *M and C,* p. 219.
[29] FL—Campbell (nd).
[30] DHL—J. B. Pinker (20 February 1917) Moore, p. 502; CUP *Letters,* vol. 3 (20 February 1917) #1377.
[31] DHL—J. B. Pinker. CUP *Letters,* vol. 3 (29 March 1917) #1390.
[32] DHI — MG (1 April 1917) Moore, p.508; CUP *Letters,* vol. 3 (1 April 1917) #1304.
[33] DHL—Kot CUP vol. 3 (4 April 1917) #1307.

[34] *Asquith*, p. 294.
[35] *Asquith* (5 March 1918).
[36] DHL—Cyril Beaumont. CUP vol. 3 (19 February 1918) #1524.
[37] DHL—MG CUP *Letters* vol. 3 [16 March 1918]. #1544. DHL—MG CUP *Letters* vol. 3 [16 March 1918] #1544.
[38] DHL—Kot CUP *Letters* vol. 3 [20 February 1918] #1525.
[39] DHL—MG CUP *Letters* vol. 3 (21 February 1918) #1528. *Moore*, p. 548.
[40] DHL—Kot CUP Letters vol. 3 (20 March 1918) #1547.
[41] DHL—OM (Easter Monday, 1918) HRC. CUP *Letters* vol. 3 (1 April 1918.) #1551.
[42] DHL—MG CUP *Letters* vol. 3 (26 June 1916).#1589.
[43] DHL—Kot CUP *Letters* vol. 3 (2 July 1918). #1593.
[44] DHL—Kot CUP *Letters* vol. 3 (6 January 1919). #1684.
[45] *Memoirs*, vol.2, p.129.

CHAPTER 19

[1] *BR Auto.*, vol. 2, p. 25.
[2] *Ibid.* p. 26.
[3] BR—OM [September 5, 1916] HRC.
[4] BR—OM (nd) HRC.
[5] BR—OM [December 3, 1916] HRC.
[6] BR *Auto.*, vol. 2, p. 27.
[7] Unpublished Memoirs.
[8] *Ibid.*
[9] *Memoirs*, vol. 2, p. 178.
[10] On envelope, BR—OM (nd) HRC.
[11] Brett —OM (15 January 1917) HRC.
[12] *Siegfried's Journey.*
[13] LS—VW (21 February 1917) *Lytton Strachey* p. 675.
[14] Seymour, pp. 282 ff.
[15] *Memoirs*, vol. 2, p. 175.
[16] Brett —OM (21 January 1917) HRC.
[17] Brett —OM (nd) HRC.
[18] *Virginia Woolf,* vol.1, p. 43.
[19] *Memoirs* (nd).
[20] BR—OM [May 5, 1917] HRC.
[21] BR—OM [May 11, 1917] HRC.
[22] LS—Carrington (28 May 1917) Strachey Trust.
[23] *Siegfried's Journey* (nd).
[24] CB—VB (nd) Charleston.
[25] *Memoirs*, vol. 2, p. 182.

[26] Unpublished Memoirs.
[27] BR—OM (June, 1917) HRC.
[28] BR—OM (June, 1917) HRC.
[29] BR—OM (June, 1917) HRC.
[30] BR—OM (July, 1917) HRC.
[31] John Middleton Murry (Murry)—OM (nd) HRC.
[32] *Memoirs,* vol. 2, p. 187.
[33] *Ibid.* p. 188.
[34] *Ibid.* p. 190.
[35] *Ibid.*
[36] *Ibid.* p. 191.
[37] *Ibid.*
[38] Murry—OM (nd) HRC.
[39] *Memoirs,* vol. 2, p. 192.
[40] Siegfried Sassoon (SS)—OM (November 13, 1917) HRC.
[41] *Memoirs,* vol. 2, p. 230.
[42] *Ibid.* p. 231.
[43] MG—OM [10 November 1917] HRC.
[44] *Memoirs,* vol. 2, p.224.
[45] *Ibid.*
[46] *Ibid.*
[47] Note on BR—OM [20 September 1917] HRC.
[48] BR—OM [17 September 1917] HRC.
[49] BR—OM [20 September 1917] HRC.
[50] Unpublished Memoirs.
[51] AH—OM (February 1916) HRC.
[52] *Memoirs,* vol. 2, p. 203.
[53] *Virginia Woolf,* vol. 2, p. 51.
[54] *Ibid.* p. 52.
[55] LS—Carrington, (21 November 1917) Strachey Trust.
[56] *Memoirs,* vol. 2, p. 232.
[57] VB— Roger Fry (nd).
[58] Unpublished Memoirs.

CHAPTER 20

[1] *Memoirs,* vol. 2, p. 233.
[2] *Ibid.* p. 237.
[3] *Memoirs,* vol. 2, p. 239.
[4] *Memoirs,* vol. 2, p. 241.
[5] SS—OM (6 March 1918) HRC.
[6] *Ibid.*

[7] SS—OM (7 June 1918) HRC.
[8] CB—OM (nd) HRC.
[9] *Memoirs*, vol. 2, p. 247.
[10] *Ibid.* p.248.
[11] MG—OM (nd) HRC.
[12] OM—DC (nd) HRC.
[13] LS—OM (3 March 1918) *Lytton Strachey*, p. 720.
[14] *Memoirs*, vol. 2, p. 251.
[15] *Ibid.* p. 252.
[16] LS—OM (3 March 1918) Holroyd, p. 718.
[17] MG—Kot [15 July 1918] *Selected Letters*, p. 160.
[18] *Ibid.*
[19] BR—OM [14 July 1918] HRC.
[20] *Ibid.*
[21] OM—DC (nd) HRC.
[22] Unpublished Memoirs.
[23] Brett —OM (nd) HRC.
[24] *BR Auto.*, vol. 2, p. 37.
[25] BR—OM (nd) HRC.
[26] *Memoirs*, vol. 2, p. 254.
[27] BR—OM (nd) HRC.
[28] *Memoirs*, vol. 2, p. 254.
[29] BR—OM (nd) HRC.
[30] *Flowers of the Forest*, p. 185.
[31] *Laughter in the Next Room*, p. 17.
[32] *Hansard* (11 November 1918).
[33] DC—Noel Carrington (NC) (November 1918) *Lytton Strachey*, p. 748.
[34] *Ibid.* pp. 748—749.
[35] *Virginia Woolf*, vol. 2, p. 62.
[36] DC—NC (18 November 1918) *Lytton Strachey* p. 749.
[37] *Laughter in the Next Room*, p. 24.
[38] *BR Auto.*, vol. 2, p. 37.

CHAPTER 21
[1] BR—OM [20 November 1918] HRC.
[2] BR—OM [18 February 1919] HRC.
[3] BR—OM (nd) HRC.
[4] BR—OM [8 January 1919] HRC.
[5] LS—OM (27 December 1918) *Lytton Strachey*, p. 750.
[6] *Ibid.* p. 752.
[7] LS—DC (11 July 1919); *Ibid.* p. 765.

[8] BR—OM [1 January 1919] HRC.
[9] BR—OM (4 September 1919) HRC.
[10] LS—Mary Hutchinson (15 May 1919) *Lytton Strachey*, p. 769.
[11] LS—VW (27 May 1919); *Ibid.* p. 771.
[12] Brett —OM (15 September 1919) HRC.
[13] OM—Brett (10 October 1919) HRC.
[14] OM—LS (nd) JV.
[15] JV interview with SJD (1972).
[16] Desmond MacCarthy —OM (nd) HRC.
[17] VW—OM (nd) HRC.
[18] BR—OM (nd) HRC.
[19] BR—OM (20 December 1919) HRC.
[20] BR—OM (27 December 1919) HRC.
[21] BR—OM (1 January 1920) HRC.
[22] *Ibid.*
[23] *Augustus John*, p. 261.
[24] *Daily News* (3 February 1920).
[25] *Truth* (6 March 1920).
[26] *The Tatler* (10 March 1920).
[27] *Everyman* (13 March 1920).
[28] *The Weekly Dispatch* (14 March 1920).
[29] PM—AJ (22 March 1920) (copy) JV.
[30] Seymour pp. 316 ff.
[31] BR—OM (nd) HRC.
[32] BR—OM (14 August 1920) HRC.
[33] OM—LS (nd) JV.
[34] PM—Mrs. Frederic Morrell (nd) JV.
[35] *BR Auto.*, vol. 2, p. 136.
[36] OM—PM (nd) JV.
[37] Original edition of *Crome Yellow*, JV.
[38] *Crome Yellow*.
[39] *Ibid.*
[40] *Ibid.*
[41] AH—OM (3 December 1921) HRC.
[42] *Memoirs*, vol. 2, p. 215.
[43] *Ibid.* p. 218.
[44] Sybille Bedford, *Aldous Huxley*, vol. 1, p. 122.
[45] *Ibid.* p. 123.
[46] *Memoirs*, vol. 2, p. 214.
[47] *Ibid.* p. 215.
[48] *Those Barren Leaves*, p. 58.

[49] *Ibid.* p. 63.
[50] *Ibid.* p. 77.

CHAPTER 22

[1] David Cecil interview with SJD (1972).
[2] L. A. G. Strong, *Green Memory*, p. 237.
[3] *Ibid.*
[4] *Ibid.*
[5] Peter Quennell, *The Sign of the Fish*, p. 125.
[6] C.M. Bowra, *Memories*, p. 195.
[7] Quennell, interview SJD (1972).
[8] Gathorne Hardy in *Memoirs*, vol. 1, p. 21.
[9] L.A.G. Strong *Green Memory*.
[10] LS—DC (3 June 1923) *Lytton Strachey*, p. 856.
[11] Blunden—OM (nd) HRC.
[12] Arnold Bennett —OM (21 November 1919) HRC.
[13] BR—OM (2 January 1922) HRC.
[14] BR—OM (11 May 1922) HRC.
[15] JV interview with SJD (1972).
[16] *Memoirs*, vol. 1, p. 29.
[17] *Ibid.*
[18] *Ibid.*
[19] Brett —OM [29 December 1921] HRC.
[20] DHL—MG [10 March 1924] *Intelligent Heart* (nd).
[21] Seymour, p. 325.
[22] LS—VW (19 September 1922) *Lytton Strachey*, p. 851.
[23] OM—LS (February, 1922) JV.
[24] LS—OM (19 September 1922) *Lytton Strachey*, p. 85.
[25] OM—BR (nd) HRC.
[26] Murry—OM [13 January 1923] HRC.
[27] Murry—OM (nd) HRC.
[28] *Memoirs*, vol. 2, p. 150.
[29] VW—Barbara Bagenal (24 June 1923); C. Bell, *Old Friends*, p. 103.
[30] LS—DC (3 June 1923) *Lytton Strachey*, p. 856.
[31] *Memoirs*, vol. 1, p. 37.
[32] Ivy Green, interview with SJD (1973).
[33] *Ibid.*
[34] C M. Bowra, *Memories*, p. 196.
[35] *Ibid.*
[36] Gilbert Spencer —OM (nd) HRC.
[37] L.A.G. Strong, *Green Memory* (nd).

[38] *Ibid.*
[39] *Memoirs*, vol. 1, p.27.
[40] *Ibid.*
[41] *Ibid.*
[42] Oxford undergraduate—OM (29 December 1924) HRC.
[43] *Memoirs*, vol. 1, p. 51.
[44] Ivy Green, interview with SJD (1973).
[45] Sir John Wheeler-Bennett, interview with SJD (1972).

CHAPTER 23

[1] *Memoirs*, vol. 1, p. 51.
[2] OM—W. J. Turner (WJT) (draft) (23 April 1927) HRC.
[3] *Ibid.*
[4] *Aesthetes* (WJ Turner), p. 36.
[5] *Ibid.* p. 41.
[6] *Ibid.*
[7] *Ibid.* p. 50.
[8] Lady Huxley, interview with SJD (1973).
[9] *Ibid.*
[10] *Memoirs*, vol. 1, p. 17.
[11] DHL—OM (8 May 1928); *Memoirs*, vol. 2, p. 129. CUP Letters vol. 6 (8 May 1928) #4421.
[12] DHL—OM (24 May 1928) HRC. CUP *Letters*, vol. 6 (24 May1928) #4437.
[13] OM—LS (nd) Strachey Trust.
[14] LS—Roger Senhouse (9 November 1928) *Lytton Strachey*, p. 970.
[15] OM—LS (nd) JV.
[16] LS—Roger Senhouse [1928] *Lytton Strachey*, p. 971.
[17] Ivy Green, interview with SJD (1973).
[18] Lady Huxley, interview with SJD (1973)
[19] JV, interview with SJD (1972)
[20] *Ibid.*
[21] DHL—OM (December 28, 1928); Huxley, p. 772. CUP *Letters*, vol. 7 (28 December 1928) #4851.
[22] *Memoirs*, vol. 1, p. 55.
[23] DHL—OM (April 3, 1929); *Memoirs*, vol. 2, p. 136.
[24] *Ibid* p. 137.
[25] Nehls, *A Composite Biography*, vol. 3, p. 383.
[26] FL—OM (nd) HRC.
[27] AJ—OM (nd) HRC.
[28] Dorelia McNeill—OM (nd) HRC.
[29] Axel Munthe —OM (nd) HRC.

30 OM—Gathorne-Hardy (GH) (copy) (5 June 1929) JV.
31 OM—GH (copy) (5 June 1929) JV.
32 DHL—OM (21 January 1930) *Memoirs*, vol 2, p. 137. CUP *Letters*, vol.7 (21 January 1930) #5484.
33 *Memoirs*, p. 138.
34 OM—VW (15 October 1932) Sussex.
35 FL—PM (nd) HRC.
36 FL—OM (2 March 1932) HRC.
37 Vivienne Eliot—OM (nd) HRC.
38 TSE—OM (14 March 1933) HRC.
39 OM—VW (20 November 1933) Sussex.
40 OM—VW (28 December 1928) Sussex.
41 Kot —OM (nd) HRC.
42 Kot —OM (nd) HRC.
43 Kot —OM (8 September 1936) HRC.
44 LS—OM (nd) JV.
45 LS—OM (8 April 1931) HRC.
46 *Memoirs*, vol. 1, p. 56, & Dilys Powell interview with SJD (1974).
47 Augustus John, *Autobiography*, p. 98.
48 DC—OM (nd) HRC.
49 DC—OM (nd) HRC.
50 Seymour, p. 373.
51 David Cecil interview with SJD.
52 OM—Sprott (6 June 1931) King's College.
53 OM—Sprott, (nd) King's College.
54 Dilys Powell, interview with SJD.
55 OM—J. Hayward (17 February 1933) King's College.
56 OM—J. Hayward (28 December 1933) King's College.
57 T. S. Moore (TSM)—OM (21 February 1938) HRC.
58 *Memoirs*, vol. l, p.16.
59 *Ibid*.
60 *World Within World*, (Stephen Spender), p. 161.
61 OM—GH (copy) (13 August 1932) JV.
62 OM—GH (copy) (13 June 1933) JV.
63 *Ibid*.
64 Lady Huxley, interview with SJD (1972)
65 *Memoirs*, vol. l, p.16.
66 In the possession of JV.
67 VW—OM (nd) HRC.
68 OM—W. B. Yeats (draft) (10 March 1937) HRC.
69 Francis Hackett —OM (nd) HRC.

[70] Hackett—OM (nd) HRC.
[71] OM—George Santayana (copy) (nd) HRC.
[72] OM—Santayana (copy) (28 June 1937) HRC.
[73] OM—Dora Sanger (nd) possession Daphne Sanger.
[74] Lady Huxley interview with SJD (1972).
[75] VW, *The Times*, (21 April 1938).
[76] Margot Asquith, *The Times*, (21 April 1938).
[77] Lady Huxley, interview with SJD (1972).

INDEX

'The Lady and the Pug' (Huxley), 409
Aesthetes, The (Turner), 371-372, 399, 413
Allen, Clifford, 322, 337, 412-413
Amores (Lawrence), 255-256, 370
Anrep, Boris, 97, 103, 134-135, 351
Apostles, the, 66, 107, 145, 172
Asquith, Cynthia (Lady), 216, 222, 257, 268, 270-271
Asquith, Herbert Henry, 28, 318, 343, 413, 415
Asquith, Margot, 302, 367, 401
Asquith, Violet, 240, 321
Athenaeum, 337, 384
Autobiography of Alice B. Toklas, The (Stein), 413
Bagenal, (see also Barbara Hiles)., 355
Bagenal, Faith, 218
Baillot, Juliette (see also Juliette Huxley), 214
Bakst, Leon, 166, 213, 246
Balzac, Honore de, 78
Barker, George, 394
Beardsley, Aubrey, 213, 324
Beaverbrook, Lord, 191, 387
Bective, Countess of, 54

Bedford, Sybille, 336, 395, 409
Beerbohm, Max, 74-75, 400
Beigel, Professor, 43
Bell, Clive, 6, 87-88, 90, 108, 144, 171, 185, 197, 218, 223, 229, 231, 233, 235, 237, 241, 249, 262, 265-266, 281, 283, 285, 296, 304, 306, 308, 316, 321-322, 329, 395, 415
Bell, Quentin, 88, 108, 408-409, 411
Bell, Vanessa see also Vanessa Stephen), 6, 78, 104, 108, 128, 137, 166, 175, 182, 185-186, 197-198, 217, 223, 234, 246, 295, 302, 415
Belloc, Hillaire, 68, 194
Bennett, Arnold, 166, 348, 409
Bentinck, Arthur (Lieutenant-General), 11, 28
Bentinck, Lady Henry, 391
Bentinck, Lady Henry (see also Birdie), 35-36
Bentinck, Lord Henry, 26, 28, 82, 160, 170, 174, 219, 223, 231-232, 281, 391
Bentinck, Lord William (see also Willie), 44, 382
Bentinck, Morven, 341
Bernhardt, Sarah, 23

Bess of Hardwick, 16
Bibesco, Prince, 77, 270
Binyon, Laurence, 55
Birrell, Augustine, 28, 50, 75, 219, 238, 324
Birrell, Francis, 194
Black, Dora (Mrs Bertrand Russell), 323, 328, 331
Bloomsbury area, i, 2, 6-7, 67, 88-90, 99-100, 102, 104, 107-108, 134, 137-138, 142, 144, 147, 154, 163-164, 166, 171, 176, 185-186, 188, 191, 194-195, 197-198, 202, 206, 218, 229, 233, 235-237, 249, 267, 278, 281, 286, 293, 295-296, 302, 307-308, 310-311, 323, 355, 365, 367, 377, 405, 411
Bloomsbury Group, The, 2, 67, 100, 107, 137, 144, 185, 191, 229
Blunden, Edmund, 347
Boer War, 44
Bollard, Clare, 354
Bolsover, Lady (see also Mrs Bentinck), 16, 22-26, 28, 36, 155, 173, 330
Bowra, C. M, 345, 359, 411
Brenan, Gerald, 354
Brenty (maid), 93, 105, 282
Brett, Dorothy, 6, 194, 222, 224, 226, 234, 236, 244-245, 249, 277-278, 283, 290, 294, 296, 302, 304, 306-307, 312, 314, 317, 325, 334, 343, 350, 355, 379, 409, 411, 415
Brooke, Rupert, 157
Broughton Grange, 2-3, 169, 272-273
Browne, H. M, 11
Browning, Robert, 27, 39, 42
Burnley Liberal Party, 95
Burrowing Duke, the (see also Portland, Fifth Duke of), 14, 19, 21
Burrows, Bessie, 179
Bussy, Simon, 102
Cameron, Dr., 383, 398, 400-401
Campbell, Beatrice, 387
Campbell, Gordon (Lord Glenavy), 267
Campbell-Bannerman (Sir Henry), 35
Cannan, Gilbert, 176, 193, 199-200, 235, 339
Carbine, 20
Carrington, Dora, 194, 235-239, 241, 247-248, 251, 268, 274, 281, 285, 288, 296, 307-308, 312, 315-316, 322, 335, 346, 353, 357, 365, 390, 409, 411, 415
Carswell, Catherine, 259
Casement, Sir Roger, 243-244, 324
Cattie (cousin), 17
Cave, Sir George, 305
Cavendish-Bentinck, Lady Victoria, 54
Cavendishes, 16

Cavendish-Holles-Harley, Margaret, 16
Cecil, David (Lord), ii, 5, 293, 340-343, 345, 354, 391, 408, 411
Celtic Twilight, The (Yeats), 326
Chadbourne, Mrs, 91
Chamberlain, Joseph, 56
Chambers, Jessie, 155, 167, 193, 228, 263-264
Chaplin, Charlie, 345, 367, 389-390
Charles I, 16
Charlie (see also Lod Charles Bentinck), 14, 17, 219, 345, 358, 367, 389-390
Churchill, Winston, 86, 135-136
Clapham Sect, the, 2, 107
Colefax, Lady Sybil, 85-86, 311, 323
Combe, Dr., 157-158, 161, 171
Conder, Charles, 52, 66, 77, 90, 317, 371
Conrad, Joseph, 177-178, 244, 317, 334, 348-349
Conscription Bill, 229
Contemporary Art Society,, 147, 245
Cooper-Willis, Irene, 204
Corsican Brothers, The, 23
Costello, Karin, 117
Courtauld, Samuel, 387
Cox, Ka, 157-158

Craig, Miss, 17, 31-32
Cramb, John Adam (J.A. Cramb), iii, 28, 61, 318, 415
Cramb, Lucy (Selby Lowndes), 64
Cresswell, D'Arcy, 397
Crome Yellow (Hixley), 334, 336-339, 409, 412
Crome Yellow (Huxley), 334, 336-339, 409, 412
Crutwell, Maud, 45
Cunard, Emerald (Lady), 85, 311, 323-324
Cuthbert Learmont (Revermort), 60-62, 64, 256, 413
D.H. Lawrence's 99 Days in Australia, 210
Dallas-Yorke, Mrs, 34
Darroch, Robert (Rob), 8-10, 19-20, 210, 272-273, 414
Davies, Compton Llewellyn, 66, 74
Davis, Mr, 212, 411
Delprat, Paul, 186
Desborough, Ettie, 358, 363
Deterding, Olga, 297-299
Devonshire, Duchess of, 24, 358
Diaghilev, Sergei, 166, 182, 314, 316-317, 325, 332
Diamand, Pamela, 404-405, 409
Dickinson, Sir John, 308
Disraeli, Benjamin, 22, 91
Douglas, Lord Alfred, 241

Douglas-Pennant, Hilda, 32, 34, 60, 65, 74, 165, 190
Drabble, Margaret, 164
Druce-Portland Case, 44, 46, 48
Dudley, Helen, 181, 184, 191, 193
Dudley, Mr, 192
Easter Uprising, 243
Edward VII, 21
Einstein, Albert, 328
Eliot, T. S, 181, 228, 311, 317, 348, 367, 385, 392, 415
Eliot, Vivienne, 229, 232, 242-243, 275-276
Ellen (maid), 32-34, 38
Eminent Victorians (Strachey), 163, 174, 310-311, 322
Epstein, Jacob, 82, 89, 409
Esher, Lord, 194
Etchells, Frederick, 166
Etherea Society, 405-406
Feilding, Percy, 52, 65
Ferdinand, Archduke, 184
Forrest, Euphemia, 100, 126, 162
Forster, E. M, 2, 97, 108, 183, 191, 202, 257, 347, 361, 409
Frou Frou (Meilhac and Halevy), 23
Fry, Roger, 89, 97, 103, 105, 108, 127, 135-136, 140, 153, 166, 180, 186, 198, 224, 233-234, 246-247, 295, 316-317, 375, 395, 404-406, 409, 415

Garnett, Angelica, 408
Garnett, David (see also Bunny Garnett), i, iii, 6, 88, 98, 108, 185-186, 194, 197-198, 200, 209, 217, 237-238, 246, 288, 296, 314, 316, 369, 408-409, 411, 415
Garsington, iv, 3, 6-7, 16, 20, 85, 100, 126, 174, 196-197, 205, 207-209, 211, 214-219, 221-228, 232-237, 240, 242-244, 246-249, 251-253, 258, 261-262, 265, 268, 269-272, 274-276, 279-281, 284-288, 290-293, 295-296, 300-309, 311-312, 314-315, 318, 320-323, 325, 330, 332, 334-337, 339-341, 343-349, 351-353, 355-357, 359-361, 363-366, 368-370, 373-374, 376-379, 387, 391, 402, 408, 412
Gathorne-Hardy, Robert, 273, 293, 343, 345, 349, 357, 361, 364, 367, 370, 375, 380, 383, 389, 394-396, 400, 402, 412, 415
Gauss, Karl Friedrich, 112, 117
George V, 150, 305
George, David Lloyd, 315, 321
Gertler, Mark, 194, 200, 202, 215, 231, 234, 236, 239, 247, 268-270, 272, 288, 291, 294, 296, 306-308, 311-312, 316-317, 319, 321-322, 333-334,

343, 349-350, 352, 354, 360, 363, 409, 411, 415
Gibbon, Edward, 55
Gide, Andre, 332, 387
Gieland, Max, 190
Gilbert and Sullivan, 23
Gill, Eric, 20, 402-403
Gimpel, Jean, 297
Gladstone League, 93, 95, 179
Gladstone, Herbert, 56
Glenavy, Lord (see also Campbell, Gordon), 267, 411
Go-Between, The (Hartley), 360
Gogarty, Oliver St. John, 325
Gomme, Lionel (see also Tiger), iii, 318, 331
Goodman, Anne, 3, 12, 23, 38, 62, 273, 374, 408, 413
Goodman, Victor (SIr), 3, 364, 374
Gore, Charles, 222, 243, 321, 400
Gorki, Maxim, 357
Gosse, Edmund, 230
Graham, James, 304
Granby, Marchioness of, 54
Grant, Duncan, 5, 87-89, 108, 166-167, 185, 195, 197-198, 202, 213, 217, 222, 231, 246, 316, 389, 401, 408
Graves, Robert, 286, 311
Green, Ivy, 359, 366, 408
Greene, Graham, 397

Grey, Sir Edward, 172, 188
Hackett, Francis, 400, 415
Hals, Franz, 396
Hamilton, Lady Hancock, 359, 413
Hardie, Keir, 188
Hardy, Thomas, 225, 386
Harrison, Jane, 97
Hatfield House, 340
Hawtrey, Ralph, 110
Hayward, John, 392
Heseltine, Philip, 222, 224, 254-255, 259
Hiles, Barbara, 194, 218, 235
Holmes, C. J, 89
Holroyd, Michael, i, 2, 144, 163-164, 239, 329, 408-409, 411-413, 415
Horner, Lady, 90
Hudson, Nan, 74
Hue and Cry After Genius, The (Garnett), 237
Hurblatt, Miss, 34
Hutchinson, Mary, 108, 217-218, 233-234, 308, 409, 411
Huxley, Aldous, 222, 234, 247, 249, 251, 262, 280, 293-294, 311, 317, 334, 336, 367, 375, 377, 381, 384, 395, 407, 409, 411-412, 415
Huxley, Juliette (Baillot), 4, 364, 374, 379, 401
Imitation of Christ (Thomas a Kempis),, 24
Ingrams, Leonard, 253
Irish nationalism, 324

Irving, Sir Henry, 23
Isaacs, Rufus, 153
Itow, 222
James I, 212
James, Henry, 66, 74, 76-77, 93, 160, 165, 177, 183, 317, 371, 400
James, William, 177
Jenkins, Roy, 43, 408, 412
John, Augustus, 77, 89, 98, 165, 186, 191, 195, 316-318, 329, 383, 389, 396, 411, 415
John, Pyramus, 104
Jones, Alice, 279-280, 369
Julian, Mother, 27, 68, 154
Kangaroo (Lawrence), 210
Kant, Immanuel, 349
Keats, John, 33, 295
Kennedy, George, 105
Keynes, J. Maynard, 108, 172, 206, 219, 223, 226, 233, 235, 240, 244, 249, 313-314, 316, 329, 347, 397
Kot (see also Koteliansky, S.S.), 203, 208, 268-270, 312, 387, 415
Kropotkin, Prince, 40, 66
Lady Chatterley's Lover (Lawrence), 331, 380
Lamb, Henry, 43, 82, 89-92, 98-99, 126, 129, 133, 135, 141-144, 148-149, 162, 175, 182, 186, 191, 232, 278, 317-318, 383, 415
Lamb, Pansy (Lady), 126, 186, 408

Lawrence, D. H, ii, 5, 164, 210, 226, 317, 319, 336, 409, 411-413, 415
Lawrence, George, 385
Lee, Vernon (see also Paget, Violet), 39, 231
Leigh Rawley, 362
Leng, Kyrle, 357, 362, 364, 367
Lewis, Wyndham, 166
Little Sisters of the Poor, 27
Litvinov, Maxim, 304
Locke, John, 27, 125
Lopokova, Lydia, 314
Macaulay, Thomas, 55
MacCarthy, Desmond, 97, 104, 108, 135, 139, 178, 214, 235, 241, 266, 270, 327, 346
MacCarthy, Molly, 171, 233
MacColl.D. S, 89
MacDonald, Ramsay, 75, 305
Maclagan, William Dalrymple, 28, 30-31, 33, 318
Maitland, Helen, 92, 96, 103, 126
Malleson, Lady Constance (see also O'Neil Colette), 243, 275-276
Malleson, Miles, 243
Manet, Edouard, 63
Manners, Lady Viola, 54
Manning, Henry Edward, 174
Mansfield, Katherine, 61, 216, 240, 252, 255-256, 275-

276, 284, 333
Margaret, first Duchess of Newcastle (Mad Madge), 16
Marie Antoinette, 25, 363, 396
Markiewicz, Constance
Marlborough, Duchess of, 243
Marples, G., 395
Marten, Dr., 346, 348, 357, 396
Masefield, John, 193
Massine, Leonide, 314, 316, 325
Massingham, Henry William, 135, 280
Masterman, Charles, 75
Matisse, Henri, 91
McMaster University, iii, 140, 408, 415
McNeill, Dorelia, 77-78, 81-84, 91-92, 96-97, 104, 383
Menasce, Jean de, 397
Merrifield, Evelyn, 280, 282, 369
Michelet, Jules, 68
Millie (maid), 208, 282, 321, 327, 343, 390
Monet, Claude, 358, 364
Moore, G. E, 107, 393
Morrell, Frederic, 40, 54
Morrell, Herbert, 56
Morrell, Hugh (OM's son), 51, 68, 239, 331, 356
Morrell, Lady Ottoline, i, ii, iii, iv, 1-56, 58-63, 64-68, 73-105, 108-111, 114-224, 226-237, 239-249, 251-252, 254-290, 292-298, 300, 302-365, 367-402, 404-406, 410-412, 415
Morrell, Mrs. Frederic, 52, 350
Morrell, Philip, iii, 3, 50, 162, 187, 220, 260, 415
Morton, Cavendish, 65
Moscrop, Mr, 179
Mrs. Dalloway (Woolf), 356
Munthe, Axel, 28, 36-41, 43, 52, 61, 65, 77, 124, 232, 318, 331, 383
Murder in the Cathedral (Eliot), 392
Murry, John Middleton, 216-217, 221, 223, 240, 255, 287-288, 317-318, 337, 354, 415
My First Fifty Years (Russell), 388
Nathan, Sir Matthew, 183
National Union of Conservative Associations, 56
Needham, Francis, 393
Newcastle, First Duke of, 15-16
Nightingale, Florence, 163, 310
Nijinsky, Vaslav, 166-167, 178, 182, 195, 308, 317, 412
No-Conscription Fellowship, 229

Norton, Harry, 108, 128, 136, 166, 179, 191, 233
Nys, Maria (see also Huxley, Maria), 193, 294
Omega Workshop, 198, 231, 275, 279
Once Upon a Vase (Jobson), 2
Oxford Movement, 174
Paget, Violet (see also Lee, Vernon), 39
Partridge, Ralph, 322, 353, 365, 409
Pearsall Smith, Alys (see also Rusell, Alys), 90, 111-113, 116-125, 131-132, 136, 138-139, 147, 151, 153-154, 168, 191, 277, 322, 328, 332-333
Peppard cottage, 69, 78, 84, 93-97, 100-105, 136, 142, 145-146, 148, 150, 152-153, 166-167, 169, 295, 389
Picasso, Pablo, 325, 332
Pitter, Ruth, 378
Plomer, William, 378, 397, 413
Point Counter Point (Huxley), 381
Ponsonby, Arthur, 188
Portland, Duchess of, 13
Portland, Fifth Duke of (see also Burrowing Duke), 13, 15, 47, 358
Portland, Sixth Duke of (Arthur Bentinck), 47, 52
Pound, Ezra, 329
Powell, Anthony, 345

Powell, Dilys, 392, 408
Powell, Nurse, 12
Poynter, Edward John, 23
Preludes (Mansfield), 312
Prewitt, Frank (see alsoToronto), 325
Principia Mathematica (Russell), 90, 112, 155
Pryde, James, 65
Quennell, Peter, 6, 344-345, 408, 413
Rau, Dr, 374, 398
Revermort, J. A, 60-61, 413
Reynolds, Mrs, 22
Richmond, Duke of, 13
Riddell, Alan, 298-299
Ripon, Lady, 166
Ritchie, D. G, 34
Roberts, Lord, 61, 210, 408
Robey, George, 291
Robinson, Jack, 336
Rochester, Bishop of, 54
Rootes, Miss, 32-34
Ross, Robbie, 160, 241, 245, 408
Rothenstein, William, 76
Rowse, A. L, 345, 413
Ruskin, John, 32-33
Russell, Bertrand, 27, 109, 118, 120, 130-132, 134-135, 138-142, 146, 148-155, 158, 161, 166-167, 173, 180, 184, 189, 191-192, 195, 201, 203-204, 215, 223, 228-229, 231-232, 238-239, 243, 246, 252, 255, 262, 271, 275-276, 278,

443

281, 285, 291-292, 300, 305, 308-310, 312-313, 315, 318, 320-321, 323-324, 328, 332-333, 348-349, 354, 378, 389
Russell, Bertrand (see also Bertie), iii, iv, 2, 10, 27, 54, 90, 97-98, 109-111, 113-125, 127, 129-130, 132-135, 137-142, 145-147, 149-151, 153-161, 167, 169, 171-172, 175-178, 180-181, 183, 186, 188-189, 191-193, 195-196, 203-206, 209, 214-217, 219-220, 223, 226-230, 232, 235-236, 242-244, 255, 262, 275-278, 285, 287, 292-293, 306, 308-310, 312-313, 316-319, 322-323, 327-329, 331, 333, 338, 341, 344, 348-349, 351, 367, 386, 388-389, 393, 400-401, 405, 408, 411, 413, 415
Sands, Ethel, 66, 74, 77, 97, 105, 110, 122, 139, 146, 165, 329, 365, 377, 380
Sanger, Charles, 66
Sanger, Dora, 401
Santayana, 223, 400
Sarawak, Ranee of, 307, 314
Sargant-Florence, Alix, 235
Sargent, John Singer, 65, 74
Sassoon, Siegfried, 230, 245, 278, 311-312, 325, 345, 352, 415
Scott, Hyacinth, 27
Scott, Mrs, 25
Senhouse, Roger, 377-378

Shaw, George Bernard, 67, 75, 221, 286, 317, 335, 364, 415
Sherman, Montague, 316
Shove, Fredegond, 294
Shove, Gerald, 194, 235, 300-301
Sickert, Walter, 74, 77, 90
Simon, Sir John, 232
Sitwell, Edith, 329
Sitwell, Osbert, 5, 314
Sitwell, Sacheverell, 314
Smallwood, Norah, 2, 164
Smart Set, 75, 77
Smith, Logan Pearsall, 52, 55, 65, 74, 90, 110, 124, 129, 139, 365
Smith, Nelson, 42, 69
Smythe, Dame Ethel, 380
Snowden, Philip, 305
Sons and Lovers (Lawrence), 199, 255, 263, 394
Spencer, Gilbert, 182, 360, 378, 408
Spencer, Stanley, 319
Spender, Stephen, 6, 374, 378, 396-397, 413
Spoils of Poynton, The (James), 66
Sprott, Sebastian, 391
St. Andrews University, 34-35, 40, 408
Stamfordham, Lord., 244
Stein, Gertrude, 91, 413
Stephen, Adrian, 108, 167
Stephen, Marlay, 2, 408

Stephen, Sir Leslie, 88
Stephen, Virginia (*see also* Woolf, Virginia), 87, 104, 135, 144, 158, 166
Stephens, James, 377
Story of San Michele, The (Munthe), 36
Strachey, Alix, 164
Strachey, James, 223, 413, 415
Strachey, Lytton, i, iv, 2, 6, 10, 43, 51, 61, 67-68, 97, 108, 128, 140-141, 146, 163-164, 196-197, 226, 239, 304, 317, 319, 361, 373, 408-409, 412-413, 415
Stravinsky, Igor, 166
Strong, Arthur, 27, 50
Strong, L. A. G., 344, 360
Sydney-Turner, Saxon, 88, 108
Tacitus, 68
Thirty-nine Articles, 61
Thomas, D, 304
Thornton, S. S., 304
Those Barren Leaves (Huxley), 338-339, 409, 412
Those Barren Leaves (Huxley., 338-339, 409, 412
Threadgill, Kenneth, 10
Tiger (see also Gomme, Lionel), 318, 320, 330-332, 339, 351
Toronto (see also Prewitt, Frank), 325-326, 351
Trevi, Bob, 115

Turner, W.J, 272, 352, 399, 415
Victoria, Queen, 22, 267, 321
Vinogradoff, Igor, 3, 272, 363, 374
Vinogradoff, Julian (see also Morrell, Julian), ii, iii, 1-2, 8-9, 163-164, 185, 272, 408, 410, 415
Vittoz, Dr., 176
Wain, Sue, 360
Walden, Lady Howard de, 54, 183
Walden, Lord Howard de, 358
Warren, Dorothy, 54, 210, 381, 408
Watts, George Frederic, 23
Webb, Sidney, 55
Weekley, Barbara, 392
Weekley, Prof. Earnest, 205
Welbeck Abbey, 13-17, 19-21, 23, 26-28, 30-31, 33, 35, 43, 46-47, 50, 53, 60, 90, 130, 155, 200, 249, 375, 393-395, 401, 403, 413
Wells, H.G, 201, 398, 400-401
Wheeler-Bennett, Lady, 251, 408
Wheeler-Bennett, Sir John, 251, 253
Whistler, James Abbott, 23
White Peacock, The (Lawrence), 199
Whiteman, Charles, 10
Wilde, Oscar, 23, 241

William of Orange, 16, 19
Willie (Lord William Bentinck), 12, 14
Willies, Joe, 395
Winn, Godfrey, 396
Wittgenstein, Ludwig, 149, 172
Women in Love (Lawrence), ii, 255-256, 258, 263-265, 267, 269-271, 274, 319, 331, 334, 336, 338, 372, 385, 412
Woolf, Leonard, 6, 53, 71, 88, 100, 158, 166, 189, 294, 361, 413, 415
Woolf, Virginia, 5, 8, 10, 98, 107-108, 195, 226, 235, 237, 279, 283, 302, 315, 335, 348, 351-352, 355, 361, 367, 373, 380, 384, 387, 395, 397, 401, 409, 411, 413, 415
Yeats, William Butler, 75, 252, 317, 326, 341, 344, 352, 360-361, 367, 377-378, 397, 399-400